The Art of Anthropology/ The Anthropology of Art

The Art of Anthropology/ The Anthropology of Art

Edited by

Brandon D. Lundy

Selected Papers from the Annual Meeting of the
Southern Anthropological Society
Richmond, Virginia
March, 2011

Robert Shanafelt, Series Editor

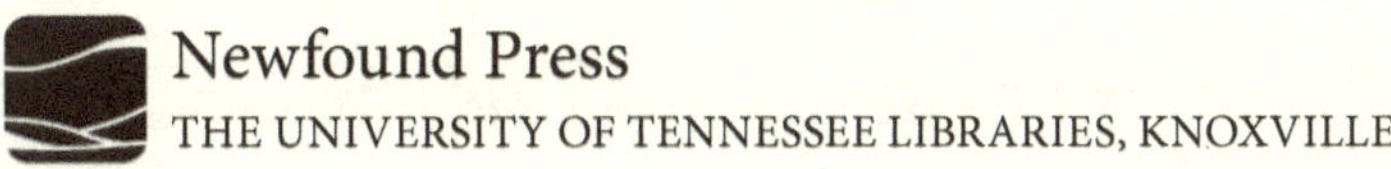

Southern Anthropological Society
Founded 1966

Digital version at www.newfoundpress.utk.edu/pubs/lundy
Print on demand available through University of Tennessee Press.

Newfound Press
University of Tennessee Libraries
1015 Volunteer Boulevard
Knoxville, TN 37996-1000
www.newfoundpress.utk.edu

ISBN-13: 978-0-9846445-6-8
ISBN-10: 0-9846445-6-3

The art of anthropology, the anthropology of art / edited by Brandon D. Lundy ; Robert Shanafelt, series editor.
Knoxville, Tenn : Newfound Press, University of Tennessee Libraries, c2013.
1 online resource (xv, 403 p.) : ill. -- (Southern Anthropological Society proceedings ; no. 42)
Includes bibliographical references and index.
1. Art and anthropology -- Congresses. 2. Ethnology -- Congresses. 3. Art and society -- Congresses. I. Lundy, Brandon D., 1976- II. Shanafelt, Robert, 1957- III. Southern Anthropological Society. Meeting.
GN302.A78 2013

Book design by Jayne W. Smith
Cover design by C. S. Jenkins

Contents

Illustrations

Figures

Photographs

Tables

Preface and Acknowledgments

Brandon D. Lundy

This volume extends the anthropological dialogue renewed at the 2011 annual meeting of the Southern Anthropological Society (SAS) in Richmond, Virginia, about the dialectical relationship between art and anthropology—how they both influence and are influenced by each other. The outgoing SAS Secretary-Treasurer of the Society, Margaret Huber of the University of Mary Washington (Emerita), organized the meeting that year. Huber also graciously contributed her paper, "Pocahontas and Rebecca: Two Tales of a Captive," to this current volume. In this paper, she voiced, "The question is not whether we should accord oral history as much trust as we do written accounts. Plainly, we cannot trust either. Rather, the comparison justifies Edmund Leach's formulation that 'history' and 'mythology' are the same."

This engagement with and deconstruction of authority foregrounds once again the problems of representation. Huber decides that the road forward out of this "crisis" is to share authorial agency with the audience—showing how the reading of history is really about the ongoing practice of meaning-making and interpretation (cf. Denzin 1997). Her choice to highlight the historical text is a direct statement about the conference theme—the production of cultural texts, whether from the perspective of art, history, or anthropology, each of which are creative acts where choices about what to put on record are made, and then those objects are examined and interpreted in a myriad of often unanticipated ways. This is, quite possibly, what makes the creative process so exciting and simultaneously so paralyzing. Artistic intent does not always create a shared message or interpretation of that message; in other words, the communicative act is not unidirectional or univocal.

The Program Chair of the 2011 meetings, Eric Gable, also at the University of Mary Washington with Huber, was responsible for conceptualizing the theme, *The Art of Anthropology/The Anthropology of Art*. He did so by describing the study of artistic practices as material, powerful, subjective, aesthetic, and contextual (i.e., situated in time and space); the study of art as consumed, displayed, political, ritualistic, and innovative; and the study of anthropology as artful, meaningful, rhetorical, persuasive, and impactful on the public's understanding(s) of humanity. In his most recent book, *Anthropology and Egalitarianism*, Gable is compelled to think about/with art as he tries to make sense of his positionality as anthropologist, authority, tourist, novice, and photographer in two distinct fields—at Monticello, the home of Thomas Jefferson, and among the Manjaco of Guinea-Bissau in West Africa. It is while residing among the Manjaco that Gable first observed:

> Taking photographs gave me aesthetic pleasure. As I looked through the lens, I imagined the way the shot would compare to photographs I had seen in books, magazines, and museums. I enjoyed composing a scene, using light and shadow and color to create "art," and I enjoyed planning how best to convey a particular moment or mood or sensibility through a fleeting image. (2011, 98)

In only a few words, Gable captures the essence of the conference and this volume. Art as *practice*, similar to how Gable sees tourism

(99); art (and anthropology) is about authenticity—a communicative act intent on capturing or critiquing "truth" about human nature or the nature of humanity. This act, while at once "aesthetically pleasing" is also disconcerting, as suggested above, as something that is axiomatically in process and, therefore, not completely "knowable." This uncertainty is both distressing and potentially empowering, as we will see.

The unsettledness of the conference topic inspired Paul Stoller of West Chester University to deliver a keynote speech titled "Finding the Right Path." He indirectly considered: How might anthropology, as a social "science," move forward after the postmodern turn of the 1980s, in which many of the theoretical and methodological foundations of the discipline were deconstructed, and as such, devalued? How can we, as anthropologists, reinvent the discipline by using the *Power of the Between* (2009) to gain a unique vantage point from which to reexamine humanity and culture? Paul Stoller, a stalwart of American Anthropology for more than three decades, has been shaping the discipline of anthropology through his artful prose. Stoller's work, including eleven books (ethnographies, biographies, memoirs, and two novels), engages with the pragmatics of livelihood, belief, sensory perceptions, and the visual arts. As a fellow "inhabiter" of the space between, Stoller was the ideal choice as the keynote speaker for this conference. For example, he once wrote:

> I suggest that when ethnographers attempt to depict social life—to write or film lives—they should incorporate the griot's historically conscientious and respectfully decentered conception and practice of ethnography, a conception and practice of ethnography that reverberates with the tension between the political and the poetic. . . . This also impels ethnographers to complement their

> explorations in social theory with tales of a people that are respectful and poetically evocative. In this way, ethnographers will understand how a mouthful of water cannot douse a fire and why griots must know themselves before they let others know them. (Stoller 1994, 354)

His message in both the keynote speech as well as his other works is clear: embrace the practice of anthropology as an act of learning, sharing, storytelling, sojourning, empathizing, and transmitting, but do so in an artful fashion that both inspires and encourages others to do the same. The chapters in this book continue Stoller's journey by embracing his message.

Over one hundred papers, posters, and ethnographic films were presented at the 2011 annual meeting of the SAS, eight of which have been revised and included in this volume (Huber, Ingersoll and Ingersoll, King, Knight, Melomo, Philen, Syka, Sheehan) alongside five new chapters (Falls, Qirko, Smith, Stephenson, Vogt). Eric Gable, the program chair of the 2011 conference, was originally slated to edit this Proceedings, No. 42, under the direction of the SAS Proceedings General Editor, Robert Shanafelt, of Georgia Southern University. Under Gable, the initial eight conference papers were collected before I was asked to assume the task of finalizing the volume. At this point, an additional call for papers was sent out, and five additional contributors were selected.

Therefore, I would like to especially thank Eric Gable, Margaret Huber, Paul Stoller, and Robert Shanafelt for their guidance, direction, and inspiration. I would also like to thank the original contributors and those who subsequently joined the project. Additionally, acknowledgment is necessary for Amanda Woomer, PhD graduate student at Kennesaw State University in International Conflict Management, and Dayton Starnes, PhD graduate student at the University of Kentucky in Anthropology, for their thorough and thoughtful editorial assistance and review of these chapters. Their judicious insights have helped shape the direction of this volume. Finally, I would like to thank the managing editor at Newfound Press, Jayne Smith, who has been helpful throughout the publication process.

References

Denzin, Norman K. 1997. *Interpretive Ethnography: Ethnographic Practices for the 21st Century*. Thousand Oaks, CA: Sage Publications.

Gable, Eric. 2011. *Anthropology and Egalitarianism: Ethnographic Encounters from Monticello to Guinea-Bissau*. Bloomington: Indiana University Press.

Stoller, Paul. 1994. "Ethnographies as Texts/Ethnographers as Griots." *American Ethnologist* 21(2): 353-66.

________. 2009. *The Power of the Between: An Anthropological Odyssey*. Chicago: University of Chicago Press.

Disciplined Aesthetics: Fashioning Art and Anthropology

Brandon D. Lundy

Repeated by artist Salvador Dalí, French poet Gérard de Nerval famously stated, "The first man who compared a woman to a rose was a poet, the second, an imbecile."[1] Many art clichés such as "art for art's sake," or even critiques of art clichés such as the one provided here by Nerval overlook two critical aspects of the artists' endeavors: art as socially and culturally constructed and interpreted, and art as fundamentally human (Geertz 1976). After all, "art imitates life," or is it, "life imitates art?" Put another way, in an online blog conversation, Jim Hurlburt suggests, "I've managed to offend 'artists' for years by saying that art *must* include communication. That at a bare minimum, one must be able to look at a piece of art and agree that the artist had something to say" ("The Uses of Cliche" 2011). Winter, in the same thread, writes, "Eternal art starts with good story telling"(ibid). As the antimetabole title implies, *The Art of Anthropology/The Anthropology of Art* engages with the complex and overlapping relationships between anthropology and art. Fashioned through cultural dialogue, anthropologists and artists help shape one another's practices, outcomes, and associated disciplines.

As several chapters in this book attest, anthropology has a long tradition of studying artistic practices—with the materiality of artwork; with art's power, as object or as act, to shape subjective states; with enduring questions of a comparative aesthetics (Ingersoll and

Ingersoll, Knight). Anthropologists study artists (Stephenson), and they study places in which art is consumed (Falls) or displayed (Syka, Vogt). In studying art, they subsume art into other categories—politics and ritual, for example—while also prompting new ways of understanding these concepts (Qirko).

If there is an anthropology of art, then there is also an art to anthropology. Good ethnographic research requires a certain artfulness; producing convincing anthropology is also an art (Philen). Therefore, by looking at the art of anthropology, some of the contributors in this volume are able to revisit older debates within the discipline about the relationship between anthropology's messages and the rhetoric that conveys those messages in new ways (Huber). These chapters ask how and why anthropology is persuasive (King, Melomo) and how artful forms of anthropology in the media and the classroom shape and shift public understandings of the human world (Sheehan; Smith, Lund, and London).

Anthropology as a social sciences discipline is tasked with observing, describing, and explaining the complexities of humanity—the human condition and human pursuits. Anthropology as a humanities discipline is tasked with probing that which makes us human through our shared experiences. As a science, anthropology's approach is systematic, but as a study in humanity, anthropology's approach is empathetic. Anthropology works to bridge the great divide between being human and becoming a human being by surpassing the mundane pursuit of meeting needs to an ongoing search for meaning.

Edward B. Tylor expressed this canonical debate in anthropology in his oft quoted tenet, "Culture, or civilization, taken in its broad, ethnographic sense, is that complex whole which includes knowledge, belief, art, morals, law, custom, and any other *capabilities* and *habits* acquired by man as a member of society" ([1871] 1929, 1; italics mine). This precept appears ad nauseam in anthropological texts for good reason. Tylor acknowledges the importance of methodology in science—the systematic and descriptive approach known as ethnography used to understand taken-for-granted routines (i.e., habits). Bourdieu, by way of Aristotle, Marcel Mauss, and others, is credited with reelaborating *habitus* as the oxymoron "the durably installed generative principle of *regulated improvisations*" (1977, 78; italics mine). Customs, then, imbibed through processes of socialization and normalization, provide the structural genres, which we strive to imitate, reproduce, revise, reenvision, or transcend be it within the artistic tradition or some other cultural custom (cf. Dissanayake 1995).

Tylor also exposed culture and its study as something that is "acquired," learned, passed on, ongoing, and processual. Scholars today consistently rely on the analogy "culture is like water" to express its fluidity. One of my favorite definitions comes from W. Jeffrey Bolster's book *Black Jacks*, where he writes:

> Culture, however, can be imagined as a river—picking up contributions from contacts along-shore and feeder streams, relegating parts of itself to back-eddies, losing yet others to silent evaporation or stranding, and constantly mixing its elements, even while it moves inexorably along a course that it continually redefines. (1997, 35)

Culture then, to some degree, is fixed through shared history, traditions, customs, norms, and the like—water is water. To some degree, culture is also ever changing due to time, individuality, agency, a shifting environment, innovation, borrowing, and catastrophe (cf. Gell 1998). This allows social scientists to trace human universals and particulars and patterns and processes over time, such as the changing hem of a woman's skirt or why tie-dye is no longer popular among teenagers.

Tylor also understood culture and its study as a complex and integrated endeavor—what is often labeled "functionalism." Today, descriptions of cultural phenomena without an explanation are pooh-poohed in academia as a thankless, yet necessary first step in the pursuit of any good science. While potentially lacking in explanatory power, a detailed understanding of how something in society works should not be undervalued. In fact, I contend that it is the *attempt* at describing a cultural artifact, event, behavior, or institution (i.e., ethnography) that promotes clarity in recognizing the complexities of human society. This *capability* to study and describe humanity leads us back to Tylor.

Recognizing the intricacy of culture allows one to shift the theoretical gaze from *habits* to *capabilities* and back again. "Social systems that disdain or discount beauty, form, mystery, meaning, value, and quality—whether in art or in life—are depriving their members of human requirements as fundamental as those for food, warmth, and shelter" (Dissanayake 1995, xx). To take it a step further:

> Those who are in love with *practice* without *knowledge* are like the sailor who gets into a ship without rudder or compass and who never can be certain whether he is going. Practice must always be founded on sound theory, and to this Perspective is the guide and the gateway; and without this nothing can be done well in the matter of drawing. . . . The painter who draws merely by practice and by eye, without any reason, is like a mirror which copies every thing placed in front of it without being conscious of their existence. (Da Vinci 1888, 19-20; italics mine)

Art then is something that is done through artifice and skill, ritual and creativity, history and innovation, literalism and interpretation, pushing boundaries and honoring tradition (i.e., authenticity). To study art is to study the ultimate contradiction between aesthetics, as culturally constructed, and function, at a minimum serving to fulfill a basic human desire for expression, continuity, creativity, and valuation—to *feel* something, in the artist and, hopefully, the audience.

Art, recognized by Tylor as an important component of culture in his well-known definition, has been inevitably studied rigorously by social scientists, including anthropologists. Beginning at the close of nineteenth century, anthropologists began to view "primitive art" first as a form of unique or shared material culture (Frazer 1900; Pitt-Rivers 1906; Tylor [1871] 1929, [1878] 1964) and subsequently, "as having the potential to reveal historical patterns and relationships between groups" (Morphy and Perkins 2006b, 5; see also Boas [1927] 1955; Fagg 1965).

For a time, sociocultural evolutionary misconceptions and misplaced stereotypes of "primitivism" downgraded these socially integrated art forms by classifying them as craft, artisanal, decorative, functional, or primitive (Clifford 1988; Vogel 1988; Price 1989; Rubin [1985] 1999). The consequence was that early investigations were divided between the study of fine arts (read: "Western") and primitive arts (read: "Other") in which the latter were claimed as the disciplinary territory of anthropology as an extension of investigations into alterity (cf. Fanon 2004; Said [1978] 1994). The "objective" study of the materiality of art within anthropology, however, eventually gave way to studies into other realms of understanding and knowledge-building relating to the *practice* of art.

What resulted from this early collaboration between "world art" (i.e., non-Western, see for example, Morphy and Perkins 2006a; Venbrux, Rosi, and Welsch 2006) and anthropology was a unique glimpse into the integrated nature of meaning-making evidenced by the elaborate descriptions of artistic creation and the sharing of symbols as purposeful and intentional cultural acts (Svašek 2007). It became less about the object or artist; anthropological investigations instead began to privilege the social act or event—recitations, dramas, storytelling, masquerades, and dances (Forge 1973; Lamp 1996; Layton 1981; Lévi-Strauss 1963; Turner 1974, 1986). As a cultural phenomenon, art continues to be explored as an aesthetic (Coote and Shelton 1995), a form of communication (Banks and Morphy 1999), a repository for social memory (Huber 2011), a point of cultural contact (Lyon and Wells 2012; Steiner 1994), a commodity (Appadurai 1986; Phillips and Steiner 1999), and a political act (Adams 2006; McGovern 2013).

Arts' influence on anthropology as a textual enterprise has also been explored as a field of study and point of departure (Clifford 1988; Clifford and Marcus 1986; Tedlock and Mannheim 1995).

> What is interesting about these borrowings is that while Western anthropologists use such theorizing unproblematically as bases for interpreting other traditions, they often do not recognize that the categories they so deploy have been contested in their own culture's historic debates about art and the aesthetic. (Marcus and Myers 1995b, 13-14)

Anthropologists, then, as interpreters of "other" traditions, inhabit what Paul Stoller describes as "indeterminate betweeness of the imagination" (2009, 174). As such, by living and working within this aperture, between *how* and *what* we study, what results is a melding of science and life (Marcus and Myers 1995a; Schneider and Wright 2006, 2010). The anthropologist who bridges the gap between anthropology and art must value "writing that delights, writing that outrages, writing that evokes the human condition in all its messiness, glory, and misery—writing that reveals the blockages that are deleterious to our social and physical environment, and is thus able to promote crosscultural understanding."[2]

There are many inroads to the study of the art of anthropology and the anthropology of art as the preceding paragraphs attest: visual anthropology, anthropology of art, the anthropological enterprise as a creative act in and of itself, not to mention the various subcategories of commodification, materiality, symbolism, aesthetics, ethnology, et cetera (van Damme 2006; Venbrux, Rosi, and Welsch 2006). To narrow the field, the original contributions in the present volume rely on preceding ethnographic studies of art and their accompanying theoretical pursuits and pick up where the conversation leaves off in four key areas: textual art, art valuation, critical art, and the art of teaching.

Chapter Summaries

PART I. Textual Art: Divergent Narratives

In the opening chapter, "Art as Distraction: Rocking the Farm," Daniel W. Ingersoll and Kathleen Butler Ingersoll present a unique look at the collapse of the Rapa Nui society of Easter Island, choosing a divergent narrative that emphasizes the ways in which Western conceptions of art and apocalypse have each played a role in obscuring further research into the subject. The chapter takes an interesting new perspective, working to turn a classical case study of ecocide into a far more complex and stimulating study of environmental innovation. The authors make the argument that from the Western perspective, the "artistic" monoliths distract from greater cultural understanding of Rapa Nui society and culture by blinding the Western eye with these monumental structures. What results is a clear narrative that looks beyond Rapa Nui monumental "art" to find the spectacular story of everyday horticultural infrastructure development that involved billions of rocks, a far more impressive form of public works with much broader implications.

Next, Robert C. Philen's "A Memoir of an Other" continues the theme of textual art as he navigates the various dilemmas involved in constructing a memoir from various pieces of writing left behind by the subject—in this case, his partner who has passed away. In this chapter, the author utilizes aspects of personal and historical narrative in order to discuss the ongoing process of creating a posthumous memoir. The general theme of the chapter centers on the manners in which, by writing a memoir of another, one can produce ethnography and, simultaneously, a creative endeavor whereby the myth of the individual is generated. Overall, the author calls attention to the overlaying aspects of writing that are at once historical, ethnographic, and creative. Thus, ethnography may at times be parallel to art. Robert engages with his identity as an anthropologist to think about how to create the fitting memoir for his poet husband, Reginald Shepherd. What he discovers is that the pieces, *bricolage*, that make up Reginald's life, in both memory and various poetic and nonfiction texts, can be used to construct *an* individual, while maybe not *the* individual. These larger questions of biography as anthropology make this story unique in that it does not emerge from an ethnographic encounter, but from a piecing together.

The final chapter in this section, "Pocahontas and Rebecca: Two Tales of a Captive," by Margaret Huber critically examines the conflicting stories of Pocahontas—one taken from the written accounts of English colonists and another from the oral history of the Powhatan Native Americans. Huber evaluates the ways in which historical narratives, while not presenting facts, can instead inform us of the contemporary cultural values of those writing or speaking. Rather than labeling these accounts as ethnography or history, Huber alternatively chooses to brand them as "myths." And, as such, they are then transformed into creative and even artistic forms of expression that provide insight into the culture from which they were created.

PART II. Art Valuation: The Creativity/Conventionality Dialectic

The second section in the book deals with art valuation and what can be called a continuum in which all art is assigned a cultural and economic importance based on both implicit and explicit criteria. These standards are often contextual, unsettled, and ephemeral. Value has many forms—historic, economic, symbolic, political, sociocultural, and the like. In her chapter "Mirror Dance: Tourists, Artists, and First People Heritage in Botswana," Jessica Stephenson shows how Bushmen touristic art transitioned from an act of commodification and reclamation into a political message of San solidarity and resistance. Stephenson analyzes the Kuru Art Project in Botswana as a form of indigenous autoethnography formed in a "contact zone" and as contemporary San "yearnings" to reclaim a nostalgic past and assert a new First People political voice. Her chapter engages with many of the themes of this book, including valuation, agency, and authenticity. Stephenson's contribution is profound since it demonstrates how an indigenous group can look beyond the short-term economic gains made available through tourism and the production of functional tourist art. These artists instead transform their artistic craft into a contemporary medium of canvas painting that bridges the prehistoric tradition of cave painting, indigenous knowledge of the localized flora and fauna, and autoethnography while simultaneously making both hidden and overt political claims for land rights, cultural recognition and assertion of cultural identity, and pleas for autonomy. What results in this chapter is a complex and nuanced journey through San history, politics, and artistic traditions.

Jennifer Vogt's "A World of Difference: Unity and Differentiation Among Ceramicists in Quinua, Ayacucho, Peru" continues Stephenson's journey toward understanding these artistic tensions by delving into the interplay between creativity and conventionality. She notes that the artisans, facing economic as well as social pressures, must balance creativity in their art with the economic push to remain "traditional." The author calls attention to the amorphous and fluid nature of the industry, rejecting rigid categorizations of artists and their work. Instead of focusing on describing the ceramic objects, Vogt works with the dialectical social and economic processes that are at play in forming the *interpretation* of these pieces.

In the chapter, "Defining Art in the Gozo International Contemporary Arts Festival," Rachel Syka uses firsthand research to identify competing definitions of art within a localized context. On the one hand, art is classified according to a set of local criterion provided by the Gozo community members of Malta, and on the other, foreign artists participating in the Contemporary Arts Festival delineate what constitutes art. Syka emphasizes the ways in which globalization changes local conceptualizations of what is valuable while also reviewing "Western" definitions of arts versus crafts. Ultimately, Syka looks at these conceptual and practical differences in arts' interpretation within a specific context through her examination of the complex ways local artists are excluded or included in the international conversation based on their social networks, personal and professional experiences, and artistic medium and subject.

In the final chapter of this section, titled "Thomas Kinkade: Money, Class, and the Aesthetic Economy," Susan Falls engages with artwork perceived to be almost entirely produced for its potential exchange value. She examines the paintings of Thomas Kinkade and the ways in which they acquire value (as compared to other, perhaps more famous or elitist artists). She frames her discussion within the theory of political economy, commenting on how neoliberal economic policies contribute to the assignment of value to, as well as the devaluation of art (evident during the recent recession). Individuals may seek to display their own value or wealth through material or visual culture, which in turn assigns some sort of value to it. Art thus becomes an investment of sorts. This is illustrated by the popularity of Kinkade's work with Middle America. For the author, art is a mirror of our society, and as such, Kinkade is shown to have capitalized on the desire for lower-income Americans to reflect the behavior of the elite, using art as an investment. The result of this (arguably) overcommodification has been an increase in the popularity of Kinkade's work as well as a change in what middle- and lower-class Americans consider investment worthy.

PART III. Critical Art: New Ways of Seeing

In the volume's third section, the evaluation of what constitutes art and how it comes to be defined as such is taken up. In the chapter on "Style and Configuration in Prehistoric Iconography," Vernon James Knight Jr. presents a new and integrated methodology for iconography that blends it with considerations of style, particularly when examining archaeological and museum collections. Knight establishes a more comprehensive method by which to undertake the processes of iconography that improves upon the interpretation of materials within a collected corpus. He concludes that in any proper consideration of art, stylistic and iconographic analyses are separate, but interdependent, techniques. In order to interpret the meaning behind an object, one must consider both style and context. Otherwise, the likelihood of misrepresentation and misinterpretation of material objects is increased.

A second critique of previous understandings of "art" is taken up by Hector Qirko in his chapter "Race and Rhythm in Rock and Roll." He argues against a racially constructed history of this music genre. Qirko asserts that all musical styles are socially constructed, similar to all racial classifications. Essentially, Qirko stresses the social processes behind categorizations and the ways in which these processes have emphasized and continue to emphasize racial differences in musical development. The chapter highlights the historical transition and emergence of rock and roll and its evolution from multiple musical, and ultimately cultural, genres into a recognized category with a prevailing myth of racial origins. With an emphasis on historical processes and the addition of music theory, the chapter goes on to reposition rock and roll (and other musical forms) as nonracially defined movements with a number of complex influences. The naïve assumption that African American and European American music evolved separately is uncorroborated although, unfortunately, it still holds sway in much popular culture and thinking.

In the third and final chapter of this section, Lindsey King asks a grand and uncomfortable question for most anthropologists: "Does Our Being There Change What We Come to Study?" Based on ethnographic fieldwork in northern Brazil, King analyzes a particular votive tradition of making *promessa*, a type of prayer at a Catholic shrine, as a viable healing strategy through the offering of a symbolic object known as a *milagre*. She encountered several difficulties during her research, such as how to define aesthetics for a genre that had no clear aesthetic criteria. What King found fascinating was that some of these folk-made objects were saved by the church museum based on a murky "technical" merit that made them recognizable and relatable to the representative problem. King argues that she eventually gained what she called a "field sight" or an ability to judge these objects by honing her capacity to share an insider's perspective when evaluating these objects. However, once she was tasked with picking out particularly fine specimens before they were destroyed, King came to the realization that she may have been affecting the "field" simply by her presence and interest in this customary healing ritual. For instance, makers started signing their work; others began to be interested in portraying certain aesthetic qualities such as a level of realism and representativeness. Upon her return to the field several years later, she witnessed a shift in which milagres were now more uniform in appearance and hung on the walls of the Casa dos Milagres instead of being burned at the close of the pilgrimage season. In other words, the milagres had shifted from being ephemeral works to permanent displays that were admired, judged, and purchased by both the viewing and participating public. King concludes by expressing the fact that cultural change is inevitable, and yet, as anthropologists, we must consider what, if any, affect our being there may have. While her findings are inconclusive thus far, King expresses her interest in continuing to assess her cultural footprint in future investigations.

PART IV. Art and Anthropology in Our Classrooms and Colleges

In the final section, Elizabeth A. Sheehan discusses "Arts Integration as Critical Pedagogy." Sheehan describes the ways in which art integration programs can enrich and even perhaps empower students, particularly those who may come from disadvantaged backgrounds. These programs are set against the stark backdrop of standardized testing and the restrictive, "teaching for the test" approaches taken in public schools. Sheehan makes an argument for the essential role of art and creativity in an education system that she believes is becoming overburdened by rules, regulations, and limiting examinations. Through the use of architectural history and arts integration in a fourth-grade class in Richmond, Virginia, students are forced to confront a history, in this case one of slavery, that had been buried, literally and figuratively, in the geography and texts of Virginia and Virginia Studies. This was made possible, not by deviating from the No Child Left Behind standardization of the curriculum but by working within the required content areas while shifting the methodological approach of its conveyance. Field trips assisted students to confront their state's past. Through photography, the students were provided the opportunity to bring history into the present by forcing it back into the public consciousness. Finally, creative writing assignments allowed these students to dialogue with these historical re-creations in individualized and meaningful ways. While the program may be difficult to pedagogically measure and evaluate, and while the program was not necessarily evidence-based, its qualitative educational value, according to the author, was undeniable.

In the next chapter in this final section, Susan Kirkpatrick Smith, Laura D. Lund, and Marilyn R. London, in "The Art of Teaching Anthropology: Examples from Biological Anthropology," provide pedagogical exercises that frame the hidden art of teaching anthropology as something that must be encouraged, nurtured, allowed time to develop, and brought to light. Ultimately, this chapter shows education for what it truly is, a social and collaborative enterprise that, analogous to art, is formulated within a specific genre or cultural domain and then communicated to others in an ongoing dialogue between the colleagues, instructors, and students. As a social enterprise, then, teaching can be improved upon by shaping the artistic skill set acquired through experience, study, and observation into something culturally meaningful for the discipline, the teacher-scholar, and the students of anthropology (which we all are). Smith et al. go on to encourage the development of a like-minded community of scholars who can advance sound curricula in a dialogic fashion through an elaboration of discipline-specific scholarship on teaching and learning. As of yet, this is something that the discipline of anthropology does not have. In other words, Smith et al. boldly display what a disciplined aesthetic, or the art of teaching anthropology, is capable of transmitting.

Last, in "The Art of Anthropology at a College in Crisis: Exploring Some Effects of Neoliberalism on Higher Education," Vincent H. Melomo makes a statement about the current condition of higher education in the United States. Liberal Arts education, as this chapter suggests, is fading in the face of a dominant neoliberal cultural logic. This chapter, by considering the undoing of an anthropology major at William Peace University in Raleigh, North Carolina, illuminates specific pressures put on universities, academic departments, and faculty by these service-oriented, market-driven ideologies. The neoliberal shift in the United States is directly influencing the professional culture of higher education from open intellectual inquiry to an institutionalized stress on what Melomo refers to as *performativity* (i.e., evidence, measurement, planning, indicators, academic audits, and quality assurance measures). Humanistic concerns are being replaced in higher education by a potentially deleterious overprofessionalization. Liberal Arts is becoming less open-minded, spontaneous, and virtuous, instead targeting economic outcomes. Melomo concludes that it is the strength of political persuasion as an art form and the neoliberal ideology pervading popular culture that led to the dismantling of the anthropology major at William Peace University. Popular perceptions about the discipline's humanistic characteristics view anthropology as somehow out of step with the new pragmatics of education, even when these popular perceptions are not necessarily based on evidence. What Melomo calls for in this chapter is an equally persuasive and artful rebuttal to the neoliberal agenda by marketing the discipline beyond disciplinary boundaries, by demonstrating how anthropology's teaching and research goals serve economic and practical goals, and by deconstructing the neoliberal logic that continues to shape our values, actions, and culture.

Conclusion

This introduction presents a case for the sociality of art as a shared and communicative act. It historicizes the study of art from the anthropological perspective and shows how art, humanity, and the creation and study of art and the humanities are intertwined. The chapters in this book explore not only art through the lens of anthropology but also anthropology through the lens of art. Given that art is a social phenomenon, the contributors to this volume interpret the complex relationships between art and anthropology as a means of fashioning novelty, continuity, and expression in everyday life. They further explore this connection by reifying customs and traditions through texts, textures, and events, thereby shaping the very artistic skills acquired by experience, study, and observation into something culturally meaningful.

Notes

1. Translated from the original French, the quote "Le premier qui compara la femme à une rose était un poète, le second un imbécile" is splashed throughout the Internet as one of the all-time most famous comments on cliché. The original source is unknown.

2. This statement is from the *Anthropology and Humanism* journal's description statement, http://www.wiley.com/WileyCDA/WileyTitle/productCd-ANHU.html, accessed June 24, 2013.

Acknowledgments

Amanda Woomer and Dayton Starnes assisted greatly with the chapter summaries. I would also like to thank Allison Garefino for commenting on an earlier draft of this chapter.

References

Adams, Kathleen M. 2006. *Art as Politics: Re-Crafting Identities, Tourism, and Power in Tana Toraja, Indonesia.* Honolulu: University of Hawaii Press.

Appadurai, Arjun, ed. 1986. *The Social Life of Things: Commodities in Cultural Perspective.* New York: Cambridge University Press.

Banks, Marcus, and Howard Morphy, eds. 1999. Rethinking Visual Anthropology. New Haven, CT: Yale University Press.

Boas, Franz. (1927) 1955. *Primitive Art.* New York: Dover Publications.

Bolster, W. Jeffrey. 1997. *Black Jacks: African American Seamen in the Age of Sail.* Cambridge, MA: Harvard University Press.

Bourdieu, Pierre. 1977. *Outline of a Theory of Practice.* Translated by Richard Nice. New York: Cambridge University Press.

Clifford, James. 1988. *The Predicament of Culture: Twentieth-Century Ethnography, Literature, and Art.* Cambridge, MA: Harvard University Press.

Clifford, James, and George E. Marcus, eds. 1986. *Writing Culture: The Poetics and Politics of Ethnography.* Berkeley: University of California Press.

Coote, Jeremy, and Anthony Shelton, eds. 1995. *Anthropology, Art and Aesthetics.* Oxford: Clarendon Press.

Da Vinci, Leonardo. 1888. *The Notebooks of Leonardo Da Vinci, Complete.* Translated by Jean Paul Richter. http://fulltextarchive.com/page/The-Notebooks-of-Leonardo-Da-Vinci-Complete1/.

Dissanayake, Ellen. 1995. *Homo Aestheticus: Where Art Comes From and Why.* Seattle: University of Washington Press.

Fagg, William Buller. 1965. *Tribes and Forms in African Art.* New York: Tudor Publishing.

Fanon, Frantz. 2004. *The Wretched of the Earth.* Translated by Richard Philcox. New York: Grove Press.

Forge, Anthony, ed. 1973. *Primitive Art and Society.* New York: Oxford University Press.

Frazer, James George. 1900. *The Golden Bough: A Study in Magic and Religion.* 2nd ed. 3 vols. London: Macmillan.

Geertz, Clifford. 1976. "Art as a Cultural System." *MLN, Comparative Literature* 91(6): 1473-99.

Gell, Alfred. 1998. *Art and Agency: Towards a New Anthropological Theory.* New York: Oxford University Press.

Huber, Margaret, ed. 2011. *Museums and Memory: Southern Anthropological Society Proceedings*, No. 39. Knoxville, TN: Newfound Press.

Lamp, Frederick. 1996. *Art of the Baga: A Drama of Cultural Reinvention.* New York: Museum for African Art.

Layton, Robert. 1981. *The Anthropology of Art.* New York: Cambridge University Press.

Lévi-Strauss, Claude. 1963. *Structural Anthropology.* New York: Basic Books.

Lyon, Sarah, and E. Christian Wells, eds. 2012. *Global Tourism: Cultural Heritage and Economic Encounters.* Lanham, MD: AltaMira Press.

Marcus, George E., and Fred R. Myers, eds. 1995a. *The Traffic in Culture: Refiguring Art and Anthropology.* Berkeley: University of California Press.

Marcus, George E., and Fred R. Myers. 1995b. "The Traffic in Art and Culture: An Introduction." In *The Traffic in Culture: Refiguring Art and Anthropology*, edited by George E. Marcus and Fred R. Myers, 1-51. Berkeley: University of California Press.

McGovern, Mike. 2013. *Unmasking the State: Making Guinea Modern*. Chicago: University of Chicago Press.

Morphy, Howard, and Morgan Perkins, eds. 2006a. *The Anthropology of Art: A Reader*. Malden, MA: Blackwell Publishing.

Morphy, Howard, and Morgan Perkins. 2006b. "The Anthropology of Art: A Reflection on its History and Contemporary Practice." In *The Anthropology of Art: A Reader*, edited by Howard Morphy and Morgan Perkins, 1-32. Malden, MA: Blackwell Publishing.

Phillips, Ruth B., and Christopher B. Steiner, eds. 1999. *Unpacking Culture: Art and Commodity in Colonial and Postcolonial Worlds*. Berkeley: University of California Press.

Pitt-Rivers, Augustus Henry Lane-Fox. 1906. *Evolution of Culture and Other Essays*, edited by J. L. Myres. Oxford: Clarendon Press.

Price, Sally. 1989. *Primitive Art in Civilized Places*. Chicago: The University of Chicago Press.

Rubin, William. (1985) 1999. *"Primitivism" in 20th Century Art: Affinity of the Tribal and Modern*. New York: Museum of Modern Art.

Said, Edward W. (1978) 1994. *Orientalism*. 25th Anniversary ed. New York: Vintage Books.

Schneider, Arnd, and Christopher Wright, eds. 2006. *Contemporary Art and Anthropology*. New York: Berg.

———. 2010. *Between Art and Anthropology: Contemporary Ethnographic Practice*. New York: Berg.

Steiner, Christopher B. 1994. *African Art in Transit*. New York: Cambridge University Press.

Stoller, Paul. 2009. *The Power of the Between: An Anthropological Odyssey*. Chicago: University of Chicago Press.

Svašek, Maruška. 2007. *Anthropology, Art and Cultural Production*. London: Pluto Press.

Tedlock, Dennis, and Bruce Mannheim, eds. 1995. *The Dialogic Emergence of Culture*. Urbana: University of Illinois Press.

"The Uses of Cliche." 2011. *Armed and Dangerous: Sex, Software, Politics, and Firearms. Life's Simple Pleasures...*, http://esr.ibiblio.org/?p=3173.

Turner, Victor W. 1974. *Dramas, Fields and Metaphors: Symbolic Action in Human Society*. Ithaca, NY: Cornell University Press.

———. 1986. *The Anthropology of Performance*. New York: PAJ Publications.

Tylor, Edward Burnett. (1871) 1929. Primitive Culture: Researches into the Development of Mythology, Philosophy, Religion, Language, Art and Custom. 5th ed. London: J. Murray.

———. (1878) 1964. *Researches into the Early History of Mankind and the Development of Civilization*. Edited and abridged with an introduction by Paul Bohannan. Chicago: University of Chicago Press.

van Damme, Wilfried. 2006. "Anthropologies of Art: Three Approaches." In *Exploring World Art*, edited by Eric Venbrux, Pamela Sheffield Rosi, and Robert L. Welsch, 69-81. Long Grove, IL: Waveland Press.

Venbrux, Eric, Pamela Sheffield Rosi, and Robert L. Welsch, eds. 2006. *Exploring World Art*. Long Grove, IL: Waveland Press.

Vogel, Susan. 1988. *ART/Artifact: African Art in Anthropology Collections*. New York: Museum for African Art.

PART I

Textual Art: Divergent Narratives

Art as Distraction: Rocking the Farm

Daniel W. Ingersoll and Kathleen Butler Ingersoll

Abstract

Monumental architecture, massive statuary, and other art forms fascinate Westerners and tend to inspire positive judgments about past cultural virtuosity and sophistication. Like the pyramids of Egypt or the stone masonry of Machu Picchu, the *moai* (the statues) and *ahu* (stone platforms supporting moai) of Rapa Nui (a.k.a. Easter Island) have impressed, mystified, and preoccupied the Western cultural imagination since their encounter by Europeans.[1] Explorers, archaeologists, anthropologists, and tourists are drawn to the monumental like moths to light—which is understandable—but that light also blinds. Here a case is made that for Rapa Nui the obsession for the monumental has led to a certain inability to perceive past Rapanui culture in a holistic fashion. For example, we contend that the labor to sculpt and move the moai has tended to be massively overestimated, in comparison with the enormous energy invested in constructing the more homely horticultural infrastructure that involved billions of rocks. We argue that the loss of the palms did not cause the culture to crash because moai could no longer be transported or because the soils eroded away, as many claim, but rather that the palms became part of that more humble but enduring subsurface realm as amendment for planting pit soil. We also argue that the Western narrative of Rapanui cultural collapse, which hinges in large part on the cessation of moai production, is not based so much on empirical data but on a ubiquitous Western mythic story form of apocalypse, here a secular, Malthusian version. The preoccupation with monumental art and the apocalyptic story model shape the perceived outcomes: cultural Armageddon, collapse, and ecocide. The collapse story tells more about us than about them.

The Monumental

When anthropologist H. Russell Bernard polls Americans (United States), most recently in Florida, on what they rank as the great accomplishments of science and social science, he finds that they tend to conceptualize science as engineering and technology, identifying "life-saving drugs, computers, space exploration, and so on" (2012, 1). Almost no respondents mention constitutions, encyclopedias, relativity theory, actuarial tables, time-motion studies, probability theory—ideas that have transformed the world and that made the technology possible. American cultural "marking" of "success" clearly gravitates toward the material, the physical, and the palpable (Bernard 2010). Ideas find themselves relegated to the dubious realm of the Ivory Tower.

Ask any Westerner: What are the wonders of the world, ancient and modern? Pyramids, temples, tunnels, bridges, cathedrals, castles, frescoes, statues, skyscrapers, et cetera, the bigger, the more complex the technology, the better. Just watch the lead-in to the popular TV show *The Big Bang Theory* that interleaves on a timeline, moai among other glimpses of the world's extraordinary material accomplishments like the wheel, the Leaning Tower of Pisa, a locomotive, automobiles, warplanes, pyramids, and the Sphinx (evolutionary life forms, images of Jesus, Einstein, Martin Luther King Jr., and the Constitution appear also). If it's monumental, it's going to grab Western attention, and if it's non-Western in origin, the mystery quest contest begins. Who built it? Surely, *these* people couldn't have engineered those massive earthen temple mounds (Southeast United States), the giant desert figures (Nasca Lines), the pyramids (Egypt, Mexico), et cetera, those marvelous statues and precise stonemasonry (Rapa Nui)! Rather, it looks like the work of the Seven Lost Tribes of Israel, Outer Space Aliens, itinerant Egyptians, or balsa-raft sailors from South America. The tightly fitted basalt blocks facing of Rapa Nui's Ahu Vinapu resembles that of Machu Picchu. If built by Peruvians, how did they get there? The moai, how did they move them? Myriad experiments follow to ascertain the technological processes: Were the moai walked (Heyerdahl 1989; Pavel 1995; Hunt and Lipo 2010), advanced with a bipod device (Mulloy 1970), or dragged on sledges, and if so, prone or supine (Van Tilburg 1994, 1995, 1996), or moved upright on rollers (Love 2000)?

Monumental architecture, massive statuary, and other art forms fascinate Westerners and tend to inspire positive judgments about past cultural virtuosity and sophistication. Like the pyramids of Egypt or the stonemasonry of Machu Picchu, the moai and ahu of Rapa Nui (you can readily find images of these on the web) have impressed, mystified, and preoccupied the Western cultural imagination since their first glimpse by Europeans. One attribute of the monumental, of course, is mass. The bigger the better; a smaller version, even if equivalent or greater skill is required to make it, rarely commands the same admiration—the craft skills required to form a contemporary five-centimeter-tall (little finger length) moai from hard obsidian, found in every tourist shop on Rapa Nui, may exceed those needed to fashion a five-meter-tall one weighing fifteen tons from tuff or basalt.

The Arts

Combine the monumental with "art," and you have the real power to move the Western audience. And what could be more artful than the enigmatic smile of Mona Lisa, or more entrancing than the gaze of *Hoa Haka Nana I'a* (view this moai by visiting the website of the British Museum) (Horley and Lee 2008, 112)? We place *art* in quotation marks here, in part because art lives in the minds of the beholders. For Westerners, art constitutes one special and segmented category of experience and meaning among many other categories. Western culture generates myriad bounded, discrete categories: species names, personality types, occupational titles, as well as disciplines such as anthropology, sociology, history, and economics. Anthropology, for example, often deploys classificatory categories like kinship, religion, myth, ritual, subsistence, and technology. Although anthropologists of the functionalist theoretical persuasion attempt to interrelate them, the categories still remain segmented (Harris 1968, 516-17, 1999, 51-52), and they are still projected onto other cultures as if the categories were universal in their distribution, which they are not.

Art exists as a bounded Western cultural category. In Western culture, art pertains to the individual. Art offers a means to excel, to achieve wealth, to signal invidious distinction, to acquire fame, recognition, and remembrance. Art should be creative and original, thought provoking, radical, and new. Art stands apart from the functional; works of art are foregrounded, framed, set off from the mundane and placed in special locations. What Western culture defines as art entrances, captivates, inspires, and rewards with respect and admiration. The artistic, the monumental, and the technologically virtuosic rivet Western attention to the point of fixation, compulsion, and blindness—resulting in tunnel vision in respect to the cultural complexity of others. An example from another culture: when Westerners view Navajo "sandpaintings," they call them paintings and label them "works of art." They watch in horror as the paintings are erased at the end of a curing ceremony. Even the anthropologist is barred from committing the sandpaintings to museums. Why is that? You need to put away the Western categories and take a holistic view of healing in Navajo culture to understand the drypaintings. Griffin-Pierce writes:

> The sandpainting is considered to be a sacred living entity. The Anglo perception of a sandpainting as an artistic achievement misses the true meaning of the sandpainting. The physical beauty of the depicted image is insignificant in comparison to the ceremonial accuracy and sacredness of the depicted forms. The emphasis of the sandpaintings is on process, the dynamic flow of action, and on its ability to summon power through the process of its creation and use. (1992, 55)

It's not about technology or art but about the power of knowledge, thought, words, mythic symbols, and the efficacy of the ritual itself to restore harmony and balance to a person or group. As the ritual unfolds, the sandpainting grows in depth and morphs, helping to tell stories and to merge past and present. You could not really exhibit a sandpainting in a museum; the upper surface of the sandpainting is just the final surface of a three-dimensional being. If you can grasp this, then not classifying sandpaintings as art makes perfect sense.

Monumental Art

If we combine the monumental and art, the attraction is magnified indeed.[2] The moai are big *and* artistic, right (images of moai are easy to find on the web, for example, at TREKEARTH and the National

Geographic sites)? Of course! How big? So big that it took forests of trees to transport them. So big that an entire transportation system had to be created to carry them. So big that the manpower draw to create these social signaling devices overtaxed the economy, as the competition to outdo the Jones clan spiraled upwards until the last palm was cut down. So big that the overtaxed economy collapsed into civil disorder. So big that with the palms gone, canoes could no longer be fashioned, and the Rapanui became island-bound.

How artistic? So artistic that the moai have become widespread icons of artistic virtuosity for millions of Americans and other Westerners. What follows is a sampling of moai madness. There are restaurants that feature moai, such as Tiki Moai House in Fort Lauderdale, Florida, and Aku Aku in Las Vegas, Nevada. Want a moai garden statue? You can order a six-foot-high replica of one from *Ahu Akivi* through *SkyMall* (a catalog available to "approximately 88% of all domestic air passengers reaching more than 650 million air travelers annually" [www.skymall.com]) or directly from Design Toscano. Design Toscano also sells moai bookends. You can try to read your books in the glow from a Lumisource Electra Phosphor table lamp made in the shape of a moai. About to sneeze? Pull a tissue out of the nose of a moai tissue dispenser, available from the Acorn or the Bits and Pieces catalogs. You can get that marvelous hospitality drink popular in Chile and Peru, the pisco sour, in moai-shaped black plastic bottles—even in the United States (you can find it easily on the web, for example, at Tiki Central). Some companies, such as Moai Technologies or the Fellows Galleries, feature moai in their advertising. Buy a Wilco moai poster and support Los Padres Forest Watch. A recent (January 2013) Microsoft TV ad for its latest operating system depicts a seacoast scene (Pacific Northwest?) with a glimpse of a giant moai-shaped rock. Send a moai greeting card featuring three conversing moai that says, "Happy Birthday from one the air moai with the caption "April 5th, 1722 Explorers discover 'Keester Island'" (American Greetings). Moai cartoons appear in magazines such as the *The New Yorker* (October 11, 2004), where a man with a moai-like head and a woman are at a bar. The woman says, "Wait. I never forget a face—Easter Island, 1722." Cartoons making the rounds on the Internet depict moai: one with two Rapanui men standing among a number of Ranao Raraku quarry-slope moai, one saying to the other, "This little vanity project of yours won't last, you know" (Creators Syndicate, Inc. 2010). In another cartoon depicting a group of moai on a grassy hill gazing at the sea, one moai says to the other moai, "Look at me while I'm talking to you" (www.CartoonStock.com). In the realm of the fine arts, one of Max Ernst's images in his graphic novel *Une Semaine de Bonté ou Les Sept Éléments Capitaux* (1934) depicts a man with a moai head looking in a hand mirror with a giant praying mantis perched on the dresser, and behind the man, a woman looking in the window from outside (shown in Kjellgren, Van Tilburg, and Kaeppler. 2001, 22, figure 7, *Jeudi le Noir Autre Example: L'Île de Pâques*). Ernst portrayed a series of humans with heads of *moai*.

We conclude our moai examples with some in-print representations. Since at least 1997, the *Rapa Nui Journal* has offered the regular feature Moai Sightings, but as early as 1992, the publication made occasional mentions of sightings. For example, in volume 25, issue 2, released in October 2011 (68), the following were featured: moai garden art from *SkyMall*, a moai atop a coffee stand in San Diego, a Starbucks cup from Chile with the Ahu Tongariki moai, battery-powered tiki pepper grinders, a moai head in the Gardens of Appletern in Holland, and a counter of a deli in Rocklin, California, with moai painted on the vertical surface. The *Rapa Nui Journal* recently decided to drop this section (last issue with the section, May 2012). In addition, many books about Easter Island feature moai on their covers: Fischer (2005), Flenley and Bahn (2003), Heyerdahl (1959, 1989), Loret and Tanacredi (2003), McCall (1994), and McAnany and Yoffee (2010). The cover of the July 2012 issue of *National Geographic* recreates the scene of ancient Rapanui walking a moai with ropes attached to the head; the cover headline reads, "Easter Island The Riddle of the Moving Statues."

The impact of the moai on Western cultural sensitivity and consciousness has been massive, we argue, to the point of distraction. The moai as monumental art have dominated interpretation. We present a brief "revisionist" history that downplays moai and diverts the focus to the greater landscape.

Our Brief Revisionist History

There are at least nine hundred moai (not including those possibly incorporated in semipyramidal and boat-shaped ahu), about 250 moai on ahu, and the remainder exist around the Raraku quarry (photograph 2.1) or beside roads (Mieth and Bork 2004a, 20; Sanger 2011). If the period of moai construction extended from around 1000 AD to ca. 1680, as some suggest, that's about 680 years, and positing regular production, about 1.3 moai per year (similar estimates can be found in Hunter-Anderson [1998, 88]). If the period of moai construction began after a later settlement date of ca. 1200 and lasted until ca. 1680, that would be about 480 years, a creation rate of about 1.9 moai per year, not sufficient to drain an island with an eventual population of five thousand to ten thousand (Flenley and Bahn 2003, 201). Employing the estimate of Jared Diamond (2005, 90 and 2007, 1693; see also Hunt and Lipo 2011, 11), who posited a population peak of around twenty or thirty thousand, surely many hands made short work. We suggest that although the moai are spectacular, they did not bankrupt the society any more than making skyscrapers has bankrupted Manhattan.

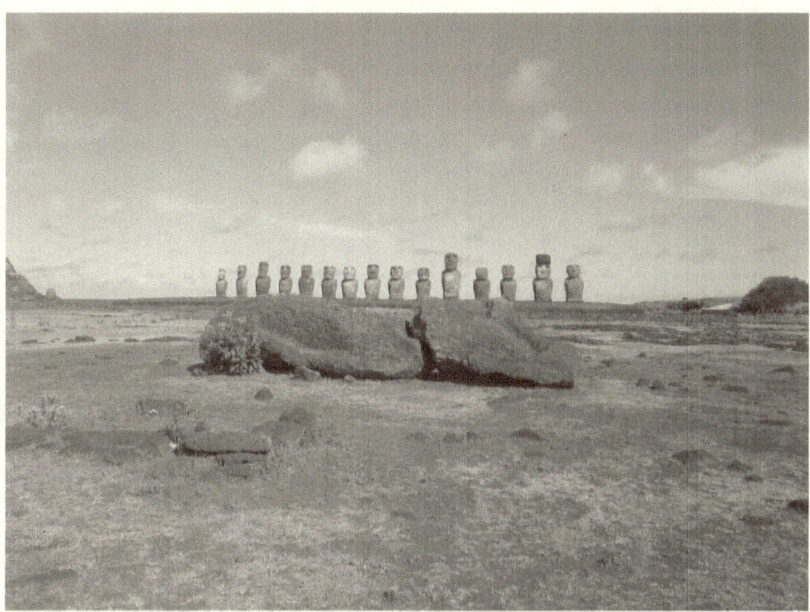

Photograph 2.1. A view of Ahu Tongariki (background) from inland looking seaward, with one supine moai (foreground). The position of the camera is within the 1960 tsunami flood plain. (Photograph by authors)

What about the ahu, about 250 of them, with both rough-cut and fitted plates on the outer surfaces and tons of basalt rubble fill within? Some of the ahu are of massive scale, as at Ahu Tongariki, which is 220 meters long (photograph 2.2). But ahu without moai on them do not evoke nearly as much awe from the Western observer. Yet, the ahu, though usually reconfigured and without moai, continued in use into the 1860s and the time of Western disruption of traditional Rapanui society. And what about all those massive basalt curbstones (slightly curved foundation stones with small insertion holes for roofing support members) for *hare paenga* (elliptical or canoe-shaped houses) and their pavements of beach cobbles (*poro*)? No doubt, substantial labor was involved for all of these and more. Yet no commentators claim that making ahu platforms, fashioning curbstones and hare paenga, transporting poro, or building roads or canoe ramps exhausted Rapa Nui resources.

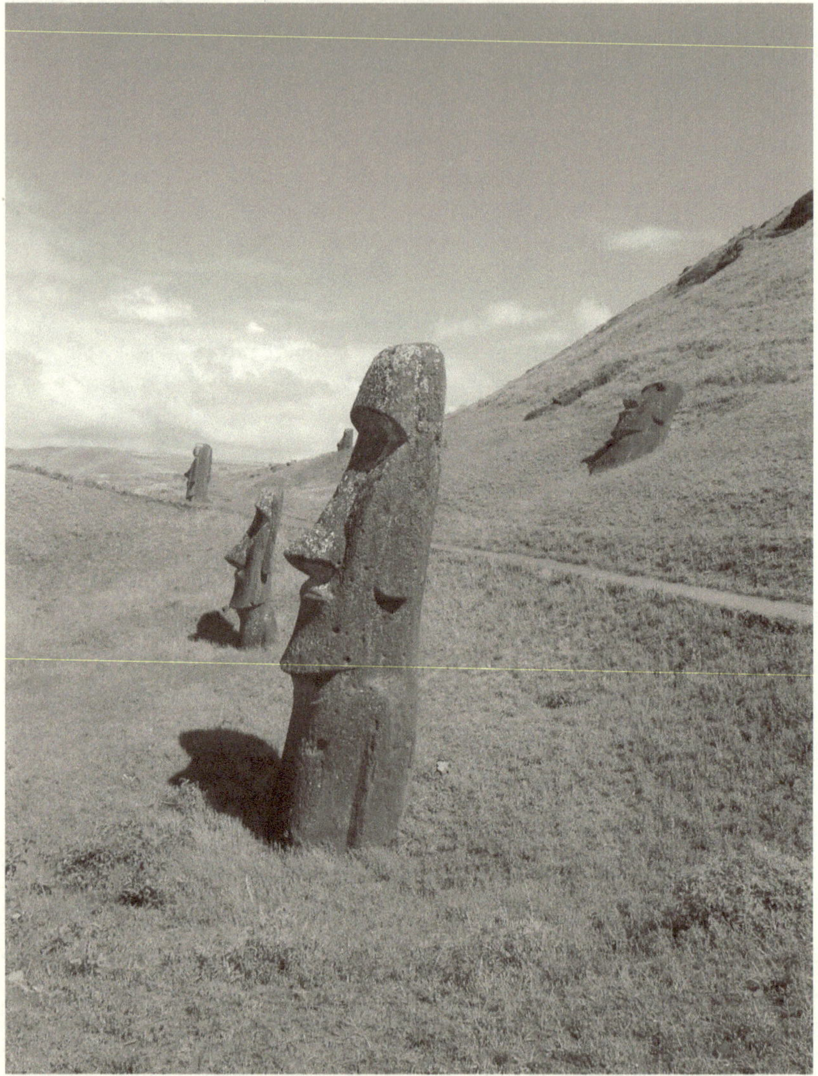

Photograph 2.2. Moai on the Rano Raraku quarry slope. (Photograph by authors)

The moai did not all fall at the same time, nor did they necessarily all ever stand at one time. And the moai on the Rano Raraku quarry slope (not on ahu) remain standing to this day. European observers from Roggeveen in 1722 through the 1830s reported moai standing on ahu (Eyzaguirre 2004; Richards 2008, 69-70). Raging civil discord often gets invoked to explain the toppling, but few researchers have considered alternative causes and the chronological parsing of the falls, with Edwards et al. (1996) a notable exception. Following Edwards, we suggest that some of the moai fell due to simple structural instability of the ahu, or from tremors or earthquakes, and in some cases tsunami. While we are not aware of any documented topplings of moai by tsunami, in 1960 a massive tsunami spawned by an earthquake in Chile destroyed Ahu Tongariki; if any moai had been standing on Ahu Tongariki at the time, they would have been knocked down. Previously fallen moai were carried inland hundreds of feet. Ahu Tongariki was rebuilt and restored with moai erect by the Japanese firm Tadano in the 1990s (E. R. Mulloy 1991; Fischer 2005, 237-238) and is one of the major tourist stops today. Many moai seem to have been deliberately reincorporated into new forms of ahu as *fill*, perhaps by their own kin group members, as the prevailing cultural symbolism gradually evolved away from moai as cultural icons (see Fischer 2005; Flenley and Bahn 2003; or McCall 1994 for descriptions of the more recent Makemake and Birdman symbolism).

Look Away: A Revisionist Landscape

Enough about moai. Step back from the ahu. Look where the coastal moai are looking: inland. What does the Western observer, the visitor, or the tourist see? According to a sampling of tourist impressions (Bove n.d.) and our own study-tour student reactions (at least initially): a barren, volcanic wasteland (photograph 2.3). In a recent book by two archaeologists, the word *barren* was used seven times, with most occurrences referring to Rapa Nui. Why? In part because the rocky appearance of the landscape suggests to the Westerner a natural volcanic rubble field, in so many places difficult to traverse. There are thought to be no trees.[3] And there are few "working" people on the landscape. The crops once tended before European contact have been replaced with imported grasses for grazing, first for sheep, now for horses and cattle, not to mention the accidental invasive species (photograph 2.4). So, you need to use your imagination to reenvision the pre-European contact landscape: put the Rapanui people, the pre-European contact plants and grasses, and the gardens back into the panorama.

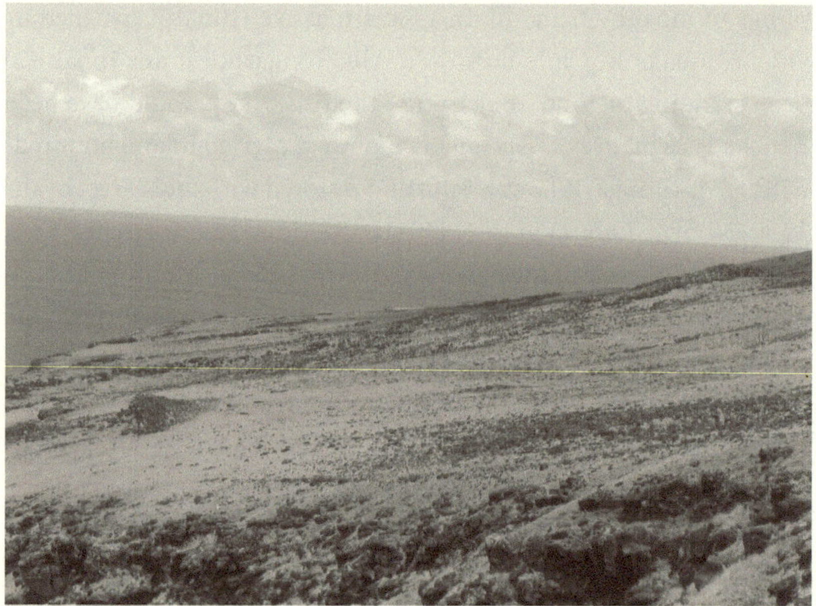

Photograph 2.3. West Coast ahu and rock-mulched gardens. (Photograph by authors)

The landscape beyond the social and ritual zones near the ahu and moai could hardly be further from a natural one. We pick up at the point where the *Jubea*-like palm no longer punctuates the landscape, perhaps due to human agency, but that's another story we will address in a separate paper. Pre-European contact cultural practices, rediscovered by archaeologists like Haoa Cardinali, Stevenson, and

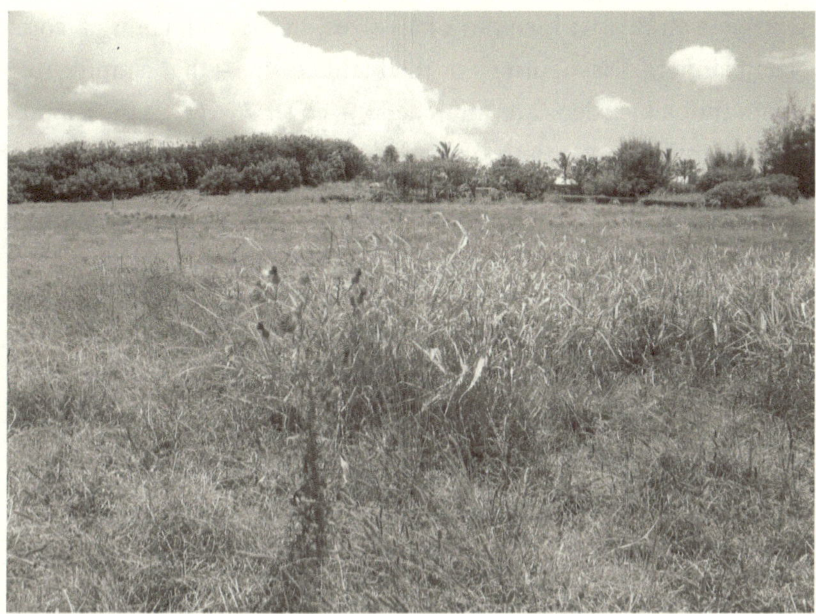

Photograph 2.4. Invasive plants: bull thistle and johnsongrass, west coast. (Photograph by authors)

Wozniak (Stevenson et al. 2005; Stevenson and Haoa Cardinali 2008a, 2008b, 2008c, 2008d; Wozniak 2005), indicate extensive quarrying and relocation of intentionally shaped and sized stone. Those scatters across the Rapa Nui landscape are human-created, as much as the burial markers in a New England cemetery surrounded by stonewalls. Think of almost every stone you see on the landscape as a manuport, placed deliberately in strategic areas by human action, for reasons Sonia Haoa Cardinali heard mentioned by the old people of the island (photograph 2.5). What many of the stone scatters mark is different kinds of gardens, such as lithic mulched, veneer, and boulder (photograph 2.6). Baer et al. (2008, 107) define six categories of rock gardens. These gardens clothe an amazing proportion of the landscape—excepting the Poike, the oldest of the island's volcanoes. Mieth and Bork (2004a, 42) estimate that "about 70% of the island surface is strewn with stones of all sizes, in places forming a complete blanket." Distributions of the blanket type—that is, mulching stones (not all gardens are "mulched")—cover 76 km^2 of the island's 166 km^2 total (Bork, Mieth, and Tschochner 2004, 12; Wozniak n.d.). Mieth and Bork write:

> The labor intensity of the stone mulching phase is certainly still underestimated in its cultural importance. Taking into account the total weight of transported stones, it is clear that the physical effort invested in the stone mulching culture probably exceeded the labor efforts of the ahu/moai phase by far. (2004b, 62)

They graphically illustrate this concept of estimated stone-transporting labor with two vertical bars (2004b, 63, figure 13), one bar in front of a moai on an ahu, and the other superimposed on a stone-mulched garden surface. The bar height/volume ratio is about 1:11.7 (ahu and moai to stone mulch). We suggest that with quantification of ahu and moai volumes, and comparison to stone-mulched surfaces and underlying amended soil volumes within sample social territorial units, the ratio would actually be much more extreme than 1:11.7.

A study conducted by Ileana Bradford and reported by Hunt and Lipo (2011, 39-41) identified 2,553 *manavai* enclosures (photograph 2.7), covering 6.4 square miles, or 10 percent of the island surface area. We think the area figure is high, both impressionistically and mathematically. Our calculations with these figures, converting to meters, give their average radius of a manavai at 137 meters, on a scale with football fields. We think the average is more like 2.5 meters in diameter. Wozniak (2005, 140) furnishes a dimension range of 2-5 meters. In terms of numbers, according to Morrison (conversation, July 2012), the initial numbers were calculated from satellite images;

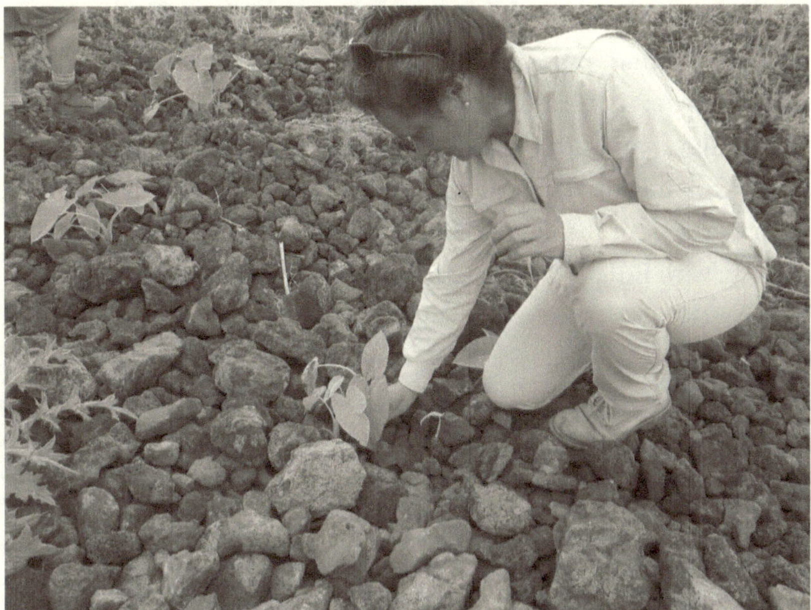

Photograph 2.5. Sonia Haoa Cardinali in a rock-mulched, veneer garden with taro. (Photograph by authors)

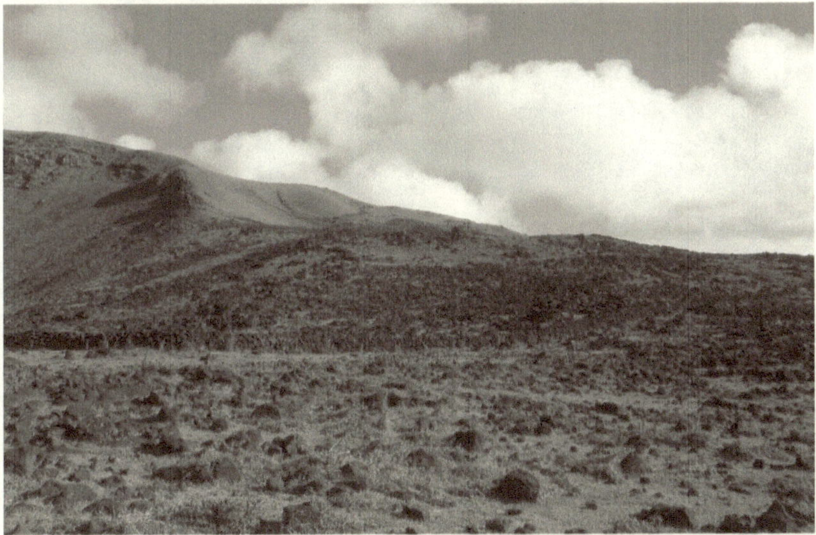

Photograph 2.6. Extensive boulder gardens, north coast, Hanga Oteo. (Photograph by authors)

he thought around 80 percent of the number quoted above would actually ground proof to manavai. However, there are inarguably many manavai, and many more manavai than ahu and moai. The manavai and lithic-mulched gardens and boulder gardens still retain functionality and higher fertility levels after nearly 150 years of internment of the cultivators and by 100 years of sheep company grazing with little or no replacement of lost nutrients.

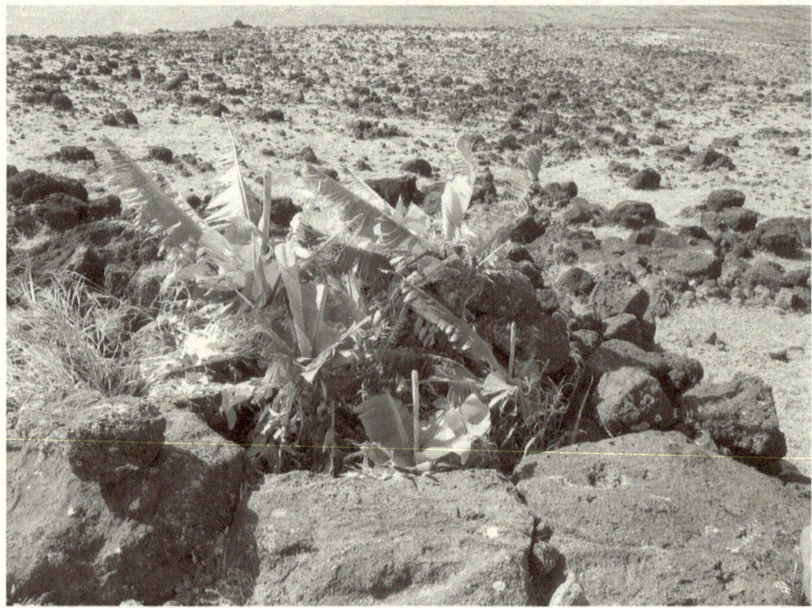

Photograph 2.7. Manavai with bananas surrounded by boulder gardens. (Photograph by authors)

Often, even when you think you are walking on natural bedrock, you are actually on a quarry's bottom, which may once have served a useful end-function of collecting and redirecting water flow. Each quarry—a volcanic flow or outcrop, mass of boulders, or extrusion—might have produced construction plates and curbs as well as thousands and thousands of stones for gardens. Mieth and Bork (2004a, 12) calculate 1.14 billion mulching stones, or 2.15 million tons for the island. Stevenson and Haoa Cardinali (2008c, 38) say billions (an estimate, not a count)—in just one area's survey—and we agree. Photograph 2.8 shows quarrying in interrupted progress. But when the rock finally is quarried down to ground level, it may serve an additional terminal function: water collection and diversion. Photograph 2.9 is a view of a large quarry in cross section. Photograph 2.10 shows a horse drinking water from a quarry taken to ground level; some terminal quarry surfaces of this type have channels cut in to direct water out. Thus, quarrying also contributed as one means of water resource management. Other means, quite dramatic in the transformation of the landscape, are being investigated now by Burkhard Vogt and his team (2012) on an intermittent watercourse on Terevaka, a location named Ava Ranga Uka A Toroke Hau.

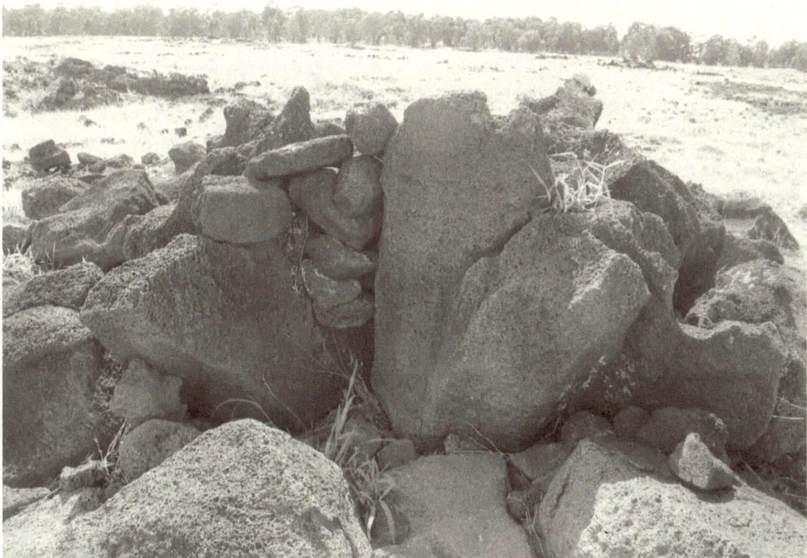

Photograph 2.8. Volcanic outcrops with wedge rocks inserted to break up basalt. (Photograph by authors)

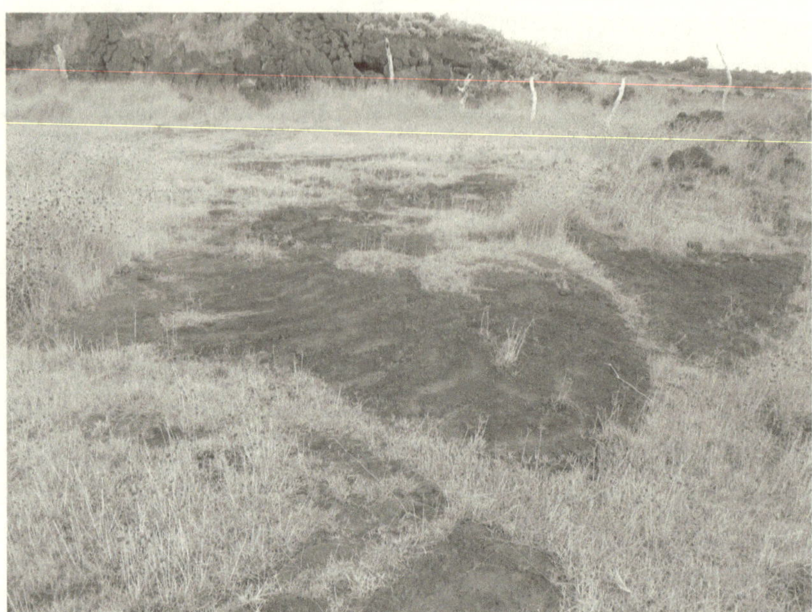

Photograph 2.9. Basalt quarry and flat surface left after quarrying. (Photograph by authors)

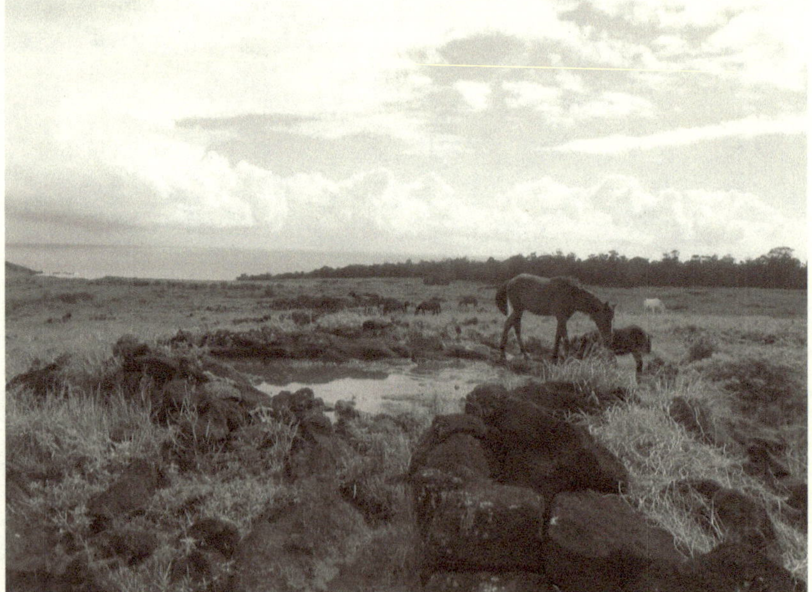

Photograph 2.10. Horse drinking from water collection basin. (Photograph by authors)

The billions of rocks serve multiple horticultural functions: protection from the wind; buffering of the soil and plant temperatures; conservation of soil moisture, moisture capture (dew condensation); control of weeds; a source of nutrients through leaching of minerals by rainfall; and prevention of soil loss by reduction of erosion (Bork, Mieth, and Tschochner 2004, 10). This sounds like the beginning of an eminently sustainable horticulture. So far, we have just scratched the surface—literally. Underlying those pesky (to Westerners) lithic- and veneer-covered surfaces, the boulder gardens, are enormous volumes of anthropogenic soils and thousands of planting pits. Under lithic mulch lies perhaps 62 cm of anthropogenic soil; under veneers, 88 cm; under boulders, 50 cm (estimated from excavation profiles in Stevenson and Haoa Cardinali [2008]). Take 70 percent of the island's area, 116 square km, at a modest 50 cm depth, or 0.5 m, and you have 58,000,000 m^3 of cultural/horticultural volume. This does not mean the rest of Rapa Nui's "un-rocked" landscape was not transformed. This is just the more visible part: the real rock art—rocking the farm—on a culturally varied landscape. The moai and ahu don't even register on this scale of demands on labor and resources.

What is in the anthropogenic soils underneath all those carefully shaped and placed rocks (photograph 2.11)? We think there is a good possibility that is where the palms and lots of other organic materials are, often as charcoal, otherwise known as biochar. The term *slash and burn* frequently occurs in the Rapa Nui literature, but we think there is widespread evidence in planting pits and anthropogenic soils underlying rock mulches for slash and char, a very different process, where biochar, *not ash*, is produced in a *reducing* atmosphere (highly limited oxygen). To differentiate, ash is mainly the remaining mineral fraction of plant materials left over after organic material has been burnt in an oxidizing atmosphere (lots of oxygen). Mineral ash is the primary product of slash and burn. Mineral ash will contain nutrients such as phosphates, iron, boron, et cetera, but not much carbon. The ash provides a quick burst of fertility, but one that might last only a few seasons.

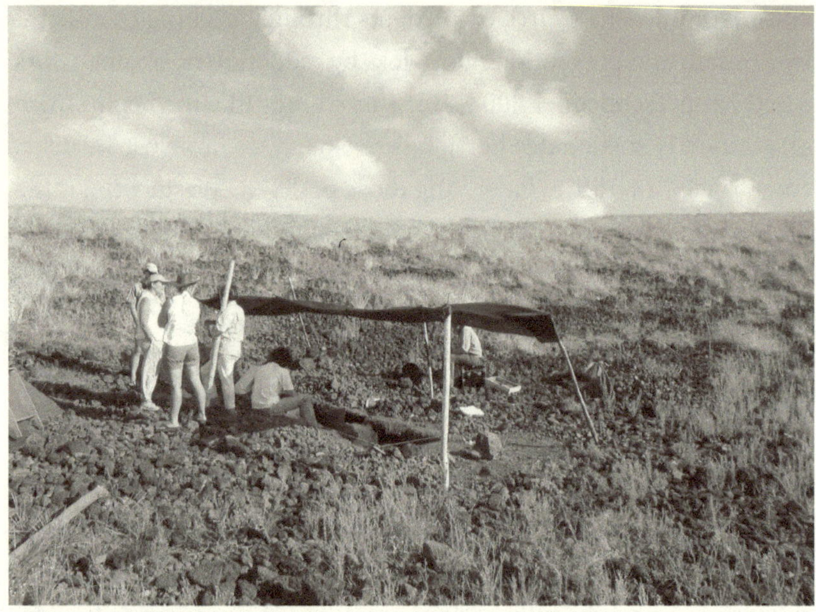

Photograph 2.11. Excavation of a rock-mulched garden showing dark amended soils. (Photograph by authors)

Charcoal, char, carbon black, or biochar results from combustion in an oxygen-low or reducing atmosphere. To produce biochar, oxygen access must be deliberately limited, here probably by burning carbon-containing materials in pits or leaf and dirt-covered piles. Then the biochar produced is added as an amendment to soils in planting pits or beneath rock veneer. The biochar amendment, while not really a fertilizer, helps hold moisture and acts like a chemical sponge to bind nutrients. Biochar resists decomposition, unlike raw compost, which readily gasses off carbon dioxide (CO_2) and methane (CH_4). Biochar can endure hundreds of years, maybe thousands (see Glaser and Woods [2004] and Woods et al. [2009] for a discussion of the characteristics of Amazonian Dark Earths). Biochar—ranging from charcoal down to carbon black—is abundant in Rapa Nui anthropogenic soils and planting pit contents. The planting pit pictured in photograph 2.12, two meters or so in diameter and over a meter deep contained perhaps forty liters of charcoal. This could be where the palms and other trees went as they fell, by whatever cause: as biochar to thousands of planting pits and thousands of cubic meters of anthropogenic soils underlying lithic mulch.

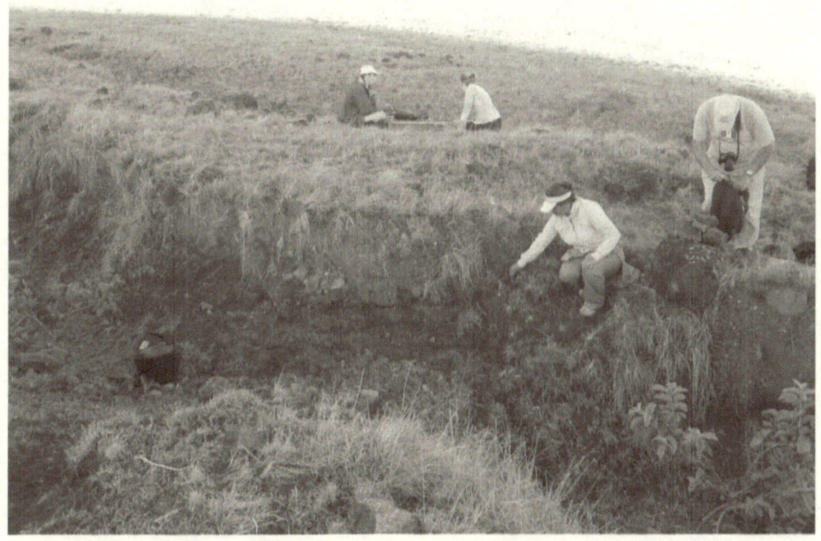

Photograph 2.12. Salvage archaeology of a planting pit exposed by an eroding gulley in Sector 26, northwest coast, with Sonia Haoa Cardinali pointing out one end of a voluminous charcoal lens. Think of this lens as a three-dimensional dish-shaped deposit. (Photograph by authors)

Now, our hypothesis about palm and other organic material ending up as biochar resulting from slash and char rather than slash-and-burn technology is not the only possible hypothesis. In response to an earlier draft of this chapter, Andreas Mieth offered these comments:

Regarding the intentional production of biocharcoal *especially for fertilizing* I am not so sure. I think that charcoal could also have been produced during slash and burn. Thick wood pieces like stumps are often under-supplied with oxygen during the burning process that causes development of ash *and* charcoal. This happened also when wood was burned in fire-pits and *umu*, where charcoal was perhaps also intentionally produced to keep the heat for longer time (as in barbecuing). We found also charred palm stumps covered by charred grass. The grass was obviously used to inflame the stump, but perhaps also for producing a slower burning process and production of glowing charcoal. We found evidence that charred palm stumps served as umu for cooking. But no doubt: the Rapanui knew about the fertilizing effect of charcoal and ash. It is no accident that this material is found in planting pits and garden soils. It is just the intentional production of [biochar] fertilizer that I do not find convincing—I argue rather for a secondary effect or use.

And another important point: apart from the charred palm stumps only very little charcoal of palms is found in the fireplaces (see publications of the Orliacs). This speaks against a simple burn history of the palms. We argue more for a *slash and use* hypothesis, which means use of palms *without* burning them—perhaps the use of the palm stems as a liquid source followed later by their biological decomposition. The burning traces we find today are mainly from other tree and shrub species, and, in the later land use phase, more from grasses. The most evident charcoal remains of the palms are the charred stumps found in situ. (Mieth, personal communication, August 30, 2012)

We still hold to the opinion that the production of biochar was deliberate, but we certainly recognize that charcoal and carbon black can also be produced by the slash and burn means described by Mieth above, and certainly, that decomposed palm could be part of the soil amendment process. The technologies are not mutually exclusive. Mieth mentions the biological decomposition of palm, something we have been documenting on Rapa Nui (yes, there are palms on Rapa Nui) and in the Hawaiian Islands. The several species of palms we are observing (coconut, royal, queen, and king palms, but unfortunately, no Jubaea palm available yet), once dead and down, decompose *very* quickly, much more quickly than trees like oaks and pines, leaving behind perhaps just their mineral content, some starch, and phytoliths. A series of experiments we have in progress on Molokai, one of the Hawaiian Islands, will test the residues left from both oxidation and reduction atmosphere palm combustion processes. We suspect that palm, a monocot, more like a weed than a tree, burns differently from dicot trees, more likely leaving fine carbon black rather than charcoal pieces as residue.

Biochar and carbon black, from whatever sources, survive in Rapa Nui anthropogenic soils to this day, helping to sustain soil fertility beyond what could ever be expected after a century and a half of horticultural hiatus and nutrient extraction by grazing. We think that the Rapanui discovery of the effectiveness of biochar could have originated in the umu and the general Polynesian practice of cooking in pits with leaf and earth coverings, automatically providing a reducing atmosphere (cf. Binford [1967] as an example for soil content analysis of features). First, it might have been observed that old cooking pits supported vigorous plant growth and then that the addition of charred materials from cooking pits to planting soils also aided plant growth. From there, the process could be generalized to a horticultural practice on a grander scale—in addition to umu, larger pits or piles of carbon-containing stuffs to make biochar. Each time a planting pit is opened or the lithic mulch pulled back and a sweet potato or taro tuber is harvested, more soil amendment is added. From repeated additions, older charcoal ends up being ground to a powder, hence the dark brown or black color of many planting pits or lithic mulch garden soils. Once a planting pit or lithic-mulch garden is created, it becomes valuable infrastructure, to be used over and over again. Biochar is a great partner to "rocking the farm" for a sustainable horticulture. The palms might be extinct, but agricultural production continued to expand, supporting population growth rather than causing a crash. Much the same as in eighteenth-century Europe and North America, aggressive forest clearing was more than balanced by the application of manure, guano, and mined phosphates, resulting in sustainable and ever-increasing crop yields. Thus, we highlight two major ingenious Rapanui contributions to sustainable horticulture: rock gardening and biochar and other soil amendments, lessons that could and should be applied elsewhere in the world.

The relationships of rock placement to horticulture by archaeologists and anthropologists did not really begin to be understood until the 1990s (Wozniak 1999, n.d.; Stevenson et al. 2006), in large part because of the focus on the monumental, about which thousands of pages had been written by then. This is what we mean by "art as distraction." Similarly, soil amendment practices are just now beginning to be explored, and at this point, we are among the very few suggesting that deliberately produced biochar amendments made a big difference—we think further research on soil composition will support our argument. All of this—the billions of rocks, the hundreds of manavai, the ubiquitous rock gardens, the staggering volume of anthropogenic soils—dwarfs the human energy and resources needed to construct the maoi. The Rapanui created a sustainable world, not one convulsed by ecocide. To fully appreciate it, follow the gaze of the moai across the landscape of a most amazing food factory (photograph 2.13).

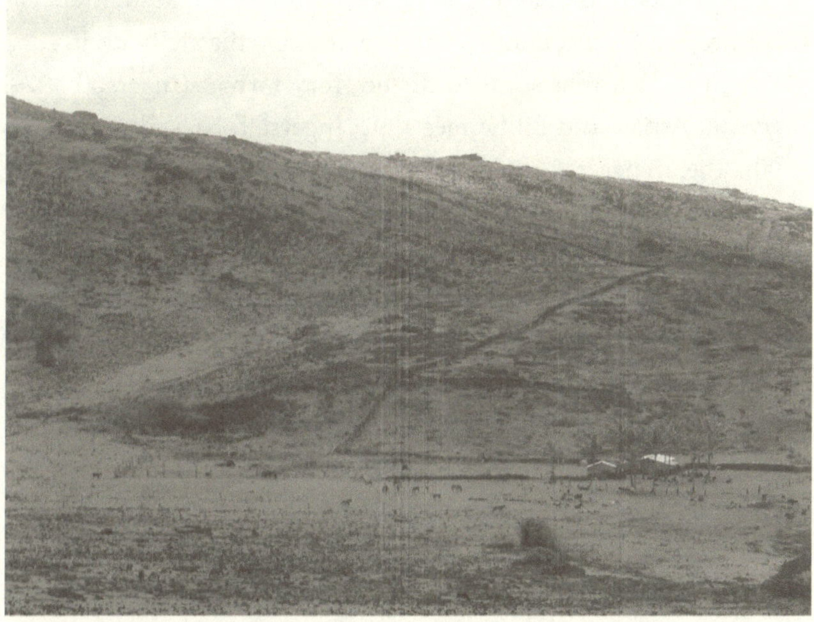

Photograph 2.13. Two stone worlds intersecting: sheep station stonewalls taken from laboriously fashioned and transported former Rapa Nui garden materials. (Photograph by authors)

Apocalypse Now

We paint a very different picture from the latter-day Malthusians, the catastrophists who proclaim ecocide. The mantra, the microcosmic world metaphor goes this way: they cut down all the palms so they can move the bigger and bigger moai. All the while, the population rises out of control, headed for the inevitable Behavioral Sink. With no palms, no moai can be moved, no canoes can be built, and with the loss of palm cover, erosion consumes the soils. Civil disorder reigns. The moai are tumbled. *Mata'a* slice and dice, soaking the island in blood. Cannibals stalk. The population crashes. A new poverty-stricken social order emerges. The culture has collapsed. Malthus was right.

This is a popular paradigmatic Western story of secular apocalypse projected onto another culture, a story that tells itself—just plug in the data that seem to fit the story format (Ingersoll 1979; Ingersoll, Attias, and Billheimer 1992; Ingersoll, Nickell, and Lewis 1980). The archetypal story, the source, is the biblical Book of Revelation, or Apocalypse. What happens is that the world as we know it ends; in the case of the Book of Revelation, people ignore or challenge the messages and warnings, which will result in the world being destroyed and reconfigured in a future that has not yet arrived, but with a present continuously vexed by dire predictions. The future-oriented biblical model adds an extension to time's arrow and history, a feature quite rare in the world's cultures and narratives. The humanities and sciences borrow and transform the model of apocalypse and future-orientation. In fiction and science fiction, worlds degrade, collapse, or crash, as for example in the popular films *Mad Max 2, Fahrenheit 451*, and *The Book of Eli* or the dystopian novels *Brave New World* (Huxley [1932] 1998), *Nineteen Eight-Four* (Orwell [1949] 2003), and *The Hunger Games* (Collins 2008).

Analogs or transforms inspired by biblical apocalypse emerge in Western science, as in the case of Malthusian theory: a population grows until it exhausts its resources and crashes. Heed the warnings: control nuclear weapon proliferation, stop pumping CO_2 into the atmosphere, cease cutting down the rain forest or there will be serious consequences. Endless variations draw on this apocalyptic theme. We received a recent mass e-mail (July 1, 2012): "The Great Methane Deposit beneath the Gulf of Mexico is melting; And its terrible gases are rolling forth! Repent, oh you people!" This apocalyptic warning combines theology and secular climatology.

On Rapa Nui, in service of rank and privilege, all the trees came down; then the moai were felled. No one could escape the island. Weapons of mass destruction (WMD) proliferated; mata'a appeared suddenly as a tool type. Rampant warfare prevailed. The people starved, as evidenced by skeletal-looking figures. Ecocide! We could apply the same apocalyptic model elsewhere, say New England, if we could not translate their writings. Perhaps archaeologists would posit that something similar occurred in New England when the forests were removed (table 2.1). Weapons of mass destruction appeared;

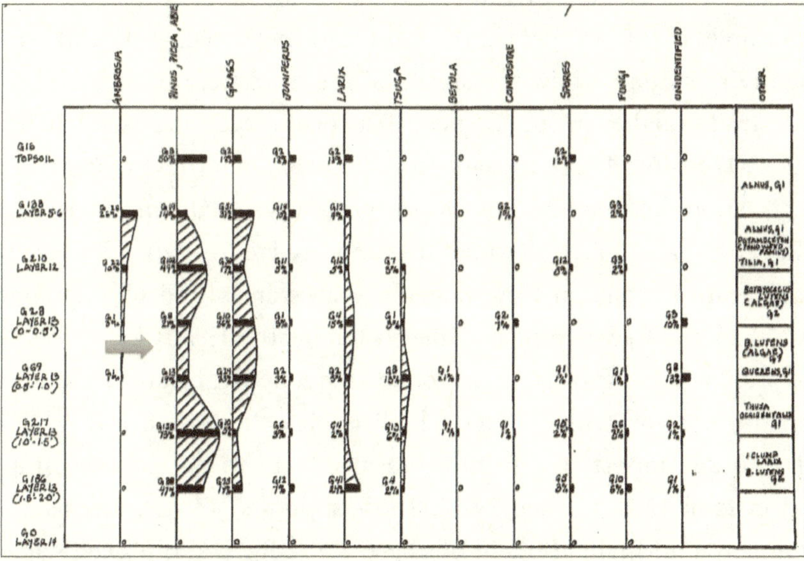

Table 2.1. Pollen diagram from Puddle Dock, Strawbery Banke, Portsmouth, New Hampshire, illustrating major loss of forest cover in this region of New England by the mid-nineteenth century (arrow) (Ingersoll 1971, plate 369). Pollen analysis by Richard Gramley. G = number of grains. Querens should be Quercus.

fearsome scythes replaced harmless sickles. The people starved as witnessed by landscapes punctuated by plots of death's head gravestones. Then New England's culture changed, leaving behind the rustic old agrarian world and evolving a new symbolism and an industrial economy. The Longfaces were replaced by the Widefaces (a play on the oft-quoted Long Ears and Short Ears Rapanui narrative). The once overharvested and burned-over forests (for barns, houses, fences, ships, and sheep pasture) of New England returned and remain to this day.

Apocalypse makes for an exciting story (see the film *Rapa Nui* [1994]), but there are other ways to read the evidence. Here we will give a few examples with the "arts." Forests come and go, but cultures may grow in spite of their loss. Did the people starve? As reported in the ethnographic literature, *kavakava* (or *moai kavakava*: view examples of this art form at the website of the British Museum) generally represented how the spirits of the dead were understood by the traditional Rapanui (Englert 1970, 60-61; Métraux and Bullock 1957, 144-146; Métraux [1940] 1971, 250-252), not those dying from starvation, as imagined by Westerners. These *akuaku*, as several Rapanui legends record, sometimes appeared to the living. Similarly, the death's heads on New England gravestones (find photographs on the web by searching for "images for Death's Heads gravestone") represented not grizzly images of death but hopeful transformations to another world, involving the biblical metaphor of the grain needing to decompose first in order to give birth to the new seedling, as in John 12:24 (Cohen 1973). Those supposed WMD, the mata'a, while not normally thought of as art, sure get a bad rap (see images of mata'a on the web by searching "Images for mata'a Easter Island"). So far, every specific technical study of mata'a we have consulted finds that use-wear, typological reconstruction studies, and provenience data indicate that mata'a are primarily tools for working with vegetal material (Bollt et al. 2006; Church 1998; Church and Ellis 1996; Church and Rigney 1994; Stevenson and Haoa Cardinali 2008a, 107). We suspect that silica gloss and blood residue analysis (see Loy and Dixon [1998] for the detection of 10,000+ year old blood residues on fluted projectile points) will detect the gloss, but only rarely human blood residue. As the landscape shifted to dominant grass and brush cover, tools like the mata'a would be just the implement to cut and scrape tubers for food, vegetation for fibers, and fuel for the newer, smaller umu fires. New England scythes, like sickles, definitely become coated with silica gloss (or as it is sometimes called "sickle gloss") from cutting grass and grain—you can see it without a microscope and feel it. Scythes function best when frequently honed, and they look pretty formidable indeed, like Death itself that scythes often explicitly symbolize. But we Westerners know that the familiar Grim Reaper symbolism is metaphoric, not literal: the scythe is not a killing weapon; rather, the Reaper harvests souls as a farmer harvests grain.

Most variants of the apocalyptic narratives for Rapa Nui claim cultural collapse and a population crash before the encounters with the first of the Europeans (such as Roggeveen in 1722). The eighteenth-century explorers Roggeveen, Gonzáles, Cook, and La Pérouse made eyeball population estimates, but the explorers never stayed more than a few days and did not see much of the island. So how can we really tell if there was a population crash? We argue that the best archeological data show only slight population decline *before* the encounters with Europeans. While no systematic census was taken on Rapa Nui pre-European contact, it is possible to use proxies to follow population growth. In our opinion, the most accurate proxy data available is from archaeological surveys quantifying occupational sites and their locations. Population growth curves indexed by number of occupations (dated by obsidian hydration or radiocarbon methods) consistently show the decline occurring quite late—just before contact or at about the time of contact (Mulrooney et al. 2010; Stevenson and Cristino Ferrando 1986, 38; Stevenson and Haoa Cardinali 2008a; Stevenson and Haoa Cardinali 2008b, 8).

But there was without doubt a population crash. It occurred *after* European contact. The decline may have begun with the first contacts with explorers in the eighteenth century: Hunt and Lipo (2011, chapter 9) implicate epidemics brought on by each successive visit for the first signs of collapse. In the first half of the nineteenth century, numerous encounters with whalers and sealers could have reintroduced disease, and during this time the first episodes of blackbirding occurred, as when the sealing ship *Nancy* (ca. 1806) captured and took away twenty-two Rapanui (Richards 2008, 23-25). Things got much worse in the second half of the nineteenth century. In December of 1862, several ships, Spanish and Peruvian, captured as many as fifteen hundred Rapanui and sold them in Peru to be plantation workers and domestics (Maude 1981, 12-20). Whereas there might have been several thousand Rapanui in 1722, by 1877 there were only 110 (McCall 1994, 64; Rainbird 2002). Might we call this "Easter Island's forgotten genocide" (Peiser 2005, 532-534)? The impact of disease, blackbirding, and forced or benevolent deportations to Tahiti and Mangareva was devastating. From the 1870s until the 1950s, the entire landscape became a sheep station occupied by firms like Williamson, Balfour and Co., the organizers of the Compañia Explotadora Isla de Pascua (Arredondo 2003, 33). At times, as many as seventy thousand sheep grazed Rapa Nui (Mieth and Bork 2004a, 32) while the dispossessed Rapanui ended up interned, for all practical purposes, in one Rapa Nui town, Hangaroa, by 1898. You can figure out for yourself what impact nearly a century of sheep safely grazing had on the existing plant species and soils. If there ever was ecocide on Rapa Nui, this was it.

Conclusion

Moai are indeed magical, but there's a very impressive world beyond and after, a world of rocks, quarries, engineered soils, water diversion systems, and brilliant land-use strategies. The Rapanui found a small island with built-in challenges to human occupation yet nevertheless developed a sustainable horticulture and a spectacular culture. The Rapanui miraculously survived against all odds: European diseases, whalers and sealers (1800-1840), Peruvian slavers (1862), rendition of their people to Peru, expropriation of their land, annexation by Chile, repression of their language and culture, and internment in Hangaroa. Due not to homespun ecocide, but the Western presence, their numbers fell from several thousand at the time of first European contact (1722) to just above one hundred in the third quarter of the nineteenth century. Today, Rapanui culture remains extraordinary, vibrant, and creative. We could be easily convinced it is the most resilient culture the world has ever seen. Or, in our hubris, we could ignore its lessons (photographs 2.14, 2.15, and figure 2.1).

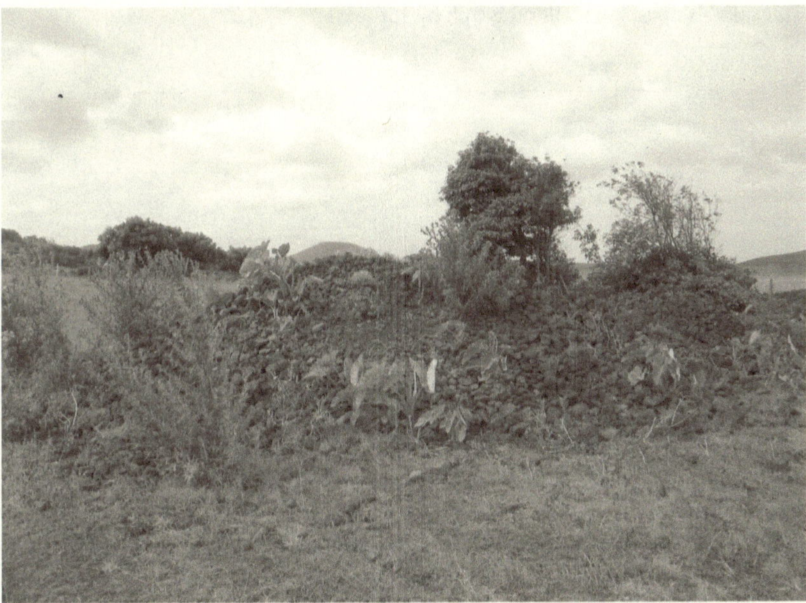

Photograph 2.14. A bulldozed pile of rocks resulting from the clearance of rocks from pre-European contact Rapa Nui veneer gardens, ironically, still growing taro. (Photograph by authors)

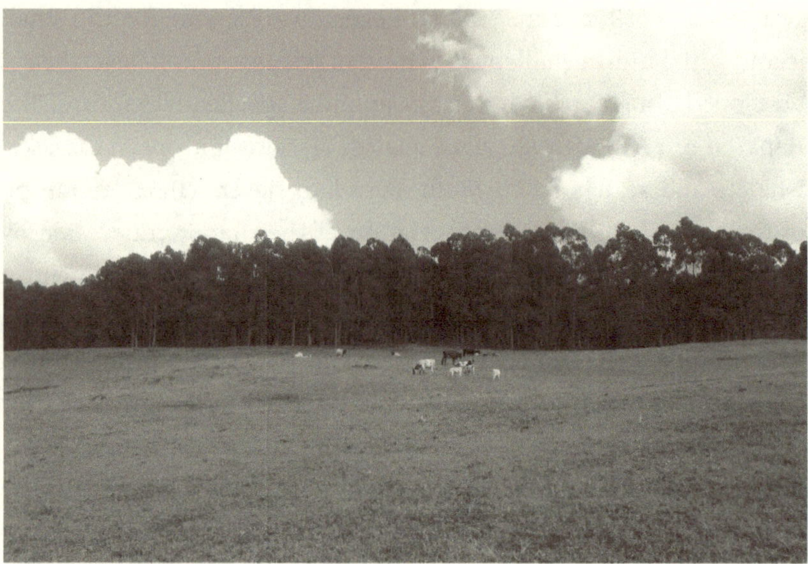

Photograph 2.15. Rapa Nui is not so barren after all: forest, pasture, and cows on Terevaka's slopes, 2011. (Photograph by authors)

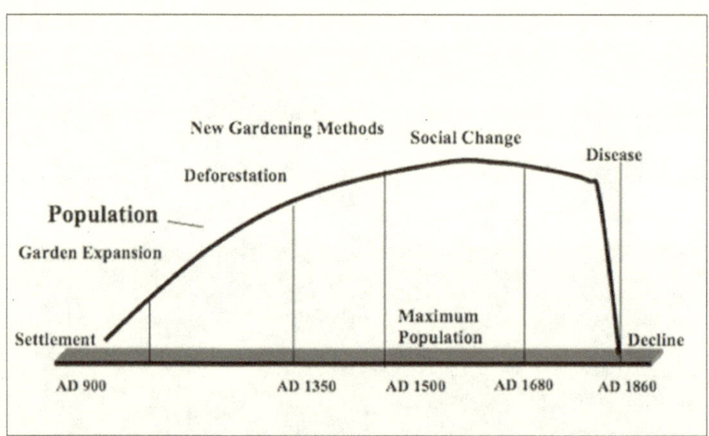

Figure 2.1. Christopher Stevenson's "alternative model" based on occupation site survey (2008). We think this is the last word: there was no "collapse" on Rapa Nui until the arrival of Europeans. (Permission by Christopher Stevenson)

Acknowledgments

Thanks to Sonia, Pancho, Chris, Tahira, Pou, Ramon, Andreas, and Josie for helping us to see things in new ways.

Notes

1. *Rapa Nui* is the residents' term for Easter Island. European languages employ some version referring to Easter, such as Isla de Pascua, Paasch Eiland, or Osterinsel. This paper employs the dominant convention in the literature of "Rapa Nui" for the island and "Rapanui" for the people, language, and culture.

2. Moai are by no means the only celebrated Rapanui "art" forms, but moai are the only one with worldwide iconic status. Other "art" forms include moai kavakava (carved wooden figures), clubs (*paoa*), chief's staffs (*ua*), paddles (*rapa* and *'ao*), feather headdresses, gorgets (*rei miro*), barkcloth images (*manu uru*), inscribed tablets (*rongorongo*), birdman carvings (*tangata manu*), and a wide range of petroglyphs. See Kjellgren et al. (2001) for illustrations published in conjunction with the exhibition "Splendid Isolation: Art of Easter Island," held at The Metropolitan Museum of Art, New York, December 2001 to August 2002. See also Heyerdahl 1959.

3. We estimate that trees or brush covers at least 10 percent of the Rapa Nui landscape, including the area of the town of Hangaroa that is rich with trees. An estimate published in the early 1980s (Rull et al. 2010, 53) was just under 10 percent trees and brush, and the area under cover has increased since then. Look at photographs 2.4, 2.8, 2.9, 2.10, 2.14, 2.15. Yes, there are trees on Rapa Nui.

References

Arredondo, Ana Maria. 2003. "Life Stories of Women in Rapanui Society in the First Half of the Twentieth Century. Gender Studies, Part 3." *Rapa Nui Journal* 17(1): 15-33.

Baer, Alexander, Thegn N. Ladefoged, Christopher M. Stevenson, and Sonia Haoa. 2008. "The Surface Rock Gardens of Prehistoric Rapa Nui." *Rapa Nui Journal* 22(2): 102-9.

Bahn, Paul, and John Flenley. 1992. *Easter Island Earth Island.* London: Thames and Hudson.

Bernard, H. Russell. 2010. "The Secret Life of Social Science." Lecture delivered at St. Mary's College of Maryland, Department of Anthropology, Distinguished Scholar Program, February 15, 2010.

———. 2012. "The Science in Social Science." *PNAS Early Edition* (Proceedings of the National Academy of Sciences of the United States of America). http://www.pnas.org/content/early/2012/11/29/1218054109, 1-4.

The Big Bang Theory TV show lead-in can be seen on YouTube, http://www.youtube.com/watch?v=4S8GOQeSlTs.

Binford, L. R. 1967. "Smudge Pits and Hide Smoking: The Role of Analogy in Archaeological Reasoning." *American Antiquity* 32(1): 1-12.

Bollt, Robert, Jesse E. Clark, Philip R. Fisher, and Hirosato K. Yoshida. 2006. "An Experiment in the Replication and Classification of Easter Island Mata'a." *Rapa Nui Journal* 20(2): 125-33.

The Book of Eli. 2010. Film distributed by Warner Bros. Pictures. Directed by The Hughes Brothers. Written by Gary Whitta.

Bork, Hans-Rudolf, Andreas Mieth, and Bernd Tschochner. 2004. "Nothing but Stones? A Review of the Extent and Technical

Efforts of Prehistoric Stone Mulching on Rapa Nui." *Rapa Nui Journal* 18(1): 10-14.

Bove, Andrew. n.d. "Easter Island as a World Heritage Site." In preparation. To be included in an edited volume, *Beyond the Moai: New Archaeological, Cultural, and Historical Perspectives on Rapa Nui*, edited by Sonia Haoa Cardinali, Daniel W. Ingersoll, Kathleen B. Ingersoll, and Christopher M. Stevenson.

Church, F., and G. Ellis. 1996. "A Use-wear Analysis of Obsidian Tools from an *Ana Kionga*." *Rapa Nui Journal* 10(4): 81-88.

Church, Flora. 1998. "Upland, Lowland, Citizen, Chief: Patterns of Use-Wear from Five Easter Island Sites." In *Easter Island in Pacific Context South Seas Symposium: Proceedings of the Fourth International Conference on Easter Island and East Polynesia* (University of New Mexico, Albuquerque, August 5-10, 1997), edited by Christopher M. Stevenson, Georgia Lee, and F. J. Morin, 312-15. Los Osos: Easter Island Foundation.

Church, Flora, and Julia Rigney. 1994. "A Microwear Analysis of Tools from Site 10-241 Easter Island—An Inland Processing Site." *Rapa Nui Journal* 8(4): 101-5.

Cohen, Kathleen R. 1973. *Metamorphosis of a Death Symbol: The Transi Tomb in the Late Middle Ages and the Renaissance.* Berkeley: University of California Press.

Collins, Suzanne. 2008. *The Hunger Games*. New York: Scholastic Press.

Diamond, Jared. 2005. "Twilight at Easter." In *Collapse: How Societies Choose to Fail or Succeed*, 79-119. New York: Viking.

———. 2007. "Easter Island Revisited." *Science* 317:1692-94.

Edwards, Edmundo, Raul Marchetti, Leopoldo Dominichetti, and Oscar Gonzáles-Ferrán. 1996. "When the Earth Trembled, the Statues Fell." *Rapa Nui Journal* 10(1): 1-15.

Englert, Father Sebastian. 1970. *Island at the Center of the World: New Light on Easter Island*. New York: Charles Scribner's Sons.

Eyzaguirre, Eduardo Ruiz-Tagle, ed. 2004. *Easter Island: The First Three Expeditions*. Rapa Nui: Museum Store, Rapanui Press.

Fahrenheit 451. 1966. Film distributed by Universal Films. Directed by François Truffaut. Based on the novel *Fahrenheit 451* by Ray Bradbury (1953).

Fischer, Steven Roger. 2005. *Island at the End of the World: The Turbulent History of Easter Island*. London: Reaktion Books.

Flenley, John, and Paul Bahn. 2003. *The Enigmas of Easter Island: Island on the Edge*. Oxford: Oxford University Press.

Glaser, Bruno, and William I. Woods, eds. 2004. *Amazonian Dark Earths: Explorations in Time and Space*. Berlin: Springer-Verlag.

Griffin-Pierce, Trudy. 1992. *Earth is My Mother, Sky is My Father: Space, Time, and Astronomy in Navajo Sandpainting*. Albuquerque: University of New Mexico Press.

Harris, Marvin. 1968. *The Rise of Anthropological Theory: A History of Theories of Culture*. New York: Thomas Y. Crowell.

———. 1999. *Theories of Culture in Postmodern Times*. Walnut Creek: Altamira Press.

Heyerdahl, Thor. 1959. *Aku-Aku, the Secret of Easter Island*. New York: Pocket Books.

———.1975. *The Art of Easter Island*. Garden City, NY: Doubleday.

———.1989. *Easter Island: The Mystery Solved*. New York: Random House.

Horley, Paul and Georgia Lee. 2008. "Rock Art of the Sacred Precinct at Mata Ngaru, 'Orongo." *Rapa Nui Journal* 22(2): 110-16.

Hunt, Terry L., and Carl P. Lipo. 2010. "Ecological Catastrophe, Collapse, and the Myth of 'Ecocide' on Rapa Nui (Easter Island)." In *Questioning Collapse: Human Resilience, Ecological Vulnerability, and the Aftermath of Empire*, edited by Patricia A. McAnany and Norman Yoffee, 21-44. Cambridge: Cambridge University Press.

———. 2011. *The Statues that Walked: Unraveling the Mystery of Easter Island*. New York: Free Press.

Hunter-Anderson, Rosalind L. 1998. "Human vs Climatic Impacts at Rapa Nui: Did the People Really Cut Down All Those Trees?" In *Easter Island in Pacific Context South Seas Symposium: Proceedings of the Fourth International Conference on Easter Island and East Polynesia*, edited by Christopher M. Stevenson, Georgia Lee, and F. J. Morin, 85-99. Los Osos, CA: Easter Island Foundation.

Huxley, Aldous. (1932)1998. *Brave New World*. New York: Perennial Classics.

Ingersoll, Daniel W., Jr. 1971. "Settlement Archaeology at Puddle Dock." PhD. diss., 2 vols. Peabody Museum Library, Harvard University.

———. 1979. "Close Encounters of the Third Kind: A Hegelian Drama." Paper delivered at the Annual Meeting of the American Anthropological Association, Washington, DC.

Ingersoll, Daniel W., Jr., J. M. Nickell, and C. D. Lewis. 1980. "Star Wars, the Future, and Christian Eschatology." *Philosophy Today* 24(4/4): 360-74.

Ingersoll, Daniel W., Jr., with Elizabeth Attias, and Catherine Gravlin Billheimer. 1992. "Divining the Future: The Toys of Star Wars." In *The Art and Mystery of Historical Archaeology: Essays in Honor of James Deetz*, edited by Mary C. Beaudry and Anne Yentsch, 427-43. Boca Raton: CRC Press.

Kjellgren, Eric, JoAnne Van Tilburg, and Adrienne Kaeppler. 2001. *Splendid Isolation: Art of Easter Island*. New York: Metropolitan Museum of Art.

Loret, John, and John T. Tanacredi, eds. 2003. *Easter Island: Scientific Exploration into the World's Environmental Problems in Microcosm*. New York: Kluwer Academic/ Plenum Publishers.

Love, Charles M. 2000. "More on Moving Easter Island Statues, with Comments on the NOVA Program." *Rapa Nui Journal* 14(4): 115-18.

Loy, Thomas H., and E. James Dixon. 1998. "Blood Residues on Fluted Points from Eastern Beringia." *American Antiquity* 63(1): 21–46.

Mad Max 2. 1981. Distributed by Warner Bros. Directed by George Miller. Written by Terry Hayes, George Miller, and Brian Hannant.

Maude, H. E. 1981. *Slavers in Paradise. The Peruvian Slave Trade in Polynesia, 1862-1864*. Canberra: Australian National University Press.

McAnany, Patricia A., and Norman Yoffee, eds. 2010. *Questioning Collapse: Human Resilience, Ecological Vulnerability, and the Aftermath of Empire*. Cambridge: Cambridge University Press.

McCall, Grant. 1994. *Rapanui: Tradition and Survival on Easter Island*. 2nd ed. Honolulu: University of Hawaii Press.

Métraux, Alfred. (1940) 1971. *Ethnology of Easter Island*. Bernice P. Bishop Museum Bulletin 160. Honolulu: Bernice P. Bishop Museum.

Métraux, Alfred, and Michael Bullock. 1957. *Easter Island: A Stone-Age Civilization of the Pacific*. Oxford: Oxford University Press.

Mieth, Andreas, and Hans-Rudolf Bork. 2004a. *Easter Island—Rapa Nui: Scientific Pathways to Secrets of the Past.* Man and Environment 1. Kiel: Schmidt and Klaunig.

———. 2004b. “Traces in the Soils: Interaction between Environmental Change, Land Use and Culture in the (Pre) History of Rapa Nui (Easter Island).” In *The Reñaca Papers: 6th International Conference on Rapa Nui and the Pacific*, edited by Christopher M. Stevenson, J.M. Ramirez, F.J. Morin, and N. Barbacci, 55-65. Los Osos: Easter Island Foundation.

Moai Sightings. 1992. *Rapa Nui Journal* 6(1): 12.

Moai Sightings. 1997. *Rapa Nui Journal* 11(4): 159.

Moai Sightings. 2012. *Rapa Nui Journal* 26(1): 82.

Mulloy, Emily Ross. 1991. “The Destruction of Tongariki.” *Rapa Nui Journal* 5(3): 33-34.

Mulloy, William. 1970. “A Speculative Reconstruction of Techniques of Carving, Transporting and Erecting Easter Island Statues.” *Journal of Archaeology and Physical Anthropology of Oceania* 5(1): 1-23.

Mulrooney, Mara A., Thegn N. Ladefoged, Christopher Stevenson, and Sonia Haoa. 2010. “Empirical Assessment of a Pre-European Societal Collapse on Rapa Nui (Easter Island).” In *The Gotland Papers: Selected Papers from the 7th International Conference on Easter Island and the Pacific: Migration, Identity, and Cultural Heritage*, edited by Paul Wallin and Helen Martinsson-Wallin, 141-53. Visby: Gotland University Press.

Orwell, George. (1949) 2003. *Nineteen Eighty-Four*. New York: Plume.

Pavel, Pavel. 1995. “Reconstruction of the Transport of the Moai Statues and Pukao Hats.” *Rapa Nui Journal* 9(3): 69-72.

Peiser, Benny. 2005. "From Genocide to Ecocide: The Rape of Rapa Nui." *Energy and Environment* 16(3/4): 513-39.

Rainbird, Paul. 2002. "A Message for the Future? The Rapa Nui (Easter Island) Ecodisaster and Pacific Island Environments." *World Archaeology* 33(3): 436-51.

Rapa Nui. 1994. Film distributed by Warner Bros. Film directed by Kevin Reynolds, produced by Kevin Costner and Jim Wilson. Written by Kevin Reynolds and Tim Rose Price.

Richards, Rhys. 2008. *Easter Island 1793 to 1861: Observations by Early Visitors before the Slave Raids*. Los Osos, California: Easter Island Foundation.

Rull, V., N. Cañellas-Boltà, A. Sáez, S. Giralt, S. Pla, and O. Margalef. 2010. "Paleoecology of Easter Island: Evidence and Uncertainties." *Earth-Science Reviews* 99:50-60.

Sanger, Kay Kenady. 2011. *Easter Island: The Essential Guide*. Los Osos, CA: Easter Island Foundation.

Stevenson, Christopher M. 2008. "Sustainability Lessons for Easter Island: Rethinking Rapa Nui's Ancient Agriculture." Lecture delivered at St. Mary's College of Maryland, November 5, 2009.

Stevenson, Christopher M., and Claudio Cristino Ferrando. 1986. "Residential Settlement History of the Rapa Nui South Coastal Plain." *Journal of New World Archaeology* 7(1): 29-38.

Stevenson, Christopher M., and Sonia Haoa Cardinali. 2008a. *Prehistoric Rapa Nui: Landscape and Settlement Archaeology at Hanga Ho'onu*. With contributions by Joan A. Wozniak, Helene Martinson-Wallin, Paul Wallin, Matthew Bampton, Linda Scott Cummings, and Pernilla Flyg. Los Osos, CA: Easter Island Foundation.

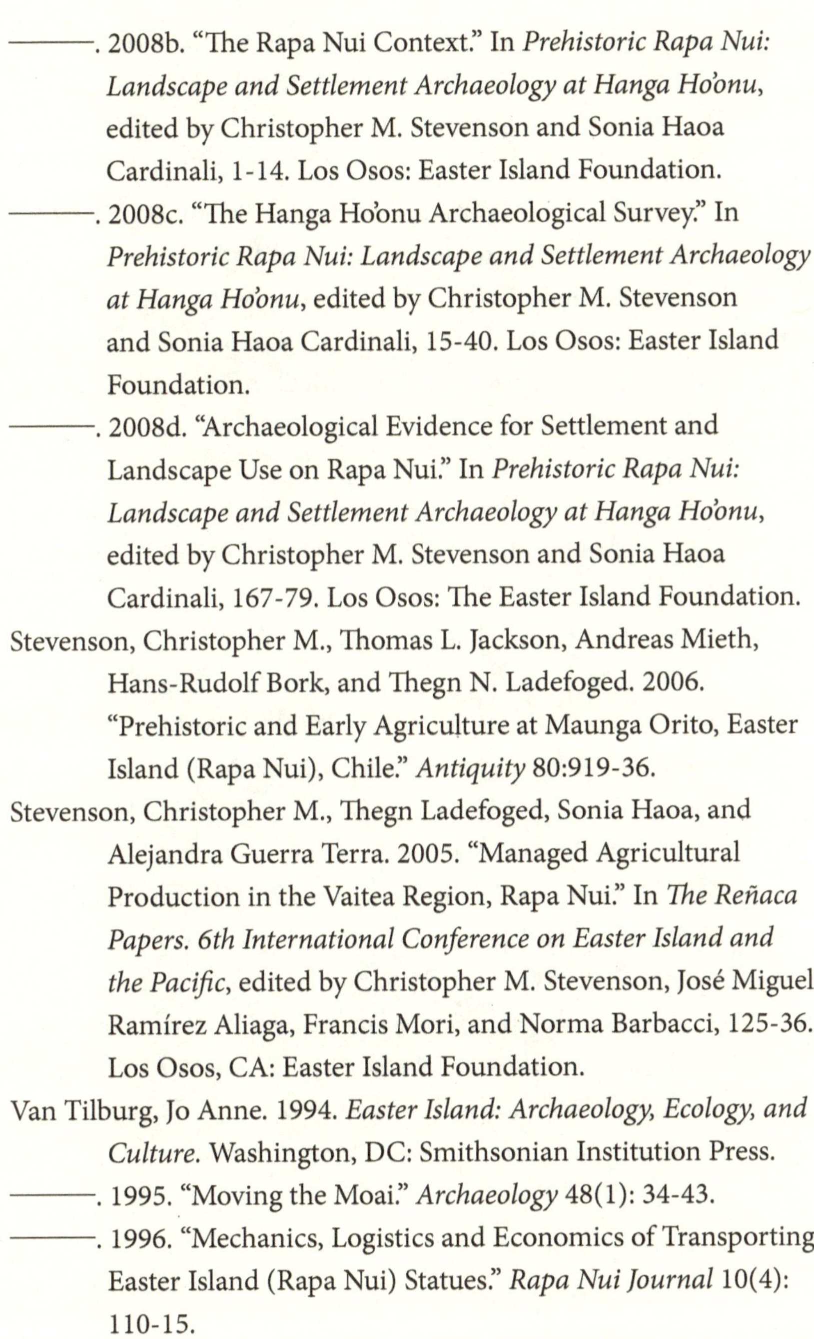

———. 2008b. "The Rapa Nui Context." In *Prehistoric Rapa Nui: Landscape and Settlement Archaeology at Hanga Ho'onu*, edited by Christopher M. Stevenson and Sonia Haoa Cardinali, 1-14. Los Osos: Easter Island Foundation.

———. 2008c. "The Hanga Ho'onu Archaeological Survey." In *Prehistoric Rapa Nui: Landscape and Settlement Archaeology at Hanga Ho'onu*, edited by Christopher M. Stevenson and Sonia Haoa Cardinali, 15-40. Los Osos: Easter Island Foundation.

———. 2008d. "Archaeological Evidence for Settlement and Landscape Use on Rapa Nui." In *Prehistoric Rapa Nui: Landscape and Settlement Archaeology at Hanga Ho'onu*, edited by Christopher M. Stevenson and Sonia Haoa Cardinali, 167-79. Los Osos: The Easter Island Foundation.

Stevenson, Christopher M., Thomas L. Jackson, Andreas Mieth, Hans-Rudolf Bork, and Thegn N. Ladefoged. 2006. "Prehistoric and Early Agriculture at Maunga Orito, Easter Island (Rapa Nui), Chile." *Antiquity* 80:919-36.

Stevenson, Christopher M., Thegn Ladefoged, Sonia Haoa, and Alejandra Guerra Terra. 2005. "Managed Agricultural Production in the Vaitea Region, Rapa Nui." In *The Reñaca Papers. 6th International Conference on Easter Island and the Pacific*, edited by Christopher M. Stevenson, José Miguel Ramírez Aliaga, Francis Mori, and Norma Barbacci, 125-36. Los Osos, CA: Easter Island Foundation.

Van Tilburg, Jo Anne. 1994. *Easter Island: Archaeology, Ecology, and Culture*. Washington, DC: Smithsonian Institution Press.

———. 1995. "Moving the Moai." *Archaeology* 48(1): 34-43.

———. 1996. "Mechanics, Logistics and Economics of Transporting Easter Island (Rapa Nui) Statues." *Rapa Nui Journal* 10(4): 110-15.

Vogt, Burkhard, Hans-Rudolph Bork, Andreas Mieth, and Annette Kühlem. 2012. "Monumental Architecture and Cultural Landscape Management at Ava Ranga Uka A Toroke Hau (Rapa Nui)." Paper delivered July 9, 2012, Session 1, The Archaeology of Rapa Nui, at the 8th International Conference on Easter Island and the Pacific, *Living in Changing Island Environments*, held at Santa Rosa, CA.

Woods, William I., Wenceslau G. Teixeira, Johannes Lehman, Christopher Steiner, Antoinette M. G. A. WinklerPrins, and Lilian Reballato, eds. 2009. *Amazonian Dark Earths: Wim Sombrek's Vision*. Berlin: Springer-Verlag.

Wozniak, Joan A. 1999. "Prehistoric Horticultural Practices on Easter Island: Lithic Mulched Gardens and Field Systems." *Rapa Nui Journal* 13:95-99.

———. 2005. "An Ethnoarchaeological Study of Horticulture on Rapa Nui." In *The Reñaca Papers. 6th International Conference on Easter Island and the Pacific*, edited by Christopher M. Stevenson, José Miguel Ramírez Aliaga, Francis Mori, and Norma Barbacci, 137-52. Los Osos, California: Easter Island Foundation.

———. n.d. "Subsistence Strategies on Rapa Nui (Easter Island): Prehistoric Gardening Practices on Rapa Nui and How They Relate to Current Farming Practices." To be included in an edited volume, *Beyond the Moai: New Archaeological, Cultural, and Historical Perspectives on Rapa Nui*, edited by Sonia Haoa Cardinali, Kathleen B. Ingersoll, Daniel W. Ingersoll, and Christopher M. Stevenson.

A Memoir of an Other

Robert C. Philen

Abstract

I am the literary executor for my late partner, the prolific poet and essayist Reginald Shepherd. Shepherd often spoke of writing a memoir but never had the chance to do so before his death. However, the essays he wrote, his poetry, his correspondences, and other writings contain many, many fragments of memoiristic material in his voice. I am in the process of assembling these fragments into his posthumous memoir, and the project bears a strong relationship to the long tradition of ethnographic biographies, as well as being a strong example of bricolage and mythic thinking. Here, I will reflect on the relationships I am encountering between memoir, myth, and ethnography as I construct/assemble this book.

April 10, 1963: Reginald Berry, later Reginald Shepherd, is born the oldest child to a single mother, Blanche Berry, in the Bronx, New York. March 31, 1978: Blanche Berry dies from an asthma-triggered heart attack, leaving Reginald Shepherd orphaned ten days shy of his fifteenth birthday. 1993: Reginald's poetry manuscript *Some Are Drowning* wins *The Nation's* "Discovery" award and is published the following year as his first poetry collection by the University of Pittsburgh Press, also winning a poetry award from the Associated

Writing Programs. 1994: Shepherd is diagnosed with HIV. December 1999: Shepherd and Robert Philen, meet at a gay book club's discussion of James Baldwin's *Giovanni's Room* at the First Baptist Church in Ithaca, New York. November 2007: Shepherd is diagnosed with Stage 4 Colon Cancer. September 10, 2008: Reginald dies.

Shepherd was a brilliant poet, one of the more significant of his generation, ultimately publishing six collections of poetry (one posthumous, Shepherd 1994, 1996, 1999, 2003, 2007a, 2011). These collections were well received and awarded. He was also a superb essayist, attested to by one of his essay collections being a finalist for a book award from the National Book Critics Circle. He was a black, gay man. He grew up exceedingly poor in public housing projects in the Bronx during his first fifteen years. He had an intensely close relationship with his single mother, a woman who died (like Reginald himself) far too young. A woman who was brilliant at working the system to get tutors and scholarships to prestigious private schools for her son while also apparently being highly dysfunctional at just about anything else other than giving her son a leg up in life (at least that was always Reginald's version of her). He was my partner for eight and a half amazing and intense years. He was intensely passionate about music (especially German opera and 80s post-punk and synth-pop), poetry (especially the Moderns, and especially Eliot and Stevens), paleontology (we had many a lively dinner-table debate about the likelihood of endo-, ecto-, or homeo- thermy for various dinosaur lineages), and history (he knew more about world history than any person I have ever encountered). In the last fourteen years of his life, he was continually poked, prodded, and surveilled by a bevy of medical professionals. In addition to HIV and colon cancer, among his "minor" maladies were a slew of kidney stones, polycythemia, osteoporosis, Bell's Palsy, near deafness in one ear, and hypertension. It almost goes without saying that just as my first paragraph's list of dates and basic facts constitutes but the merest wires to hang a life from, this second just begins to clothe his multifaceted life and identities.

In the last few years of life, Shepherd intended to write a memoir. He had gotten as far as writing a proposal for a potential manuscript and had made some start on it. He had led an interesting life. Although he had not cared so much for nonfiction prose writing earlier in his life, in his later years as he wrote more essays, he developed a significant taste for that form of writing. And finally, given the current publishing trend in which memoirs comprise a significant portion of the nonfiction market, he figured that so long as he had to deal with the psychological baggage that came from growing up the poor, black, gay son of a single mother (when that wasn't a "normal" thing—he always identified strongly with the Supremes' song "Love Child") as well as the physical baggage of his various bodily complaints, he might as well profit a bit from it. I have no doubt that he would have completed this project if cancer had not cut his time short.

At the same time, while he never actually wrote that memoir, he wrote a few memoir essays—and his writings of all sorts, essays, poems, e-mails, and unpublished drafts—contain much memoiristic detail. I am in the process of assembling a memoir in his words from this material, to be titled *To Make Me What I Was* (a modification of the title of one of his more memoiristic essays, "To Make Me What I Am" (Shepherd 2007b).

I have a number of motivations and intentions in this project. First, in my roles as Reginald's partner and his literary executor, I see this process as a fulfillment of one aspect of his work. Further, I see this as a project of inherent interest to the literary community, insofar as he was a significant literary and critical figure.

I also approach this project as an anthropologist. There is a long history in ethnographic writing of giving voice to the "other" in autobiographical form, whether Ruth Mary Underhill's *Papago Woman* (1926), Paul Radin's *Autobiography of a Winnebago Indian* (1920), Oscar Lewis' *The Children of Sanchez: Autobiography of a Mexican Family* (1961), or Vincent Crapanzano's *Tuhami: Portrait of a Moroccan* (1980). I see this work as fitting within that subgenre of ethnographic writing, though the nature of my source material is different, coming as it does from Reginald's words that were written for different purposes, as opposed to spoken words arising in the context of ethnographic interviewing. To use a musical analogy, while those earlier projects might be seen as duets in which the autobiographical words arose in the context of the ethnographic encounter, my project might be seen more as re-mixing. Shepherd's words will be assembled in the context of a particular literary and ethnographic project, but they were in no way prompted by that project.

This memoir project also has an interesting relation to a perennial topic of anthropological interest: myth. I am creating a myth of Reginald Shepherd—no doubt motivated consciously and subconsciously to put the fragments back together to make him what he was in a process no doubt doomed to fail at some level. I am engaging in a process Lévi-Strauss identified as central to mythic thinking, *bricolage*, in the attempt to assemble a coherent whole out of preexisting odds and ends of language. (Incidentally, this process strongly mirrors the process Reginald used in writing most of his poems. While he clearly had what might as well be termed a *Muse*, regardless of one's thoughts on the metaphysics and epistemology of Musical inspiration, he was, like many poets, continually struck by poetic bits of language that he had to write down quickly or lose forever. Most of his poems were the result of assembling the already existing bits of musically inspired language he had written down.)

Bricolage, whether in the forms of myth-telling or the work of the handyman bricoleur, can always result in multiple forms—the same odds and ends might be put to building a table or a chair, the same culturally significant narrative bits might be incorporated into multiple mythic forms. No doubt, others or I could craft many possible myths out of Shepherd's words—part of the power of bricolage is its ability to craft indefinite numbers of forms out of limited material. At the same time, for *any*thing to result, *some* organizing theme has to be at play, though this might involve either applying a given theme to the material at hand or discerning from that material a theme to build with. I am in the process of discerning the key themes around which to sift through all of Shepherd's words (or I should say all his written words that remain within my access) and assemble his memoir.

In doing so, I am currently attempting to triangulate between three sources of conceptualization of the significant themes orienting his writing. First is my sense of who he was and what the organizing themes were in his writing. Second is his sense of the same thing, as seen in his own proposal for a memoir manuscript or in the surface organization of some of his memoir essays. I am also searching for latent themes, for organizing elements that might not have been so explicitly recognized by him or myself, but which might nonetheless play a powerfully structuring role in his thoughts expressed in written word. As Lévi-Strauss (1995) recognized in his work on myth, much that structures myth isn't necessarily in the conscious and explicit thought of those engaged in mythic thought. While Lévi-Strauss used the language of "mythemes" and "sonemes," he wasn't particularly interested in the "emic" in the simplistic sense of the "Native's point of view." I am very much interested in this case in my particular native's point of view, as well as my view of his view, but I'm also interested to uncover less clearly noticed, but nonetheless significant, underlying themes in Reginald's work, and to do so I am currently using the interpretive software package NVivo to draw out key patterns in his writing.

An equally important conceptual process as I engage in this project involves thinking through the relationship between Shepherd's poetry, his life, and his memoir. In his essays, he wrote much about poetry and much about writing poetry; and poetry was a key part of him and frankly one of the main reasons, alongside his essays, that someone who hadn't known him personally might be likely to want to know more about him. Therefore, his poetry can't very well be left out, though figuring out exactly how to include it is a difficult and fraught task.

Shepherd was against what he called identity poetry. He was against the notion that poetry was straightforward self-expression, or that it should reflect biography or a poet's identity—for example, the idea that because he was a black, gay poet, he should stick to writing "black" and/or "gay" poetry. In his essay, "The Other's Other: Against Identity Poetry, For Possibility" (2007c), he further stressed the ways in which poetry or other art might enable critical and alternative thinking. He stressed the role of encountering Eliot's "Love Song of J. Alfred Prufrock" and the difficulties he encountered in "figuring it out" as an adolescent, as instrumental in opening his thinking to possibilities outside the poverty of his Bronx neighborhood. Though a skeptical materialist, such as myself (or Shepherd at times), might wonder whether it wasn't also attending a richly endowed private school on scholarship that took him literally and well outside his ghetto home life thanks to his mother's bureaucratic hustling that was also particularly instrumental in opening his thinking.

In any case, it is clear his poetry cannot be easily reduced to his particular life circumstances at the moment of the poem's writing —nor can I imagine why one would want to. To take one example, in April 2008, in a particularly nasty phase of Reginald's cancer, he entered a semicomatose state for two weeks. When he was just coming out of it, and at a time when he was only semiconscious and unable to talk, he scrawled a poem on a sheet of paper on a clipboard, one of the purest examples of poetry as musically inspired as I can imagine. He was not even aware of having written this poem after the fact, and I found it only after his death. As I discussed in the introduction to Shepherd's posthumous essay collection, *A Martian Muse* (Shepherd 2010, 6), and where this poetic fragment was also published, most of it is completely illegible, as his handwriting was extremely unsteady at that moment, but a fragment of it can be read:

> A palmful of Persian peaches,
> the world is a work of wish and
> human circumstance,
> this history of being rusted, being burned
> rusting, being burned
> years burned up, not down
> burned off to the night

The biographic circumstances of the writing of that poem are perhaps of interest, but it is not clear how this writing relates to memoir, nor how the poem itself relates to him or his circumstances.

At the same time, often his poetry was powerfully influenced by circumstances, and often his poetry did express significant things about himself. How could it not? Even while he was against the determinism of identity poetry, that poetry *should* or *must* reflect biography or identity, he in no way rejected the notion that it *could* do such a thing. In his own proposal for a memoir, he even included some of his more autobiographical poetry, and many of the key themes that show up in his essays and memoiristic writing (whether discerned by himself, me, or the NVivo software package) show up as key elements of his poetry. For example, "Mother" shows up as a continual preoccupation in his poetry, essays, and the conversations I had with him. As such, I'd like to leave with the words of one of his poems (from Shepherd 2011) that I hope demonstrates the significance of poetic writing to his memoir and my mythic project to make him who he was while also indicating the lack of straightforward clarity in so construing him, because of course, the poem (and his other words) is its own object and not him, and its meaning irreducible to events outside it. (As T. S. Eliot, when asked what he had meant by the line in "Ash Wednesday," "Lady, three white leopards sat under a Juniper tree," simply reiterated, "Lady, three white leopards sat under a Juniper tree.")

"My Mother Was No White Dove" from *Red Clay Weather*, by Reginald Shepherd, © 2011. (Reprinted by permission of the University of Pittsburgh Press.)

no dove at all, coo-rooing through the dusk
and foraging for small seeds
My mother was the clouded-over night
a moon swims through, the dark against which stars
switch themselves on, so many already dead
by now (stars switch themselves off
and are my mother, she was never
so celestial, so clearly seen)

My mother was the murderous flight of crows
stilled, black plumage gleaming
among black branches, taken
for nocturnal leaves, the difference
between two darks:

a cacophony of needs
in the bare tree silhouette,
a flight of feathers, scattering
black. She was the night
streetlights oppose (perch
for the crows, their purchase on sight),

obscure bruise across the sky
making up names for rain

My mother always falling
was never snow, no kind
of bird, pigeon or crow

Acknowledgments

Much love and thanks to Reginald Shepherd and Carlos Goebels, without whom this piece would not have been written and without whom my life would be radically different and much less enriched.

References

Crapanzano, Vincent. 1980. *Tuhami: Portrait of a Moroccan.* Chicago: University of Chicago Press.

Lewis, Oscar. 1961. *The Children of Sánchez: Autobiography of a Mexican Family*. New York: Random House.

Radin, Paul. 1920. *Autobiography of a Winnebago Indian: Life, Ways, Acculturation, and the Peyote Cult.* Berkeley: University of California Press.

Shepherd, Reginald. 1994. *Some Are Drowning*. Pittsburgh: University of Pittsburgh Press.

———. 1996. *Angel, Interrupted.* Pittsburgh: University of Pittsburgh Press.

———. 1999. *Wrong*. Pittsburgh: University of Pittsburgh Press.

———. 2003. *Otherhood.* Pittsburgh: University of Pittsburgh Press.

———. 2007a. *Fata Morgana*. Pittsburgh: University of Pittsburgh Press.

———. 2007b. "To Make Me Who I Am." In *Orpheus in the Bronx: Essays on Identity, Politics, and the Freedom of Poetry*, 7-40. Ann Arbor: University of Michigan Press.

———. 2007c. "The Other's Other: Against Identity Poetry, For Possibility." In *Orpheus in the Bronx: Essays on Identity, Politics, and the Freedom of Poetry*, 41-55. Ann Arbor: University of Michigan Press.

———. 2010. *A Martian Muse: Further Essays on Identity, Politics, and the Freedom of Poetry*, edited by Robert Philen. Ann Arbor: University of Michigan Press.

———. 2011. *Red Clay Weather*, edited by Robert Philen. Pittsburgh: University of Pittsburgh Press.

Levi-Strauss, Claude. 1995. *Myth and Meaning: Cracking the Code of Culture*. Berlin: Schocken.

Underhill, Ruth Mary. 1936. *Papago Woman*. Stanford: Stanford University Press.

Pocahontas and Rebecca: Two Tales of a Captive

Margaret Williamson Huber

Abstract

The Jamestown colonists' accounts of their capture of Pocahontas, her reactions to life among them, and the consequences for the success of the colony differ radically from the Mattaponi Indian oral history of the same events, published in 2007. Both versions present themselves as "true"—that is, objective reporting of real events; but the fact that each inverts the other raises questions of validity and, ultimately, of historiography in general. This paper argues that the question of veracity is irrelevant to our interpretation of these accounts. Instead, we must take them as representations of a culturally conceived reality—that is, as myth. Each Pocahontas narrative represents events in terms of contemporary cultural assumptions and agendas: in the case of the English, ideas about savagery and redemption; for the Mattaponi, the moral and economic primacy of native Virginians in the history of the foundation of the colonies and, thus, of the United States. The analysis confirms the idea that the conventional distinction between history and myth is invalid because it depends on Western (i.e., "scientific") notions about reality and its representation.

The English colonial tale of Pocahontas is familiar to many modern Americans, in general outlines, if not in detail. Briefly, it goes like this: she was the favorite daughter of Wahunsenaca (or Powhatan), the paramount chief in Tidewater Virginia (Hamor [1615] 1957, 4; Smith [1624] 1986, 151), who in late 1607 captured the leader of the Jamestown colony, Captain John Smith (Smith [1608] 1986, 47). When Wahunsenaca ordered Smith to be put to death, his ten-year-old daughter, Pocahontas, intervened, causing her father to relent and to befriend the English (Smith [1624] 1986, 151-152). Until Smith's departure in 1609, she came frequently to James Fort, usually with lavish gifts of food without which the colony would have foundered (Smith [1624] 1986, 152; cf. Smith [1608] 1986, 61). Smith also claimed that months later, when he had escaped an assassination at her father's hands, she suddenly appeared to Smith and his men in the woods nearby and begged him to depart if he valued his life (Smith [1624] 1986, 198-199). From the time Smith left until 1613, she disappears from the English record except for a brief notice that in about 1611 she had married an Indian "captain" named Kokoum (Strachey [1612] 1953, 62). In 1612, Captain Samuel Argall discovered that she was visiting a Potomac chief and, as he himself later reported, he decided "to possesse my selfe of her by any stratagem that I could use, for the ransoming of so many Englishmen as were prisoners with Powhatan: as also to get such armes [and] tooles, as hee, and other Indians had got by murther and stealing from others of our Nation, with some quantitie of Corne, for the Colonies relief" (Purchas [1625] 1906, 92-93). Argall's attempt was successful and he brought Pocahontas triumphantly to Jamestown (Hamor [1615] 1957, 2). During her residence there, she eagerly adopted English manners and dress; and she agreed to be instructed in English and in Christian religion, which led to her baptism and the assumption of the name Rebecca (Dale [1614] 1957, in Hamor [1615] 1957, 53-56).

In April of 1614, she married John Rolfe, with whom she was in love (Hamor [1615] 1957, 10); they had a son, Thomas (Smith [1624] 1986, 258). In 1616, they went to England, where she developed a fatal illness and died, being buried at Gravesend Church.

This Anglo-American narrative has recently been countered by a published version derived from the Mattaponi Indian sacred oral history, written by the Mattaponi Oral Historian Dr. Lin "Little Bear" Custalow and his assistant, Angela Daniel "Silver Star" (Custalow and Daniel 2007). For the most part, their version does agree about what the events were: that Pocahontas probably became aware of Smith during his captivity; that she came to the fort with provisions following his release—although the history says that these were gifts from her father and that she was present merely as a "peace gesture" (24, 26); that she married a man named Kokoum (42); and that she was captured by Argall (47) and, while a captive, came to marry John Rolfe; that she had a son named Thomas; and that she visited England, where she died.

But there are divergences between the two accounts. Here I summarize these and defer detailed discussion until later in the paper. The Mattaponi Historians reject both stories of Pocahontas rescuing Smith. They say that the famous episode wherein she forced her father to release Smith could not have happened because Smith was never really in any danger from the Powhatan; in fact, they insist that Wahunsenaca liked Smith, and that the Powhatan as a whole were favorably inclined to the English, at least initially (Custalow and Daniel 2007, 12, 18-19). Smith, they state, could not have needed rescuing; and even if he had, his rescuer would not have been a child (20). The second rescue is improbable because, as the young daughter of a paramount chief, Pocahontas would have been too important to be allowed to run around by herself, especially on a dark stormy winter night; nor could she have eluded those who had her in their care or have escaped through the palisades of Werowocomoco unnoticed (30-31).

These differences are comparatively trivial, echoing the objections of a number of Anglo-American scholars to the rescue stories (most recently, Rountree [2001, 2005]; Townsend [2004]; see Lemay [1992] for an extended discussion of the issue). Much more serious is the difference between the Anglo and Mattaponi accounts concerning Pocahontas's life as a captive. So far from enjoying her life at James Fort, as the English say she did, the oral history says that she sank into a profound depression amounting to a nervous breakdown because of separation from her family, including her husband, Kokoum, and their child; brainwashing from the English (who told her that her father didn't love her); and—not least—being repeatedly raped by several of the colonists (Custalow and Daniel 2007, 56-57, 61-63). Among her violators was the Governor, Sir Thomas Dale, who was probably the father of her son, who was born out of wedlock (64). The English did not want an unwed mother on their hands, so they made her marry Rolfe (65). (Sir Thomas was already married.) Since they knew that Dale and not Rolfe was the father of the infant, however, they named him Thomas instead of John (64). Although Pocahontas hardly knew Rolfe and certainly did not love him, she consented to marry him for the good of her people, knowing that such an alliance would result in peace between them and the English (65). This theme, that Pocahontas willingly sacrificed her happiness for the good of her people, infuses the Mattaponi version in contrast to the English account, which suggests that she happily repudiated her "barbaric" life to adopt English ways. Finally, according to the Mattaponi sacred oral history, her death was caused not by microbes, but by poison administered by the English in London, a measure taken to prevent her making a true report about the English to her father in Virginia (Custalow and Daniel 2007, 83).

How to think about the radical differences in these narratives forms the substance of this paper. Because the accounts contradict each other so extensively, historical method insists that we cannot accept both. We want to know which is true so we can dismiss the other, a reaction that arises from the historian's reasonable assumption that there is a series of events that really happened to people who really existed that can be recovered from the past. Even as historians acknowledge that the resources available make that ideal impossible (Evans 1999, 75; McNeill 1986, 18-19; Portelli 1990, viii-ix), the concept of "truth" informs their discussions. They debate the notion of what is to be accepted as truth, but they do not question that there is an objective, verifiable reality that one ought to seek and that one's success as a historian is a function of how closely one comes to representing that reality.

But a strict adherence to this premise has as a corollary that anything that cannot be verified, that owes much to imagining, that smacks of the physically impossible, becomes relegated to the less-than-historical: the legend, the tradition, the folktale, the myth. This is a regrettable point of view (Burridge 1969, xvii-xxi; Heusch 1982, 8; Leach 1970, 54; Vansina 1985, 20; White 1983, 3n). "History" and "myth" are Western categories of narrative, and so we cannot trust them to be reliable keys to understanding other people's stories or, indeed, our own. The distinction prejudices us against accepting as history what to a Western mind seem fantastical stories that informants tell about their past, even though they themselves clearly accept them as true and produce the evidence to prove it. The fact that the narratives describe marvelous events such as trees turning into human beings or women married to heavenly bodies does not in itself justify distinguishing the narrative from history since tales only appear marvelous to those who are not used to them. And, in any case, mythology is not really about the marvelous. We have to take it as a representation about the culturally imposed order of the world. Another way of putting this is to say that although the narrative may describe a past, the structure of the narrative—the things it includes (or excludes) and the ways that it arranges those things in relation to each other—reflects present ideas about how the world is organized and how it works. There is good reason to regard historical sources, and even histories, in the same light.

I am not saying that histories are only about the present, although the subjects they choose to treat and the ways they treat them reflect current concerns among historians (Evans 1999, 73). My position is that there is a past to discover, that that discovery is possible, and that it can be represented in such a way as to make the best sense out of the facts at one's disposal. This is the historian's analogue of the cultural anthropologist's mandate. Yet it leaves open the question of what exactly the "best sense" would be, and that will depend on one's theoretical perspective. To a functionalist, what people make of their own actions is irrelevant to anthropological understanding, while to a structuralist it is essential. In history as in anthropology, the same facts may be submitted to different interpretations, with different results. This is not to say a priori that one will be right and the other wrong but rather that each approach seeks to answer different questions; judging the outcome has to rest on whether the question is valid and, if so, how well it is answered. But regardless of the questions asked and the theories employed, there is a "there" there that the writer is attempting to describe and understand; neither the history nor the ethnography is simply a projection of the writer's imaginings. As Dumézil sapiently observed, the system is inherent in the facts (1988, 17).

Here I may seem to be begging a question, however. May we legitimately assume that there is such a thing as a fact? Surely we can. Evans defines a historical fact as "something that happened in history and can be verified as such through the traces history has left behind" (1999, 66). Ethnographic facts may be harder to verify, if only because of the difficulties of getting to many research sites; but even in the most vigorously criticized ethnographies—for instance, Colin Turnbull's disturbing *The Mountain People* (1972)—we have descriptions of people's activities and the landscape in which they take place, so that it is possible to arrive at alternative interpretations of the material and even identify things that contradict the author's own conclusions. Or, to take different situation, Annette Weiner's work in the Trobriand Islands (1976) shows that Malinowski's reporting was accurate so far as it went; it just did not go far enough. Reality leaves its impress in the minds of those who will describe it.

But this leaves hanging the original point of this argument: that we should think of myth and history as the same kind of narrative. The proposition is not that history is invention but rather that what we like to call myth is *not* invention, that it *is* factual, at least to the people who tell it. McNeill suggests, "Myth and history are close kin inasmuch as both explain how things got to be the way they are by telling some sort of story" (1986, 3). I propose that myth and history are more than kin—they are the same kind of cultural form—and that the dichotomy myth/history is invalid. Leach's argument is compelling:

> An indefinitely large number of events have actually occurred in the past. Only a tiny selection of these events can ever come to be perpetuated as 'history.' The process by which the selection is made is a complex combination of pure accident and editorial interest, but the net result is quite arbitrary. . . . Of 'history' as of 'myth,' it is quite sensible for the sociological inquirer to ask himself: 'Why does this particular incident (rather than some other) occur in the story in this particular form (rather than

> in some other)?' It is not sufficient to give the orthodox historian's answer which is: 'Well that is what really happened,' for many other things also really happened which do not appear in the story at all. (Leach 1969, 42; cf. Lévi-Strauss 1966, 257; contra, Evans-Pritchard 1965, 179)

What we conventionally call history and myth both rely on the conceptual and the empirical, and any attempt to classify narratives according to their degree of either is bound to interfere with our understanding of them. On the contrary, to regard them all as narrative ways of talking about the conceptual order of the world proves more useful to their understanding (Burridge 1969, xx; cf. Beidelman 1970, 75).

As the summaries given above show, most of the facts about Pocahontas's relationship to the English are not at issue. (The famous "rescue" of Captain Smith is an exception.) Rather it is in the interpretation of those facts that we find the profound contradictions that force us to think about which is acceptable and for what reasons. One obvious approach is to subject both to meticulous historical analysis and demonstrate the greater validity of one of them. Verifying oral history in the absence of contemporary documents is difficult, though (cf. Vansina 1985, 29), and in this case, the contemporary documents are precisely those whose reliability the Mattaponi oral history questions. We have no easy or conclusive way to prove which of these narratives we must accept as the more valid.

Instead, I have chosen to take them as reflections of their respective contemporary concerns rather than as disinterestedly objective descriptions—that is, to read them as myths, which use experience to form a narrative that will make experience intelligible (Lévi-Strauss 1966). These are not tales devoid of fact—far from it; but their narrators have selected facts (persons, events, things), described them, and related them to each other so as to convey a metamessage about relations between Anglos and indigenes. It is possible to unpack that implicit message by the same methods we use to reveal the structure of a myth.

But first, we should ask to what extent these two tales of a captive—a collection of seventeenth century colonial documents and an oral history, the one written by English colonists, the other preserved by their adversaries the Mattaponi—are comparable. Given the differences, the answer might appear to be "not at all," but I hope to show that comparison is not only possible but also legitimate.

Historians regard the Jamestown documents as eyewitness accounts. If their writing is not a streamed coverage of the events, still the time between experience and recording is in many cases quite short—hours, or a day or two. One might argue, too, that the vividness of such unusual experiences would remain with the witness longer than that of everyday happenings, particularly when the witnesses really want to remember and report what has happened. The comparative immediacy of these narratives makes it seem reasonable to trust them to tell us what went on in Jamestown.

The Mattaponi sacred oral history, on the contrary, is an oral tradition transmitted from one historian to another since the seventeenth-century (Custalow and Daniel 2007, xxiii). This lays it open to all the criticisms of the genre, of which the principal is that memory, however carefully cherished, is malleable and therefore not a trustworthy record (Abrams 2010, 5; Allen and Montell 1981, 68; Portelli 1990, 52; Vansina 1985, 5). Another objection is that there can be no scientific test of how reliable an oral account is (Abrams 2010, 5). Even Vansina, that vigorous supporter of the value of oral history, cautions that such historical information is reliable only if confirmed by some independent (i.e., material) source, preferably a written document (1985, 29). At its simplest, this attitude implies that historical documents reflect the truth while oral histories necessarily distort.

Over the past few decades, however, practitioners of oral history have come to see that its value is not its objectivity but its subjectivity (Abrams 2010, 7, 22-24; Allen and Montell 1981, 21; Passerini 1979; Portelli 1990, xi; Thomson 1998, 582-584). The sort of truth one gets in an oral history is not the literal and unemotional sequencing of events but is instead a representation of those events from the speaker's point of view. And that it is subjective detracts not at all from its value as a narrative about the past.

The opposition between objective and subjective, apparently assimilable to that between truth and fiction or history and mythology, deserves careful thought. What might *subjective* mean? Portelli calls it "the cultural forms and processes by which individuals express their sense of themselves in history" (1990; cf. Passerini 1979, 84-85; Vansina 1985, 124), a phrasing that recalls Dumont's definition of the person as "a more or less autonomous point of emergence of a particular collective humanity, of a *society*" (1970, 39). That is, "subjective" does not mean purely personal or idiosyncratic (e.g., Ginzburg 1980). The oral historians cited here seem to agree with Halbwachs that society shapes personal memory to such an extent that without a society no one could have any memory (Halbwachs 1980 [1950]; cf. Burridge 1969, 198). A person's story about the past is a conjuncture between her or his own memories of the event and the cultural forms that affect how it is remembered and how it is told. Even vastly differing versions of the same event may be understood as expressions of cultural ideas about narrative and narrators—for instance, that the culture places a premium on individuality or that the different versions reflect political divisions of the larger society. The story responds to the people who tell it at least as much as it responds to the interviewer.

But if oral histories and traditions are subjective, so too are written historical sources and histories that depend on those written sources. In fact, extended consideration forces one to ask why anybody bothers to distinguish oral from written sources, except that oral history offers rather more in the way of ethnographic information (cf. Allen and Montell 1981, ix; Passerini 1979, 84; Portelli 1990, viii). Historiographers now take it as axiomatic that nothing is written without a point of view—not even an eyewitness report, and eyewitnesses are demonstrably unreliable (e.g., Evans 1999, 2, 18, 89ff; Loftus 1996; Vansina 1985, 5; Wright and Loftus 2008). The source document may have gaps, or gloss over or whitewash difficult points; it may report a "truth" that is based on the writer's complete misunderstanding of a situation; it will stress what the writer considered important and leave out material she or he judged to be irrelevant, dull, or dangerous; it will be colored by the writer's various biases, which may have motivated its creation to begin with. Compounding these difficulties is the fact that writers vary considerably in their abilities to describe ideas or experiences, even if they remember them correctly. Tones of voice and nonverbal cues do not transmit themselves easily to the page; the reader must imagine them, and there is no guarantee that mentally adding any of them to a passage restores the writer's intention. In short, the historical source, like the history that uses it, is an interpretation (Abrams 2010, 22-23; Allen and Montell 1981, 21; Collingwood 1939, 31, 114, et passim; Evans-Pritchard 1962, 147; Howell and Prevenier 2001, 149; McNeill 1986, 4; Vansina 1985, 83ff; White 1983).

These observations are pertinent to the present case. Questions have arisen for centuries about how much we should trust the Jamestown documents, in particular those of Smith, whose veracity has been not simply challenged (e.g., Rowse 1957, xvi) but denied outright (see Barbour 1986, lxiiiff). But most of these documents were meant as encouragements to actual and potential investors in this colonial enterprise rather than as records for posterity. The writers promote themselves as they denigrate their rivals among the colonists; they minimize the difficulties of the colony and make much of its small successes. Among the latter, they insist on the imminent "civilizing" of the natives, whom they represent as something not (yet) quite English, but close enough that political, economic, religious, and perhaps even kinship ties can be established and maintained. Knowing the points of view of these writers—their mutual hostility, their desperate wish for financial support, and their desire to represent the native Virginians as a civil society (Williamson 2003, 73)—allows us to add the requisite grains of salt to the narratives. We do not make the mistake of thinking that these documents are a form of debriefing, much less modern ethnography.

This argument means that as far as the documents relating to Pocahontas are concerned, there is no basis for favoring either the written "eyewitness" accounts or the Mattaponi sacred oral history as being the more truthful. Both are subjective, in the sense outlined above; the written documents are no more, and no less, representations of the true state of affairs than the oral account. But they are not therefore useless as sources of information. As expressions of contemporary cultural ideas—in Burridge's phrase, "modes of cognition [that] communicate awareness" (1969, xxi)—they reveal a great deal. Considering them in this light, we are forced to conclude that they differ not at all from the anthropological understanding of mythology—that is, a representation, in narrative form, of relations among currently accepted cultural categories.

So my propositions are these: most generally, there is no utility in distinguishing narratives as history or as mythology. Narrative is narrative, and it obeys the same imperatives in its construction and delivery no matter what its subject is. Second, narrative exists to convey information at a variety of levels, and it will incorporate, omit, and arrange material in order to achieve that end. The two tales of Pocahontas that I turn to now demonstrate the virtue of my arguments.

I take these differing accounts as narratives that describe events in such a way as to make them make sense to the people who know the myth, and I have tried to figure out what that sense is. The Jamestown documents reflect the period when England was still influenced by the reign of Elizabeth but increasingly under the domination of James I. For the Mattaponi, the reference is the later twentieth and early twenty-first centuries. But before I go on, a word is in order justifying my assumption that the Mattaponi sacred oral history—despite its name—is about the present. The Mattaponi themselves say that this history has been learned in each generation by the designated historian and that teaching the history stressed accuracy above all else. They consider that the tale as told today is the same as the narrative of events formulated by their priestly body in the seventeenth century (Custalow 2008, personal communication). But, as I have been arguing, insisting on the veracity of the narrative is beside the point. Whether it is the exact truth or not, it persists, and has been published today, because it has meaning to the Mattaponi in the present, whatever its debt to the past may be. To see it as a document about the present does not do violence to the Mattaponi insistence that it represents the past.

Because it comes first in time and because the Mattaponi sacred oral history refers to it, I begin with a consideration of the Jamestown colonists' story of Pocahontas.

In a "little booke" that Captain John Smith wrote for Queen Anne at the time Pocahontas visited England, he says that

> during the time of two or three yeeres [i.e., 1607-1609], she next under God, was still the instrument to preserve this Colonie from death, famine and utter confusion, which if in those times had once beene dissolved,

> Virginia might have line [lain] as it was at our first arrivall to this day. . . . This Kingdome [i.e., England] may rightly have a Kingdome [i.e., Tsenacomaco, or Virginia] by her meanes. (Smith [1624] 1986, 259-260, my interpolations; see ibid. 152)[1]

He describes in sufficient detail her several contributions to the colony, and he concludes by describing her as "the first Christian ever of that Nation, the first Virginian ever spake English, or had a childe in mariage by an Englishman" (Smith [1624] 1986, 258-259).

Smith's panegyric summarized the elements of the continuing Anglo tale of Pocahontas. He offered several explanations for what he regarded as uncharacteristically generous actions on the part of a "savage." We can be sure which of them he preferred when he described her as "at last rejecting her barbarous condition" (Smith [1624] 1986, 259). The image of her turning her back on her own people, rebelling against the domination of her father and his ways, and adopting English religion and customs as if they were the truth revealed at last encapsulates Smith's understanding of Pocahontas, as it did for his contemporaries.

So we find Sir Thomas Dale, who assumed the governance of Jamestown in 1611, describing her actions on the occasion of his taking her up the Pamunkey River in an attempt to goad her father into responding to the Governor's demands for the return of English tools, weapons, and men, and a shipload of corn: "The King's daughter went ashore, but would not talke to any of them scarce to them of the best sort, and to them onely, that if her father had loued her, he would not value her lesse then olde swords, peeces, or axes: wherefore she would stil dwel with the English men, who loued her." Later, Dale said, he

> caused [Pocahontas] to be carefully instructed in Christian Religion, who after shee had made some good

> progresse therein, renounced publickly her countrey Idolatry, openly confessed her Christian faith, was, as she desired, baptised, and is since married to an English Gentleman of good vnderstanding . . . she liues ciuilly and louingly with him. (Dale [1614] 1957, in Hamor [1615] 1957, 53-56)

The Reverend Alexander Whitaker, chaplain to the colony and Pocahontas's instructor in Christian religion, wrote in similar terms to a fellow minister in London (Whitaker [1614] 1957, 59-60). In his letter to Sir Thomas Dale requesting permission to marry her, John Rolfe described her as "one whose education hath been rude, her manners barbarous, her generation accursed, and . . . discrepant in all nurtriture from my selfe," language rather startling in an avowed lover (Rolfe [1615] 1957, 64). And that he loved her there can be no doubt, given another passage in which he said that she was one "to whom my hartie and best thoughts are, and have a long time bin so intangled, and inthralled in so intricate a laborinth, that I was even awearied to unwinde my selfe thereout." Other passages in his letter, however, make clear that to him, the political and religious implications of the proposed union were more important. He called the possibility of the marriage a "mightie ... matter," and he insisted that it is not "the unbridled desire of carnall affection: but for the good of this plantation, for the honour of our countrie, for the glory of God, for my owne salvation, and for the converting to the true knowledge of God and Jesus Christ, an unbeleeving creature" (Rolfe [1615] 1957, 61-64).

Hamor's book, to which Rolfe's letter was appended, was explicitly designed to persuade people that the colony was succeeding. Hamor offered Pocahontas as the principal evidence in support of his argument. All these men saw in her the possibility of converting and civilizing the whole of indigenous North America, who—like herself—would come to welcome the English presence among them. The name Rebecca reflects this. The original Rebecca, like Pocahontas, offered succor to strangers and left her own family to marry among them (see Alter 2004, 119-26).

From the beginning, then, as a symbol of the triumph of Protestant civilization over pagan savagery, Pocahontas assumed mythic status.[2] That is, she represented to the English of her day the relationship between civilization and savagery, true religion and error, just domination and submission, masculine and feminine—in short, the order of the world. For this reason, then, I argue that we need to see these so-called "historical" documents as myth, not history—not ethnography, either—because their writers have chosen to include only what is related to their abiding concern to bring Protestantism, English commodities, and civility to the newfound land; their choices reflect, confirm, and sustain established cultural categories that have their own structural relations to each other. And it worked, because the "wild Indian" still persists in popular imagery, as does the idea of this continent as a wild land needing to be tamed (that is, developed), and of Pocahontas as a cultural mediator that made the taming possible (Donaldson 1999; Kidwell 1992; Strong 1999; cf. Green 1980).

In their narratives, the colonists represent the Powhatan as essentially savage, which is to say irrational and governed only by "the undifferentiated rage that they released upon anyone foolish enough to come within reach" (Sheehan 1980, 37). Not surprisingly, the same narratives represent the colonists as virtuous and—when victims of this rage—unfairly put-upon. Or, in McNeill's terms, the good guys and the bad guys (1986, 13). To them, Pocahontas is wonderful because she is able to break out of that savagery and become a civilized person. The same stereotypical relationship obtains in the Mattaponi sacred oral history, but the roles are reversed: the English are unremittingly savage and the Powhatan virtuous and, when victims of this savagery, unfairly put-upon. And the history presents Pocahontas's role, in keeping with this relationship, as a principal agent in the attempt to civilize the English. In structuralist terms, each of these tales is an inversion of the other.

The Mattaponi historians stress repeatedly that the Powhatan and their leader regarded the English as friends and potential allies; that they went out of their way to welcome and succor the English and, eventually, to try by various means to incorporate the English into their own empire; and that the English, habitually paranoid and aggressive, were incapable of understanding these overtures in the spirit in which they were offered, and therefore rejected a relationship that might have been mutually productive, bringing ruin to the native Virginians at the same time. The historians write that "from the Powhatan perspective, the Powhatan showed friendship to the English colonists from the beginning of their arrival" (Custalow and Daniel 2007, 13); "[Wahunsenaca] viewed the English at that time as having come in peace. They were welcome to stay as long as they wished" (19); "Wahunsenaca truly liked Smith. He offered Smith a position to be a werowance of the English colonists, to be the leader of the English within the Powhatan nation" (18).

The English, according to the *History*, did not reciprocate this kindness. A sample passage about their actions states:

> Many of the Powhatan people were afraid of the English because they used 'thunder sticks' to kill them. . . . When Smith went into any village, he would take four or five armed English colonists with him. They would traumatize the people with their weapons to the point that they would give Smith what he wanted to get him to leave. For instance, Smith would pretend to come into a village in a friendly manner. When he was in close proximity

> to the chief of the village, he would put his pistol to the chief's head, demanding a ransom of food in exchange for the chief's release. Smith and his men would proceed to take all the corn and food in the village. As they left, Smith would throw down a few blue beads, claiming to have 'traded' with the Powhatan people. (Custalow and Daniel 2007, 14)

The whole import of Mattaponi sacred oral history is that if there were savages in Virginia in the early seventeenth century, they were the English (59). The history consistently paints a positive picture of Powhatan culture, saying that its basic guideline was a respect for life; rape was abhorrent, and women were never forced into marriage; generosity, hospitality, and the common good concerned everyone, the chiefs most of all; deception, greed, and selfishness were unknown; and rule, including the discipline of children, took the form of love rather than force because violence was always to be avoided. These qualities stand in opposition to those that the *History* says were typical of the English at Jamestown. Smith's violence, greed, and deception are obvious in the passage just quoted. I have mentioned already that the history says that the men at the fort raped Pocahontas; it says too that they raped Powhatan women and children at will (35). It asserts, more generally, that without the assistance of the Powhatan Indians, the Mattaponi and the Pamunkey in particular, the colony could never have survived. Not only did Wahunseneca provide food for them but also his priests taught them how to grow and cure tobacco (71ff). The whole success of the Virginia colony—and, by implication, the United States—is due to the natives of Virginia, not to the Jamestown colonists.

In each case—the English narratives, the Mattaponi sacred oral history—the implicit message is that the writers are superior to those whom they write about. The English represent themselves as God's gift—literally—to the New World. The Mattaponi sacred oral history counters the claim by representing the native Virginians as the true custodians of the knowledge of how best to live in this land and the English as a scourge and a blot. The Mattaponi description of precontact Powhatan life implicitly sets it in opposition to what many see as the ills of modern Anglo society—for instance, the prevalence of violence and rape, the greed of corporations, the corruption of politicians, the use of force rather than consensus-building to govern. And it counters the consistent modern Anglo refusal to acknowledge Native Virginian contributions to the success of Jamestown and the Virginia colony in such contexts as the Jamestown Settlement Museum and various websites devoted to Jamestown.[3] It also alludes to the wish of the Virginia tribes for state and national recognition.

Taken as histories, the Jamestown documents and the Mattaponi sacred oral history cannot be reconciled. But viewed in the same way as we look at myths—that is, ways of talking about the writers' contemporary ideas—they become equally valid. The Mattaponi history reflects current concerns among the Mattaponi just as surely as the original Jamestown documents represent their contemporary concerns and cultural categories. The sources operate in the same way as the myths that we interpret as expressing the relations between cultural categories. In this case, the important ones include savage/civilized, ignorant/informed, generous/stingy, spiritual/materialistic, nurturing/destructive. But each tale characterizes its tellers in terms of the positive side of these oppositions, representing the "others" in these negative terms.

What the Mattaponi history says about Pocahontas is likewise completely contrary to what the English say. Some sense of this appears in the opening paragraphs of this paper. The Jamestown version has her choosing and emphatically preferring the English way of life over that in which she was brought up, from which it rhetorically separates her. The Mattaponi sacred oral history says explicitly that she did not turn her back on her father and that she "did not betray her own people" (Custalow and Daniel 2007, 60). The Mattaponi historians point out that for a Powhatan woman to accommodate herself to a different culture was quite usual since the capture of women and children was an accepted consequence of Powhatan warfare and one that she had been raised to expect (58). Thus she could easily figure out how to adapt herself to the demands of the situation in order to save her own life and—more important—to prevent retaliations against her people because of her intransigence. She hoped that the English would come to realize how amenable the Powhatan were to accepting the English, provided they (the English) abandoned their uncivil ways. What the English took for cultural conversion is, by this account, simple accommodation. The Mattaponi historians understand in the same way her accepting Christianity, which was made easier by the fact that "the Powhatan people lived the principles of Christianity more than those who professed faith in it" (59). The English praise her willingness to adopt English clothing and manners; the Mattaponi historians say that she constantly shed her heavy English garments—forced upon her to hide her swelling belly—so that her keepers had to keep dressing her up again (57, 63). John Smith says that her son Thomas was the first legitimate child of a Powhatan-English union; the Mattaponi are explicit that baby Thomas was a bastard. In every possible way, the Mattaponi history contradicts and inverts the Anglo-American history of Pocahontas, and in doing so, it argues that the superior people in this drawn-out encounter were not the victors, the English, but the indigenous Virginians.

It is interesting, then, given this contrary picture, that it incorporates an Anglo understanding of our heroine. To the Mattaponi, she is quite as mythic (in the sense I am using it here) as she is to

Anglo-Americans. She is their cultural mediator, the one who bridged the gap between nations and brought peace between them. Her actions came at considerable personal cost, but then that's what women do: they sacrifice themselves for the greater good. Or in Anglo mythology they do. What this means is that however much the Mattaponi sacred oral history insists on its native integrity, we must at least suspect that it has acquired an Anglo gloss. The difference is that while the English saw Pocahontas's conversion and marriage as evidence of her prescience in recognizing a superior way of life and true religion, the Mattaponi say that she was doing the English a favor by agreeing to live among them. As a gift of inestimable price, one for which a comparable return cannot be made, she establishes the superiority of the Native Virginians over the Anglos for all time (Donaldson 1999).

More generally, this comparison suggests that, as I proposed in the beginning, searching for a historical truth in one or the other of these narratives is unnecessary. Treated like myths, they give us quite a lot of information, if not information that we originally hoped to garner from them. It is worth proposing, then, that we should analyze all historical sources in this way—that is, as narratives which by their choice of matter and its arrangement replicate, however unconsciously, their writers' cultural categories. A result of such an operation must be that the past made available to us is even richer than otherwise because our understanding of the past will include how our writers thought about things as well as the things themselves.

Acknowledgments

My thanks to Robert Shanafelt for including me in his session "Systems, Cultural Areas, Poetry and Myth: Insights Worth Keeping?" at the 2011 SAS Conference and to Eric Gable for encouraging me to expand the conference paper for publication.

Notes

1. What Smith means is that no development of the "natural" land would have occurred. A constant justification for colonizing Virginia was that the natives had made no improvements to the land God had given them, and therefore they had no further rights to it (e.g., Strachey [1612] 1953, 24-27; but see Cronon 1983).

2. Many scholars have addressed this point: Custalow and Daniel (2007); Donaldson (1999); Gleach (1997); Lemay (1992); Puglisi (1991); Quitt (1995); Rountree (1998, 2001, 2005); Strong (1999); Townsend (2004); Williamson (1992).

3. E.g., Jamestown Settlement website (http://www.historyisfun.org/History Jamestown.htm), Jamestown National Historic Site page of the Virginia Travel website (http://www.virginia.org/Listings/OutdoorsAndSports/JamestownNationalHistoricSite), the Historic Jamestowne page of the Visit Williamsburg website (http://www.visitwilliamsburg.com/williamsburg-attractions/historic-jamestowne/index.aspx), and the Jamestown page of the about.com website (http://dc.about.com/od/daytripsgetaways/a/Jamestown.htm). Wikipedia does mention the Powhatan but stresses their antipathy to the English at the expense of their friendly overtures (http://en.wikipedia.org/wiki/Jamestown,_Virginia).

References

Abrams, Lynn. 2010. *Oral History Theory*. New York: Routledge.

Allen, Barbara, and William Lynwood Montell. 1981. *From Memory to History: Using Oral Sources in Local Historical Research*. Nashville, TN: American Association for State and Local History.

Alter, Robert. 2004. *The Five Books of Moses*. A translation with commentary. New York: W. W. Norton.

Barbour, Philip L. 1986. "Brief Biography of Captain John Smith." In *The Complete Works of Captain John Smith (1580-1631)*, vol. 1, edited by Philip L. Barbour, lv-lxi. Chapel Hill: University of North Carolina Press.

Beidelman, Thomas O. 1970. "Myth, Legend and Oral History: A Kaguru Traditional Text." *Anthropos* 65(1/2): 74-97.

Burridge, K. O. L. 1969. *Tangu Traditions*. New York: Oxford University Press.

Collingwood, R. G. 1939. *An Autobiography*. New York: Oxford University Press.

Cooper, Rachel. 2012. "Jamestown, Virginia: A Visitor's Guide." About.com, Washington, DC, http://dc.about.com/od/daytripsgetaways/a/Jamestown.htm.

Cronon, William. 1983. *Changes in the Land*. New York: Hill and Wang.

Custalow, Linwood "Little Bear," and Angela L. "Silver Star" Daniel. 2007. *The True Story of Pocahontas: The Other Side of History*. Golden, CO: Fulcrum Publishing.

Dale, Sir Thomas. (1614) 1957. "Letter." In *A Trve Discovrse of the Present Estate of Virginia*, by Ralph Hamor, 51-59. Reprinted from the London edition, 1615, with an introduction by A. L. Rowse. Richmond: Virginia State Library.

Donaldson, Beth. 1999. "Pocahontas as Gift: Gender and Diplomacy on the Anglo-Powhatan Frontier." *Journal of the American Studies Association of Texas* 30:1-17.

Dumézil, Georges. 1988. *Mitra-Varuna*. Translated by Derek Coleman. New York: Zone Books.

Dumont, Louis. 1970. *Homo Hierarchicus*. London: Paladin.

Evans, Richard J. 1999. *In Defense of History*. New York: W. W. Norton.

Evans-Pritchard, E. E. 1962. *Social Anthropology and Other Essays*. New York: Free Press.

———. 1965. *Theories of Primitive Religion*. New York: Oxford University Press.

Ginzburg, Carlo. 1980. *The Cheese and the Worms: The Cosmos of a Sixteenth-Century Miller*. Translated by John Tedesci and Anne Tedesci. London: Routledge and Kegan Paul.

Gleach, Frederic W. 1997. *Powhatan's World and Colonial Virginia: A Conflict of Cultures*. Lincoln: University of Nebraska Press.

Green, Rayna. 1980. "Native American Women." *Signs* 6(2): 248-67.

Halbwachs, Maurice. (1950) 1980. *The Collective Memory*. Translated by Francis J. Ditter Jr. and Vida Yazdi Ditter. New York: Harper and Row.

Hamor, Ralph. (1615) 1957. *A Trve Discovrse of the Present Estate of Virginia, and the Successe of the Affaires There Till the 18 of Iune, 1614*. Reprinted from the London edition, 1615, with an introduction by A. L. Rowse. Richmond: Virginia State Library.

Heusch, Luc de. 1982. *The Drunken King or The Origin of the State*. Translated and annotated by Roy Willis. Bloomington: Indiana University Press.

Historic Jamestowne. 2012. "Visit Williamsburg," http://www.visitwilliamsburg.com/williamsburg-attractions/historic-jamestowne/index.aspx.

Howell, Martha, and Walter Prevenier. 2001. *From Reliable Sources: An Introduction to Historical Methods*. Ithaca: Cornell University Press.

Jamestown National Historic Site. 2012. "Virginia is for Lovers," http://www.virginia.org/Listings/OutdoorsAndSports/JamestownNationalHistoricSite/.

Jamestown Settlement. 2012. "Jamestown Settlement & Yorktown Victory Center," http://www.historyisfun.org/History-Jamestown.htm.

Kidwell, Clara Sue. 1992. "Indian Women as Cultural Mediators." *Ethnohistory* 39(2): 97-107.

Leach, Edmund. 1969. *Genesis as Myth and Other Essays*. London: Jonathan Cape.

———. 1970. *Lévi-Strauss*. London: Fontana/Collins.

Lemay, J. A. Leo. 1992. *Did Pocahontas Save Captain John Smith?* Athens: University of Georgia Press.

Lévi-Strauss, Claude. 1966. *The Savage Mind*. Translated ed. Chicago: University of Chicago Press.

Loftus, Elizabeth F. 1996. *Eyewitness Testimony*. Cambridge: Harvard University Press.

McNeill, William H. 1986. *Mythistory and Other Essays*. Chicago: University of Chicago Press.

Passerini, Luisa. 1979. "Work, Ideology and Consensus Under Italian Fascism." *History Workshop* 8:82-108.

Portelli, Alessandro. 1990. *The Death of Luigi Trastulli and Other Stories: Form and Meaning in Oral History*. Albany: State University of New York Press.

Puglisi, Michael J. 1991. "Capt. John Smith, Pocahontas and a Clash of Cultures: A Case for the Ethnohistorical Perspective." *History Teacher* 25(1): 97-103.

Purchas, Samuel. (1625) 1906. *Hakluytus Posthumus, or Purchas His Pilgrimes*, 20 vols. Glasgow: James MacLehose and Sons.

Quitt, Martin H. 1995. "Trade and Acculturation at Jamestown, 1607-1609: The Limits of Understanding." *William and Mary Quarterly* 52(2): 227-58.

Rolfe, John. (1615) 1957. "The coppie of the Gentle-mans letters to Sir Thomas Dale, that after maried Powhatans daughter, containing the reasons mou-ing him thereunto." In *A Trve Discovrse of the Present Estate of Virginia, and the Successe of the Affaires There Till the 18 of Iune, 1614*, by Ralph Hamor. Reprinted from the London edition, 1615, with an introduction by A. L. Rowse. Richmond: Virginia State Library.

Rountree, Helen C. 1998. "Powhatan Indian Women: The People Captain John Smith Barely Saw." *Ethnohistory* 45(1): 1-29.

———. 2001. "Pocahontas: The Hostage Who Became Famous." In *Sifters*, edited by Theda Perdue, 14-28. New York: Oxford University Press.

———. 2005. *Pocahontas, Powhatan, Opechancanough: Three Indian Lives Changed by Jamestown*. Charlottesville: University Press of Virginia.

Rowse, A. L. 1957. Introduction to *A Trve Discovrse of the Present Estate of Virginia, and the Successe of the Affaires There Till the 18 of Iune, 1614*, by Ralph Hamor. Reprinted from the London edition, 1615. Richmond: Virginia State Library.

Sheehan, Bernard. 1980. *Savagism and Civility: Indians and Englishmen in Colonial Virginia*. London: Cambridge University Press.

Smith, John. (1608) 1986. "A True Relation of such occurrences and accidents of noate as hath hapned in Virginia since the first planting of that Collony, which is now resident in the South part thereof, till the last returne from thence." In *The Complete Works of Captain John Smith*, edited by Philip L. Barbour, vol. 1, 21-117. Chapel Hill: University of North Carolina Press.

———. (1624) 1986. "The Generall Historie of Virginia, New England and the Summer Isles." In six books. In *The Complete Works of Captain John Smith*, edited by Philip L. Barbour, vol. 2, 26-488. Chapel Hill: University of North Carolina Press.

Strachey, William. (1612) 1953. *The Historie of Travell into Virginia Britania*, edited by Louis B. Wright and Virginia Freund. London: Hakluyt Society.

Strong, Pauline Turner. 1999. *Captive Selves, Captivating Others: The Politics and Poetics of Colonial American Captivity Narratives.* New York: Westview Press.

Thomson, Alistair. 1998. "Fifty Years On: An International Perspective on Oral History." *Journal of American History* 85(2): 581-95.

Townsend, Camilla. 2004. *Pocahontas and the Powhatan Dilemma.* New York: Hill and Wang.

Turnbull, Colin. 1972. *The Mountain People.* New York: Touchstone Books.

Vansina, Jan. 1985. *Oral Tradition as History.* Madison: University of Wisconsin Press.

Weiner, Annette. 1976. *Women of Value, Men of Renown.* Austin: University of Texas Press.

Whitaker, Alexander. (1614) 1957. "To my verie deere and louing Cosen M. G. Minister of the B. F. in London." In *A Trve*

Discovrse of the Present Estate of Virginia, and the Successe of the Affaires There Till the 18 of Iune, 1614, by Ralph Hamor. Reprinted from the London edition, 1615, with an introduction by A. L. Rowse, 59-61. Richmond: Virginia State Library.

White, Hayden. 1983. *Metahistory*. Baltimore: Johns Hopkins University Press.

Wikipedia. 2012. "Jamestown, Virginia," http://en.wikipedia.org/wiki/Jamestown,_Virginia.

Williamson, Margaret Holmes. 1992. "Pocahontas and Captain John Smith: Examining an Historical Myth." *History and Anthropology* 5(3-4): 365-402.

———. 2003. *Powhatan Lords of Life and Death*. Lincoln: University of Nebraska Press.

Wright, Daniel, and Elizabeth Loftus. 2008. "Eyewitness Memory." In *Memory in the Real World*, edited by Gillian Cohen and Martin Conway, 91-106. New York: Psychology Press.

PART II

Art Valuation: The Creativity/ Conventionality Dialectic

Mirror Dance: Tourists, Artists, and First People Heritage in Botswana

Jessica Stephenson

Abstract

Arts destined for the tourist market have long been devalued and set aside from serious study. They are considered mass-produced, artistically uninteresting, and inferior in quality. Recent scholarship counters these views; many forms of tourist art can be recognized as artistically inventive and conceptually complex authentic objects of significance to both client and artist. Here the paintings and prints created by artists affiliated with the Kuru Art Project in Botswana are considered as forms of autoethnography, after Mary Louis Pratt's term for indigenous autobiographies created in the context of "contact zones." Autoethnographies are received heterogeneously—in this case, as both nostalgic images of longing that drive the touristic quest in southern Africa, but also as contemporary San yearnings for the reclamation of a hunter-gatherer past in the assertion of a new First People political voice.

> Some films can kill. One such film was the blockbuster *The Gods Must Be Crazy*, which played to packed houses in the United States, South Africa and elsewhere. This film, with its pseudoscientific narrator describing Bushmen as living in a state of primitive affluence, without the worries of paying taxes, crime, police and other hassles of urban alienation, has had a disastrous impact on those people whom we call "Bushmen."
> — Robert Gordon[1]

In 1997, I visited D'Kar in Botswana to interview artists affiliated with the Kuru Art Project. Near the end of my visit, I purchased a souvenir, a color print by Dada Coex'ae Qgam. Fresh off the printer, Dada explained that the work depicted the edible Xoru plant and a species of Kalahari Desert bird that favors the berries of this plant (figure 5.1). She also identified a small schematic human figure at the bottom left-hand corner as a representation of herself as mother and grandmother. Below the figure are two series of short parallel lines that denote the number of children and grandchildren that Dada has nurtured. Yet this interesting autobiographical detail disappeared when the artist signed and titled the work *Xoru Plant and Birds*.

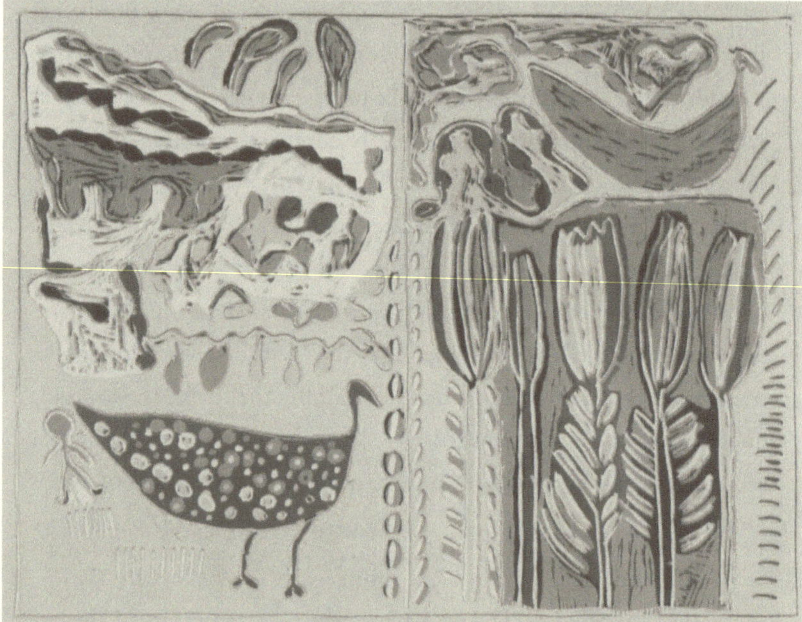

Figure 5.1. Dada Coex'ae Qgam (1934-2008), *Xoru Plant and Birds*. Silkscreen. 1997. (Photograph by Shane McDonald)

Images of grandmothers do not sell art, but references to Bushman indigenous knowledge and nature do—topics that are equally of value to the artists themselves. Dada went on to explain:

> I like to depict the things that bring me joy, like the plants from the Kalahari that can fill an empty stomach when you are hungry or can satisfy your thirst when there is no water to be found. I like to show the women collecting veldfood, the houses we live in, and the children who are always present. I like to depict the simplicity of our lives and the beauty that can be found in it, even though we have so many hardships.[2]

These two reflections, the first by an anthropologist and the second by a contemporary Bushman artist, highlight the complex relationship that exists between the images of, and those made by, people identified as Bushmen or San, images that are more often than not produced, disseminated, and consumed through popular culture mediums such as film and tourism.[3] Here I consider the paintings and prints created by Dada and fellow artists affiliated with the Kuru Art Project for consumption within the southern African tourist industry. Since 1990, a small group of male and female artists have created colorful, decorative, and semiabstract images of edible wild plants and animals, folkloric activities, mythological beings, and the iconic image of the hunter. Marketed through local tourist and ethnic art galleries within Botswana and neighboring Namibia, this body of work tends to be framed as the creation of nonliterate rural visionaries engaged in unmediated, intuitive, and naïve endeavors. Popular media articles use language such as "lack of sophistication and appealing innocence," "clumsy yet magical," "primitive charm," "innocence of vision," and "unselfconscious immediacy," which authenticates the work according to criteria often associated with folk, self-taught, or outsider artists whose art caters to touristic needs for souvenirs and mementos of southern Africa.

While contemporary art from D'Kar is often purchased as tourist art, it has been unfortunately set aside from serious study because of this. Arts destined for the tourist market tend to be devalued because they are perceived to be mass-produced, artistically uninteresting, and inferior in quality. They are also devalued as inauthentic because the rationale for artistic creation is believed to be economically motivated and guided by the consumer's desires, rather than those of the artist.[4] Recent scholarship has countered these views; many forms of tourist art are now recognized to be artistically inventive and conceptually complex objects.[5] Here, I acknowledge contemporary San art's function as souvenirs for tourists and unpack how they successfully fulfill the demands of their clientele. Yet this study also stresses that, beyond their touristic appeal, the works exhibit alternative significance for the artists and their local communities. I begin by analyzing how the artworks' formal aspects and imagery read as a nostalgic language of longing, recalling Susan Stewart's concept, for tourists seeking souvenirs of a sojourn to southern Africa. Then, drawing upon bell hooks' notion of yearning, I consider this body of work as assertions of cultural reclamation and a critical voice. Toward this end, I reconstruct the contexts for the emergence of Kuru art in the Kalahari region of Botswana, a "contact zone" that fostered the distinctive social identity of various Bushman communities that by the 1990s were claiming the memory of a hunter-gatherer past to assert a new critical First People voice.

Contemporary Art from D'Kar as Souvenir of Nostalgic Longing

In style and subject matter, Kuru Art Project arts appeal to tourist tastes. The images are naïvely rendered, brightly colored, and convey images such as African animals and scenes of scantily clad hunters and gatherers that correspond to mythic ideas about Africa (figure 5.2). As a souvenir for its buyer, Kuru artworks serve as mementos of a sojourn in southern Africa. Sidney Kasfir defines the souvenir as "an object of memory; a token of remembrance of a person, a place, or an event—that is, an object that stands for something remembered" (1999, 69). As objects of memory, souvenirs have two functions: they are mnemonic devices and repositories for nostalgia. As mnemonic devices, souvenirs serve as a touchstone for the memory of an experience, and as a repository of nostalgia, they represent qualities that tourists long for that do not exist in their own everyday world. For Susan Stewart, the souvenir therefore generates an inward narrative suggesting the personal, internalized meanings that a souvenir may bear (1984, 135). Dean MacCannell theorizes that when life in modern society is perceived to be devoid of meaning, people embark on a journey, seeking places and cultures that fulfill their longing for spirituality and authenticity. Through an encounter with people or places that are perceived to be "pristine, primitive, natural and, as yet untouched by modernity" the traveler is himself or herself transformed (MacCannell 1976, 373-74).

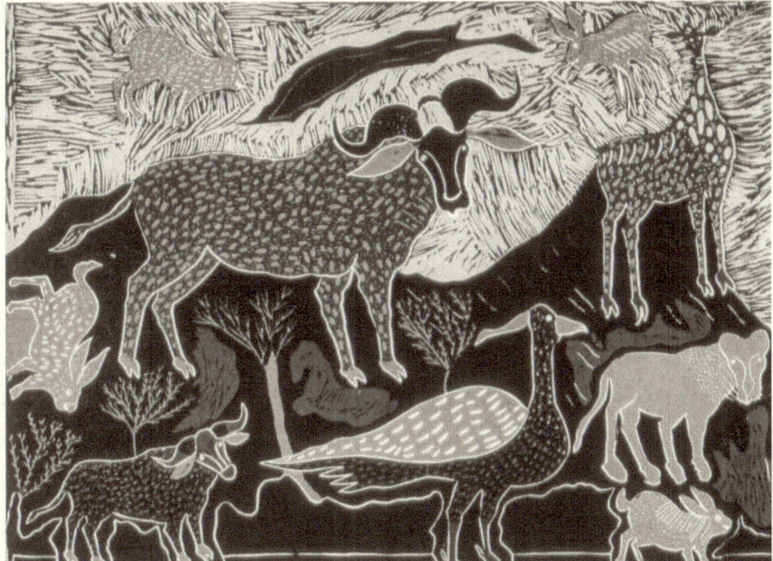

Figure 5.2. Thamae Kaashe, *Giraffe, Buffalo and Other Creatures.* Color linocut. (Photograph by author)

Kuru paintings and prints depict fauna, flora, and primal Africans, scenes that a tourist might witness, hope to encounter, or only imagine. As anthropologist Kenneth Little has argued, "Tourists come to Africa with a perspective and a story in mind and they try to find scenes that resemble these prior images that evoke recognition and an easy sense of familiarity" (1977, 156). As destinations for safari and ecotourism, Botswana and Namibia where one can purchase paintings and prints from D'Kar, cater to a tourist's nostalgic longing for difference. Before departing on vacations, tourists are likely to have engaged with representations of southern Africa through media productions on *Discovery Channel* and *National Geographic,* and national tourist ministries as well as private companies draw on the same types of tropes circulating in popular media. For example, the current website for Botswana national tourism focuses on its natural resources—the fauna and flora of the Okavango Delta and the Kalahari Desert. The only Botswanans featured are a group of leather-clad Bushmen, their backs to the viewer, heading off into the landscape, no doubt on a hunting or gathering excursion.[6] An unmediated encounter with both nature and primitive peoples is thus implied as achievable by the tourist.

Souvenirs tourists buy convey concepts of difference and longing (whether defined as the exotic, the foreign, the primitive, or the natural) that the tourist seeks (Jules-Rosette 1984, 18). The postcard, as the most ubiquitous souvenir, is one example of how the tourist market shapes and caters to touristic desires for the above-mentioned qualities. A preponderance of southern African regional postcards depicts individual species of fauna and flora, or scenes of the veld and sunsets: all images appealing to those tourists who invest in the idea of an Africa pristine, primitive, natural, and, as yet, untouched by modernity. The use of cropped, compressed, image-packed compositions also projects desirable qualities and ideas about Africa as a place that teems with energy and life. Postcards often replicate the look of tourists' photographic snapshots, underscoring their function as an authentic souvenir of potential or actual experiences.

Contemporary Kuru artworks as souvenirs replicate some of the formal and iconographic elements circulating in southern African tourist media. As I found when visiting D'Kar in 1997, artists such as Sobe Sobe and Thamae Kaashe actively appropriated and reworked popular literature on southern Africa—for example, images from *National Geographic* and popular books, such as Anthony Bannister's *The Bushmen* (1987), images that are in turn replicated in tourist media that shape tourists' desires and expectations about their destinations (figure 5.2). As Kasfir has observed, souvenirs "exist as fragments of something else—they are metonymic references to a larger cultural experience that is being remembered and objectified" (1999, 68). Souvenirs are designed to evoke memories or sought-after experiences and therefore need not be realistic representations of the actual places visited by the tourist. While the subject matter seen in Kuru art resonates with tourist imagery, the styles depart from photographic realism. Kuru artists tend to favor flat, decorative, and abstract approaches to representation. Schematic representations of an African naturescape such as we see in Kuru art therefore offer a highly flexible mnemonic for an experience of Africa on a more abstract level. Like the typical southern African postcard, the image-packed, high-contrast, color-saturated scenes of nature can memorialize Africa as a vital, wild, and exotic place. Similarly, the naïve pictorial qualities and decorative two-dimensional handling of space come to signify similar qualities and ideas about Africa.

However, it is the image of the Bushman hunter-gatherer depicted and, even more importantly, the Bushman identity of the artists that make these paintings and prints particularly well-suited souvenirs of the safari experience (figure 5.3). Beginning in the 1960s, the Kalahari

Desert and its Bushman inhabitants increasingly became the place and people through which tourists sought to fulfill a yearning for those qualities cited by MacCannell. Laurens van der Post (1958, 1961), the Jungian writer and filmmaker, was the most influential figure in the creation of this practice, largely as a result of his representation of Bushmen as the consummate egalitarians, spiritualists, and naturalists. Numerous others were to follow Van der Post—for example, more recently Paul Myburgh, the filmmaker who "claims to have become Bushman in order to represent the Bushmen."[7] A common feature of much popular filmography and literature on the Bushman is its narrative structure around a physical journey into the desert, where a sought-after or chance encounter with Bushmen leads to a spiritual or existential journey of self-discovery, and hence the attainment of a more essential humanity and community now lost to modern society.

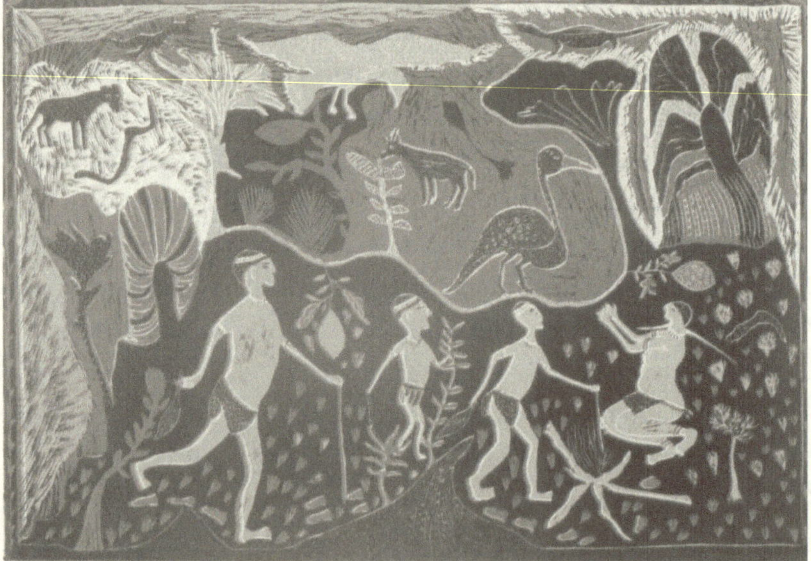

Figure 5.3. Thamae Kaashe, *Eland Dance*. Color linocut. Date unknown. (Photograph by author)

It is thus not surprising to find that the Botswanan and Namibian tourist industry within which Kuru art circulates draws extensively on the trope of the Bushman in its marketing material. For example, the internationally distributed tourist guide *Insight Guide: Namibia*, published in the mid-1990s, offers the opportunity to meet "still almost thoroughly traditional Bushman family groups [that] offer an image of unspoiled human existence." "[W]ithout class distinctions, . . . men and women know and perform their own tasks. Even today, the Bushman require[s] only a minimum of laws" (Garland and Gordon n.d., 6). Another contemporary publication, the *Spectrum Guide*, declares that Bushmen are "natural conservationists in an ever more polluted world, [who] take great care of their harsh habitat, at home in a terrain where few other human beings could survive." The description goes on, "Those who continue the tribe's 20,000 years of traditions even use utensils that have not noticeably altered during the past few thousand years" (Garland and Gordon n.d., 6).

An artwork created by a Bushman artist is thus a mnemonic for a set of ideas about the safari experience as nostalgic longing. Many tourists go on safari in order to get "back to nature," but few tourists actually achieve this. A nature scene painted by a Bushman artist can therefore serve as a repository of nostalgia, if the tourist yearns for the "at-one-with-nature" lifestyle depicted in the artwork that he or she assumes is actually lived by the artist. I suggest, therefore, that souvenirs metaphorically and metonymically come to signify nostalgic longing for an always-allusive authentic experience. Stewart argues that because authentic experience is ultimately unattainable, tourists inscribe it in objects connected with fictive domains of the antique, the pastoral, and the exotic, and in the case of contemporary San art, the naïve (1984, 133). Thus, the painting of an African Eden created by a Bushman artist is the consummate souvenir by which to transport the tourist to a nostalgic domain of longing.

I now turn to consider the local significance of contemporary San paintings and prints. I contend that, even though destined for tourist consumers, Kuru paintings and prints are forms of resistance to the social realities of the day, and in order to understand how this may be, I consider the "contact zone" out of which the work emerged.

I suggest that the persistent presence of bucolic images of wild animals and plants, mythological subject matter, and the hunter serve to remedy and counter a "collective sense of loss" that transpired among San peoples over the course of the twentieth century.

In my reading of Kuru contemporary art from the perspective of the artist, I am influenced by bell hooks' notion of "yearning" (1990, 36). Yearning can be synonymous with longing, but Stewart's (1984) concept of "longing" functions for the consumer as a place of escape, while hooks' "yearning" serves for the artist as a place of confrontation and encounter (1990, 4). *Yearning* is a term that refers to a depth of longing felt by those who struggle for the freedom to control destiny, not through a return to the past, but through a reclaiming of and appeal to old world values (1990, 6). Hooks observes that a sense of yearning occurs in contexts of dramatic social change and, as I will show, Kuru art emerges out of historical experiences of radical rupture leading up to the 1990s when this new art form emerged. For hooks, yearning is more than longing's domesticated nostalgia; rather it offers a cultural space to do cultural, indeed political, critique (1990, 6).

Tourism and Ethnic Mobilization in the Kalahari Contact Zone

The Ghanzi district in which Kuru paintings and prints of the 1990s emerged has long been and continues to be a *contact zone*. Mary Louise Pratt uses this term to describe "the space of colonial encounters, the space in which peoples geographically and historically separated come into contact with each other and establish ongoing relations, usually involving conditions of coercion, radical inequality, and intractable conflict" (1992, 6). Contact zones are places were colonizer and the colonized, the foreigner and the indigene, the tourist and the tourist worker, the national and the international encounter, struggle with, and influence one another. Contact zone is often synonymous with *colonial frontier*, but while the latter term is grounded within a European expansionist perspective, Pratt employs "contact zone" in an attempt to involve the spatial and temporal copresence of subjects previously separated by geographic and historical disjunctions, and whose trajectories now intersect. By using the term *contact*, the interactive, improvisational dimension of encounters is foregrounded. A "contact" perspective emphasizes how subjects are constituted in and by relations to each other. It treats the relations among colonizers and colonized, or travelers and "travelees," not in terms of separateness, but in terms of copresence, interaction, and interlocking understandings, often within radically asymmetrical relations of power (Pratt 1992, 7).

People commonly identified as Bushmen entered Botswana's colonial contact zone in one of two ways. They were sequestered in game reserves—the situation for G/wi and related groups living in the Central Kalahari Game Reserve of Botswana, where they were drawn into tourism. Alternatively, colonial rule was experienced as a process of land dispossession and incorporation into the lowest stratum of a racialized and ethnically hierarchical class system. The latter was the occurrence for Nharo and G/wi living in the Ghanzi district of Botswana where the mission station of D'Kar is situated, and where Kuru Art Project painting and prints emerged. The process of G/wi and Nharo incorporation into colonial society started a century ago when farms began to spring up in 1898 as numerous Boer families trekked northwards from the Marico area of southern Africa, seeking fertile pastures (le Roux 2000, 22). In the well-watered grasslands of the Ghanzi region, cattle ranchers began to utilize land inhabited predominantly by bands of Nharo and G/wi. By the late nineteenth century, big-game hunters and explorers had all but decimated Ghanzi's herds of wildlife. So, with the arrival of cattle, Nharo and G/wi began to work as farm laborers. In exchange for food, shelter, and some livestock, Nharo and G/wi men performed general farm work and trekked cattle, "cowboy style," to farflung grazing grounds. Women fulfilled domestic duties in Boer homes and gathered veld foods, like the *marama* bean, to feed Boer and Bushman families (Guenther 1996, 234). Referred to as *Basarwa*, a Tswana term for "people without cattle," Ghanzi Bushmen were at the bottom of a cattle-centered economic and social landscape.

The style of dress called *tanana*, after the multicolored cattle farmed in the region, adopted by Ghanzi farm Bush(wo)men in the early twentieth century, reflects their cultural sensibilities as farm Bushman people and their sense of place within Ghanzi's hierarchical class system. This dress form, as described to me in 1997 by Tumba Bob, a young Nharo woman then working at the Kuru Art Gallery in D'Kar, is similar to, and based on, the better-known Herero "long dress." According to Tumba, the tanana is like this Herero long dress, only the skirt is shorter, falling to midcalf. Both the tanana and the longer dress are made from patchwork fabric, a product of Ghanzi farm Bushman women's work and training within Boer households. The tanana emerged as a distinctive Ghanzi farm Bushman dress form during the early twentieth century in a context of competition over jobs between farm Nharo and G/wi and immigrant Herero coming from neighboring southwest Africa. The name of the Basarwa dress also relates to Ghanzi Bushman people's ties to cattle, both as herders and as owners (actually or desirably).[8] These references to class through cattle ownership therefore refute the pejorative connotations of the word *Basarwa*. The tanana can also be understood as a style of dress by which Ghanzi farm Bushmen differentiated themselves from the so-called veld Bushmen. Farm Bushmen had, by the 1950s, developed attitudes of alienation and ambivalence toward the culture of the veld Bushmen—those peoples who resided within the unfarmable central Kalahari Desert region bordering Ghanzi district, and who subsisted on a mix of tourism, and hunting and gathering (Guenther 1996, 238). However, the line between farm and veld Bushmen was in reality blurred, as the status and identity of individual Nharo and G/wi often shifted back and forth between these two categories, depending upon their access to farm labor and material goods. But here the important point is that Ghanzi Bushmen viewed the status and hunter-gatherer culture of veld Bushmen with some ambivalence, as a sign of poverty and exclusion from the broader class-based society, even though the two groups continued to share many cultural traits, such as language, religion, and the practice of veld foraging for food and medicines. This ambivalence was also likely tied to the attitudes of cultural outsiders, including Boer and Tswana farmers, who viewed veld Bushmen in negative terms as backward and primitive.

Yet after the complete loss of access to land and employment by the late 1960s, the farm Bushmen began to look to the veld Bushmen for inspiration as part of a process of cultural revitalization. During the 1950s, wealthier South Africans who utilized industrial-style farming techniques bought out Ghanzi Boer farmers; their preferred farm laborers were now Herero, Tswana, Kwena, or Kgalagadi Bantu speakers, thought to be "stronger, more reliable, better educated" (Guenther 1996, 234). Many third- and fourth-generation farm Nharo and G/wi lost their patrons and their homes. Unemployed, landless families drifted from farm to farm and flocked into the regional town of Ghanzi, where they survived on missionary and government aid handouts. During the same time, the Central Kalahari Game Reserve was established, in part due to the work of an anthropologist and government official who lobbied to protect veld Bushman culture. Beginning in the 1960s, the Kalahari Desert and its Bushman inhabitants increasingly became the place and people through whom tourists sought to fulfill the nostalgic longings that motivate touristic travel.

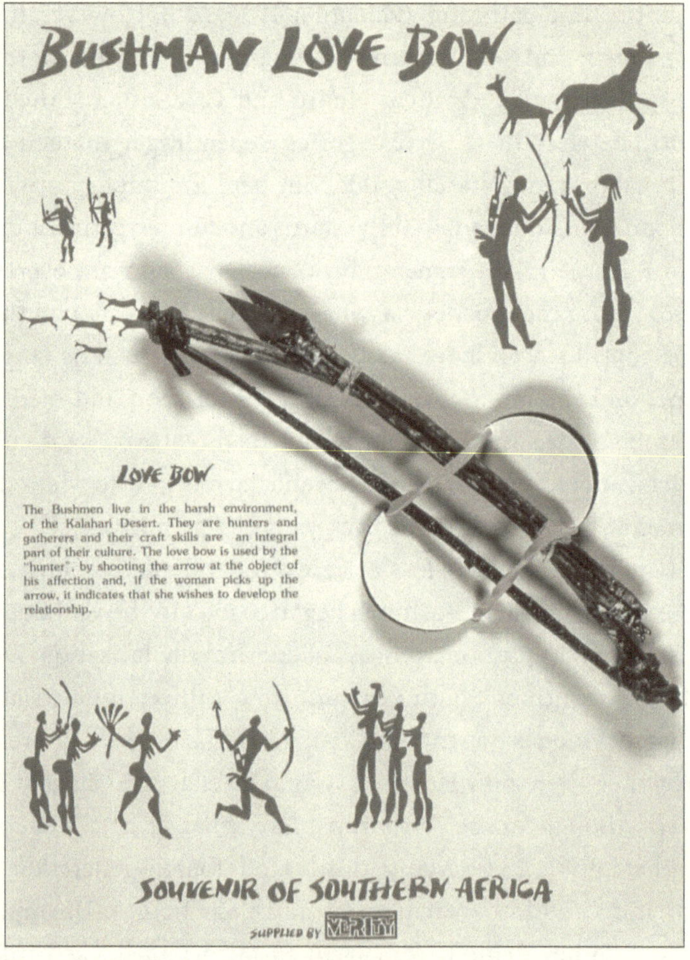

Figure 5.4. Bushman love bow, souvenir of southern Africa. (Photograph by author)

Bushmen have long produced and tailored aspects of their material culture for sale to Kalahari tourists and travelers seeking souvenirs to commemorate those qualities that they deemed authentic. Objects associated with hunting and gathering, such as miniature bow-and-arrow sets and gathering bags made from leather and decorated with glass beads, proved highly appropriate for this market (figure 5.4). Through a process of miniaturization, these once functional objects were transformed into nonfunctional aesthetic objects. For tourists seeking encounters with the primitive and the natural, these particular items represented a set of ideas about a lifestyle seen to exist in opposition to modernity. The fact that they were handmade from natural materials made them valuable in an age of mechanical reproduction.

In the face of this process of total land dispossession and economic marginalization, Ghanzi's farm Bushmen utilized various cultural resources as coping mechanisms. Since the establishment of game reserves within Botswana was accompanied by an increase in tourism, farm Bushmen transformed the visual elements of the veld Bushman's hunter-gatherer lifestyle into commodities. The involvement in this trade may have been partly instrumental in their subsequent positive reevaluation of veld Bushman material culture, for tourism conferred upon it positive values. As Ruth Phillips observed among native North American groups:

> The marketability of souvenirs depends on their success in conveying recognizable—and acceptable—concepts of difference. To succeed in this task, aboriginal makers had to re-imagine themselves in terms of the conventions of Indianness current among the consumer group, an exercise that profoundly destabilized indigenous concepts of identity. (1998, 9)

The production of those types of objects that I described previously, therefore represent an appropriative act of veld Bushman culture by the farm Bushmen. Over time, the new inclusive manufacture of miniature bow-and-arrow sets and gathering bags transformed what previously stood as signs and symbols of veld Bushmen into symbols of an emerging Ghanzi pan-Bushman ethnicity.

A sense of ethnic identity emerged over the course of the 1960s and 1970s, as farm Bushmen looked to the veld Bushmen with feelings of solidarity as peoples united in suffering. Attitudes toward the lifestyle of the veld Bushmen also changed among another distinct group of Bushmen—the "mission Bushmen" of D'Kar—who began to assess the old ways represented by the veld Bushmen with nostalgia and pride. These mission Bushmen constructed a nostalgic image (through the lens of Christianity?) of the hunter-gatherer lifestyle as a utopia of plenty, peace, and harmony in a world otherwise marked by inequality and conflict (Guenther 1979, 169, 172). By the 1960s, the performance of the trance dance, the Bushman's medicine, also rose substantially in intensity and instance, as a response to an increase in physical and psychosomatic illnesses. It was transformed into a cultural event that defined the identity of all Ghanzi Bushmen within a pluralist society as Bushman healers became professionalized, working for cultural outsiders, most notably for Herero and Tswana clients but also for European farmers for whom they performed rainmaking ceremonies. The trance and the trance dancer served as a vicarious and powerful integrating force among the Ghanzi farm Bushmen and between them and the veld Bushmen (Guenther 1979, 168).

The 1980s witnessed a group of D'Kar mission Bushmen begin the process of politically consolidating all Botswana's Bushman groups into one nation around the issue of land ownership, political representation within the nation-state, and rights to language-based education. D'Kar Dutch Reformed Church deacon Khomtsa Khomtsa was the first to actively lobby to reclaim territory based on original ownership when in a 1986 letter to Queen Elizabeth II of Great Britain he wrote:

> When you [the British] came to our land you saw the eland and the gemsbok, the grasses and the trees, but you recognized only the black man. You never saw us —maybe because we are so small—but we were always there with the land and the grass and now you have given the black man our land and today we have no rights, no land. (Gall 2001, 44)

Concurrent with the emergence of this politicized group of Ghanzi Bushmen was the adoption of a new pan-ethnic form of heritage dress that Tumba Bob modeled for me in 1997. This leather hunter-gatherer-style garb is a late twentieth-century reinvention of a precolonial dress style. In the past, hunter-gatherer Nharo and G/wi women would have gone bare-chested. But, when the dress style was revived during the 1990s, Nharo and G/wi women added a leather bikini top to the ensemble. The bikini top reflects modern and Christian notions of bodily modesty while marking the costume as a new form of cultural dress. Worn at cultural festivals, the dress represents a pan-Bushman identity that unites farm, mission, and veld Bushmen as opposed to the tanana, which while retained as traditional dress, is not worn in contexts where pan-Bushman identity is articulated at national events where Bushmen present themselves to audiences of cultural outsiders.

The emergence of a politicized Ghanzi Bushman community occurred over several decades as a response to experiences of economic and social marginalization. Tourism first provided positive affirmation that veld Bushman culture was of value, in contrast to the lack of cultural recognition provided by the Botswana state. The transformation of the Ghanzi Bushmen into First Peoples represented another stage in this process but occurred in a bigger regional and global context. It happened through contact with Namibian groups who, in collaboration with development workers and anthropologists, began in the 1980s to lobby for land rights based on indigenous identity. For example, anthropologist Megan Biesele's book *Shaken Roots* (1990), which deals with the emergence of San activism during the 1980s in Namibia in the context of donor aid and development, documents the Bushman critical voice as that of First People. One quote by Tsamkxao =Toma reads:

> We are not a people who buy land. We ourselves do not buy land. Instead we are born on land. My father taught me about his father, who taught him about the foods of our land. Your father's father teaches you. People have taught each other and taught each other and taught each other. People have died but the teaching goes on. (Biesele 1990, 45)

In 1992, the first Botswanan Bushman political group, Kgeikani Kwei (First Peoples of Kalahari), was established. The Kgeikani Kwei logo illustrates the transformation of hunter-gatherer imagery into symbols of a politicized First People ethnicity (figure 5.5). The fire encircled by footprints framed by a digging stick and an arrow represents two unique aspects of Bushman culture—the trance or communal healing dance and the hunter-gatherer lifestyle. Here the trance dance serves as a symbol for the unity of all Bushman peoples, and the digging stick and arrow are symbols of self-sufficiency and productivity and are key to the concept of the First Peoples' strong ties to land. Rejecting the colonialist term *Bushman*, the term *San* is embraced as a pan-ethnic designator.

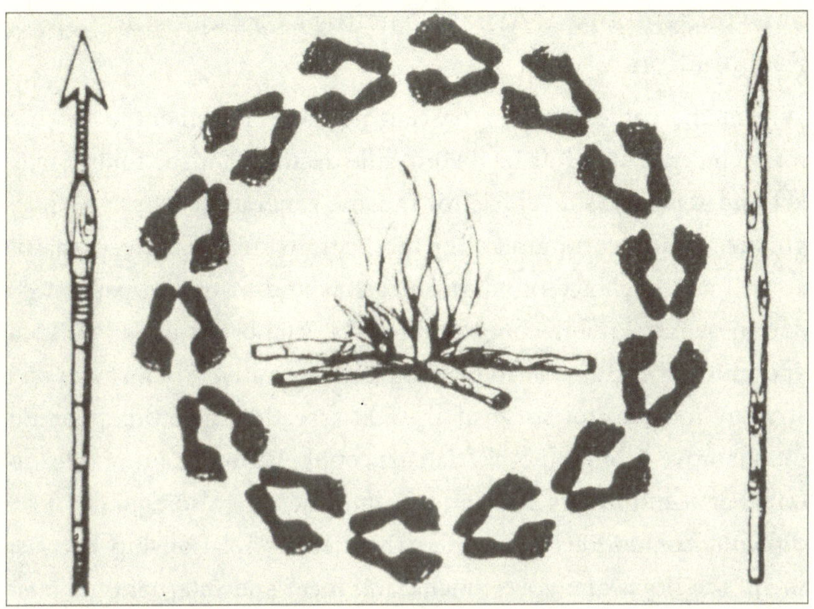

Figure 5.5. Kgeikani Kwei (First Peoples of Kalahari) logo. (Photograph by author)

Kgeikani Kwei, collaborating with other regional San political groups and international organizations such as Survival International, effectively lobbied against land dispossession and marginalization that continued through the 1990s often as a result of international mining interests, as was the experience for Q/wi residents of central Botswana, forcibly removed from their hunting territories to clear the way for exploratory forays by the diamond company De Beers. In 2001, overnight in London, activists from Survival International replaced a De Beers billboard featuring supermodel Iman decked out in diamonds with a photograph of Sana Kruiper, the wife of a well-known #Khomani leader. The De Beers slogan "Diamonds are forever" became "The Bushmen aren't forever," illustrating the strategic use of a stereotypical representation for political ends.

San Contemporary Art as Yearning's Critique and Reclamation

Within the context of this nascent political movement, a new art form emerged at D'Kar in 1990. While destined for the tourist market and serving as a vehicle for income generation in a hypermarginalized rural community, the motivations shaping subject matter as well as the choice of paint on canvas and prints on paper were driven by more than economic interests. Supporters of San political and cultural rights considered the new figurative art form to be a strategy for cultural survival and self-assertion, given its potential for narrative. Contemporary San art could play a mediating role, not only between tourists and San communities but also equally in the difficult, contentious, and often threatening relationship between them, the Botswana government, and local and international business interests. Supporters within the art community considered it a modern aesthetic idiom to replace the anonymous genres of objects that had become linked to touristic trade on the one hand, and to ethnographic artifact on the other. The embrace of modern art mediums—paint and various print techniques—could provide talented members of the D'Kar community with the means to refashion themselves as innovators and singular artists with an outlet appropriate to the contemporaneity of their aesthetic and political goals.

The relationships between the producers and promoters of the Kuru Art Project are dialogic and collaborative. Although Nharo and G/wi artists created the work, many others provided incentives and pressures that helped shape it. As the product of collaborative interactions between artists, patrons, and consumers, contemporary San art exemplifies products of the contact zone. Three events paved the way for these innovations. First, in 1989 Aaron Johannnes, a young politically engaged community leader, led a group from D'Kar to the Tsodilo Hills in northern Botswana. Today a UNESCO-protected

World Heritage site, scores of ephemeral paintings and engravings on rock surfaces at Tsodilo feature Kalahari region fauna including lions, elephants, rhinoceroses, elands, and various antelope. Of indeterminate age, contemporary scholars attribute such pictorial images to hunter-gatherer San artists of the precolonial and early colonial period. Johannes proposed a revival of this figurative tradition. Subsequently, the Kuru Cultural Project was launched later that same year, funded by an NGO, the Kuru Development Trust, initially staffed by missionary and international aid workers working together with the local community. The goals of the Cultural Project were to reclaim, revive, and preserve San lifeways and cultural practices, including visual art, folklore, music, dance, and foraging and hunting skills of the veld Bushmen.[9] The Cultural Project initiated an intervention and critical language around culture and performance that would shape the future of pictorial arts at D'Kar with their emphasis on visualizing the unique attributes of Nharo and G/wi veld culture.

The third and most significant event in the birth of contemporary art at D'Kar occurred in 1990. That year, Catharina Scheepers-Meyer, a young South African artist and high school teacher, embarked on a journey to find what she described as "a healthy place to live," far from urban life and the tensions of late era apartheid South Africa.[10] She happened upon the small mission station at D'Kar where she met Qwaa Mangana, a local Q/wi musician and trance dancer of note. Both were critical of the prevailing tourist trade in standardized, anonymous, mass-produced bow-and-arrow sets, ostrich-egg-shell necklaces, and leather gathering bags decorated with abstract motifs. Scheepers shared her paints, canvas, pencils, and paper with Mangana, thereby setting the stage for the realization of Aaron Johannes' call for a rebirth of San figurative imagery. Within a few years, additional artists joined Scheepers and Mangana. Many, such

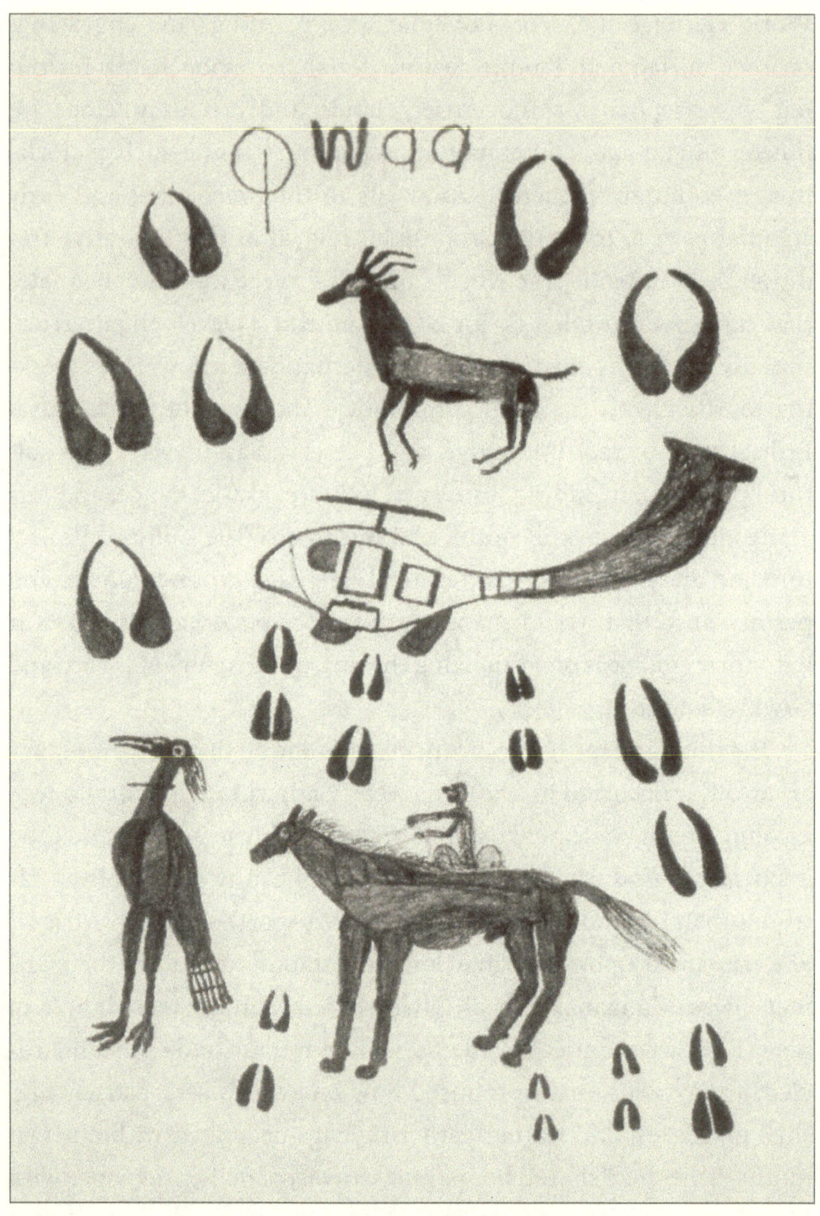

Figure 5.6. Qwaa Mangana (1920s-1997), *Hunter*. Drawing. 1991. (Photograph by author)

as Dada, were respected community elders and products of the early contact zone when Nharo and G/wi territory was first penetrated and settled by European and African cattle owners. They lived and worked within the hybrid borderland between San, European, and African cultures. The younger artists, by and large, as products of Botswana's assimilationist education system, were equally motivated to record and preserve local histories and traditional practices.[11]

I now turn to consider individual artworks in the light of bell hooks' notion of "yearning." For hooks, yearning is a springboard for resistance, for affirming the self, and it offers a critical voice. The hunter-gatherer imagery, combined with other relevant elements, signifies artistic resistance to European and African and colonial and postcolonial pressures and marginalizations. Consider a drawing by Qwaa Mangana (figure 5.6).

In this hunting-related scene, we see, front and center, a helicopter surrounded by antelope spoor and, below, a mounted San hunter. For tourists who purchase this work, the helicopter serves as evidence for their presence and experience of the Kalahari world as an exotic primitive place experienced from above. For the artist, other meanings are possible. The helicopter, circling above the mounted Bushman hunter, is either a mechanism for tourism and its related practice of trophy hunting or a vehicle of state control and restriction of local San hunting practices. Either way it represents surveillance and modernity's intervention into the Kalahari region of Botswana. Yet the way the image of this machine of power that lifts tourists and government officials up into the air appears in Qwaa's picture compositionally qualifies and diminishes it in size, thereby demystifying the power it holds. In amongst the animal tracks, the modern machine is dwarfed and contained. Here the artist returns the surveyor's gaze and in so doing challenges and suggests that such signs of authority are perhaps not as stable as they may conventionally seem.

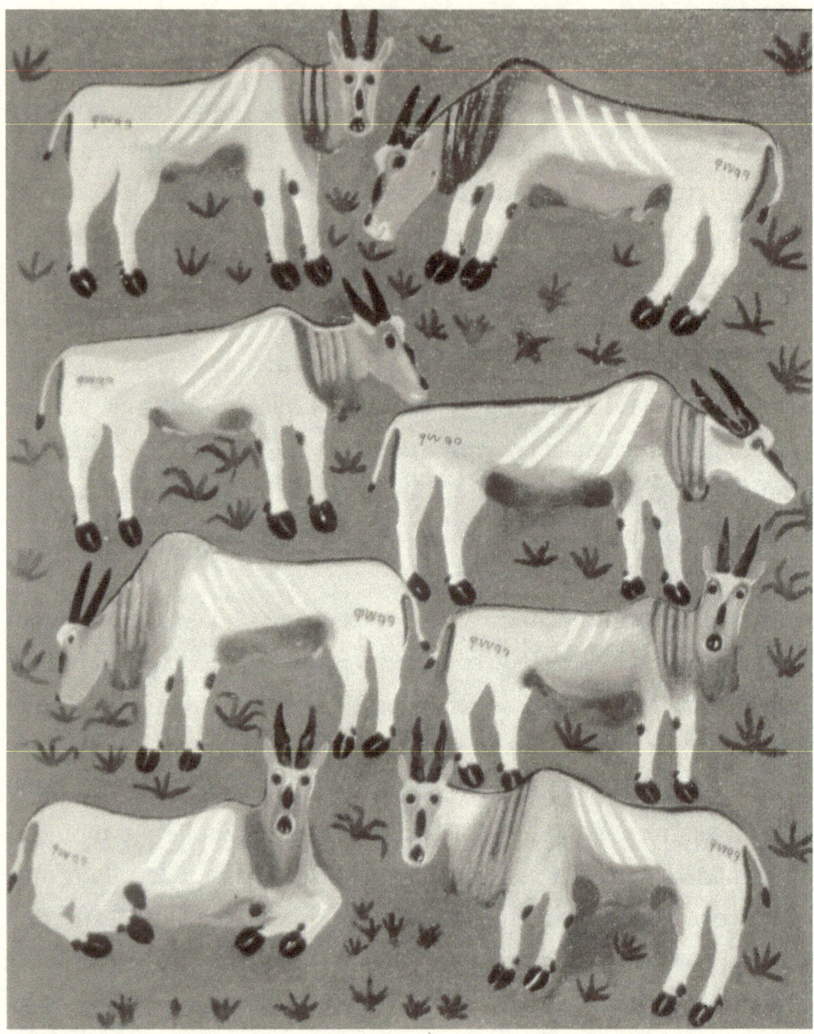

Figure 5.7. Qwaa Mangana (1920s-1997), *Eland*. Paint on canvas. 1994. (Photograph by author)

Equally fitting as a tourist souvenir is a picturesque group of eland, a large placid herbivore unique to Africa, the subject of a painting by Mangana (figure 5.7). Besides being a distinctly African animal, eland have a privileged role in San cosmology. They possess large amounts of *n//um* or spiritual potency, said to be stored in the large fat sack of the animal's neck, which enables it to endure during lengthy droughts. In trance, San healers journey below the water to seek the Rain Animal that sometimes takes the form of their Rain Animal Eland. The healer's union with or transformation into this spiritual Rain Animal is the vehicle for enacting actions for clients, the environment, and living plants and animals upon which San communities historically subsisted. The eland is also an anomalous antelope, preferring to live a solitary existence in contrast to most African antelope species. Yet here we see a herd of grazing eland, recalling herds of British-, Boer-, and African-owned cattle that forced the San off of their lands over the course of the twentieth century. The placement of the artist's signature repeated over and over, on the flanks of each animal like a branding drives home the message: eland are San cattle, and they, like the San, are indigenous—they were there first. This work demonstrates that the creative output of contemporary San art offers space where dominant power loses authority and subordinates can instigate agency and critique.

Visual images related to folklore provided another resource to protest the marginalized position of Ghanzi San. For example, the titles of Qmao's works, such as *!Xrii*, *The Old People*, and *Jackal Ancestor*, are clues to the dominant theme of his work—namely, depictions of the First Order, the primal world of San cosmology. The First Order is a time of cosmic inversion in which //Guawa, the trickster god, transforms, distorts, and inverts things that he created. In his works, Qmao populates this primal world of ambivalence with hybrid surreal beings and plant forms. The central character in Qmao's works is usually the trickster as Jackals. According to Guenther, *Jackal-jong* (Jackal-boy), a common character in contemporary farm Bushman stories, is "as flouter and saboteur of the new rules brought into the land by the oppressive colonists who had taken this land from the

Bushmen and decimated its game and plants" (1999, 103). The trickster-as-wayward-farmhand thus became a symbol of resistance in the postcolonial context. By setting Jackal-jong, a contemporary character, within the First Order of time, Qmao draws on the transformative and subversive power of myth and religion. While his critique is oblique, it suggests that contemporary San art cannot be so easily described or dismissed as innocuous souvenir scenes.

Even the seemingly naïve and decorative images of plants offer political voice. Identified with titles such as *Qare* (edible plant) and *Wild Xgam-tsinxabo Plant*, these colorful artworks can be read in political terms as statements about San cultural knowledge, relationship to land, and consequently First People status (figure 5.1). By giving the Nharo or G/wi term for medicinal or edible plants in the title of an artwork, rather than the Western scientific name, authority over economically and politically valuable resources is asserted, astutely protecting this knowledge from pharmaceutical companies that have recently looked to San knowledge of medicinal plants in the development of new diet drugs, for example. Furthermore, vegetal imagery provides a channel for the continuing expression of indigenous values and beliefs that is more than politically strategic. Plants occupy an important place in San cosmologies, constituting cognitive categories. Plant life is a potential locus for medicinal power for healing and an integral link in the chain of life, transforming the sun's energy into food for animals and humans. In 1995, Khomtsa Khomsta's political group, Kgeikani Kwei (First Peoples of the Kalahari), collaborated with Dada and other Nharo women, to map the historical uses of veld foods and plants, a project that aimed to both record and preserve oral histories of medicinal plant use, location, and, consequently, land rights.

The densely packed, flat, obscure images seen in these works by artist Dada stand in marked contrast to the meticulous precision evident in work by the artist Qwaa Mangana. Besides reflecting individual artistic preferences, style choices may be politically expedient —Dada's images of plants are intentionally difficult to read to protect indigenous knowledge, while Qwaa's descriptive style recalls the historical body of rock art attributed to San artists of many centuries prior to the onset of colonial rule.

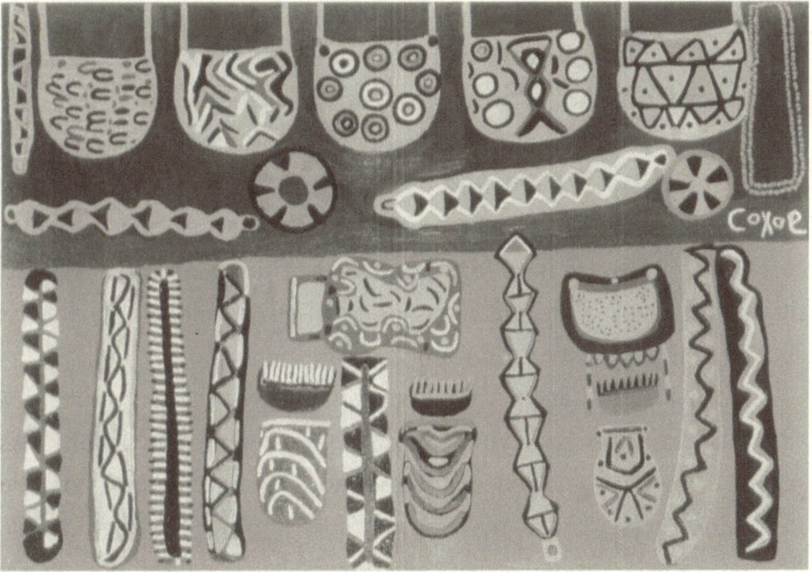

Figure 5.8. Coex'ae Bob, *Skin Bags and Beads*, oil paint on canvas, date unknown. (Photograph by author)

A painting by Coex'ae Bob, or Ennie, illustrates the subtle mirror dance that is San contemporary art as a form of what Pratt calls *autoethnography*, a term for autobiographies created in the context of "contact zones." In the colorful work in figure 5.8, Ennie carefully organizes rows of bead headbands, leather bags, and necklaces. The painting simultaneously recalls the displays of souvenirs to visiting tourists that one encounters along the road to D'Kar, yet also reads as a catalog of Nharo women's art forms to be seen in the local community museum established by the Kuru Cultural Project. Thus, a self-conscious awareness of identity and tradition is being articulated here, addressing both local and visiting audiences. Ennie's painting, like all contemporary art from D'Kar, is multivocal, simultaneously fulfilling the differing needs of audience and artist. For tourist and folk art collectors, the art does fulfill people's needs for a romantic "Other" that exists in a world nostalgically seen as primordial and unspoiled. This is indisputably part of what has made contemporary San art a viable financial business. But at the same time, we must not lose sight of the fact that for a community of a handful of artists, these novel art forms are one mode of cultural criticism. As bell hooks has observed, "yearning" has historically functioned as a force promoting critical resistance, enabling marginalized communities to cultivate in everyday life a practice of critique and analysis that disrupts and even deconstructs cultural productions (the tourist souvenir) that promote and reinforce domination.

In conclusion, I argue that it is profitable to consider contemporary San paintings and prints as examples of "autoethnography." As proposed by Pratt, autoethnographies are works in which colonized individuals represent themselves in modes familiar to the colonizer, or in this postcolonial case, the tourist. Kuru contemporary art certainly resonates with tourist media. Yet because autoethnographies "appropriate and transform the idioms of travel and exploration writing, merged or infiltrated with indigenous modes" they are "bilingual and dialogic," being "addressed both to cultural outsiders and to sectors of the speaker's [or artist's] own social group, and bound to be received very differently by each" (1992, 7). As autoethnography, contemporary art from the Kuru Art Project reads simultaneously as souvenir of domesticated longing and nostalgia and as site for yearning and cultural resistance.

Acknowledgments

I would like to thank Robert Gordon and Mathias Guenther for their insight and guidance during fieldwork, and my father, Richard Taplin, for being such a wise travel companion. Peter Brown and Willemien le Roux must be thanked for their hospitality when I visited D'Kar, where Dada opened many doors for me. Sandra Klopper and Sidney Kasfir offered useful feedback on an earlier draft of this paper; Maude Brown assisted with copyright permission for the images; and my mother, Sally Taplin, contributed invaluable editorial assistance.

Notes

1. Gordon and Douglas (2000, 1).

2. Quote from http://www.africaserver.nl/kuru/english/artists/dada.htm, accessed June 11, 2013.

3. !Xun artist /Thaalu Bernardo Rumao once said, "The people say they are not Bushmen anymore. They do not wear skins and they do not live in the bush. They say they are now the San." Rumao's reading of "Bushman" as primitive and "San" as modern is one perspective on the complex meaning and use of these terms. San and Bushman remain hotly contested in political and academic circles; their meanings are not stable and their uses never neutral. Gordon and Douglas (2000) note that *Bushman* is derived from the Dutch settler word *bossiesman*, which may connote bandit or outlaw. It was coined in the former Cape Dutch colony to describe economically marginal peoples who were placed in a lumpen category because they did not easily fit a prescribed ethnic designation (Gordon and Douglas 2000, 6). By the nineteenth century, scholars began using the term to identify various groups living across southern Africa seen to share

a number of cultural and social (hunter-gathering activities), linguistic (click languages), and physical (small stature and light skin tone) traits. By the twentieth century, the term entered popular culture as a descriptor for premodern hunter-gatherers associated with desert terrains in Botswana and southwest Africa (now Namibia). While some contemporary scholars such as Mathias Guenther and Robert Gordon continue to use the term *Bushman*, others object to its pejorative connotations, and racist and sexist overtones. As a substitute, anthropologists such as Ed Wilmsen began using the term *San*. Derived from *Sonqua*, the name given by Hottentot/Khoi-Khoi/Nama pastoralists to foragers living in the Cape of Good Hope, *San* has been translated to mean original people (Wilmsen 1989). Gordon notes that the academic preference for San occurred after the 1950s when ethnographers became interested in hunter-gatherers as representatives of the Paleolithic, so it too promotes romantic ahistorical representations (Gordon and Douglas 2000, 5). In Botswana, groups such as the Nharo and G/wi are popularly referred to as *Basarwa*, considered by the latter peoples as a pejorative term; they favor their own self-designation of N'coakhoe or red people. More recently, both Bushman and San have been embraced as ethnic self-designations. Since the early 1990s, a southern African aboriginal or first peoples movement has emerged as a collaborative venture between community elites and cultural outsiders affiliated with NGOs. SASI, the South African San Institute, for example, embraces the word *San*, as does the Kuru Development Trust that oversees the Kuru Art Project that is discussed in this article. Here, *Bushman* will be used when discussing art from Kuru as tourist souvenir since *Bushman* is the term that dominates popular media. *San* is used when discussing the emergence of a politicized first nation ideology at D'Kar. Local self-designations such as Nharo or G/wi are used when referring to the cultural affiliations of individual Kuru artists.

4. See for example the introduction to Jules-Rosette (1984).

5. See Phillips (1998). The literature treating tourist-destined and other commodified art forms as worthy subjects of study is a rapidly growing field. See for example Phillips and Steiner (1999).

6. See http://www.botswanatourism.co.bw/, accessed June 11, 2013.

7. Van der Post's writings include *The Lost World of the Kalahari* (1958) and *The Heart of the Hunter* (1961). See also, Edwin N. Wilmsen (1995) and Alan Barnard (1989) for a discussion of the development and iconography of Bushman as Rousseauesque pre-modern innocent and more recently as Stone Age first peoples.

8. The Herero long dress is based on Victorian-era clothing introduced to the Herero by German missionaries. Today, Bushman girls in the Omaheke district of Namibia wear the Herero long dress during their initiation into womanhood. Here their passage into a higher social role is equated with upward class mobility.

9. See http://www.kuru.co.bw/Kuru_Dkar.html for information on Kuru D'Kar Trust.

10. Catharina Scheepers-Meyer, interview with author, August 11, 2000.

11. See http://www.kuruart.com/about.php for further information on the art project.

References

Bannister, Anthony. 1987. *The Bushmen*. Struik Publishers.

Barnard, Alan. 1989. "The Lost World of Laurens van der Post?" *Current Anthropology* 30(1): 104-14.

Biesele, Megan. 1990. *Shaken Roots: The Bushmen of Namibia*. Marshallton, South Africa: EDA Publications.

Gall, Sandy. 2001. *The Bushmen of Southern Africa*. London: Chatto and Windus.

Garland, Elizabeth, and Robert Gordon. n.d. "Up the Sepik and into the Kalahari: Mining for Tourist Dollars in Namibia." *Spectrum Guide*, 1-25.

Gordon, Robert, and Stuart Douglas. 2000. *The Bushman Myth: The Making of a Namibian Underclass*. Boulder: Westview Press.

Guenther, Mathias. 1979. *The Farm Bushmen of the Ghanzi District, Botswana*. Stuttgart: HochschulVerlag.

Guenther, Mathias. 1996. "From 'Lords of the Desert' to 'Rubbish People': The Colonial and Contemporary State of the Nharo of Botswana." In *Miscast: Negotiating the Presence of the Bushmen*, edited by Pippa Skotnes, 225-38. Cape Town: University of Cape Town Press.

———. 1999. *Tricksters and Trancers: Bushmen Religion and Society*. Bloomington: Indiana University Press.

hooks, bell. 1990. *Yearning: Race, Gender, and Cultural Politics*. Boston: South End Press.

Jules-Rosette, Bennetta. 1984. *The Messages of Tourist Art: An African Semiotic System in Comparative Perspective*. New York: Plenum Press.

Kasfir, Sydney. 1999. "Samburu Souvenirs: Representations of a Land in Amber." In *Unpacking Culture: Art and Commodity in Colonial and Postcolonial Worlds*, edited by Ruth Phillips and Christopher Steiner, 67-86. Berkeley: University of California Press.

le Roux, Willemien. 2000. *Shadow Bird*. Cape Town: Kwela Books.

Little, Kenneth. 1977. "On Safari: The Visual Politics of a Tourist Representation." In *The Varieties of Sensory Experience*, edited by David Howes, 148-63. Toronto: University of California Press.

MacCannell, Dean. 1976. *The Tourist*. New York: Schocken Books.

Phillips, Ruth. 1998. *Trading Identities: The Souvenir in Native North American Art from the Northeast, 1700-1900*. Seattle: University of Washington Press.

Pratt, Mary Louise. 1992. *Imperial Eyes: Travel Writing and Transculturation*. London: Routledge.

Smith, Andy. 2000. *The Bushmen of Southern Africa: A Foraging Society in Transition*. Cape Town: David Phillip.

Stewart, Susan. 1984. *On Longing: Narratives of the Miniature, the Gigantic, the Souvenir, the Collection*. Durham: Duke University Press.

van der Post, Laurens. 1958. *The Lost World of the Kalahari*. New York: Harcourt Brace.

———. 1961. *The Heart of the Hunter: Customs and Myths of the African Bushman*. New York: Harcourt Brace.

Wilmsen, Edwin N. 1989. *Land Filled With Flies*. Chicago: Chicago University Press.

———. 1995. "First Peoples?: Images and Imaginations in South African Iconography." *Critical Arts* 9(2): 1-27.

A World of Difference: Unity and Differentiation Among Ceramicists in Quinua, Ayacucho, Peru

Jennifer A. Vogt

Abstract

This chapter analyzes local notions of authenticity drawing on ethnographic data collected during thirteen months of fieldwork in the rural village of Quinua, Peru. The author highlights how local ceramic artisans conceived of authenticity, which, it is argued, is encapsulated by local terms and material practices surrounding the concept of *artesano verdadero.* Artisans in Quinua share, borrow, and even "steal" designs from others. Within this context, artisans persistently evaluated each other based on these practices. Ultimately, the narratives artisans tell themselves and others about who they are, and are not, as artisans, thereby put forth claims about who counts and who does not as an artisan. This chapter shows that to be a "true" and thus successful artisan, one must strike a delicate balance of maintaining control over his or her craft and cultural heritage while engaging fickle markets.

In October of 2010, regional government officials from Ayacucho city, Peru, asked two prominent artisans in the rural district of Quinua to instruct a two-month course in ceramic design. The request came as part of a regional development project sponsored by the Peruvian government to promote innovation of artisan products for exportation. Although the two artisans would have received financial compensation, they declined the offer. They reasoned, among other things, that the artisans participating in the course (who had been producing for no more than two years) needed to develop their creativity independently; they were not yet *artesanos verdaderos* (i.e., true or real artisans). During more than a year of fieldwork (2010-2011) in the rural district of Quinua in the southern Andes of Peru, I quickly discovered that such evaluations of who is "real" or "true" between producers were not uncommon and often were intensely personal.

Certainly, not everyone expressed it exactly the same. Some artisans, for instance, summed up their sentiments in the following way: "You may copy me, but you will never equal me."[1] Still, every artisan explained to me in some way or another that if a person is to be a "true artisan," he must develop his own style.[2] Keeping such phrases in mind, I will discuss in this chapter local notions of authenticity. I want to highlight how artisans in Quinua conceived of authenticity, which, I argue, is encapsulated by local terms, ideas, and material practices surrounding artesano verdadero. Specifically, artisans self-consciously struggle to balance crafting daringly close replicas of others' designs, mixing and matching their own and others' stylistic elements, and creating new designs. They simultaneously employ shared aesthetic conventions, techniques, and symbols. Within this context, artisans persistently evaluate each other based on these practices.

This chapter then also analyzes artisans' struggles of appropriation—seemingly mimetic encounters between artisans who share, borrow, reuse, and even "steal" stylistic and technical elements from others. I am not necessarily interested in similarities and differences between ceramic objects themselves, or in whether these constitute "authentic" manifestations of a cultural heritage of ceramic making in the Quinua area. Rather, I highlight the relationships between artisans as they debate, negotiate, and even overlook material practices of and meanings surrounding appropriation. What makes these relationships particularly tense lies in how artisans differently, and sometimes contradictorily, interpret their and others' practices of appropriation: appropriation may be a way of maintaining a community's craft tradition, a livelihood strategy, a socially offensive act, a sign of unoriginality, or even a creative technique. Within this context, I focus on narratives artisans tell themselves and others about who they are, and are not, as artisans, and thereby make claims about and debate who counts and who does not as an artisan.

Background: Quinua, Ayacucho Department, Peru

The 6,115 Quechua/Spanish-speaking inhabitants of the rural district of Quinua live in twenty-four dispersed hamlets and one more densely populated town center (Perú Posible 2010). Located at an altitude of 3,270 meters in the department of Ayacucho in the southern Andes, the district is buttressed by a mountain range forming the eastern wall of the Ayacucho valley and, 40 kilometers southwest, by the city of Ayacucho (Arnold 1972a, 1972b, 1975, 1985, 1993; Mitchell 1972, 1973, 1991, 1999; Tschopik 1947). Most families produce food (potatoes, corn, fava beans, squash) in their own fields, but they rarely have enough land to achieve self-sufficiency. Although virtually everyone sells or exchanges surplus produce or other foodstuffs on occasion (usually in small quantities with neighbors or during Sunday markets), only a few townspeople produce crops or raise livestock in any commercially significant way. All families ultimately build livelihoods through diverse strategies (e.g., agricultural and unskilled wage labor, food vending, providing transportation services, migration and remittances from migrants, and craft production). Providing some degree of regularity in cash-earning opportunities, artisan production, primarily ceramic making, is the largest source of cash flow for about one-fourth of the population (approximately twelve hundred people) in Quinua (Municipalidad Distrital de Quinua 2001).

While organization and relations of production in ceramics are too complex to elaborate fully here, they tend to fall under three main patterns. In one scenario, an owner of a workshop prepares primary materials (clay, designs) but pays men and women to transform them into finished ceramic pieces. Alternatively, an owner of a workshop or tourist shop may informally subcontract another person to make unpainted, but fired, ceramic pieces in the latter's own home workshop; the first owner buys these pieces to later paint and sell. In the final scenario, an artisan who owns his own workshop or tourist shop prepares primary materials and executes the main body of ceramic pieces. Older women in the family balance household work (and its allocation to children) with decorating, painting, and shining ceramic pieces. For families living in the town center, women tend also to manage prices and make sales to tourists and other clients in the family gallery or in rented kiosks in the town marketplace. Most families sell their products to local artisans or tourists, while less than ten sell to vendors or export companies in Lima. If the family business requires travel to Ayacucho city or Lima (to visit potential buyers, travel to artisan fairs, or turn in completed orders to clients), men usually undertake these trips. Children may spend some of their free time helping with light tasks (e.g., painting, selling, stocking the shop, and loading kilns).

Authentic Objects to Authentic People

In recent years, anthropologists working with artisans in different parts of the world have shown how authenticity is a weighty concept with diverse meanings. In his work on "tourist art" in Africa, anthropologist Christopher Steiner (1999) finds that uniqueness of artisanal works is not what defines their authenticity. Instead, it is the redundancy of pieces—the quality of looking-alike so that they all reference a well-known model—that is essential to their authenticity. Other scholars, like sociologist Frederick F. Wherry (2006) and anthropologist Les Field (2009), have argued for different understandings of authenticity, which may overlap and conflict in complex ways. Different definitions and their use is shaped by the social situations that artisans, sellers, buyers, museum curators, collectors, and even anthropologists inhabit, thus forming the substance of their judgments (Marcus and Myers 1995; Phillips and Steiner 1999). Thus, if we follow objects as they are created, bought and sold, used, modified, and even destroyed within complex, dynamic networks, we may arrive at more complex and shifting understandings of authenticity (Appadurai 1986). Artistic production then is necessarily embedded in "art worlds"—that is, networks of people whose artistic activities are organized around shared conventions and agreed ways of doing things (Becker 1982, 34). These scholars have obliged us to show how diverse agents—as necessarily interested individuals, groups, or institutions—work to tell stories to authenticate the nature and value of particular objects. In this sense, authenticities are never objective, but are always culturally and politically conditioned by the contexts in which they emerge.

This framework enables a complex understanding of authenticity, wherein seemingly opposed concepts like tradition and modernity, personal and the collective, as well as conventionality and innovation, may be mutually constituted in unexpected ways. It has also been useful in overcoming subject-object dualism by emphasizing that inanimate things, too, may possess agency (Gell 1998; Latour 2005). Building on this framework, I shift analysis from how people create a world of authentic or, in Kopytoff's (1986) terms, *genuine objects*, to focus on how people create a world of authentic selves, and by implication, less than authentic others. Artisans in Quinua indeed make ceramic objects through discourse and material practices into authentic High art, popular art, and tourist art. Further, museum curators, art collectors, and even anthropologists and other scholars play a part in telling these stories (e.g., Lauer 1982; Mauldin 2011; Ravines and Villiger 1989; Stastny 1968; Torres 2010). I, however, want to build on these analyses, putting analytical pressure on the relationship between artisan as creator and material objects produced (Gell 1998). In plying this point of convergence, I show how artisans' identities as creative laborers directly articulate with the objects they produce. I then explore how this dynamic shapes relations between different artisans, as creative laborers contributing to objects' creation (Becker 1982).

This framework helps to expand notions of authenticity when talking about artisanship. For one, it pushes beyond long-standing tendencies to counterpoise "legitimate" or "authentic" works of art, commercial crafts, and "pure" traditional artifacts. Recent scholarly works have made significant analytical strides in complicating this approach (e.g., Phillips and Steiner 1999). I draw on and extend such works by also analyzing ideas about creativity, which also shapes how people define, construct and pursue values of authenticity.[3] Creativity, like aesthetic criteria and notions about cultural purity of objects, has also provided a basis for denying the aesthetic traditions of many peoples as witnessed in the status of authenticity in many Latin American contexts. This denial is particularly at issue for what is disparagingly called, time and again, "tourist art" or "airport art." I show, by contrast, that producers prioritize creativity in making even these sorts of mass-produced and standardized objects.

Secondly, this framework opens analytical space for showing one very important way in which *who*, rather than *what*, may be considered authentic in certain contexts, particularly in Latin America and amongst artisan populations. Rather than asking how "that honorific title" art is fought over, what actions it justifies, and what users of it can get away with (Becker 1982, 131-64), I ask in this chapter how the title "artesano verdadero" is fought over and debated, what actions are justified as well as contested, and what contradictions emerge within narratives told by users of it. I ground one such view in ideas about creative people. Artisans I interviewed in Quinua consistently linked creativity with authenticity and, specifically, with "artesano verdadero." In this local language of authenticity, originality, uniqueness, and seemingly nonreplicable qualities conspicuously stand out. Yet, the requirement of shared tradition, in claiming that a ceramic object distinctly originated from Quinua, means that no person can innovate so uniquely as to be considered entirely outside the local cultural calculus.

During my time in Quinua, I often saw artisans reuse older elements, combining them in new ways. They also shared these new designs with family members or sold them to friends and neighbors. Even one well-known ceramic maker, Efraín, locally referred to as a "true artisan," draws inspiration from older ceramic styles and techniques known to Quinua, using naturally derived red and white pigments and modeling each piece by hand.[4] He learned these techniques and styles from his father and grandfather, from which he later developed his personal creative style. Similarly, other people identified as "true artisans" remarked how they too learned technical skills and some stylistic elements as apprentices of Efraín, but later developed their own style. All artisans, even "true artisans," in this way depend on each other to recreate the styles of a recognizable craft, and from this shared repertoire, every artisan not only fashioned his business, but also his sense of self as an artisan-producer (Colloredo-Mansfeld 2002). In this context, local notions of authenticity are constituted by both: (1) personal creativity (innovative qualities) and (2) collective ideas and practices (imitative qualities), but not unambiguously or comfortably so. In this way, claims to authenticity involve much social commentary and debate. When people in Quinua try to define "artisan verdadero," we find inconsistencies in which people and their material practices of production meet some, but not all, of the criteria expressed by the ideal of "artesano verdadero."

Allure of "Tradition"

Wandering through any tourist marketplace in Peru, one immediately notes the rows of seemingly identical objects, placed side by side on display shelves and tables. One likewise observes similarities between hand-produced artifacts while perusing a popular art gallery in Lima. Such repetition and seriality of a craft, often glossed as "tradition" or "cultural heritage," emerges, in part, from shared material production practices and aesthetic conventions. Specifically in Quinua, the majority of artisans use fine-grained clays of a somewhat-dark red color, although artisans play with tones by combining other mineral elements. The majority of artisans apply decorative elements (e.g., plant shapes, facial features of figures, and other small details) using creamy white, red ochre and dark brown slips. Shapes most commonly identified with the Quinua tradition include *toro* (bull) pitchers, *qarqacha* (two-headed llama) pitchers, musicians, *chismosas* (gossiping women), and *ukumari* (half-woman, half-bear mythical creatures). The miniature churches, for instance, commonly seen on the rooftops of homes in Quinua, are perhaps the most emblematic design/shape for Quinua ceramics (Mauldin 2011; Stastny 1968).[5] We also find to a lesser extent in contemporary Quinua plates of different sizes, *toqtoq* (vessels for toasting corn), as well as spherical and curved-contoured vessels for carrying liquids (e.g., *aysaku*, *yukupuynu*, *tachu*, and *tumin*). In making these vessels, artisans have traditionally employed coiling and hand-modeling techniques; paints and slips are applied with fine-tipped brushes made from chicken feathers or cat hair. Many artisans continue these practices today but have also incorporated new technologies to aid production.[6]

Such imitation and seriality of designs, as Steiner (1999) argues, give coherence and visibility to a shared craft in markets.[7] Even tourists, after one or two trips to a Peruvian craft market, may be able to identify the miniature churches or typical white-on-red color scheme identified with Quinua ceramics. Aesthetic repetition, as a marketing strategy, is thus crucial to making products by artisans in Quinua identifiable to a broad population. In this context, it is artisans' strategies of appropriation—sharing, borrowing, reusing, and even "stealing" stylistic and technical details—that gives a sense of contiguity to artisan products.

Scholars of expressive cultural production in Peru—whether called *artesanía*, *arte popular*, *arte vernacular*, or *expresión plástica* —have repeatedly called attention to the unique cultural, stylistic, and technical characters of Quinua pottery (e.g., Fuente, et al. 1992; Ravines and Villiger 1989; Sabogal Wiesse 1979; Spahni 1966; Tschopik 1949). In one of the most well-read books on arte popular in Peru, Francisco Stastny tells us that "[a]mong present-day potters villages, one of the most active and successful is Quinua, in Ayacucho" (Stastny 1968, 111). Dean E. Arnold, in an ethnoarchaeological and ecological analysis of pottery making, states:

> Quinua ceramics are unique in the Ayacucho Valley. No other pottery made in the valley approaches that of Quinua in the diversity of vessel shapes, flexibility of expression, and the complexity of its decoration. These characteristics also make Quinua Pottery one of the most complex and diverse contemporary ceramic products of

> the entire Peruvian highlands. Quinua pottery is also unique to Latin America. Its pottery (churches, bulls, and other shapes) is exported to worldwide markets and is available in import shops in New York, Chicago, San Diego, Milwaukee and Europe. (1993, 15)

Fuente et al. relate how the craft has been passed down between generations:

> In the past, Quinua was a center inhabited by '*olleros*' . . . It is difficult to discern exactly when ceramic objects in Quinua began to have a ceremonial function. The ceramicist Otccochocco initiated the production of these objects, who was followed by Dionisio Lope and Faustino Nolasco, of the Inkacasa community, located below Quinua. Another follower of the idea [to make ceramics for ceremonial use] was Francisco Sanchez, known by the nickname '*Al aire*' [literally meaning "to the air"] . . . According to artisans in the area, this name was given to him because his ceramics were so fine that they appeared as if blown by air. His son Santos Sanchez, known as '*Niño al aire*' ["Child to the air"], was a fine ceramicist . . . The son of [Santos] is Mamerto Sánchez, creator of so many new forms we see today. (1992, 80-81)

Various government administrations too have pursued the economic and symbolic potential of ceramic production in Quinua (see Hernando and Van Hulsen 2001; Indacochea 2001; Villantoy Valverde 2011). A recent government-backed development project *Di mi tierra, Un producto*, for instance, selected Quinua to receive development assistance, describing Quinua as "one of the most enchanting villages of Ayacucho . . . inhabited by talented artisans that mold clay with mastery, creating works of art whose motifs represent and express daily life and emotion, just as their Huarpa and Wari ancestors did" (PromPerú 2012). While these brief accounts importantly demonstrate cultural significance of ceramic production in Quinua, they convey a sense of unproblematic "sameness" and continuity of artistic styles and technical forms, downplaying differences between producers and styles.

To reconcile these differences, Quinua ceramics have been categorized into objects for ritual use, for domestic use, and for decorative use (e.g., Arnold 1993; Fuente et al. 1992; Ravines and Villiger 1989; Stastny 1968). Similarly, many scholars and development specialists have attempted to identify different sorts of producers. For instance, Sabogal Wiesse distinguishes between "indigenous artisan," "artisan-worker," "pseudo-artisan," and "vernacular artist" (1979, 6). A 2001 International Labor Organization study of development potentials of artisan work in the Ayacucho region distinguishes between "master artisan," "innovator artisan," and "local artisan" (Hernando and van Hulsen 2001, i). Although classifying phenomena into categories is useful in many situations, it hinders our understanding of locally constructed concepts as well as how people in artisan communities seek to make sense of anomalous cases—that is, cases that meet some, but not all, of the criteria expressed by such concepts (Becker 1982). In this way, externally derived categories obscure ambiguities, contradictions, and slippage between them. By attending to how people in Quinua socially construct or create social types, we are better positioned to see "the ambiguities of [folk] terms and the contradictions between what they predict and what the world exhibits" (Becker 1978, 863). Thus, while much has been written about artisan production in Quinua, far less understood is how people working to make ceramic products experience, talk about, and try to come to grips with the ambiguities of sameness and differentness of objects and, further, how these understandings articulate with their sense of who they are as creative laborers.

Multiple Significations

Over a year of working with artisans in workshops, market stalls, and even during strictly nonmarket activities, I heard all artisans recount, often with frustration, experiences with design copying and theft. Many artisans in different parts of the world are similarly preoccupied with copying and daringly close replicas of their products but, importantly, for different reasons. As Steiner argues for African art markets, for instance, acts of imitation may enable strategic market positioning. Indeed, a part of Quinua ceramic object's value "depends not on its originality or uniqueness but on its conformity to 'traditional' style, [where] displays of nearly identical objects side by side [in a market] underscore to prospective tourist buyers that these artworks indeed 'fit the mold,'" or conform to a "traditional" style (Steiner 1999, 95). This critique, however, offers only a partial view, and a particular understanding of a creator's relationship to objects he or she produces as market-oriented. It therefore does not help explain why producers in Quinua make distinctions between not only their products but also each other as creators.

Many artisans in Quinua, in some respects, also view imitation as a way of legitimating the skill of a predecessor, paying homage to generations before them, or keeping their cultural heritage alive. An artisan named Juan described this to me: "*Los antiguos* have to be followed, too. . . . Waiting for new works so that these too give value to their [los antiguos'] works. If we continue using the same designs, we are not valuing los antiguos." This cultural phenomenon has been found to operate similarly amongst Asante woodcarvers (Silver 1981, 1983). Yet in their conversations with each other and me, artisans drew implicit distinctions between copying and sharing designs. An artisan, on one hand, may explain how he preserves technical aspects, spiritual myths, and everyday practices—elements that are said to belong to the community—by reusing older design elements in his pieces. He may also, however, criticize others' pieces as mere copies, explaining they offer little economic and cultural value. The point I want to make for the case of Quinua, therefore, is that anxieties about design copying are not the same as positive feelings associated with sharing a craft tradition.

Writers on the sociology of art and culture provide a framework that opens analytical space for both negotiations of values and a relational understanding of aesthetic criteria (e.g., Becker 1974, 1976, 1982; Bourdieu 1983). Becker (1982) for instance, points out that even the most apparently individual of works can be the result of collaboration (even if the work is attributed to one author), while Bourdieu (1983) focuses on struggles occurring between individuals. Colloredo-Mansfeld, Andtrosio, and Jones (2011), through an analysis of Otavalan weavers, highlight both cooperation and conflict:

> Amid the robbery of designs, the lost earnings, and the mutual suspicions, artisans were also materializing a foundation of a market. This base drew from the changeability of fashion, commitments to an economy with an indigenous identity, and interdependence of working side-by-side in a provincial market town. The circulation of ideas . . . contribute to a kind of economic commons. . . a base of designs and goods with value linked with some notion of indigenousness—although (and this is crucial) such contributions are rarely intentional. (41)

The authors further show that while many complain of rivals who "sent someone to their showroom to buy a sample under false pretenses, or 'spied on their shop windows from the street corner,'" just as many producers perceived copying as a "reassuring sign of connection" (Colloredo-Mansfeld, Andtrosio, and Jones 2011, 45). The shared value of ideas contributes both to an artisan's enterprise and to an individual's sense of personal and collective self.

Simultaneously, copying and conflicts over appropriating ideas reflect concerns about market value and competition: the more daringly close ceramic objects appear, the more they are likely to compete for the attention of prospective buyers. Artisan producers thus seek to capture the economic value by differentiating their products from one another through creativity and innovation. What differs between the Ecuadorian case and the Peruvian case is that producers in Quinua are particularly adamant about personal identity, particularly linked to the notion of creativity. So while creativity is oriented toward innovating to create new and better products, it is also socially imbued with a particularly nonmonetary value (although these different valuations are inextricably intertwined).

Ethnographic Beginnings

Once, in describing why he enjoyed making ceramics and why he had done so for more than twenty years, Manuel said that in working with clay, "*Uno se deja sus huellas con sus dedos.*" That is, quite literally, the artisan leaves behind the marks of his fingers after having used them to massage, pinch, and pull wet clay in shaping an object (photograph 6.1). Here, we begin to see how people's impressions of themselves, of who they are as artisans, begin to emerge from direct bodily engagement with the material of clay. Objects made from clay, I suggest, become a kind of extended person, an argument derived from Alfred Gell's (1998) conception of art as a transfer of properties and agency of persons to things. Rather than simply a transfer, however, where the objects themselves may possess capacity to affect certain processes while circulating in different networks, engagement between person-as-creator and clay-material is a mutually constituted extension.

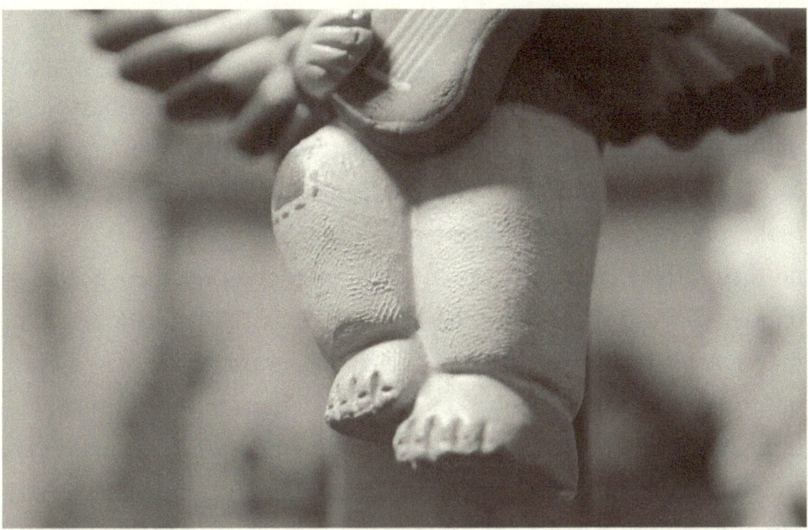

Photograph 6.1. "*Uno se deja sus huellas con sus dedos.*" That is, quite literally, the artisan leaves behind the marks of his fingers after having used them to massage, pinch, and pull wet clay in shaping an object. (Photograph by author)

On one hand, the raw material of clay, particularly as it is shaped from an abstract mass of raw material to a specified form, extends the body-person of the artisan, leaving imprints on the surface of the clay (Gowlland 2009).[8] For Manuel, his fingers, and, by extension, his hands and the rest of his embodied person, leave one very observable and physical manifestation of himself as creator. He later fires the clay, after maybe shaping it into an animal figure or miniature church, and puts it up for display in his shop or market stall. In this way, then, these personal markings of the creator and thus a sense of who he is as a maker become more permanent and visible for future artisans, buyers, and other observers.

On the other hand, the clay material, its physical properties bearing a kind of agency, affects the artisan as creator. Artisans' narratives reflected in various ways the importance of this mutual engagement with clay. Producers, for instance, often complained that many producers "*hacer por hacer*" ("make for the sake of making"). One artisan elaborated on this idea, explaining that such producers are not engaging the head (*la cabeza*) while engaging the hands (*los manos*).[9] Another artisan described it thus: "Without emotion one can have ability, but there is no art, there is no creativity." People make objects, which necessarily require their hands, but they are not using their creativity, which necessarily requires their head and hands working in conjunction (photographs 6.2*A* and 6.2*B*). One may master technical skills in manipulating materials of the craft, but to become a true artisan one must also master nontechnical faculties locally referenced as *emoción* (emotion) or *espíritu de creatividad* (spirit of creativity) or simply as *mi creatividad* (my creativity). Artisans in Quinua consistently stressed the importance of creatividad in setting a true artisan apart from all others working in ceramic production.

One artisan named Carlos helped me understand this process. He explained learning creativity as the following: "With your hands you make different little models, and you learn more too. You learn what difficulties you have in making ceramics. You learn what small differences you can make. And so I have to model using my hands, to get more practice." The clay and person are mutually constituted, each being transformed by the other in their conjunction. Artisans continually emphasized this predilection for creativity for making objects and curiosity for the clay as a fundamental aspect of artisan identities in Quinua.

Creatividad, moreover, was cited as an essential element in the longer process of learning to make ceramics. In making an object, there is a clearly definable task at hand, which is to be achieved by one person in conjunction with a mass of clay. This single act of creating, suspended in time and place, in which materials, tools, and maker interact, however, may be, and often is, for many producers,

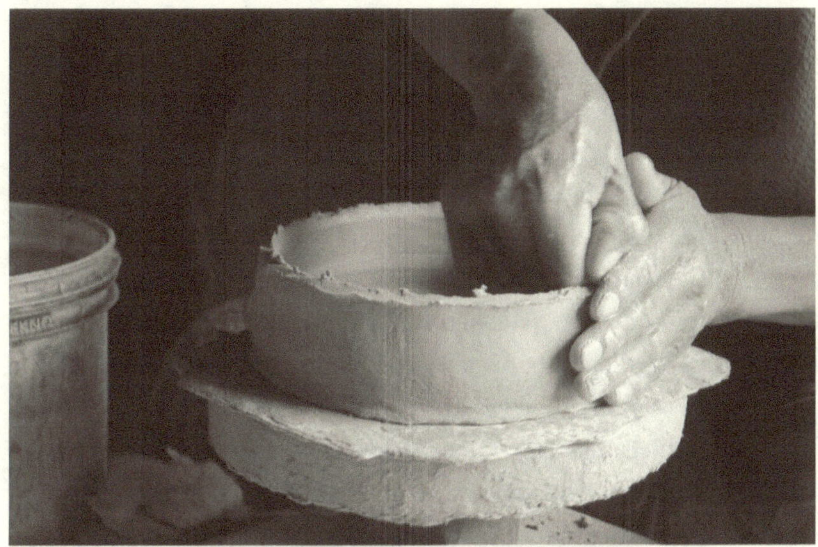

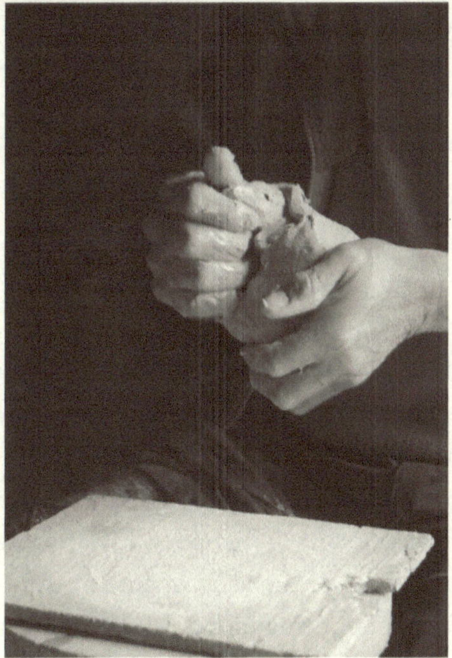

Photographs 6.2*A* and 6.2*B*. People make objects, which necessarily require their hands, but they are not using their creativity, which necessarily requires their head and hands working in conjunction. (Photographs by author)

part of a longer process of ceramic making. In describing how they learned to make ceramics, every artisan emphasized how their physical engagement with clay often spanned over many years, perhaps four, ten, or twenty years, and sometimes more. Thus, finger impressions literally and metaphorically reference this process, just as they reference the more momentary mutually constituted relationship between clay-material and body-person-maker. In this long process, if a person is to be a "true artisan," he must become familiar with the physical malleability of clay, to learn directly with the hands and other bodily senses the clay's limits and potential for creating things. With embodied mastery of technical skills, an artisan must, at the same time, self-consciously familiarize himself with the malleability of his own imaginative faculties. He must learn directly, through exploration and experimentation as the artisan's hands engage the immediacy of clay and the limits and potential of his creativity.

Social Commitment and Values of Personal Authenticity

At this point in my analysis, one might conclude that local conceptions of authenticity, grounded in ideas about personal creativity, support modern views of authenticity in the context of artistic practices. In these views, authentically creative persons are defined as special individuals, whose work distinguishes them as persons set apart, or better, above the masses.[10] But this view is problematic because it sets the authentic creative person against tradition, where the creative person must struggle for originality over imposed cultural rules. "What gets lost," as Charles Taylor argues, "in this critique is the moral force of the ideal of authenticity" (1992, 17). My analysis thus far hints of this moral force in local understandings of authenticity, since artisans define and evaluate personal identity of themselves and each other within a set of shared values (for creativity). Following Becker and Bourdieu, I now shift to an explicit focus on the *socially* constructed and agreed upon moral nature of authenticity. In other words, creative laborers in Quinua are necessarily enmeshed in a broader social space or arena.

While imprints left by fingers reference a person's physical engagement and personal identity, for artisans, they are also symbolic of their social identity. As these marks materialize on ceramic objects, referencing personal artisan identities, they are also up for display, as I mentioned before, for other artisans and observers. Along with these marks of the body are made other marks of the creator, such as the particular color combinations he chooses, in the particular way he forms the shape of an eye or paints on a plant design, and in other small details. This fluid convergence of personal marks are thus also up for display in public spaces. Artisans insisted, for instance, that each artisan has his *sello* (stamp) or *estilo* (style). Each artist's style of executing the complex combination of colors visibly distinguishes his work and accentuates the individual character of Quinua ceramics.[11] Developing a personal style depends on both individual, creative flair and technical mastery of manipulating clay. It also depends on manipulation of established, albeit flexible, conventions governing the use of materials, the choice of colors, the use of local cultural themes, and other elements of design and content (Becker 1982).

For example, consider these bull pitchers, each made by a different artisan (photographs 6.3*A*, 6.3*B*, 6.3*C*, and 6.3*D*). Each artisan worked within a similar set of stylistic and symbolic elements, most prominently, the typical white-on-red color scheme and the bull form of the pitcher used to serve *chicha* at community fiestas. Yet we also see that these four artisans used similar elements to create four distinct pieces. Artisans thus "use available materials to produce works which, in size, form, design, color, and content, fit into the available spaces and into people's ability to respond appropriately" (Becker

1984, 229). Notably, when I showed a photograph of these pieces (which were all on public display) to several artisans, most were fairly accurate in naming the creator of each piece.[12] Each clay object often bears socially recognizable marks of the artist who made it.

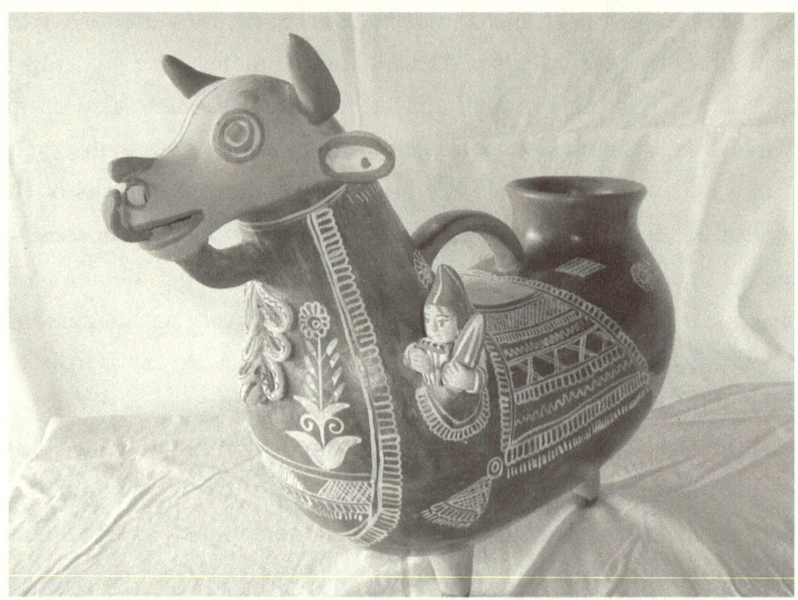

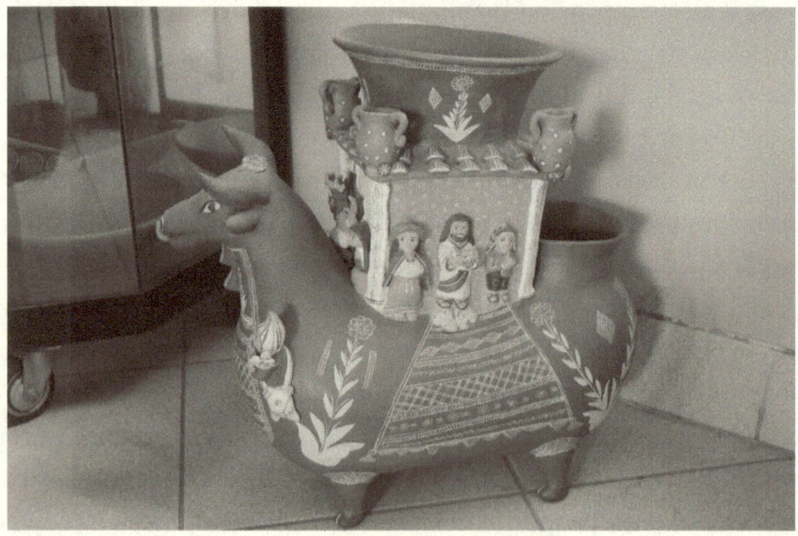

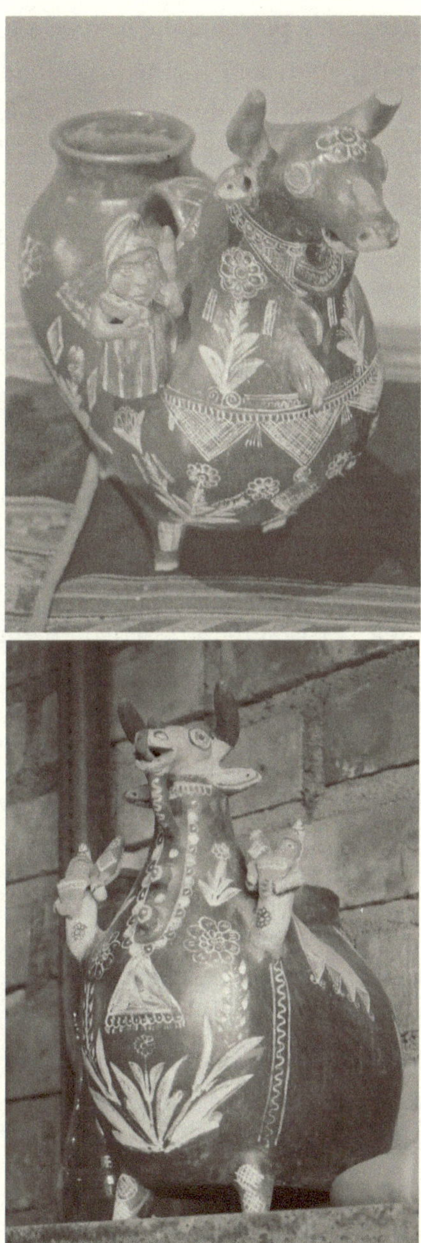

Photographs 6.3*A*, 6.3*B*, 6.3*C*, and 6.3*D*. Bull pitchers, each made by a different artisan. (Photographs by author)

Artisans insisted that a person, if he is to be a true artisan, must develop this personal style, and further, continue to do so to set himself apart in a world of social others who all draw on a shared repertoire of symbols and styles of a recognizable Quinua tradition of ceramic making. The individual who puts the piece up for sale or buys it advertises his proficiency. Displaying and selling ceramic objects therefore put artisans' personal identities on the line, exposing their creative choices to public scrutiny and judgment. Ceramic objects in the rural Quinua district, much as Blenda Femenías (2005) found for producers of bordados in rural Coylloma Province of Peru, become a ground for social evaluation where people must prove their creativity in seeking to gain respect as a "true artisan."

"You May Copy Me, But You Will Never Equal Me."

Artisans in Quinua persistently stressed the connection between shared technical skills and symbols used in making ceramics and the creative skills, talent, and vision of the individual creator. Many even acknowledged that, practically speaking, it is entirely impossible to execute an exact replication of another person's work or style, given individual tastes and abilities. So if each artisan is said to have his or her own style, why do artisans make social distinctions and argumentative claims about one's own and others' authenticity? Part of the explanation, I argue next, is grounded in ideas about copying, specifically in relation to values for creativity. For this argument, I turn to Bourdieu, who, like Becker, conceives of creative practices as occurring within certain social relations, but these are characterized by antagonism and power struggles rather than cooperation.

The primary source of inspiration, artisans reported, is other pieces of ceramics.[13] Skilled artisans design them in clay, using tools, without looking at a model. Well-trained artisans, therefore, need not directly copy other's work to be directly influenced by it, or they may design from memory a design seen only once, especially since most pieces draw on shared aesthetic conventions. An artisan named Eduardo, for instance, who produced small piggy banks, told me how he came across this design while working, and simultaneously learning how to make ceramics, in a larger workshop for another artisan. Eduardo made a small change to produce his personal design. As he reconstructed the pig form in clay from memory, he bent its ears to make them appear "floppy" and "realistic," a detail, Eduardo said, based on countless observations of living pigs. This process of conservative modification, or "editing" (Becker 1982), characterizes creative practices in Quinua; artisans orient themselves according to a shared repertoire of a Quinua style, gained from countless observations of other people's ceramic works, which enables innovation and improvisation. Importantly, however, such impressions of personal style are not always reliable proof of its creator, particularly given apparently small changes and variation in design details marking personal styles. It is these apparently minor variations within a common currency of designs that give rise to conflicts; artisans accuse each other of copying their original, unique design. In this context of quasi-identical objects, seemingly small variations and changes become socially significant details.

When artisans spoke of others as copying or described others' accusations of copying, these discourses almost always articulated with ideas about authenticity grounded in moral and social values. The family owning the workshop in which Eduardo had seen the piggy bank design, for instance, approached Eduardo, asking him why he copied their design. Eduardo rejoined that the design did not belong exclusively to them, explaining that "the design belongs to Quinua . . . everyone makes it now." Eduardo legitimated his use of the design by citing a social fact—that is, aesthetic conventions shared within the district. Accusations about design imitation, artisans said, also indicated that a person lacked self-esteem. "If an artisan is worried about others copying his work," one artisan explained, "then he is not confident in himself and his creativity," implying that only a true artisan is unconcerned when others copy his work because he knows and demonstrates that, as a craftsman, he and his creative skills are equal to no other. And conversely, no one can equal him even if he dares try.

One aspect of ceramic production in Quinua that provided a particularly salient source of conversation and debate about copying as well as in artisans' desires to show how they were true artisans is plaster molds (photograph 6.4). I recall one afternoon when I asked an artisan named Efraín, who was working at the time on hand coiling a water pitcher, if he used molds.[14] At the time, it seemed a common enough question, since I had seen every artisan use plaster molds in some way or another. Further, molds allowed artisans to produce in a standardized way and at a much faster pace than did modeling each piece by hand alone. Yet Efraín stated, after laying down the rock he used to evenly smooth the coiled-clay walls of the pitcher, "No. I only make pieces by hand. Handmade pieces have their value. Each piece is unique. With molds, there's no difference in the pieces." One might stop here to argue that artisans defined authenticity as based in objects that are unique, purely made by hand, and carry a higher market value. Objects made with molds are, by contrast, serial copies, inauthentic, and cheap. But, consider this statement made by Efraín as our conversation about molds and artisan work in general in Quinua unfolded: "Nobody equals me. Nobody!" he exclaimed. "I can't say I'm the only one making ceramics, but these people, they don't equal me." Within Efraín's exclamation, market values ambiguously infuse with values for a sense of self, of Efraín's perception that he is a uniquely creative person. For most artisans, too, this material practice of using molds versus hand modeling techniques was a constant source of social evaluation, bringing the value of one-of-a-kind creative person into the social realm.

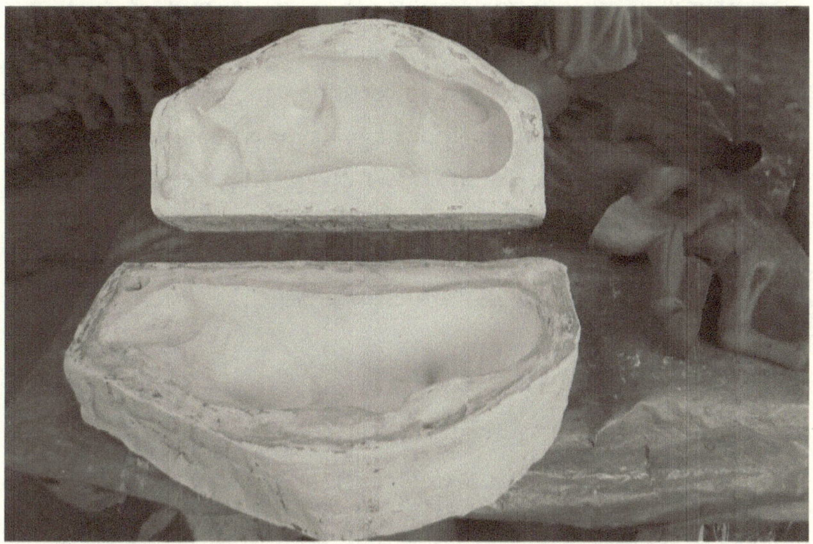

Photograph 6.4. Plaster mold, plaster artisan. (Photograph by author)

Additional contextual clues relating to Efraín's assertion that he definitively does not use molds reveals the ambiguous and often contradictory nature of imitation and innovation. Later I found out that Efraín had asked his daughter-in-law to make small people figures using her plaster molds. Efraín integrated these molded figures into a piece that he wanted to use to enter a national artisan contest. A few other artisans in Quinua, when they saw this piece, remarked that Efraín had used molds to make this piece. "So why should he win?" they asked. In doing so, they attempted to diminish Efraín's authenticity as an artisan. In general, it is not uncommon to find such contradictions among artisans in Quinua. Many artisans criticize others' use of molds or downplay their own use of molds, even though every artisan either used molds to produce or bought plaster-molded pieces from others to quickly fill their shops. My question is thus: If molds practically help artisans produce and earn a better living for themselves and their families, why do they attempt to downplay their own and/or devalue others' use of molds?

Artisans who used molds, a type of technology for duplication, and could thus produce faster, certainly increased competition between each other for sales. Indeed, artisans complained about lost sales due to introduction of mold technology in general.

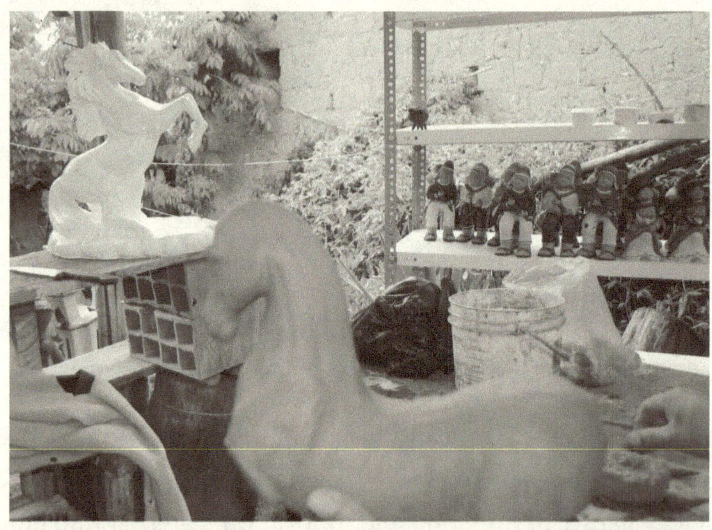

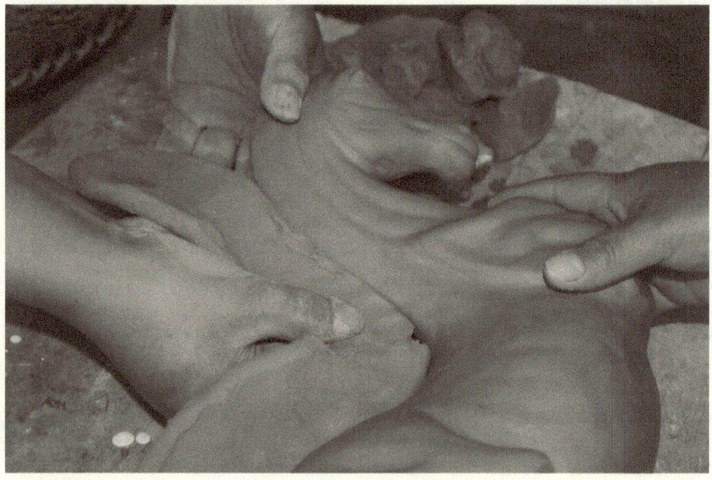

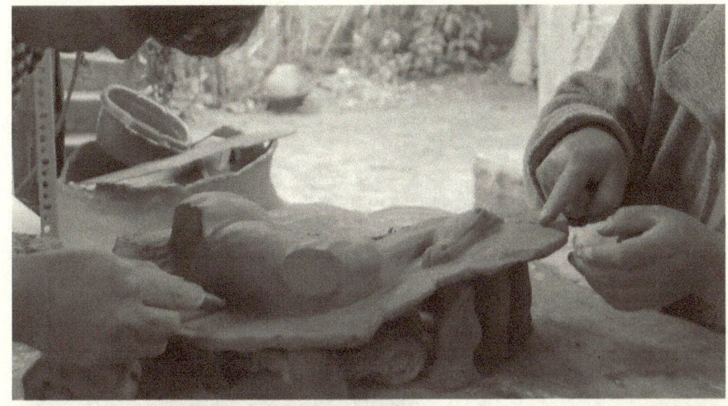

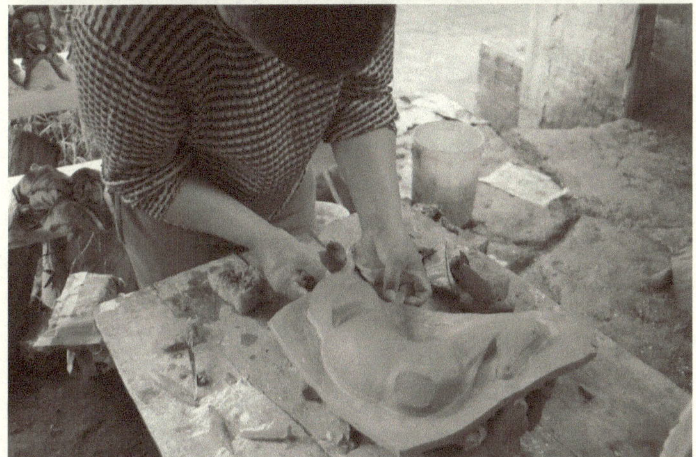

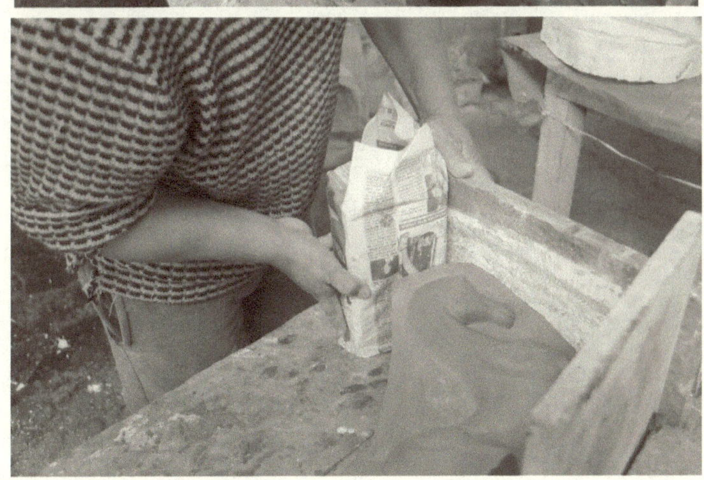

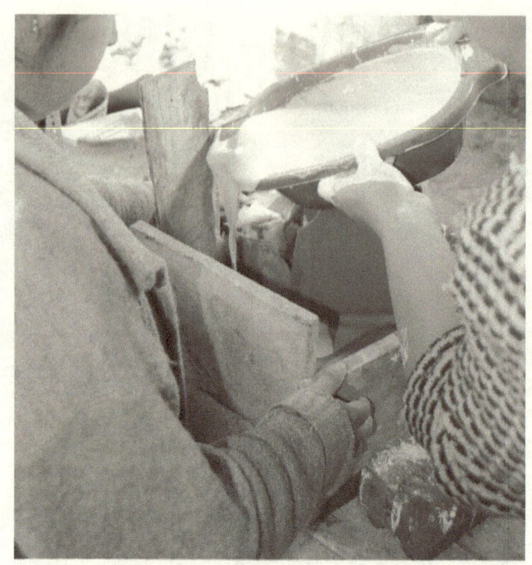

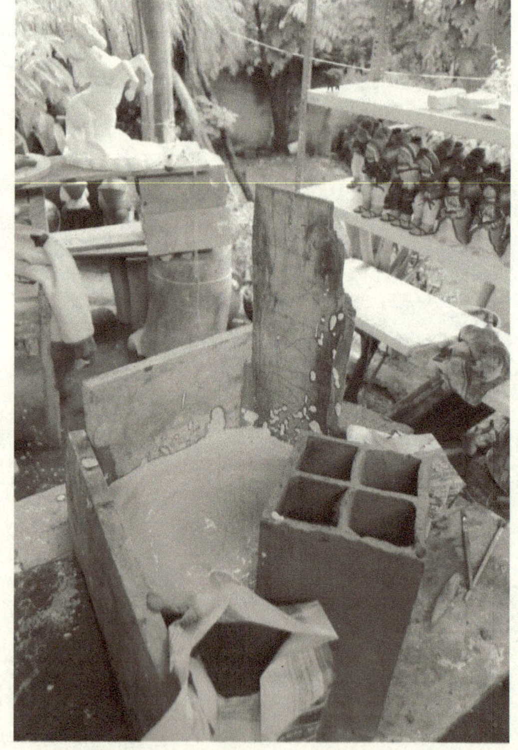

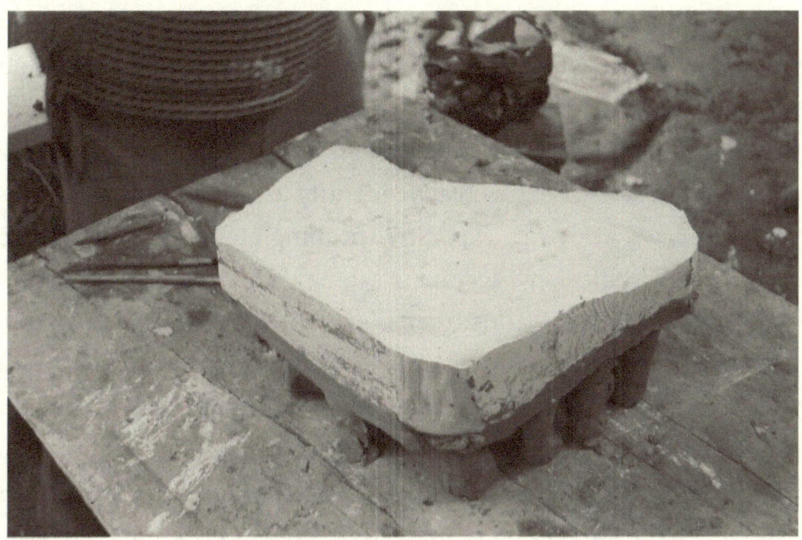

Photographs 6.5*A*, 6.5*B*, 6.5*C*, 6.5*D*, 6.5*E*, 6.5*F*, 6.5*G*, and 6.5*H*. Felipe using mold technology for faster duplication of a stallion sculpture. (Photographs by author)

Felipe made a mold from a stallion sculpture that he himself designed and modeled in clay (photographs 6.5*A*-6.5*H*). As he and his wife, Felicita, worked to create the mold, he conveyed that he enjoyed designing such unique pieces because it allowed him to be creative. Making the mold, Felipe said, would help him produce faster without working so hard to make each piece entirely by hand. Many other artisans made plaster molds from one "original" design, which, an artisan may tell you, originated in his workshop. From these molds were made serial copies to increase his and his family's production output, which increased his ability to compete with his neighbors for attention from prospective buyers.

The anxieties around molds, however, most prominently emerged when the so-called original piece presumably belonged to an artisan other than the one who created the plaster mold. Specifically, producers often talked about molds in the context of copying and robbery of designs (*robar mi diseño*) as a moral and social offense. My conversation with the artisan Carlos (mentioned previously) helped me to understand why imitating others was such a social, moral, and personal offense. His comments, to remind the reader, relate back to my argument that finger impressions and details marked on clay objects reflect an artisan's creative identity, but what I did not mention was that Carlos was explicitly speaking about the relationship between creativity, copying, and mold use. "One is not an artisan, if he uses only molds," Carlos further explained. "He is not thinking, not using his creativity. Molds are to advance in one's work. With your hands, you make different little models, and you learn more too. You learn what difficulties you have in making ceramics. You learn what small differences you can make. And so, I have to model using my hands, to get more practice. If not . . . if I am just making with plaster molds . . . then I am settling on the same." Comments like Carlos' express a kind of awareness that molds, as a form of technology, affected confluent processes of separation.

In one sense, molds physically separated the artisan from his clay medium because the artisan used his hands less to form the clay, the mold acting as a partial proxy. But this contracted experience of direct contact with clay also meant that the artisan spent less time and energy thinking and creating in clay since the mold, in bearing a predetermined design, did a good part of the image-making and creative work for the artisan. Carlos further pointed out to me the material signs of this process of separation. "Handmade pieces cost you a little more time. You need higher temperature [for the kiln]. And when it's fired well, it sounds like metal," he explained, knocking on a fired, hand-modeled piece of ceramic. "If it's not fired well, it doesn't sound like this," he continued, knocking for comparative purposes on a plaster-molded ceramic piece. Indeed, I could hear the difference, the latter being a more muted sound. Inhering in the material properties of a finished ceramic object was an irrefutable test of technical mastery, accessible to human sensory experience and thus a materially grounded source for social evaluation and proving oneself to be a true artisan. Carlos continued further: "Molds leave these small seams here, within," he points out on a plaster-molded piece, "Just by looking at it, this was made with a mold. If you look inside this [hand-modeled] piece, it doesn't have seams. With a mold, it looks like this. Wiping with a sponge, you can see it." Herein also lay a material test of creativity, wherein one substitutes impressions of fingers with nonhuman marks (e.g., seams of a plaster mold); wherein one simultaneously risks replacing creativity with mere copying and ultimately risks being evaluated as anything but a true artisan. Deeper anxieties lie at the heart of much of artisans' struggles to minimize others work as unoriginal and mold-made. Molds separated artisans from their creative potential and mastery of technical skills and by extension their identities as authentic and true artisans.

Final Comments

Right now in Peru, and in other Latin American countries, state development policies celebrate local artisan enterprises. They ostensibly do so to stimulate creative market strategies, revitalize traditional technologies, and encourage disintermediation. By grafting onto products, like ceramics, narratives of origin, shared "tradition," "authenticity," as well as quality, artisans in Latin America may be able to create symbolic value (Bourdieu 1984, 1986; Brown 2003; Coombe 2011; Harvey 2009). As Coombe, Schnoor, and Ahmed argue, "Places of historical and contemporary disadvantage may thereby be transformed into places of competitive advantage" (2006, 896). Yet assertions of collective patrimony may also figure in political projects that idealize concepts of artisan communities and authentic culture.

When examined from a local perspective, as I have tried to do in this chapter, authenticity may look very different from how it is conceived by policymakers and development. Perhaps above all, artisans' narratives about authenticity function as projections of future trajectories and about becoming. In this sense, constructions of authenticity reflect emotional investments and desires for attachments. After all, artisans are caught up within wanting to belong to national and global economies, to be recognized as authentic artisans or entrepreneurs, and to capture a share of the market value that inheres in claims to creating "authentic" cultural products. But they are also emotionally invested in local communities composed of present as well as future creative laborers. It would seem that it is this emotional component to people's constructions of themselves and identities that escapes apparently simple definitions of authenticity in a context in which external agents are redrawing where and how artisans' identities are expressed. I will save an extended discussion of these wider political economic implications of shifting authenticities for future essays. Instead, I would like to end this chapter with the following, an extended excerpt from my conversation with the artisan Juan (mentioned previously), which, I believe, reflects these difficulties artisans face in struggles to define who they are, where they come from, and where they are going, both personally and collectively, in terms of both material livelihood and social relationships:

> It's difficult [to protect our designs]. We artisans, we live from this, no? We can't say 'don't do that [copy this design].' The artisans who come before us, well, we live from them. Los antiguos [the ancient ones] have to be followed, too . . . Waiting for new works so that these too give value to their [los antiguos'] works. If we continue using the same designs, we're not valuing los antiguos . . .

> and what other option is there for us? There is no other option. So I say, if I sell more of these [pieces that everyone sells], I'm just settling. But if I don't sell these, I have to look for another [design]. This is how I'm inspired. This work I no longer sell, but it's better that I make another. So this little thing inspires me. The traditional or whatever can inspire me. And it's even better if I can sell to the public, no? And so, one makes a decision this way. If not, I'm settling for what I'm already making. I'm not thinking how to create new and better works. An artisan has to look for new values, to look for new prestige.

Acknowledgments

This research has been made possible through the artisans and families in Quinua, who shared their stories and lives with the author. Professors Edward F. Fischer and Miriam Shakow provided invaluable guidance and support for this project. This project was funded by the Inter-American Foundation, Fulbright-Hays, and Vanderbilt University.

Notes

1. Translations from Spanish sources are my own.

2. This chapter is a tentative exploration of the implications of everyday practices of and debates over local meanings of authenticity. As such, the analysis here constitutes a focus on adult men working in ceramic production. This focus offers a particularly fruitful place to begin, I believe, since people generally referred to as "artisan" during my fieldwork in Quinua were predominantly male adults. A discussion of how already-existing inequalities—in this case, class, gender, and generational differences—translate into competing ideas about

cultural authority and authenticity would overextend my analysis in this chapter.

3. The ideas and practices surrounding creativity and authenticity that I discuss in this chapter are a recent phenomenon in Quinua and in Peru in general. Their most prominent forms have emerged in the last decade or two but are historically linked to a conjunction of wider processes—for example, early twentieth-century *indigenista* movement, subsequent state industrial and development policies, and programs carried out by different Peruvian administrations, and shrinking land base and other livelihood opportunities for rural people.

4. I have used pseudonyms, except for artisans' names that appear in published scholarly works (i.e., Mamerto Sánchez, Francisco Sánchez).

5. During my conversations with artisans, they too singled out the significance of these objects, describing how the *padrino* (godfather) of a *zafacasa* (house-raising ceremony) contracts an artisan to make a church. The family building the home holds a fiesta, where they provide food and music for dancing for those invited (e.g., extended family members, friends, and neighbors). The church is later adhered to the roof of the new home, saying something to this effect: "May this house be blessed with this church."

6. I will discuss one such technology—that is, plaster molds—later in the chapter.

7. Steiner (1999) argues, drawing on principles of mass-production, that "authenticity [of tourist art] is measured generally through redundancy [of a particular ethnic style] rather than originality" (101). This is a different, yet mutually influential, form of authenticity than notions of authenticity I discuss in this chapter.

8. See Gowlland (2009) for a comparative case of *Zisha* pottery making in China.

9. This conceptualization is different from the mind/body dualism so often critiqued by anthropologists and other scholars. Rather than viewing creativity as located in an immaterial mind and distinguishable from a material body, artisans conceptualized creativity in terms of materiality of the head-hands and distinguishable from materiality of hands making alone. This is a process recognized by several writers and commentators on creativity in artistic practices (e.g., Sennett 2008).

10. See Taylor (1992) for an extended discussion.

11. Also see Femenías (2005) and Gowlland (2009) for comparison. Gowlland, for instance, argues that "the actions of the body-person imprints on the surface of the clay; the sum of skilled movements performed in proper sequence comes to mark the pot with the signs of the maker" (2009, 138).

12. Other scholars have similarly noted the ability of artisans to differentiate their styles by visual cues (e.g., Femenías 2005, Gowlland 2009).

13. Artisans also mentioned newspapers, television, and books as well as everyday events and special occasions in the community as other sources for inspiration. Artisans in Quinua, however, most often appropriate design and stylistic elements from other artisans' goods.

14. A plaster mold is used to create duplicate copies of utilitarian, decorative, or even more complex works of art through a process called casting. The mold itself is a negative or mirror image of the final work.

References

Appadurai, Arjun. 1986. "Introduction: Commodities and the Politics of Value." In *The Social Life of Things: Commodities in Cultural Perspective*, edited by Arjun Appadurai, 3-63. Cambridge: Cambridge University Press.

Arnold, Dean E. 1972a. "Mineralogical Analyses of Ceramic Materials from Quinua, Department of Ayacucho, Peru." *Arachaeometry* 14(1): 93-102.

———. 1972b. "Native Pottery Making in Quinua, Peru." *Anthropos* 67:858-72.

———. 1975. "Ceramic Ecology in the Ayacucho Basin, Peru: Implications for Prehistory." *Current Anthropology* 16(2): 183-203.

———. 1985. *Ceramic Theory and Cultural Process*. New York: Cambridge University Press.

———. 1993. *Ecology and Ceramic Production in an Andean Community*. New York: Cambridge University Press.

Becker, Howard Saul. 1974. "Art as Collective Action." *American Sociological Review* 39:767-76.

———. 1976. "Art Worlds and Social Types." *American Behavioral Scientist* 19(6): 703-18.

———. 1978. "Arts and Crafts." *American Journal of Sociology* 83(4): 862-89.

———. 1982. *Art Worlds*. Berkeley: University of California Press.

Bourdieu, Pierre. 1983. "The Field of Cultural Production, or: The Economic World Reversed." *Poetics* 12(4): 311-56.

———. 1984. *Distinction: A Social Critique of the Judgement of Taste*. Cambridge, MA: Harvard University Press.

———. 1986. "The Forms of Capital." In *Handbook of Theory and Research for the Sociology of Education*, edited by J. G. Richardson, 241-58. New York: Greenwood.

Brown, Michael F. 2003. *Who Owns Native Culture?* Cambridge, MA: Harvard University Press.

Colloredo-Mansfeld, Rudi, Jason Antrosio, and Eric C. Jones. 2011. "Creativity, Place, and Commodities: The Making of Public Economies in Andean Apparel Industries." In *Textile Economies: Power and Value from the Local to the Transnational*, edited by Walter E. Little, 39-55. Lanham, MD: Rowman Altamira.

Colloredo-Mansfeld, Rudolf. 2002. "An Ethnography of Neoliberalism: Understanding Competition in Artisan Economies." *Current Anthropology* 43(1): 113-37.

Coombe, Rosemary J. 2011. "'Possessing Culture': Political Economies of Community Subjects and their Properties." In *Ownership and Appropriation*, edited by M. B. Veronica Strang, 105-27. New York: Berg.

Coombe, Rosemary J., Steven Schnoor, and Mohsen Ahmed. 2006. "Bearing Cultural Distinction: Informational Capitalism and New Expectations for Intellectual Property." *UC Davis Law Review* 40:891-917.

Femenías, Blenda. 2005. *Gender and the Boundaries of Dress in Contemporary Peru*. Austin: University of Texas Press.

Field, Les W. 2009. "Four Kinds of Authenticity? Regarding Nicaraguan Pottery in Scandinavian Museums, 2006–08." *American Ethnologist* 36(3): 507-20.

Fuente, María del Carmen de la, María Josefa Nolte, Lucy Nuñez Rebaza, and Roberto Villegas Robles. 1992. *Artesanía peruana: orígenes y evolución*. Lima, Perú: Allpa.

Gell, Alfred. 1998. *Art and Agency: An Anthropological Theory.* Oxford: Clarendon Press.

Gowlland, Geoffrey. 2009. "Style, Skill and Modernity in the Zisha Pottery of China." *Journal of Modern Craft* 2(2): 129-41.

Harvey, David. 2009. "The Art of Rent: Globalisation, Monopoly and the Commodification of Culture." *Socialist Register* 38:38.

Hernando, Nelly, and Sandra Van Hulsen. 2001. *Investigación del cluster de Artesanía en Ayacucho; sus características y potencial de desarrollo (Investigation of the handicraft cluster in Ayacucho: Its characteristics and development potential).* Lima, Perú: ILO.

Indacochea, Alejandro. 2001. *Ayacucho Competitivo.* Lima, Perú: CARE-Peru/USAID.

Kopytoff, Igor. 1986. "The Cultural Biography of Things: Commoditization as Process." In *The Social Life of Things: Commodities in Cultural Perspective*, edited by Arjun Appadurai, 64-91. Cambridge: Cambridge University Press.

Latour, Bruno. 2005. *Reassembling the Social: An Introduction to Actor-Network-Theory.* New York: Oxford University Press.

Lauer, Mirko. 1982. *Crítica de la artesanía: Plástica y sociedad en los Andes peruanos.* Lima, Perú: Desco.

Marcus, George E., and Fred R. Myers, eds. 1995. *The Traffic in Culture: Refiguring Art and Anthropology.* Berkeley: University of California Press.

Mauldin, Barbara. 2011. *Folk Art of the Andes.* Santa Fe: Museum of New Mexico Press.

Mitchell, William P. 1972. *The System of Power in Quinua: A Community of the Central Peruvian Highlands.* PhD diss. University of Pittsburgh, Pittsburgh.

———. 1973. "A Preliminary Report on Irrigation and Community of the Central Peruvian Highlands." Paper presented at the *Symposium on Irrigation and Communal Organization*, 72nd annual meeting of the American Anthropological Association, New Orleans.

———. 1991. *Peasants on the Edge: Crop, Cult, and Crisis in the Andes*. Austin: University of Texas Press.

———. 1999. "Detour onto the Shining Path: Obscuring the Social Revolution in the Andes." In *Deadly Developments: Capitalism, States, and War*, edited by S. P. Reyna and R. E. Downs, 235-78. Amsterdam: Gordon and Breach Publishers.

"Municipalidad Distrital de Quinua." 2001. *Balance Poblacional de la Municipalidad de Quinua*. Quinua, Peru.

"Perú Posible." 2010. *Plan de Gobierno Municipal de Distrito de Quinua 2011-2014*. Partido Político "Perú Posible." Quinua, Peru.

Phillips, Ruth B., and Christopher Burghard Steiner. 1999. *Unpacking Culture: Art and Commodity in Colonial and Postcolonial Worlds*. Berkeley: University of California Press.

PromPerú. 2012. "Quinua, De mi Tierra, Un Producto." http://www.demitierraunproducto.gob.pe/quinua.html. Ravines, Rogger, and Fernando Villiger. 1989. *La Cerámica Tradicional del Perú*. Lima, Perú: Editorial Los Pinos.

Sabogal Wiesse, José R. 1979. *Arte Vernáculo en Huamanga: Testimonio de Tres Artesanos*. La Molina, Perú: Universidad Nacional Agraria.

Sennett, Richard. 2008. *The Craftsman*. London: Allen Lane.

Silver, Harry R. 1981. "Calculating Risks: The Socioeconomic Foundations of Aesthetic Innovation in an Ashanti Carving Community." *Ethnology* 20(2): 101-14.

———. 1983. "Foreign Art and Asante Aesthetics." *African Arts* 16(3): 64-80.

Spahni, Jean-Christian. 1966. *La cerámica popular del Péru*. Lima, Perú: Peruano Suiza.

Stastny, Francisco. 1968. *La artesanía del Perú y sus orígenes*. Madrid, Spain: Fundacion del Banco Continental para el Fomento de la Educacion y la Cultura.

Steiner, Christopher B. 1999. "Authenticity, Repetition, and the Aesthetics of Seriality." In *Unpacking Culture: Art and Commodity in Colonial and Postcolonial Worlds*, edited by Ruth B. Phillips and Christopher B. Steiner, 87-103. Berkeley: University of California Press.

Taylor, Charles. 1992. *The Ethics of Authenticity*. Cambridge, MA: Harvard University Press.

Torres, Fernando, ed. 2010. *Arte de Ayacucho: Celebración de la vida*. Lima, Perú: Universidad Ricardo Palma/Instituto Cultural Peruano Norteamericano.

Tschopik, Harry. 1947. *Highland Communities of Central Peru: A Regional Survey*, vol. 5. Washington, DC: Smithonsonian Institute.

———. 1949. *Peruvian Folk Art*. Washington, DC: American Federation of Arts.

Villantoy Valverde, Janett. 2011. "Colocan primera piedra para construcción del CITE en Quinua." *Diaro de La Voz de Huamanga*, October 18.

Wherry, Frederick F. F. 2006. "The Social Sources of Authenticity in Global Handicraft Markets: Evidence from Northern Thailand." *Journal of Consumer Culture* 6(1): 5-32.

Defining Art in the Gozo International Contemporary Arts Festival

Rachel Syka

Abstract

This chapter explores the role of identity, place, and origin of the artists in the Gozo International Contemporary Arts Festival in Gozo, Malta. Based on research conducted in July 2010 for a summer field school in sociocultural anthropology, I draw on conversations with several of the artists showing their work, as well as interactions with local organizing officials, arts instructors, and Gozitan artists and craftspeople not directly involved in the exhibit. I argue that the event is a space in which central questions of Gozitan identity are actively addressed and negotiated, focusing particularly on the manner in which the international artists participating in the festival construct both conceptual and visual images of Gozo and Malta. I suggest that the origin of the artist, in tandem with the purpose and medium of their artwork, plays a major role in how the work is incorporated into the exhibit. Framed in part as a cosmopolitan attraction alongside the historical sites of the island, the exhibition acknowledges the increasingly global nature of Gozo. Ultimately, I aim to address questions pertinent to postcolonial identity and tourism on Gozo and Malta. How is the island viewed by visitors from abroad? What cultural resources is it assumed to possess (or lack)? How do Gozitan artists interact with and respond to such expectations through events like the Arts Festival?

This chapter explores definitions of art and the inclusion and exclusion of certain artists in the first Gozo International Contemporary Arts Festival in Gozo, Malta, in the summer of 2010. Based on research undertaken for three weeks in July for a field school in sociocultural anthropology, I draw on conversations with Gozitan artists, international artists who had come to Gozo to make and exhibit their work, and local organizing officials affiliated with the arts.[1] Within the context of tourism, which is the thriving industry on Gozo, I argue that the selection of artists exhibiting their work at this event was determined in part by varying definitions of what constitutes "art" and the artists' claimed or perceived proximity to the "global art scene." By proximity, I refer to the degree to which a given artist's work aligns with the modern, individualistic, and personally expressive goals and means of Western-focused "art for arts' sake," or "fine art."

Malta, located south of Sicily and northeast of Tunisia in the center of the Mediterranean Sea, gained independence from Britain in 1965 and European Union membership in 2004. Gozo, the smaller of the two inhabited islands in the Maltese archipelago, is separated from the main island of Malta by a thirty-minute ferry ride. With a population of about thirty thousand, Gozo is characterized as more rural than Malta, with a comparatively relaxed pace of life.

The International Arts Festival, which was slated to become an annual event, was held in the Citadel in Victoria, the main town in the center of the island. The remains of the original fortified city, the Citadel (or Citadella) now functions as both historical attraction and cultural center for visitors. It houses the Gozo Cathedral, several museums, various shops, and a Maltese restaurant. The space hosts events throughout the year, including concerts and reenactments, and boasts an impressive view of the island from its place atop a hill in the town center. For the portion used to exhibit the works in the

International Arts Festival, the wall hangings, altars, and other features typically present in the Citadel's hallways were left in place, with art pieces arranged around them. Admission to the festival was free.

Through my conversations with several of the participants in the Arts Festival about the presence of arts and crafts on the island and the nature of their own work, I noticed a distinction between the perspectives of those coming to Gozo from the global circuit and other artists that I met on the island who were not included in the activities of the festival. Foreign artists' assumptions about what could be considered adequate arts resources (education, exposure overseas, events, etc.), along with different expectations regarding function, purpose, and style, distanced groups of foreign and Gozitan artists from one another. Ultimately, this helped to exclude several Gozitan artists' pieces from display in the International Arts Festival.

International Artists

The International Contemporary Arts Festival was envisioned and organized by French digital photographer, painter, and sculptor Raphael Labro.[2] He had moved to the island with his family several years before, describing the area as a kind of paradise with limestone beaches and quaint towns, distinct from busy metropolitan areas elsewhere in Europe. Although Raphael had organized numerous private exhibitions since moving to Gozo, this was his first large-scale event that included artists from abroad. Moving to the island as an established artist, Raphael made it clear that he wished to bring the ethos of a more international art perspective to Gozo.

When I spoke with several of the exhibitors in the Arts Festival, Raphael's view of Gozo was described as a potential crux for the artistic world—because it was located at the center of the Mediterranean, Raphael wished to make Gozo what he described as the "center of the art world" as well. While Malta's geographic location has been perhaps its greatest point of interest throughout history, Gozo itself has only recently been exposed to many globalizing influences: two shopping malls, one containing the first McDonald's for the island, had opened several years before my visit. Although tourism is the main industry throughout Malta, Gozo in particular remains a place with a distinctly local way of life. Because of this, Raphael's agenda to make the island the "center of the art world" through the International Contemporary Arts Festival had little to do with Gozo's own cosmopolitanism.

The title of the event evokes the idea of Gozo as a global place, yet this was a more accurate description of the festival itself. Many of the artists exhibiting their work were Raphael's friends and acquaintances, including artists from Peru, France, Bulgaria, Japan, Germany, Macedonia, and Gozo and Malta. Some were foreign residents living on Malta and Gozo, several were local artists, and many flew in from overseas to participate.

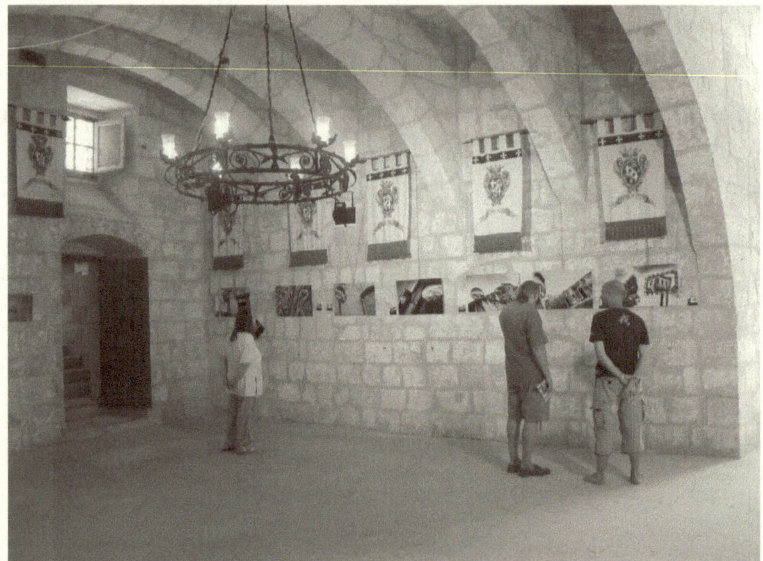

Photograph 7.1. Marc Bartolo welcomes visitors to his *Mirozo* exhibit at the Gozo International Contemporary Arts Festival, July 19, 2010. (Photograph by author)

Marc Bartolo, a photographer from Canada who now works out of Germany, was one such exhibitor who had traveled to Gozo for the festival (photograph 7.1). I spoke with him as he looked after the gallery in which his pieces were displayed. The series he exhibited, *Mirozo*, featured digitally manipulated images of the ubiquitous traffic mirrors on the island (hence the title for, "mirror + Gozo"). Reflected in the mirrors were features of buildings and the Gozitan landscape that were historical, iconic, or paradoxical in nature.

Marc stands in an interesting relationship to Gozo, however—although he was raised abroad and works in the global art circuit of fashion and fine art photography, his father is Gozitan. Thus, he claimed a certain familiarity with and ownership of Gozo as a place, implying a level of Gozitan identity. It seemed that his choice of subject matter was in part a revisiting of childhood experiences on the island, which perhaps explains his focus on the characteristic details of the streets.

The inclusion of the work of Dana Krantz, a German glass artist, provides another interesting example of the way in which international artists were selected for the festival. Although her primary medium is glass-painting, she now mostly produces jewelry and beads, selling mainly to tourists. Dana learned glasswork by studying at a school in Germany for three years and decided to move to Gozo after having visited on holiday as a child. Because the cost of renting a space for both a studio and a shop were less expensive on Gozo, it was more feasible for her to start her own business there rather than in Germany, where it would have been prohibitively expensive.

I spoke with Dana one afternoon in her studio and shop near the main square in Victoria. At the time, I was interested in distinctions between arts and crafts on Gozo, and Dana noted that she would personally classify her work as a craft. Nevertheless, she was grouped into the community of artists in the International Arts Festival, in part because of a preexisting connection to Raphael and her identity as an artist with an international background.

Gozitan Artists

In addition to the international artists, I also spoke with many Gozitan artists. Two of my main contacts were sculptor Paul Aquilina and painter Manuel Farrugia; both are active in producing materials for display during village *festas*, the annual celebration of Catholic patron saints (photograph 7.2). Every village or town in Malta has a patron saint, and in the case of larger locales, there are often saints for different districts or neighborhoods. The various festas (also referred to as "feasts") are staggered throughout the summer months, and each aims to put on a celebration more opulent than their neighbors'. Festivities include a series of street processions, fireworks, religious events, and plenty of eating, drinking, and socializing in the streets.

Paul was the very first artist on Gozo that I was introduced to; I met his mother through their family shop in Victoria that sells "religious articles," or small images and statuettes of saints to decorate the home. While asking her about the pieces in the shop (which were mostly made in Spain, Italy, and China), I inquired about the brightly painted statues I had seen lining the streets in preparation for the Saint George (San Gorg) feast. Hearing my question, she began to laugh—by coincidence, her son was one of several makers still producing these festa pieces throughout Gozo and Malta.

She described her son's interest in sculpture as a passion beginning in childhood. When I expressed a desire to speak with him, she suggested that I see his studio and offered to take me there, insisting that I really needed to see the statues and his workspace in order to understand his art. She told me that it is impossible to learn the artistic abilities that her son has "from a book." Rather, one must be born with the deep emotional connection and personal beliefs that, as she explained, allowed Paul to bring the images of festa saints into the physical world.

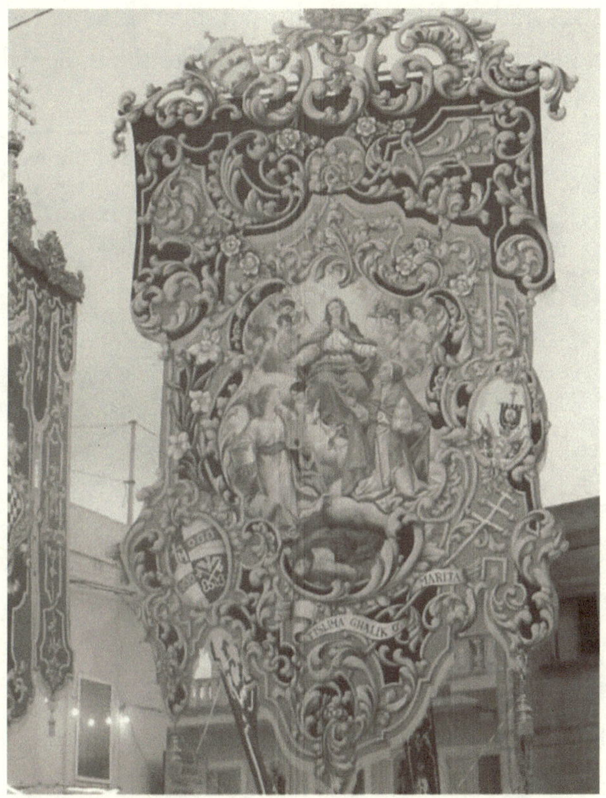

Photograph 7.2. Festa banner with center painting by Manuel Farrugia at the St. Gregory (San Girgor) festa in the town of Kercem, Gozo, July 10, 2010. (Photograph by author)

When I visited Paul's studio and spoke with him later, he often emphasized the self-taught nature of his sculpting abilities; this was a particular point of pride for him (photograph 7.3). He grew up admiring the statues of festa and wanted to reproduce the deep, personal connection he had with the experiences of growing up and living on Gozo. Indeed, his work and role as an artist were intimately tied to the yearly cycles of festa, and at the time, he was hurrying to complete a commission featuring three figures to be picked up for display on Malta. As I looked at the busts shaped in clay amongst the plaster mixes and wire frames in his hot, dusty studio, I was struck by the detailed, expressive faces that spoke to the undeniable talent of their maker.

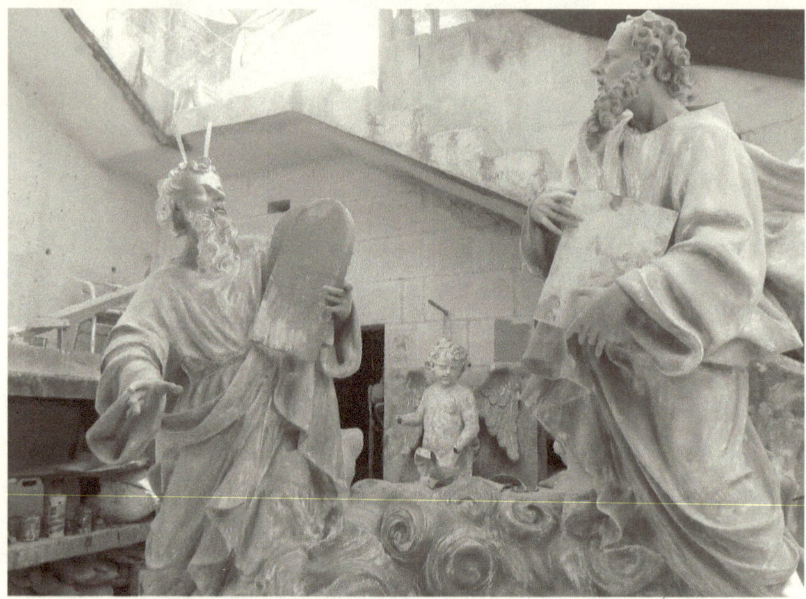

Photograph 7.3. Work-in-progress statues in Paul Aquilina's workshop, July 14, 2010. (Photograph by author)

It was through Paul that I met Manuel, who on occasion helps Paul paint his statues, especially when he is rushing to finish a commission. Although they differ in age (Manuel is in his early twenties, while Paul is older), they are good friends and remarked that when they are together, they constantly discuss art. Manuel, like Paul, works on commission to produce portraits of saints for festas throughout Gozo and Malta, although his medium is different: he works in oils, painting large images on canvases that are set into banners marking the procession routes. Working out of a basement studio at his parents' house in Victoria, he was also commuting to Malta for school (and art courses, in particular) several times per week. Manuel strives to make his paintings unique by using original poses sketched from his own photos; his friends and family have all been incorporated into the basis of his many pieces. Even though he creates images on commission according to his clients' expectations, he often includes tiny details from the original human portrait as a mark of his own distinction.

While discussing his work at his studio one afternoon, Manuel emphasized the need to travel beyond Gozo for further training. Early on, he took courses at the Wistin Camilleri Gozo Centre for Art & Crafts, Gozo's main source for arts education. However, he quickly felt he had surpassed the basic skills taught at the school and preferred to improve on his own before deciding to make the expensive and time-consuming commute to Malta. He spoke specifically about figure drawing classes, which he was attending at the time in order to improve his knowledge of human anatomy.

Although Manuel explained that schools on the main island provide more offerings than the Centre on Gozo, he said that training abroad is even more desirable. However, it seemed to be financially unattainable for him at the time—he almost had an opportunity to study art in Italy, but the government grant he had received fell through. He seemed frustrated by his inability to expand his resources further and expressed a desire to paint portraits and images of his own conception, free from the expectations of clients or the necessary imagery that accompanies festa saints. Nevertheless, he maintained a steady stream of festa commissions, often taking on projects from former teachers and older artists who could not accept every portrait they were asked to paint. He used the opportunities from commissions to practice his technique and sought to improve through classes available domestically and by reading and studying on his own.

Both Paul and Manuel base their livelihoods on their passion for producing works of art; however, they remained outside the circle of artists included in the International Contemporary Arts Festival. They were aware that the exhibit was currently on display, yet neither had gone to see it at the time that I spoke with them.

One of the Gozitan artists whose work was included in the International Arts Festival was George Vella, the owner of a painting supply and framing shop in Victoria. Raphael, the festival organizer, met George when he bought supplies from George's store upon first moving to Gozo, and he later approached George about exhibiting his work. George showed me a painting and two terra cotta busts that he had done, kept in the back room of his shop. With managing his business in order to support his growing family, however, he had no time to produce work of his own on a regular basis. The three terra cotta pieces on display in the International Arts Festival seemed to be the result of Raphael's encouragement; they had elemental themes and resembled masks or wall hangings, beautifully shaped and smoothly sculpted. Tellingly, the pieces that George showed me in the back room of his shop were of a decidedly religious nature—depictions of the Virgin Mary and Jesus. When left to his own creative devices, George seemed to gravitate toward the familiar imagery of the church, much in the same way that Paul (the festa sculptor) developed his sense of artistry at festas throughout his early life.

Other Artists and Arts Affiliates

Several of my other contacts were art instructors and local officials working with organizations related to the arts. I spoke with Kevin Sciberras, of the Culture Office for the Ministry for Gozo, at his office off one of the main squares in Victoria. The Culture Office's role is to "promote, organize and enhance cultural activities on the

Island of Gozo," as well as to work with local art galleries, church-affiliated band clubs, theatres, and other groups.[3] With the activities of festa artists, craftspeople making and selling their work to tourists, the Gozo Centre for Art & Crafts, and other events, Kevin described the arts scene on Gozo as "very vibrant," especially for such a small island. He also viewed the internationally informed Arts Festival in the Citadel as an attractive event to encourage tourists to visit the island, alongside the island's appealing historic sites and sunny beaches.

Kevin and the Culture Office put me in touch with Joseph Attard, director of the Wistin Camilleri Gozo Centre for Art & Crafts. As the major arts education resource on the island, the school offers a number of courses in a variety of mediums, including painting, ceramics, stained glass, and silverwork. I was also able to talk with Justin Falzon, a Gozitan painter with experience abroad who now teaches at the Centre for Art & Crafts, during my meeting at the school. Speaking about the goals of the Centre, Joseph emphasized the attainment of "professionalism" in the arts. While he acknowledged that achieving this was not possible for all students, he repeatedly invoked the desirability of such a status. Producing professional artists whose abilities could compete with those of artists abroad seemed to be an imperative that he, as the director, advocated.

Justin, a painting teacher at the center who had studied in Italy and the United States, expressed the need for increased educational resources for artists on Gozo and Malta. When I asked both Joseph and Justin about the décor of festa (they knew Paul, Manuel, and the other festa artists), they cited having to conform to a set of expected imagery in the depiction of religious subjects as artistically limiting. This mentality was echoed by several of the international artists of the Arts Festival in the Citadel; several people referred to festa sculptures as if they were less creative than their own work.

Joseph, Justin, and the other Centre affiliates that I spoke with more briefly represent an interesting position distinct from either the international artists on Gozo or their Gozitan counterparts. They inhabit a space between the local and the international; they are Gozitan, and yet they tapped into a wider, more global "fine arts" sensibility.

At the time that I visited the Centre for Art & Crafts, Joseph and the other officials were working on a press release announcing the first nude figure drawing class to be offered at the school. Joseph, Justin, and another former director (who remained involved after his retirement) described the resistance to the class from older, conservative members of the community with exasperation. Justin seemed especially frustrated. All three framed the community's conservatism partly in terms of a sense of religious modesty.

While the Gozitan artists and teachers at the Centre for Art & Crafts echoed the view of the international artists of the International Contemporary Arts Festival—namely, that the "art scene" and its resources on Gozo were inadequate—their perspective was far more complex. At once thoroughly Gozitan, and yet connected to a view of art that originated beyond Gozo, they also understood intimately the significance of festa (one of the other teachers I was introduced to made pedestals for festa statues in addition to teaching at the school). Even though aspects of traditional, Catholic culture on Malta and Gozo conflicted with their more global ideas of art, they were working within their own home communities to improve the resources that they thought should be available to artists locally.

By contrast, the international artists on Gozo, with little understanding of, or connection to the traditions of festa, tended to see only the limitations of the arts community on the island without knowledge of the long-standing artistic traditions of festa.

Defining Art: Foreign Standards and Local Talent

While some Gozitan artists were struggling to reconcile the expectations of a view of "art" defined elsewhere with the traditions and practices of their local communities, the international artists of the Contemporary Arts Festival frequently brought their own conception of "Gozitanness" or "Malteseness" to the island and, interestingly, incorporated it into their work.

The most poignant example of this I encountered was a strange coincidence that came up in a conversation with Marc (the photographer) and Dana (the German glass artist). While I was chatting with Dana in her shop, Marc dropped by to tell her, excitedly, that he had "found the perfect model" for his "Venus of Malta photo shoot." Several of the most popular historical attractions in Malta include Neolithic statues of "fertility goddesses" found throughout the archipelago, similar to the famous Venus of Willendorf; the most prominent of these is referred to as the "Venus of Malta." In fact, these figures were a popular theme in the art of the International Contemporary Arts Festival. Raphael and others had created paintings and other works depicting "Venus of Malta" figures in reference to the history and culture of the islands. Yet these works did not appear to reflect an authentically Maltese or Gozitan experience in that they shared no similarities in style with festa artwork or other local cultural imagery. Malta and Gozo may have been the subject being explored in these pieces, but their conception was clearly informed by a more pan-European or global "fine art" aesthetic.

For his photo shoot, Marc wanted to create a photograph of a nude woman at the edge of one of Gozo's characteristic limestone beaches, but it seemed as though he had trouble finding a model for the image he had in mind. As he described the woman he had just met, we realized that she was, in fact, one of the directors of my field school—a Scottish woman with long, blonde hair and blue eyes.

While the photo-shoot never actually materialized, I found Marc's vision of the "perfect" Venus of Malta fascinating—her fair complexion perfectly matched a classically Eurocentric notion of beauty befitting a "Venus" figure, yet she was completely unlike the dark-haired, olive-skinned people that actually populate Malta and Gozo. It was clear that Marc was comfortable interacting with people from abroad while on the island, but I speculated that he had made little effort to approach Maltese women in his search for a model.

The preconceptions about art and its aesthetic, technical, and functional standards that enabled this interaction to take place also created the dividing line between artists included within the International Contemporary Arts Festival and those left outside of its exhibits. While the Arts Festival was based initially on Raphael's own network of international artists and those he had met since moving to Gozo, assumptions about the religious artworks for festa and Gozo's artistic communities also worked to distance artists like Paul and Manuel, with their depictions of saints, from the activities of the international artists (photograph 7.4).

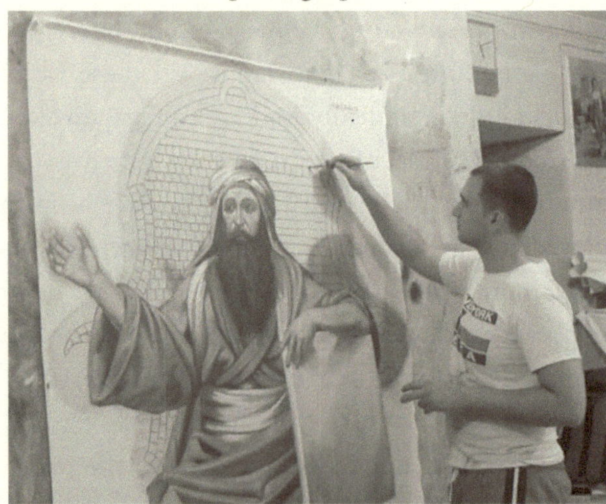

Photograph 7.4. Manuel painting a commissioned piece in his studio in Victoria, Gozo, July 22, 2010. (Photograph by author)

Many of the international artists criticized the skills of local artists based on a lack of "proper" or "official" arts training, both directly and indirectly. It was frequently implied that little artistic vision and minimal technical skills were required to reproduce the imagery of Catholic saints (an opinion strongly contrasting my own observations while visiting Paul's workshop and Manuel's studio). Not only were the art courses and training available on the island considered inadequate compared to standards abroad, but also foreign artists often distinguished their work in ways that contained negative opinions about the talent required to create pieces for display in festas.

While I was speaking to one person, she gestured toward a festa statue in the street and told me that some Maltese people would point to that and say it was "really good art." She then shrugged and said, "It depends on what you call art." When I asked her about the "art scene" on Gozo, she also insisted that there was not much of an arts community. She said that anyone who had "held a brush in their hand" or "taken an art class for two weeks" considered themselves an artist. However, this person had also considered enrolling in a goldsmithing class at the School of Art & Crafts to learn some basics to incorporate into her work. Nevertheless, she implied that the school was not a legitimate source of rigorous arts education beyond a basic, introductory level and left much to be desired compared to training she had undertaken elsewhere.

Several of the local artists echoed the viewpoint that the education and exhibition opportunities for artists were limited on Gozo. While this may seem paradoxical, I suggest that Manuel, Joseph Attard, Justin Falzon, and others expressed this perspective in part because of their own exposure to outside views of art that connected them to expectations of the international mainstream. And unlike the visiting or expatriate foreign artists, they are intimately connected to their Gozitan communities. For Manuel, this means that pursuing a passion for painting manifests as a career in painting festa banners; for Justin and Joseph, it means actively striving to improve available art classes on the island through teaching and administrative work at the Centre for Art & Crafts.

Meanwhile, Paul emphasized the self-taught nature of his sculpting abilities, occupying the furthest position from international influence. This is not to imply that he is in any way naïve or sheltered from international perspectives; rather, he is instead focused on the Maltese and Gozitan communities around him. His status as an artist is based upon the traditions of festa and therefore local, thoroughly *Gozitan*, definitions of art.

Another part of the distinction international artists made between local art and their own dealt with the subject matter and purpose of the work. Marc emphasized that his work was "about an emotional moment," a very personal and fleeting experience. By contrast, he characterized festa décor as "functional." This was a descriptive word that people often applied to the difference between objects of "craft" and objects of "art," although most of the people that I successfully engaged this topic with were foreigners or Maltese and Gozitan artists and craftspeople who had lived abroad. Nevertheless, Marc qualifying the festa statues and banners as "functional" (in that they serve a decorative purpose for a community event) effectively distanced them from objects that reside in museums and galleries.

Paul and Manuel's audiences are the communities of Gozo and Malta, rather than the elite, global network of museum-oriented "fine" art makers and critics. Thus, they were not in contact with Raphael and were not within the scope of those considered for the International Contemporary Arts Festival. This is illustrated interestingly in the case of George Vella's pieces—those that Raphael encouraged him to exhibit in the International Arts Festival appealed to the aesthetics and expressive philosophy of "art for art's sake," while his equally impressive sculptures and paintings of religious figures were left to the cluttered back room of his framing shop.

The assumptions of the international artists, as well as the frustrations of Justin and Joseph of the Centre for Art & Crafts, often rested on criticisms of the canon religious imagery of festa artwork. Yet the emphasis on reproducing familiar symbolism in festa-related work seemed to be more a question of style than a matter of stifling religious restrictions. Rather, notions of individualism, expressiveness, and innovation that come from a mainstream, foreign sense of "art" seemed to be more crucial in determining what works were considered art and what works were not for the purposes of the International Contemporary Arts Festival.

The expectation that art should express the individual rather than the collective, or be innovative rather than reiterative, belongs to an international perspective. Paul's festa sculptures derive their meaning in part by communicating a set of established symbols affiliated with each saint; likewise, Manuel's work does this in order to fulfill his clients' expectations, even while he strives simultaneously to make their interpretation his own.

Paul also emphasized the importance of copying famous Maltese statues to learn about form or create reproductions to keep in the home. When I first met his mother in their family shop, she likened the practice of displaying images of saints to having pictures of your family nearby—a vital part of daily life. Paul's pieces that depict Jesus, the Virgin Mary, and patron saints are reflective of the aesthetic, religious, and traditional values and experiences shared with his community. Yet these same pieces, informed by a Gozitan way of life, had no place in the International Contemporary Arts Festival's definition of "art."

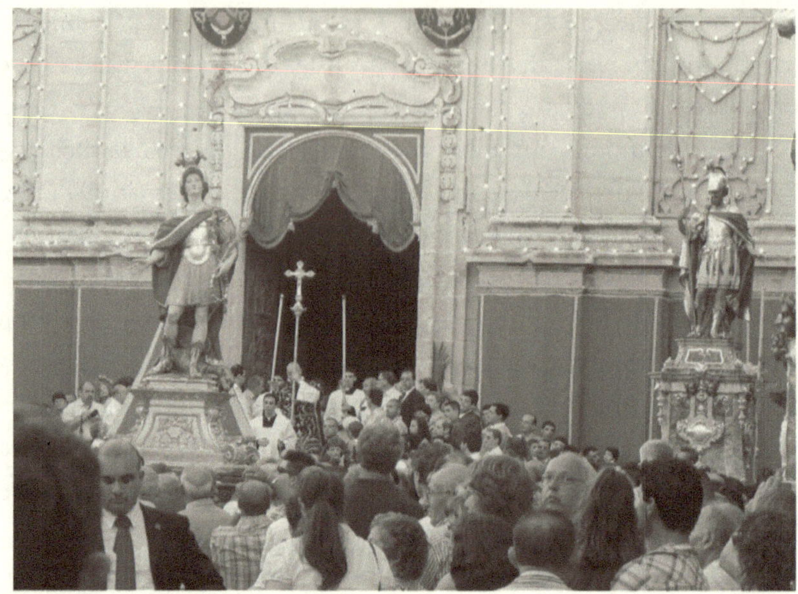

Photograph 7.5. Festa procession carrying the statue of St. George (San Gorg) in Victoria, July 18, 2010. (Photograph by author)

By examining the ways in which the parameters of "art" were defined in the first Gozo International Contemporary Arts Festival, it is possible to glimpse a portion of the truly abundant activities of artists and artisans working and creating on Gozo and Malta. The tensions between global and local present in the international artists' definitions of art, and the separation between local traditions and the activities of the International Contemporary Arts Festival, ultimately speak to broader dynamics of globalization occurring throughout the Maltese islands today.

Although many of the international artists coming to Gozo may overlook the images of saints in festa as gaudy or formulaic, perhaps it is Kevin Sciberras' view of the "vibrant" arts scene on Gozo that includes room for the statues and banners of festa, as well as the photographs, sculptures, and paintings of the International Contemporary Arts Festival.

Notes

1. This field school is run by Sam Janssen and Marc Vanlangendonck and affiliated with the Katholieke Universiteit Leuven. For more information, visit http://www.anthropologyfieldschool.org/.

2. All names that appear in this chapter are used with the permission of the individual; for instances in which permission was not obtained, I have omitted the names entirely (no pseudonyms are used).

3. See http://www.gozo.gov.mt/gozoportal/ministry_for_gozo/departments/dted/cultureoffice.aspx, accessed June 1, 2012.

Thomas Kinkade: Money, Class, and the Aesthetic Economy

Susan Falls

Abstract

Contemporary art is seldom given sustained anthropological analysis despite its tantalizing potential. As a response, this essay examines the work of Thomas Kinkade to cast an oblique light on the production of value. Kinkade's mechanically reproduced opus representing Cotswold cottages, quaint city scenes, and Disney fantasies are sold by authorized dealers in malls, along tourist strips, and online. Rather than operating as kitsch, lowbrow, or a new model for art-making, Kinkade's overt profit motive, self-celebration, and evangelical Christianity refract political, economic, and especially aesthetic constructions that undergird contemporary markets. A bad boy of the aesthetic economy, Kinkade's work, mostly dismissed by the established art world, nevertheless has much to say about it, and about us. Ultimately, I suggest that The Painter of Light's™ success shows that aesthetic sensibility is integral to political economy, rather than epiphenomenal to it, and that we must therefore pay attention to the role of art therein.

I have been fascinated by the question of value for some time. Some kinds of art are quite valuable, at least from a monetary perspective: Picasso's *Nude, Green Leaves and Bust* for example, sold on the secondary market at Christie's May 2010 auction for $95 million. But how do we get from a conglomeration of relatively inexpensive paint, wood, and canvas to expensive art? What is actually being sold? Where does its value come from? How is aesthetic value defined, produced, and recognized? What is "value" anyway? Where do aesthetics meet money?[1]

Moving beyond standard economic models of value that hinge upon exchange, anthropological theories take on many forms and consider a broad range of variables such as labor, use, class, sentimentality, morality, semiotics, and so forth. The anthropological lens is multivalent, even kaleidoscopic: "From Smith and Ricardo to Marx and Mauss, and by way of Simmel and Saussure, the category has been used in varied ways to illuminate ethical, economic, aesthetic, logical, linguistic, and political dimensions of human life . . . The value of value may lie in its ability to elucidate and move across boundaries of many kinds" (Eiss and Pedersen 2008, 283, 287). Value is, thus, a foundational category and deserving of exploration across all domains of activity and experience.

Many anthropological theories start with Marx and develop "value" in ways that attend to some aspect of labor, use, or exchange with regard to contemporary capitalism. David Graeber, in *Toward An Anthropological Theory of Value: The False Coin of Our Own Dreams*, for example, combines theoretical treatments by Mauss, Bhaskar, and Piaget to argue for value as a form of creative action (2001). Contributors to Meyer's edited *Empire of Things: Regimes of Value and Material Culture* (2002) take on implications of Weiner's theory of inalienability within a capitalist context alongside Appadurai's demonstration that objects take on different meanings as they move through different cultural contexts (Appadurai 1986; Weiner 1992). Taking a completely different angle, Foster (2007) explores how consumers, in the act of consumption, add value to goods over and above that promoted by marketing. Each of these texts show that value can be used as a theoretical lens to transcend restrictive binary categories (like production vs. consumption or gift vs. commodity) and can provide an analytic device to address how social groups are connected by their interaction with a set or kind of good even when separated by time or space. Using value in this way, however, usually requires a sustained consideration of historical context.

Now, there is a small, but important, set of anthropological studies that take on art from the perspective of value and political economy; for example, Adler (1979) examined art as a form of labor while Plattner (1996) performed an ethnography of midlevel art markets. In connecting aesthetic to historical dynamics, Winegar (2006) wields value theory to investigate international markets for art, showing how the value of art operates as both an index and a tool in the negotiation of postcolonial identities and relationships. And Falls and Smith (2011a, 2011b) show that a colonialist legacy of ideas about the Khmer person, the historical migration of weaving practices, and the waxing and waning of dyeing technologies, all nested within the consumption practices of capitalism, enhance exchange value for both tourist and couture Cambodian *ikat* textiles. All of these anthropologies of art show how expressive culture is deeply entwined with other regimes of value and meaning.

Just as different notions of *value* appear in theory and analysis, the construction of the term varies in everyday talk. It is a word whose meaning at once expands and dissolves upon closer inspection, "value" is never inert. Its force is felt in every domain of social life—from the political and economic to the aesthetic, religious, scientific, semantic, and personal. And so, any study of value should consider a range of questions about relationships between various forms of value. I am specifically interested in examining the relationship between art and value: How is art valued? How much is value about content, and how much is it about context? What are the short- and long-term consequences—to art, to artists, and to the publics they activate—of art becoming a financial instrument? What are the larger functions of art markets? The invisible logic that allows us to attach monetary value to visual culture can be penetrated by examining market extremes through the lens of political economy. Understanding recent movements in financial markets can help us understand why a screen print, paper collage of Jacqueline Kennedy by Andy Warhol sold at a 2012 auction for $626,000, more than twice the price of an average house sold in that same year in the United States. To illustrate the scales at which questions of art and value might to be considered, this essay focuses on a shallow slice of time for the market and addresses the work of (the recently deceased) American artist Thomas Kinkade.[2]

The Art Market

In 2007, the Dow Jones Industrial Average peaked at 14,198 points, and the art market reached unprecedented highs, with global revenue for fine art approaching $9.4 billion, more than double the $4.2 billion total for 2005 (Artprice 2010, 7). It seemed that the sky was the limit for both, so I followed with great interest how the 2008 financial crisis affected the contemporary art market (which makes up about 10 percent of the auction market), the total value of which has soared from $82 to $955 million in the last decade. Artwork by Hirst, Koons, and Murakami, which had done well in the years leading up to 2008, lost value and became scarcer in secondary (auction) sales.

Apropos of these shifts, Chris Burden's 2009 Gagosian LA show, in which he planned to mount 3.3 million dollars worth of gold bars, was suspended because the bars, which were to serve as a reflection on the notion of value itself as well as on cultural behavior surrounding things of value, were confiscated by the SEC as part of an investigation of Allen Stanford, the "Bernie Madoff" of LA, with whom Larry Gagosian had invested. The text on the Gagosian website explaining the problem read:

> We regret to inform you that the opening reception on Saturday, March 7 must be cancelled.
>
> 100 kilos of gold bricks bought by Gagosian Gallery for CHRIS BURDEN: *One Ton One Kilo* was purchased from Stanford Coins and Bullion, a subsidiary of Stanford Financial Group, which as widely reported in the press, is now in receivership. Unfortunately, the gallery's gold has been frozen while the SEC investigates Stanford.
>
> CHRIS BURDEN: *One Ton One Kilo* cannot be mounted until the gold bullion is released. Please continue to check our website for a new opening date.[3]

This notice, ironically, is perhaps an even more powerful meditation on the relationship between material and ideological weights and measures, the art market, and hierarchies of value than Burden's work itself. In fact, the constructed nature of value in the art world became acutely visible across the world as the larger financial crisis deepened, with real estate, investment portfolios, and artworks losing significant value.

There were more tectonic changes during the following year, 2010. As the Dow Jones continued to plunge and unemployment and foreclosure rates rose, Thomas Kinkade declared bankruptcy. China overtook the United States and the United Kingdom as the world's largest auction-place for Fine Art (Artprice 2010). Many of the new buyers were the emerging Chinese million- and billionaire-class, and several Chinese artists acquired top-selling status. Today, the Occupy Wall Street movement should give the art world pause since the trading practices being protested, especially complex deals on the derivatives market, have been in play with regard to skyrocketing art prices ever since the deregulation of financial markets (Tett 2009).[4]

Scholars tracking the dialogue between political economy and aesthetic shifts have productively understood art as labor, as a tool of the state, or even as a social world unto itself (Alexander and Rueschemeyer 2005; Becker 1984; Thornton 2008; Wolff 1993). Even more intriguing is work by art world insiders who have investigated the dynamics of commoditization (Eiss and Pedersen 2008; Graw 2010; Stallybrass 2004). Werner's (2005) devastating analysis of the Guggenheim franchise *Museum, Inc.* argues that museum leadership, in keeping with best practices in neoliberal governance, began treating their collection as financial capital, thus undermining arts' aesthetic and even academic character. When art becomes *primarily* an investment vehicle, it becomes an alibi for the institution whose main function it is to maintain the status quo. Here, content recedes into the background, and the art dematerializes. Could dematerialization be a new condition for art in a neoliberal context?

Insights drawn from both Walter Benjamin (1968) and Thorstein Veblen ([1894] 1964) can help us to understand better the work of Thomas Kinkade (Bush 1978). Sitting at the opposite end of the spectrum of critical acclaim from unique works included in the Guggenheim collection, the work sold as Kinkade art exemplifies mechanical reproduction in the age of neoliberalism. Together, the means of production and class-based collecting practices for Kinkade pieces cast into visibility a special relationship between art and political economy.

But, first, who is Thomas Kinkade, and why discuss him in the same paper with critically acclaimed artists who show in A-list galleries and museums and sell work at record-breaking prices? If you are searching your Art History 101 memory for some reference to this work, you will likely not find it, although an excellent collection of essays, mostly by art historians, on *Thomas Kinkade: The Artist in the Mall* was just published by a prestigious academic press (Boylan 2011). Kinkade, self-proclaimed Painter of Light™ and "most collected living artist" in America, is rarely mentioned in college courses and certainly not in the company of respected collectables like Warhol, Murakami, or Hirst, although there are striking similarities, if not in the work itself, then in the context by which their work accrues value, and thus meaning. In fact, most critics have completely ignored Kinkade, whose work is completely disengaged with contemporary art trends.[5]

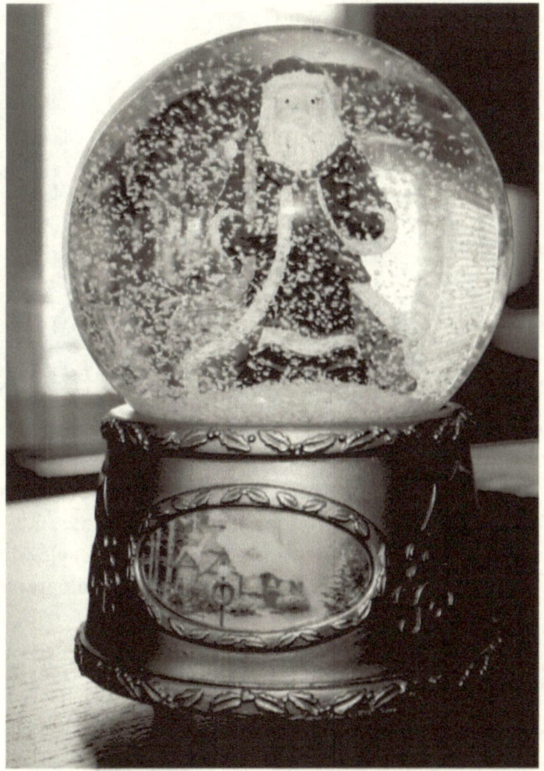

Photograph 8.1. In this example of Kinkade merchandise, Santa weathers the storm. (Photograph by author)

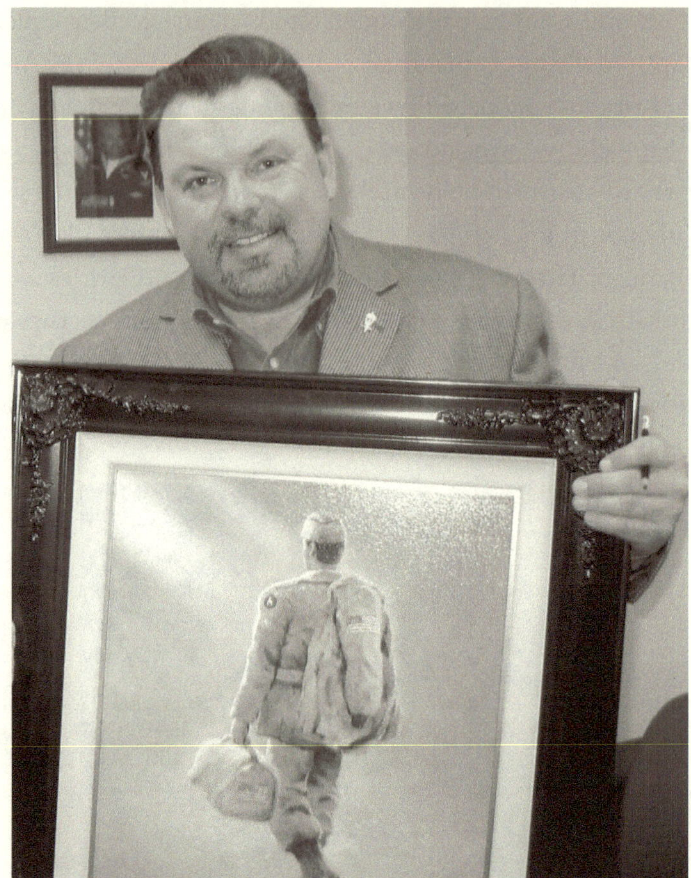

Photograph 8.2. Thomas Kinkade posing with *Coming Home* in 2005 said, "Peace and safety go hand in hand. The joy of living is the joy of freedom. Without freedom, there is no joy in life . . . I paint a world free from war, free from terrorism, free from fear and hatred and anger. The world I paint, I think it's very affirming of the beliefs of people in this country and of the service people who are overseas waging a war to protect those beliefs" (Quigley 2005). (Photograph in the public domain)

Though he has been called a naïve postmodernist, and perhaps for good reason, Kinkade has described his own work as antimodernist. He says he is following in the plein air, impressionist tradition, with most of his work representing unpeopled dramatic landscapes and cottage scenes. Thomas Kinkade products contain relentlessly sanitized images of romantic nature, cozy home life, and apple-pie Americana without any trace of irony or pastiche. God, nature, and family are not dead; none of that ever happened. In his more performative moments, he assumed a vaguely French persona, wearing a beret or taking the name Robert Girrard. Recent work has an overtly evangelical and/or patriotic bent, sometimes veering toward NASCAR or Disney.

You will not find this work at Gagosian or white cube-style galleries, taste-making museums, art fairs, or major auctions, although the artist Jeffrey Vallance did put together what turned out to be a rather controversial installation of Kinkade's works at California State at Fullerton's Grand Central Art Center. This fascinating exhibit, *Heaven on Earth*, displayed a vast array of original paintings and "Kinkadia," bric-a-brac modeled on Kinkade's aesthetic that was to serve as a shrine as well as a contemporary installation work. The strength of the exhibit was in its ambiguous position on the painter and the work, with Vallance intimating that Kinkade is the ultimate trickster (Vallance 2011; Vallance and Kinkade 2004).

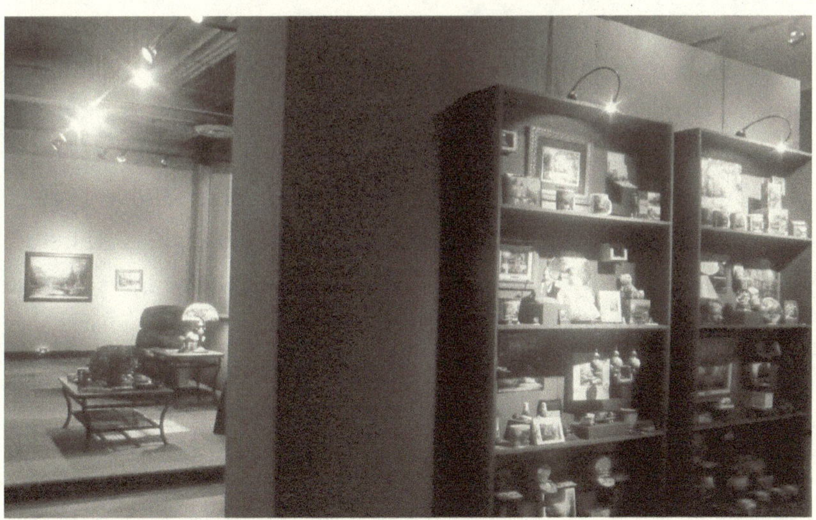

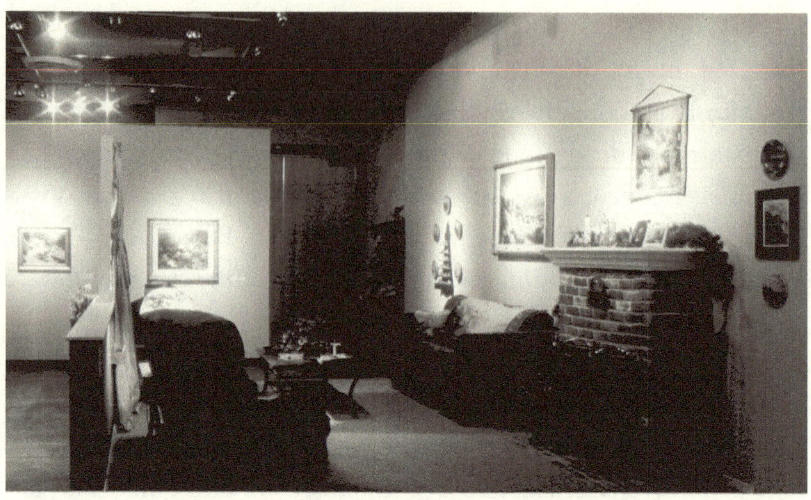

Photographs 8.3 and 8.4. Installation views of *Heaven on Earth,* curated by Jeffrey Vallance, Grand Central Art Center, Santa Ana, California. (Used by permission of Jeffrey Vallance)

But most of Kinkade's fans meet him in "Gold" and "Silver" Signature stores in malls, along tourist strips, and at QVC and online. Here in Savannah, Georgia (where I teach anthropology at an art and design school), a Kinkade "Gallery Of Light" appears alongside horse and buggy rides, trinket stores, and fudge shoppes to complete the old-timey tourist scene that makes up City Market. Exemplary of what anthropologist David Howes (2005) calls the "experience economy," this carpeted, family room simulacra houses chatty franchise owners who (seem to) believe in the "paintings" and less pricey "merch" like night-lights, teddy bears, and fridge magnets. The store is busy; tourists come in to browse, turn the gallery lights up and down to view the luminescent effect on the pictures, and visit pieces that they already have or aspire to buy. The interior design, friendliness, and Muzak are deliberate semiotic departures from silent "white-cube" spaces that are sparse, brightly lit, and overseen by hushed galleristas.

That there is a cash register in plain view is no mistake; anyone can purchase these objects (supposedly, one in twenty American homes boasts a "Living the Light" lifestyle item), in contrast to the pedigree needed to purchase work from elite galleries who ask potential buyers (Thornton 2008): What else do you own? What will you do with it? Can you be trusted not to negatively impact the price of other works? Many, if not most, of Kinkade's customers have never owned anything they considered to be art, a fact that the Kinkade franchise promotes as a democratization of the aesthetic economy.

Given these facts, it is interesting to note that Kinkade is himself no art world outsider, at least by virtue of training or contacts, but he is a rogue of sorts. Born in northern California under modest circumstances, he serendipitously met and apprenticed under the painter Glenn Wessels, who helped arrange for his admission to the University of California at Berkeley. Kinkade later attended Pasadena Art Center College of Design, where his tightly choreographed narrative reports, he became "bored" when asked to draw a nude model and had a religious conversion experience, producing a veiled Jesus instead (although he reportedly does have a collection of erotic paintings that are not for sale).[6] Later, Hollywood fantasy illustrator Frank Frazetta hired him to paint background images for Ralph Bakshi's now canonical rotoscope feature *Fire and Ice*, which has been convincingly described as a spectacular example of "batshit crazy" pornokitsch (Anne 2010).[7]

But, in spite of his insider background and training, his work—repetitive, sugary, and formulaic almost to the point of parody—is wholly detached from concepts or trends that receive critical attention in the art world. He claims to reject what he characterizes as a postmodern, antiChristian, antimoral Establishment that has failed to embrace him. But, finding that his small "impressionistic" renderings of the Carmel seaside did have a market, Kinkade and a partner started Lighthouse Publishing in 1989, eventually selling mechanically reproduced giclees upon which workers he calls "master highlighters" dab bits of paint to make the piece look like a painting that supposedly accrues value over time. The few giclees that have been dabbed by Kinkade himself, thus imparting his aura, are the most expensive, while the thousands of giclees touched only by lowly workshop staff are the least pricey. These giclees are pointedly sold as investments; potential customers are given a price sheet and educated about how the relative rarity impacts the price of the "editions" of each painting.

Kinkade models his sales strategy on the idea that art is a financial investment while simultaneously shunning the kind of art for which this strategy works best. And while investors of Kinkade products are still waiting for their investments to pay off, Kinkade himself was making a fortune until 2010 when his company, then called Media Arts, filed for bankruptcy. That the fall of Kinkade's business is related to the collapse of the global economy that also put the kibosh on Burden's show and impacted the value of Hirst's opus is a given. But what kind of artist is Kinkade, and how does political economy link him to A-list figures?

Commenting on the admixture of art theory and finance, Andy Warhol remarked that "being good in business is the most fascinating kind of art. Making money is art and working is art and good business is the best art" (Stiles 1996, 342). So perhaps making money through franchised aesthetics is Kinkade's revenge against what he calls the critical elite. Perhaps his business is his art. Is this all an elaborate performance meant to cast cultural trends into critical relief? While the idea represents an intriguing possibility, I suspect this would be giving Kinkade too much credit.

When Joseph Beuys, another art world darling with a famous definition of the artist, said that everyone is an artist, what he meant was that there could be artistry to funneling the inchoate into order, through material or language. An artist is one who expresses or transforms, the medium is not important. One might even argue, like Goebbels did, that the political order is the plastic art of the state (Frankl [1946] 2006). In a similar vein, Giorgio Agamben (2009), in his essay "What is Contemporary," defines an artist as one who is not only reflexive but also "sees into the darkness," understanding what others do not and bringing an alternative vista to our attention (44-47). Kinkade certainly sees himself in this role, or at least pretends to, and in this sense, is perhaps more interesting, even if he is unwitting, than Warhol's businessman or Beuys' everyman. But, I would like to sidestep debates about intention and what a "real" artist is like, and instead levy Agamben's claim to explore the value of Kinkade's work, which is where the Gordian knot of aesthetics and political economy really comes into play.

With the rise of commodity capitalism, where identity is produced and maintained by displaying the mass-produced goods that we purchase, art has emerged as a major category of investment and consumption. Forget about Marxian notions of labor, use, and surplus value, as well as the twinned notions of supply and demand (traditional categories through which economists have understood value). The relevant categories are now sign and exchange value. Semiotically, visual culture has shifted from ornament to index under capitalist conditions, where its salient characteristics are novelty, obtuseness, and the collapse of meaning into price. In other words, relatively "useless" objects can obtain social meaning by virtue of cost and the degree to which it is new, unique, or hard to acquire. That Kinkade explicitly advances the decorative value of his work by instructing consumers on the imaginative steps they should take to appreciate it and attempts to imbue the work with a spiritual aura through linguistic and marketing gymnastics is testament to the threat of art as ornament.

On the other hand, with regard to exchange value, Kinkade's prices adhere to a highly managed pyramid scale, with a relatively expensive and "rare" giclee highlighted by "master apprentices" valued at about $1,000. At the other end of the art market, Damien Hirst's *The Physical Impossibility of Death in the Mind of Someone Living*, or the stuffed shark, sold for $12 million, and Tranquility, a butterfly series painting, also executed by assistants, recently fetched over $1.7 million. What I want to suggest is that although they are positioned at opposite ends of the art world, Kinkade, Hirst, and their respective consumers are all enabled and codefined by the context of consumer capitalism in which they are equally ensconced. Like two sides of the same coin, Kinkade is the anti-Hirst.

What do I mean by this? Many new millionaires and even billionaires were produced as a result of Reagan's and Thatcher's economic policies, sometimes referred to as postmodern capitalism or advanced neoliberal capitalism (Harvey 2005). Neoliberalism, the dominant political economic practice (first in the United States and the United Kingdom, and then elsewhere in the politically "relevant" world) since the 1980s, proposes that "human well-being is best advanced by liberating individual entrepreneurial freedoms and skills within an institutional framework characterized by strong private property rights, free markets, and free trade" (Harvey 2005, 2). This policy includes deregulation of the financial markets, a sector I mention in particular because now hedge fund managers and other money wizards, like Steve Cohen who purchased Hirst's shark, can make upwards of $90,000 an hour (Thompson 2008). And what are these financial wizards to do with this wealth? How can a new millionaire distinguish himself? One way is to compete for what Veblen calls status granting "conspicuous consumption" through the purchase of fine art. Here, prestige—political, economic, social, and aesthetic—is simultaneously generated, exchanged, intermingled, and displayed.

Clearly, aesthetic activity belies political and economic capital and is foundational to contemporary capitalism. I say foundational because aesthetic sociality provides a medium through which people display, claim, or even negotiate, an ethos of worthiness, taste, "beauty," and genius. And it is not a mere coincidence that the fine art market has, in many ways, become as attractive a place for elites to invest as the stock trade. The big money game of contemporary art is deeply implicated in the conspicuous consumption around which neoliberal capitalism revolves.

But what is perhaps even more significant is emulation of the higher by the lower classes because it represents overall buy in to a system of status making, a buy in to deepening class inequality by middle and working classes who, by the way, constitute Kinkade's customer base. For most of them, buying power of wages has been flat since the 1980s, while worker productivity is up in the face of offshoring, temporary and contract work, layoffs, forced vacation, and unpaid furlough, which have all contributed to massive increases in wealth for top earners. As one snarky Salon critic put it, Kinkade's work is created for "very, very worn-out and perhaps even traumatized people" (Miller 2002), and perhaps there is some truth to this. Frankfurt School scholars like Benjamin, Horkheimer, and Adorno certainly understood mass-produced culture as functioning to help wrecked workers refuel for the next day of industrialized drudgery.

Seen from another angle, the distance between Kinkade and more expensive market artists reflects the culture-wars world where educated critique has become "elitist"; citizens are flattened into consumer types, and nostalgia for disinfected nature, safe hometowns, and old-fashioned morality is a reigning mode of collective identity. Here, actual politics—the making of decisions by an informed public for the greater good—is reduced to a popularity contest between candidates whose positions differ only in the most superficial of ways. And it is small wonder that people suffering from such structural violence might be drawn to the kind of refuge Kinkade explicitly says he is creating.

Kinkade's work, however, is different from that of artists like Hirst or Koons, because while, like a good auctioneer, store personnel perform an elaborate sales pitch to explicate content and even build art historical value, they work particularly hard to position his products as an "investment" for a public who have no or very little experience with venture art. This is important because it recapitulates the idea that content can become secondary to exchange value, even at this level. So far, their efforts have been wildly successful. Between 1997 and 2005, Thomas Kinkade earned more than $50 million dollars in royalties (Christenson 2006).

Mechanical Reproduction in the Age of Neoliberalism

The art market invites exploration of larger contexts because buying and selling art is a rarified universe in which cultural dynamics are cast into relief. Kinkade's work—mechanical reproduction in the age of neoliberalism—is a powerfully literal expression of contemporary values, and it tells us who we are, just as Hirst's, Murakami's, or Warhol's does. The same dynamics that produce soaring prices for stuffed sharks, masturbating cowboys, and screen prints of soup cans, make possible the "Most Collected Artist in America." They are mirror images, extremes at the ends of a single continuum.

Our interactions with aesthetics, especially in the arena of venture art, operate within a system that transfers wealth toward the top one to two percent. Investment in hedge funds and real estate has been augmented by investing in art—paintings, for example, are unique instruments that confer status as well as potentially making money. As Veblen had pointed out by 1899, the proletariat emulates consumption by the leisure class. Kinkade has rightly expected and exploited this behavior, promoting his work as investment-grade art for the working person.

While a few exceptional texts are out there, the social and economic context of the art world remains largely unexamined by anthropologists. But the aesthetic economy, as an object of study and as an activity, is critical to the reproduction of social realities. So while we do not have to like or respect them, it is for this reason that aesthetic workers like Thomas Kinkade and his constituents must be taken seriously.

Acknowledgments

I would like to thank Capri Rosenberg, Aseel Sawalha, Lisa Young, Craig Campbell, Mary Doll, and Dare Dukes for their insightful commentary on this chapter. I would also like to thank two reviewers whose careful reading and feedback enhanced the chapter. This project was funded in part through a Presidential Fellowship for Faculty Development from the Savannah College of Art and Design.

Notes

1. Research for this paper was funded by a Savannah College of Art and Design Presidential Fellowship. I would also like to thank Capri Rosenberg, Jeffrey Vallance, Chris Campbell, Geoff Taylor, Lisa Young, Mary Doll, Dare Dukes, the two anonymous reviewers, and the Thomas Kinkade gallery in Savannah, Georgia, for their generous help. All errors remain my own.

2. Thomas Kinkade died in 2012 of acute intoxication of alcohol and Valium. He was at the time with Amy Pinto-Walsh, his live-in girlfriend of eighteen months. Galleries reported an uptick in sales following his death (Cox 2012).

3. This notice was taken from the Gagosian website, http://www.gagosian.com/exhibitions/chris-burden, accessed January 1, 2012.

4. For play-by-play on the deregulation of the financial markets, see http://www.marketoracle.co.uk/Article8210.html.

5. Critic Dave Hickey, friendlier to the popular than most, said of Kinkade that he "pretended to make terrible, disingenuous paintings that were mostly cranked out in a factory in China. You can tell by the excessive use of thalo green and alizarin crimson-Chinese restaurant colors. Also, they are all pastiche; Saxon cottages do not have bay windows." Even this dismissal of Kinkade was more than most critics were willing to state. (For the complete Hickey interview, see http://www.planetjh.com/music_arts_culture/A_108312.aspx.)

6. I recently heard Kinkade describe this experience on a YouTube video of the Press Conference for the Vallance installation. Kinkade reports that he was not aware that he was drawing Jesus. When he looked down and saw the image, he was surprised. It was as if the hand of God had drawn it. Kinkade then went on to preempt any "postmodern critics" who will say this sounds hokey by suggesting that in the modern era it was not that uncommon for people

to experience such spiritual events. This narrative was very much in keeping with Kinkade's ongoing efforts to position himself as an artist representing values of a bygone time. In his decidedly modernist posing, he weirdly appears to inhabit a postmodern sensibility. One does wonder at times if the entire exercise is not an elaborate ruse. (See Jeffrey Vallance's "Thomas Kinkade: Heaven on Earth," which was curated by Jeffrey Vallance http://www.youtube.com/watch?v=64m0i6a8wPY.)

7. *Fire and Ice* has been rated the 99th greatest film of all time by the online film critics society. (See "OFCS Top 100: Top 100 Animated Features," http://www.ofcs.org/2010/09/ofcs-top-100-top-100-animated-features.html, accessed October 17, 2011.)

References

Adler, Judith. 1979. *Artists in Offices: An Ethnography of an Academic Art Scene.* New Brunswick, NJ: Transaction Books.

Agamben, Giorgio. 2009. "What is the Contemporary?" In *What is an Apparatus?: And Other Essays*, translated by David Kishik and Stefan Pedatella, 39-54. Stanford, CA: Stanford University Press.

Alexander, Victoria D., and Marilyn Rueschemeyer. 2005. *Art and the State: The Visual Arts in Comparative Perspective.* London: Palgrave.

Anne. 2010. "Monsters & Mullets: Fire and Ice (1983)." *Pornokitsch*, http://www.pornokitsch.com/2010/12/monsters-mullets-fire-and-ice-1983.html.

Appadurai, Arjun. 1986. "Introduction: Commodities and the Politics of Value." In *The Social Life of Things: Commodities in Cultural Perspective*, edited by Arjun Appadurai, 3-63. Cambridge: Cambridge University Press.

Artprice. 2010. "China: The New Global Leader." In *Artprice: Art Market Trends*, pp. 11-15, http://imgpublic.artprice.com/pdf/trends2010_en.pdf.

Becker, Howard S. 1984. *Art Worlds*. Berkeley, CA: University of California Press.

Benjamin, Walter. 1968. "The Work of Art in the Age of Mechanical Reproduction." In *Illuminations: Essays and Reflections*, 217-52. New York: Schocken.

Boylan, Alexis, ed. 2011. *Thomas Kinkade: The Artist in the Mall*. Durham, NC: Duke University Press.

Bush, Donald. 1978. "Thorstein Veblen's Economic Aesthetic." *Leonardo* 11(4): 281-85.

Christenson, Kim. 2006. "Thomas Kinkade Accused of Bad Business Dealings, Behavior." *Dallas Morning News / LA Times*, March 17.

Cox, Laura. 2012. "Painter of Light Thomas Kinkade's wife and girlfriend head to court for showdown over $60m estate as judge rules it will remain public." *MailOnline News*, July 2, http://www.dailymail.co.uk/news/article-2167911/Thomas-Kinkade-Painters-mistress-Amy-Pinto-Walsh-wife-Nanette-head-court-60m-estate.html#ixzz2PVXwelBb.

Eiss, Paul, and David Pedersen. 2008. "Introduction: Values of Value." *Cultural Anthropology* 17(3): 283-90.

Falls, Susan, and Jessica Smith. 2011a. "Branding Authenticity: Cambodian Ikat in Transnational Artisan Partnerships (TAPs)." *Journal of Design History* 24(3): 255-71.

———. 2011b. "Good Hands: Transnational Artisan Partnerships (TAPS) in Cambodia." In *Textile Economies: Power and Value from the Local to the Transnational*, edited by Walter Little and Patricia A. McAnany, 201-22. Society for Economic Anthropology Monograph Series. Lanham, MD: Altamira Press.

Foster, Robert. 2007. "The Work of the New Economy: Consumers, Brands and Value Creation." *Cultural Anthropology* 22(4): 707-31.

Frankl, Viktor E. (1946) 2006. *Man's Search for Meaning: An Introduction to Logotherapy*. New York: Beacon Press.

Graeber, David. 2001. *Toward An Anthropological Theory of Value: The False Coin of Our Own Dreams*. New York: Palgrave.

Graw, Isabelle. 2010. *High Price: Art Between the Market and Celebrity Culture*. New York: Sternberg Press.

Harvey, David. 2005. *A Brief History of Neoliberalism*. New York: Oxford University Press.

Howes, David. 2005. "Hyperesthesia, or The Sensual Logic of Late Capitalism." In E*mpire of the Senses: The Sensual Culture Reader*, edited by David Howes, 281-303. Oxford: Oxford University Press.

Meyers, Fred, ed. 2002. *The Empire of Things: Regimes of Value and Material Culture*. Santa Fe: SAR Press.

Miller, Laura. 2002. "The Writer of Dreck™: With his appalling new novel, Thomas Kinkade, 'The Painter of Light™,' makes a strong bid to become the world champion of vapid, money-grubbing kitsch." *Salon Media Group*, March 18, http://www.salon.com/2002/03/18/light_4/.

Plattner, Stuart. 1996. *High Art Down Home: An Economic Ethnography of a Local Art Market*. Chicago: University of Chicago Press.

Quigley, Samantha L. 2005. "America Supports You: Artist Brightens Day at Naval Hospital." *American Forces Press Service*, US Department of Defense, Washington, DC., Oct. 21, http://www.defense.gov/News/NewsArticle.aspx?ID=18000.

Stallybrass, Julian. 2004. *Art Incorporated: The Story of Contemporary Art*. New York: Oxford University Press.

Stiles, Kristine. 1996. *Theories and Documents of Contemporary Art: A Sourcebook of Artists' Writings*. Berkeley, CA: University of California Press.

Tett, Gillian. 2009. *Fool's Gold: How the Bold Dream of a Small Tribe at J. P. Morgan Was Corrupted by Wall Street Greed and Unleashed a Catastrophe*. New York: Free Press.

Thompson, Don. 2008. *The $12 Million Stuffed Shark: The Curious Economics of Contemporary Art*. New York: Palgrave.

Thornton, Sarah. 2008. *Seven Days in the Art World*. New York: W. W. Norton.

Vallance, Jeffrey. 2011. "Thomas Kinkade's Heaven on Earth." In *Thomas Kinkade: The Artist in the Mall*, edited by A. Boylan, 191-205. Durham, NC: Duke University Press.

Vallance, Jeffrey, and Thomas Kinkade. 2004. *Press Conference on Thomas Kinkade: Heaven on Earth*, curated by Jeffrey Vallance at Grand Central Art Center. Fullerton, CA: California State University Fullerton.

Veblen, Thorstein. (1894) 1964. "The Economic Theory of Women's Dress." In *Essays in Our Changing Order*, edited by L. Ardzrooni, 66. New York: Augustus M Kelly.

Weiner, Annette B. 1992. *Inalienable Possessions: The Paradox of Keeping-While-Giving*. Berkeley, CA: University of California Press.

Werner, Paul. 2005. *Museum, Inc.: Inside the Global Art Market*. Chicago: Prickly Paradigm Press.

Winegar, Jessica. 2006. "Cultural Sovereignty in a Global Art Economy: Egyptian Cultural Policy and the New Western Interest in Art from the Middle East." *Cultural Anthropology* 21(2): 173-204.

Wolff, Janet. 1993. *The Social Production of Art*. New York: New York University Press.

PART III

Critical Art: New Ways of Seeing

Style and Configuration in Prehistoric Iconography

Vernon James Knight Jr.

Abstract

The iconography of ancient art has to do with making propositions about what that art depicts. Stylistic studies, in contrast, make propositions about the sharedness of formal properties with other objects. These can be done separately. Although many iconographic analyses of ancient art proceed with little or no consideration of style, I argue that the two modes of analysis are interdependent. I offer a methodological case that stylistic analysis is logically prior to iconographic study in the domain of ancient art. This observation argues for a distinctively staged approach to the iconography of ancient objects, one in which detailed stylistic study is a necessary prerequisite to success in determining the referents of representations.

In this chapter, I wish to make what is really a fairly simple methodological point concerning the relationship between the iconography of ancient art and the study of style. I think the point is worth making because I have found that there is far less consensus about method among prehistoric iconographers than many would readily admit. I argue that stylistic and iconographic analyses are interdependent and that stylistic analysis is an indispensable prerequisite to a more confident, successful iconography. This suggests, in turn, a staged methodology incorporating both.

Before going any further, let me situate myself, so to speak, in order to reveal some of my biases. In the New World, pre-Columbian iconography of art is divided between two sets of practitioners: one trained in the field of art history and a somewhat larger group trained as anthropologists. These two groups, however crisply divided by their training, nevertheless do interact extensively and borrow methodologically from one another. Personally, by training I am an anthropologist, one who works in eastern North America and the Greater Antilles. Further, I am one of the original members of the Mississippian Iconographic Workshop, originally a spinoff of Linda Schele's Maya Hieroglyphic Workshop, which has met annually since 1993 in Texas. At the moment, the group is responsible for three edited volumes (Lankford, Reilly, and Garber 2011; Reilly and Garber 2007; Townsend and Sharp 2004) and a number of additional articles. My interest in methods is fresh in that I spent the greater part of 2010 working on a book manuscript on the subject (Knight 2013), having received a stipend for that purpose by Dumbarton Oaks in Washington, DC; I have taught the subject as a graduate seminar for twenty years.

As for my theoretical perspective, it comes ultimately from a background in symbolic and structural anthropology acquired during the 1970s. My view of the nature and role of culture has a great deal in common with cognitive anthropology as outlined by D'Andrade (1987) and others. In short, I view both style and iconographic communication as governed by schematic cultural models of differentially distributed knowledge.

Iconography is fundamentally about the relationship between representational images and whatever they refer to, outside of themselves. I use the term *referent* intentionally, as opposed to the more slippery term *meaning*. Iconography is therefore completely different from the study of style (Panofsky 1939), which has to do with cultural models governing the manner in which images are depicted. I further restrict myself to the iconography of prehistoric images. These are images to which any contemporaneously written record is completely denied. The subject matter therefore includes imagery produced by such pre-Columbian groups as the Olmec, Teotihuacán, and Izapa of ancient Mexico, Coclé of Panama, the Marajoara of the Amazon Basin, the Chavín and Moche of Peru, and many others. These ancient peoples, all of whom left a wonderful variety of art for our modern contemplation, have in common that they were organized as what most archaeologists would call "complex societies," meaning simply that they were socially differentiated to some degree, and their communities were politically organized. I exclude such groups as the Classic Maya, who had a well-developed glottographic writing system. In Classic Maya art, imagery is often combined directly with text so that the burden of communication is shared. This creates entirely new genres (e.g., Berlo 1983), and in a very real sense, it changes the rules of iconographic interpretation. Further, iconography can be considered a subset of cognitive archaeology, although our practice diverges very much from standard descriptions of what cognitive archaeology is by such worthies as Colin Renfrew (1994), Kent Flannery, and Joyce Marcus (1998). From the art historical perspective, what we are doing could be considered a facet of what Erwin Panofsky (1939) called "iconology," although Panofsky himself might not recognize it as that, were he alive today.

I claim that where ancient images are at stake, there is a special methodological relationship between the study of styles and the study of representations. Let me introduce the matter with a paradox. In North and South America respectively, among the most profound sources of iconographic insights published to date are two research projects. First, for North America, is Philip Phillips's and James Brown's (1975-1982) magnificent six-volume set concerning the corpus of Mississippian engraved shells from the Craig Mound at the Spiro site in Oklahoma. For South America, the corresponding work is the extraordinarily influential two-volume set on Moche fineline painted ceramics by Christopher Donnan, Donna McClelland, and Donald McClelland (Donnan and McClelland 1999; McClelland, and Donnan 2007). These two studies have much in common, including the sheer amount of labor that went into collecting the corpus in both, a methodological imperative inherited from art history (Kubler 1967, 1969). The Spiro shell volumes brought together 791 artifacts, presented in a common format, as rubbings gathered from numerous scattered collections by a team of four artists working over a six-year period. The Moche fineline pottery database is even more impressive in this regard. It is a photographic archive documenting over 2,300 pottery vessels from museums and private collections worldwide assembled over a period of thirty years. As many as twenty to thirty photographs of each vessel were taken. Because these paintings were most often done in the round, for the purpose of analysis and publication, the photographed paintings were converted into inked two-dimensional rollouts. The paradox concerning these volumes is as follows. Although both the North and South American studies have been extraordinarily fertile sources of iconographic interpretation in the years since their publication, neither study mainly concerns iconography. Instead, they are fundamentally stylistic studies, which subdivide their materials into style groups and style phases using formal traits of execution and layout. Their concern with the subject matter of the art is secondary in both cases, and its discussion develops only after sufficient control of style and stylistic change over time has been achieved. Both studies are extraordinarily conservative in regard to interpretation of the imagery, especially in their shared disavowal of any sort of ethnographic analogy to help interpret what is being depicted.

The importance of this is that many of the attitudes expressed in these volumes are at odds with dominant tendencies among practicing prehistoric iconographers. Many ignore the imperative to collect a full corpus of a single genre before proceeding. Instead, they are content to move interpretively from object to object, skip from genre to genre, and follow alleged motifs or themes across great distances in time and space. They tend to employ ethnographic analogy promiscuously, using documentation from the ethnographic present that they project backwards in time with little regard for the possibility that forms might become disjoined from their subject matter over time. In doing so, these practitioners appear satisfied to interpret ancient images merely as illustrations of already known ethnographic concepts. More to the point of this chapter, they tend to shun the laborious work of stylistic analysis, preferring to jump headlong into the arena of iconographic subject matter. They tend to assume the existence of styles, especially so-called "international styles" such as the Olmec or Teotihuacano, where there has been no such formal demonstration. Even a casual look at such "styles" reveals enormous diversity and complexity. I believe these shortcuts are a mistake and that detailed stylistic analysis is methodologically essential as a precursor to practicing iconography with ancient images.

Before zeroing in on this relationship more precisely, I need to say just a bit about methodology in iconographic work itself. In simple terms, like stylistic analysis, it begins with a collected corpus of works of the same time period and ideally of the same genre. Insistence on working within one genre at a time—say engraved shell cups or fineline painted pots—echoes what the art historian Ernst Gombrich (1972) called the "principle of the primacy of genres," which says that representations change as genres change. To take an extreme example, a representation of the Greek goddess Athena on a coin is not to be compared with the image of Athena as the central object of devotion in the Parthenon. The referents are very different at anything other than a superficial level. With a corpus of work assembled in a format favorable to comparison, analysis begins by deconstructing images into their parts, using a series of defined suprastylistic concepts, such as salient element, motif, filler motif, identifying attribute, classifying attribute, and ideograph. Most of these terms come directly from the vocabulary of art history, but with definitions refined and tailored over the years to the tasks at hand. By giving the discovered elements neutral names and by tracing their occurrences, relative positions, and clustering completely throughout the corpus, one arrives at sets of apparent common subject matter. Depending on the circumstance, these sets are labeled as visual themes and visual narratives and are again given neutral names so as not to bias the outcome of analysis. The art historian George Kubler (1967, 1969) called this method "configurational analysis."

Importantly, configurational analysis is conducted entirely without reference to ethnographic analogy (or more accurately, historical homology [Berlo 1983], since what is being compared are chronologically distant manifestations of the same cultural phenomena rather than merely analogous traits). Avoidance of historic documentation at this stage of analysis is deliberate. Kubler (1969) believed that historical disjunction between form and referent was such a persistent danger that complete avoidance was the prudent course. Nowadays, nearly all anthropologically trained iconographers, and probably most of the art historians as well, would not go that far. They would argue that historically recorded myths, rituals, beliefs, cosmologies, and so forth grant an indispensable foothold into the past. Methodologically then, the issue is to carefully control the application of these later sources, to minimize the possibility of simply reading the present into the past and irreversibly biasing the outcome. Past configurations are, to some degree, allowed to speak for themselves, being systematically compared with later information, noting both what seems to fit and what does not. Procedurally, the configurational analysis must both come first and must be analytically separate from any consideration of historical homologies.

Because configurational analysis relies on internal information embedded within the images, it is fair to ask to what degree one can reliably say anything about subject matter and therefore do iconography. Art historians of Panofsky's generation assumed that some kinds of subject matter recognition were universal, with factual understandings requiring no cultural knowledge. But a subsequent generation of theorists (e.g., Gombrich 1977; Hermerén 1969; Kippenberg 1987) pointed out the fallacy of factual recognition, even in art that we might think of as being naturalistic. So clearly, in images we see only what we are conditioned to see by shared cultural models—in this case, stylistic models of depiction. On this basis, Robert Layton (1977) has argued that there is no such thing as "naturalism" in art; all depiction is conventionalized. The one distinction that can be made is the degree to which the style in question is, or is not, obedient to perspective, in the sense of showing the contours of what the eye sees from a fixed vantage point. Some style systems ignore perspective almost entirely.

Thus, our recognition of anything at all, iconographically, depends on how much of the stylistic model in question we happen to grasp. As in other aspects of iconography, success is largely a matter of knowing the context.

My contention is that stylistic and iconographic analyses are separate but interdependent endeavors. I am arguing that an explicit grasp of the stylistic canons governing a corpus of related imagery is fundamentally prerequisite to any successful iconographic analysis of that corpus. To further drive home this point, let us consider three things essential to prehistoric iconography that a study of stylistic conventions can tell us: what is what, what is contemporaneous with what, and what is local.

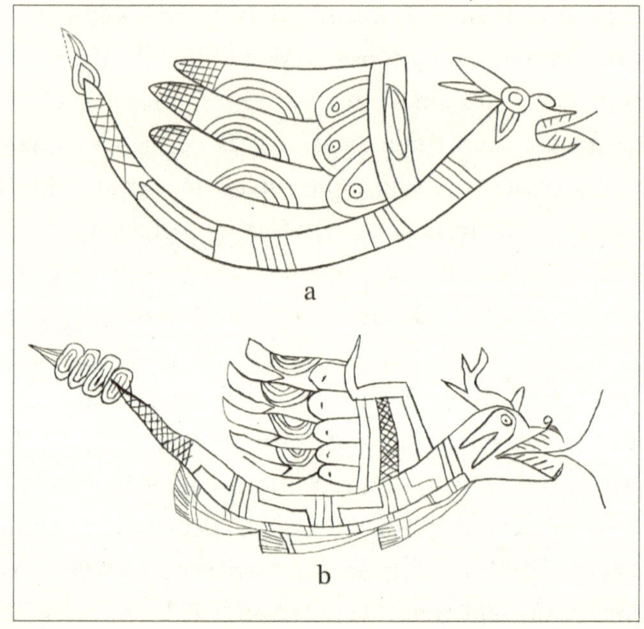

Figure 9.1. Two winged serpents, from engraved pottery vessels from the Moundville site, Alabama ([a] from Moore [1907, figure 59]; [b] drawing by Erin E. Phillips). (Drawing and permission courtesy of Erin E. Phillips)

First, an understanding of stylistic conventions can tell us what is what. Consider the two images given in figure 9.1, both drawn from the corpus of engraved pottery in the Hemphill style from the Moundville site in Alabama. Arguably, these Mississippian engravings depict the same theme, which is a winged serpent. The uppermost is a well-known illustration. It was published by Clarence B. Moore in 1907, and it has been occasionally reproduced in publications ever since. At times, this particular snake has been referred to in figure captions as a "plumed serpent," with the objects on the head viewed as feathers. The unspoken comparison here is obviously with the "feathered serpents" of Mesoamerica. The lower image, in contrast, is commonly understood as "horned," with the corresponding objects on the head seen as antlers. Again, there is an unspoken comparison, in this case with the horned underwater serpents of Native American myth in the eastern United States. The question is, does the upper configuration really depict plumes, or instead is it merely another convention for antlers?

Fortunately, we have a comparative stylistic study of all thirty-nine known winged serpent depictions from Moundville (Schatte 1997), and that study reveals the answer. It gives us empirical grounds to state with complete confidence that all such configurations on the head are to be interpreted as the same thing (antlers), which show a full range of schematization from fully to barely recognizable. It so happens that the lower example is chronologically early and the upper is late (E. Phillips 2011). Viewing images in isolation leads to incorrect conclusions, but systematic stylistic study of an entire corpus reveals a continuous range of conventional depiction. Figure 9.2 provides a second illustration of the idea, again taken from the engraved art on pottery from Moundville. I once gave a talk where I used this drawing to illustrate another of the common themes on Moundville pottery, which we call the crested bird. As I was explaining that this does, in fact, depict the head of a crested bird, a gentleman in the back of the audience raised an objection. While he saw that it could be a crested bird, he thought it much more likely to depict a fish in the process of consuming something large. He was seeing the hachures at the border between the beak and head as the teeth of a fish, and the crest as the fish's dorsal fin. And frankly, if this were the only image we had of the subject, his interpretation could be as easily defended as mine. Obviously, we do not all necessarily see the same thing. In my case, if I had been armed at that moment with the full repertoire of engravings of the crested bird theme, I could have explained the stylistic canons that govern its depiction. Because the remaining examples of the crested bird theme show nothing even remotely fish-like, my case could easily have been made. Even in cases where the analyst cannot identify the natural referent, stylistic analysis can still allow us to make informed choices about what is the same subject versus what is something else. Style informs the critical same-versus-different distinctions that make iconography possible.

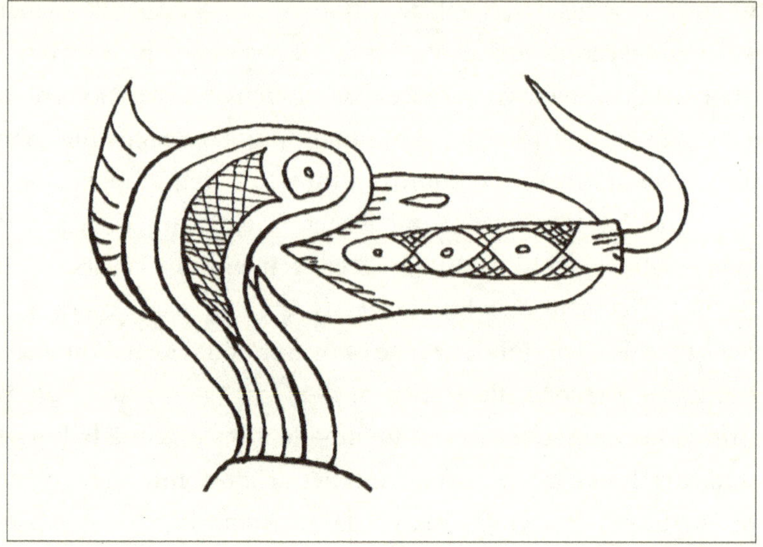

Figure 9.2. Detail from a depiction of a crested bird on engraved pottery from the Moundville site, Alabama (Moore 1905, figure 9). (Image in the public domain)

Second, style helps us to decide what is contemporaneous with what. Stylistic seriation is an indispensable tool for arranging images in a chronology. The creation of style phases within traditions grants us "analytical moments" so to speak—synchronic units that give us a framework within which we can capture the local, potentially temporary, relations between images and their referents. Our recognition of style horizons also allows us to link contemporaneous works across larger geographical spans in order to consider whether their referents are the same or different. Conversely, a lack of attention to these details can lead only to jumbled comparisons of images drawn from different times and places, leading to false assumptions about continuity of forms and referents. In short, iconography is meaningless without the control of time, and style is a major contributor to the building of chronologies.

Third, stylistic analysis can tell us what is local. Prehistoric complex societies were not isolated systems. In these societies, skillfully crafted goods were often sought from afar, or perhaps brought as gifts by emissaries seeking alliance. Nonlocal goods were ultimately distributed among both elites and non-elites, during feasts, marriages, funerals, and other consequential social events. As a result, the total assemblage of portable imagery at any given site, particularly at large civic-ceremonial centers, is a mix of goods produced locally and goods manufactured elsewhere. Among these nonlocal goods, typically there are images that not only are foreign to the local style but also bear subject matter that would have had no particular significance in the local context. In any effort to isolate local systems of images and referents, as a practical matter it is necessary to winnow out the nonlocal "noise," simplifying the universe of images and eliminating from consideration much that would otherwise confound the analysis. Among the key tools for accomplishing this winnowing out of the foreign material is stylistic analysis (another being the chemical or geological sourcing of raw materials). Consider the two large stone effigy smoking pipes shown in photograph 9.1, depicting a supernatural panther. Although four such pipes have been found at the Moundville site in west Alabama, stylistically they are out of place. They do not belong to any of Moundville's styles, but rather to a style known as Bellaire A that properly belongs in the Lower Mississippi Valley (Steponaitis et al. 2009), where many more examples have been found. In confirmation of this, the limestone from which they are made has been sourced to outcrops near Vicksburg on the Mississippi River. Not only are the objects foreign at Moundville, but so is the subject matter. Of the many hundreds of locally produced images in several media at Moundville, none shows the long-tailed panther. It is a foreign subject but one that was probably reinterpreted according to local cultural models and incorporated into Moundville ritual practice in a limited way.

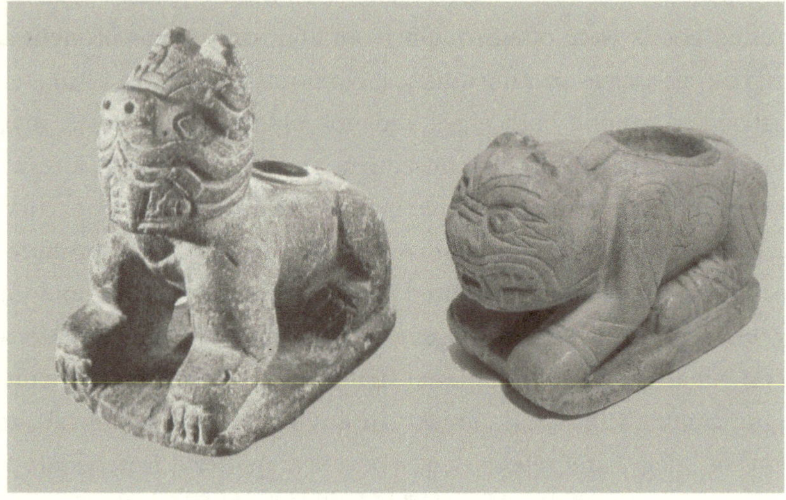

Photograph 9.1. Limestone effigy pipes from the Moundville site, Alabama, depicting long-tailed panthers. (Photograph courtesy of Vincas Steponaitis)

In summary, style, as pure form, can profitably be analyzed entirely apart from subject matter, and much work along these lines has been done. Nonetheless, the results of stylistic analysis have much to do with an understanding of referents. Style has the potential to inform us on what is what, what is contemporaneous with what, and what is local, all of which have a strong bearing on understanding suprastylistic configurations. In that sense, stylistic analysis is logically prior to configurational analysis and any considerations of iconographic reference. Aspects of iconography thus have a methodologically dependent relationship to aspects of style, just as configurational analysis of images is logically prior to the application of historic homologies. All of this argues for a distinctly staged approach to prehistoric iconography which is sometimes hinted at and other times carried out in practice, but is seldom explicitly laid out as I think it should be. I envision the ideal approach as having several stages: first, assembly of the corpus; second, organization of the material according to stylistic analysis; third, incorporation of natural history and archaeological field data; fourth, configurational analysis of suprastylistic units; fifth, careful application of ethnographic analogy; sixth, building of iconographic models; and seventh, testing these iconographic models. This last is because, after all, we do have to verify our claims.

References

Berlo, Janet C. 1983. "Conceptual Categories for the Study of Texts and Images in Mesoamerica." In *Text and Image in Pre-Columbian Art: Essays on the Interrelationship of the Verbal and Visual Arts*, edited by J. C. Berlo, 1-40. Oxford: BAR International Series 180.

D'Andrade, Roy G. 1987. "Cultural Meaning Systems." In *Culture Theory: Essays in Mind, Self, and Emotion*, edited by Richard Schweder and Robert Levine, 88-119. Cambridge: Cambridge University Press.

Donnan, Christopher B., and Donna McClelland. 1999. *Moche Fineline Painting: Its Artists and Its Evolution.* Los Angeles: UCLA Fowler Museum of Cultural History.

Flannery, Kent V., and Joyce Marcus. 1998. "Cognitive Archaeology." In *Reader in Archaeological Theory*, edited by David S. Whitley, 35-48. London: Routledge.

Gombrich, Ernst H. 1972. *Symbolic Images: Studies in the Art of the Renaissance*. London: Phaidon.

———. 1977. *Art and Illusion: A Study in the Psychology of Pictorial Representation*. 5th ed. London: Phaidon.

Hermerén, Göran. 1969. *Representation and Meaning in the Visual Arts: A Study in the Methodology of Iconography and Iconology*. Lund: Berlingska Boktryckeriet.

Kippenberg, H. G. 1987. "Iconography as Visible Religion." In *The Encyclopedia of Religion*, edited by Mircea Eliade, vol. 7, 3-7. New York: Macmillan.

Knight, Vernon James, Jr. 2013. *Iconographic Method in New World Prehistory*. Cambridge: Cambridge University Press.

Kubler, George. 1967. *The Iconography of the Art of Teotihuacán*. Studies in Pre-Columbian Art and Archaeology, No. 4. Washington, DC: Dumbarton Oaks.

———. 1969. *Studies in Classic Maya Iconography*. Memoirs of the Connecticut Academy of Arts and Sciences, No. 18. New Haven: Connecticut Academy of Arts and Sciences.

Lankford, George E., F. Kent Reilly, and James F. Garber, eds. 2011. *Visualizing the Sacred: Cosmic Visions, Regionalism, and the Art of the Mississippian World*. Austin: University of Texas Press.

Layton, Robert. 1977. "Naturalism and Cultural Relativity in Art." In *Form in Indigenous Art: Schematisation in the Art of Aboriginal Australia and Prehistoric Europe*, edited by Peter J. Ucko, 33-43. Canberra: Australian Institute of Aboriginal Studies.

McClelland, Donna, Donald McClelland, and Christopher B. Donnan. 2007. *Moche Fineline Painting from San José de Moro*. Los Angeles: Cotsen Institute of Archaeology at UCLA, University of California.

Moore, Clarence B. 1905. "Certain Aboriginal Remains of the Black Warrior River." *Journal of the Academy of Natural Sciences of Philadelphia* 13:125-224.

———. 1907. "Moundville Revisited." *Journal of the Academy of Natural Sciences of Philadelphia* 13:337-405.

Panofsky, Erwin. 1939. *Studies in Iconology: Humanistic Themes in the Art of the Renaissance.* New York: Oxford University Press.

Phillips, Erin E. 2011. "Social Contexts of the Production and Consumption of Hemphill-Style Pottery at Moundville." PhD diss. Tuscaloosa: Department of Anthropology, University of Alabama.

Phillips, Philip, and James A. Brown. 1975-1982. *Pre-Columbian Shell Engravings from the Craig Mound at Spiro, Oklahoma.* Hardbound ed., 6 vols. Cambridge: Peabody Museum Press.

Reilly, F. Kent, and James F. Garber, eds. 2007. *Ancient Objects and Sacred Realms: Interpretations of Mississippian Iconography.* Austin: University of Texas Press.

Renfrew, Colin. 1994. "Towards a Cognitive Archaeology." In *The Ancient Mind: Elements of Cognitive Archaeology*, edited by Colin Renfrew and Ezra Zubrow, 3-12. Cambridge: Cambridge University Press.

Schatte, Kevin E. 1997. "Stylistic Analysis of the Winged Serpent Theme at Moundville." Master's thesis. Tuscaloosa: Department of Anthropology, University of Alabama.

Steponaitis, Vincas P., George Lankford, Vernon J. Knight, and Robert Sharp. 2009. "Iconography, Style, and Function of Effigy Pipes in the Lower Mississippi Valley." Paper presented at the 66th Annual Southeastern Archaeological Conference, Mobile, Alabama.

Townsend, Richard F., and Robert V. Sharp, eds. 2004. *Hero, Hawk, and Open Hand: American Indian Art of the Ancient Midwest and South.* Art Institute of Chicago. New Haven: Yale University Press.

Race and Rhythm in Rock and Roll

Hector Qirko

Abstract

This chapter argues that contrary to conventional wisdom and the views of many scholars and critics, rock and roll's most important rhythmic elements are derived from a complex blend of African, American, and European musical traditions. There is therefore no objective support for racialized characterizations of the "beat" that often serve, however unintentionally, to perpetuate stereotypes in discussions of both the genre and American popular music more broadly.

You take a white right hand, and a black left hand, and what do you got? Son, you got rock and roll. —Sam Phillips (purportedly)

The mysteries of black and white in American music are just not that simple. —Greil Marcus

Tracking the origins of rock and roll is as difficult as identifying the headwaters of a large river. As Robert Palmer observed, "It would take at least one book, if not a library, to trace various kinds of rock 'n' roll back through their myriad sources" (1992, 6). Attempts to do so are complicated by the fact that musical genres are ultimately defined socially, as a consequence of economic, political and, above all, cultural processes. The "true" origins and characteristics of any genre at any point in time, much less over time, cannot be determined objectively (Moore 2002; Peterson 1997). Unsurprisingly, then, attempts to associate specific musical features (as well as artists and dates) with the birth of rock and roll often depend on which social factors are perceived to be most important to its development (D'Anjou 2003).

A good illustration of these difficulties is the relationship between race and rock and roll, in particular regarding the genre's rhythmic characteristics, or "beat." At the outset of rock and roll's development as an independent genre in the United States in the 1950s, popular opposition to the music was couched in racial as well as generational terms. Many adult whites perceived rock and roll as "black music," no doubt in part because initially it was predominantly performed by African American artists (Martin and Segrave 1993). However, the characterization was also due to the music's purported "jungle beat," the volume and intensity of which were perceived as alien and even dangerous to rock and roll's young, white audience (Altschuler 2003; Kamin 1975). This was, as Michelle Hamilton notes, simply a long-held belief in a new context:

> Since the mid-nineteenth century, more than any other music worldwide, that of African Americans has worked its way into white imaginations. It has been a development that racial reactionaries have regarded with apprehension, even horror. In that cross-racial attraction they could see only evil, a barbaric jungle beat that had the power to remake its listeners—not just to move their bodies, but to reshape their minds. (1999, 650)

It is easy to dismiss a racialized reaction to rock and roll as stemming from ignorance and racism. However, many music scholars and critics also racialize when they describe the rhythmic character of rock and roll as derived primarily from its African American, and often ultimately African, roots. This paper argues instead that rock and roll's most important rhythmic elements, like the genre as a whole, result from a complex blend of cultural traditions, and that as strong a case can be made for the importance of "white" influences as for those derived from African American and African sources. With respect to rhythm, as with the genre's other features, there is therefore no objective support for dichotomous characterizations of racial contributions which ultimately serve, however unintentionally, to perpetuate stereotypes in discussions of not only rock and roll but other genres of American popular music. As Greil Marcus (1997, 155) noted about the notion that Elvis Presley was successful because he was a white man performing black music: "It's just not that simple."

Rock and Roll and R&B

Rock and roll is typically viewed by scholars and critics as originating from a blend of various styles, particularly rhythm and blues (R&B) and country (or country and western) (e.g., Belz 1972; Friedlander 2006; Shaw 1974; E. Ward 1986; Wilgus 1970). Sometimes the influence of pop is also emphasized (e.g., Stuessy and Lipscomb 2009; Wicke 1990). Other views focus on R&B and country's antecedents—thus, Charles Brown (1983) calls rock and roll a mixture of folk, pop, and jazz, subsuming R&B in his third category, while Evans (1987) describes only blues and country as rock and roll's root styles. In some cases, researchers deemphasize the contributions of specific genres by focusing instead on their shared core. For example, Hatch and Millward state that the "musical family blues-boogie-gospel . . . contains virtually all the elements out of which the musical types in the pop tradition [including rock and roll] have been constructed" (1987, 5), and Palmer emphasizes "myriad forms of boogie-woogie," aimed at both black and white audiences, in his version of the story (1995, 16).

However, some scholars describe rock and roll not as a hybrid form at all, but simply R&B marketed to and appropriated by white audiences (e.g., DeCurtis 1996; Ewen 1977; George 1989; Redd 1985). For example, Szatmary (2000) argues that rock and roll is the result of a short leap from up-tempo, frantic R&B taken by a handful of artists, notably Little Richard and Chuck Berry. Others counter that the country and western influence on rockabilly, one of the earliest forms of rock and roll (most famously recorded by Carl Perkins, Elvis Presley, and other artists from Sam Phillips's Sun Records in Memphis), is undeniable (e.g., Morrison 1996). Perhaps the most reasoned view is that while disc jockey Alan Freed's use of the term *rock 'n' roll* to describe the R&B he played in Cleveland in the early 1950s launched the genre, very shortly thereafter there developed variants influenced by other styles (Campbell 2008; Friedlander 2006; Gillett 1996).

At any rate, whether or not descriptions of early rock and roll invoke some blend of genres typically associated with white or black popular music (or both), virtually all share the view that R&B or its African American antecedents contributed importantly to the rhythmic foundation of the music. To Wicke, "Right from the start rock and roll was nothing but black music played by white musicians," with African American rhythms playing the "decisive role" in the development of the new genre (1990, 18). Similarly, Gillett notes that the many early forms of rock and roll all "depended for their dance beat on contemporary Negro dance rhythms" (1996, 29). Many scholars see these rhythms as ultimately African in origin. Thus Palmer argues that transplanted African music provided several important elements that survived in rock and roll, including both "remarkable polyrhythmic complexity [and] a kind of percussive directionality or rhythmic drive" (1992, 4). Gracyk agrees, noting that the rock beat "preserves an African attitude toward basic accents, rejecting the standard Western assumption that the first beat of the measure is the strongest" (1996, 135). This "irresistible and implacable rhythmic drive, that never [loses] momentum" (Ewen 1977, 555) is also often specifically attributed to R&B, and many early rock and roll songs, for example Elvis Presley's "Blue Moon of Kentucky," are seen as emblematic of the genre because of their R&B-derived "chugging rhythm" (E. Ward 1986, 81). In short, a common view regarding the rhythm of rock and roll can be summed up in the first quotation that introduces this paper. In the movie *Great Balls of Fire*, Sam Phillips describes rock and roll to pianist Jerry Lee Lewis in terms he will understand: the melody (right hand) may be white pop- or country-influenced, but the rhythm (left hand) is straight out of the black, R&B tradition (Plasketes 1989, 75).

The Rock and Roll Beat

Clearly, R&B influenced 1950s rock and roll in many ways. Powerful singing styles, typical instrumentation, and call and response vocal/vocal and vocal/instrument patterns are all important features in rock and roll's development (C. T. Brown 1983, 42-45). And there is much in the rhythm of R&B that is important as well. One element is a dynamic intensity that was not typically found in pop or country at the time. As Leo Mintz noted (in E. Ward 1986, 69), white kids began buying R&B music because "the beat is so strong that anyone could dance to it without a lesson." R&B rhythmic styles certainly utilized more forceful rhythm sections than any other styles of the times, and the influence of that approach on rock and roll is undeniable.

A related element is what Belz calls the "Big Beat," which involves not only a hard-driving beat, but also a "totality of impact" (1972, 29) created by the close relationship between vocals and instrumentation, both in terms of arrangements and recording "mix," that "projected a fabric of sound in which everything struck the listener at once—instrumental sound, lyrics, fragmentary or improvised lyrics, and all with a powerful incessant beat" (1972, 29-30). Unquestionably, the "total rhythm" R&B style contributed immensely to early rock and roll. In fact, later rock and roll (and, subsequently, rock) took this approach a step further by emphasizing the repetitive and even unison playing of various instruments to reinforce the beat, in comparison to R&B's more individualistic ensemble playing.

In addition, and most obviously, many of rock and roll's basic rhythmic figures, particularly the "backbeat" accenting of beats 2 and 4 and the emphases on triplet figures and dotted eight-notes, sprang from R&B and earlier blues and boogie-woogie patterns (C. T. Brown 1983; Campbell 2008).

However, other claims for R&B's rhythmic contributions to rock and roll may not be as valid. One is Palmer's "remarkable polyrhythmic complexity." Here Horowitz may be correct in arguing that "the first stage in the development of rock was the sacrifice of musical complexity for the sake of capturing an audience" (2010, 141). In his view, rock is notable for its "rejection of complication for its own sake [and] the return to a more direct expression of emotions" (Horowitz 2010, 142). While popular music as a whole may be noted for these features, it is certainly clear that rhythmically much R&B, as well as early rock and roll, was obviously and intentionally simple and repetitive.

Another element to be considered is the average tempo of rock and roll songs, which is generally faster than that of R&B and is thought by some to relate, at least in part, to the influence of country music (Belz 1972; Tosches 1999). While the dynamic force of rock and roll is certainly traceable to R&B, then, another vehicle for its ability to convey excitement—the tempo—is not as clearly derived from the same source.

The most important point, however, involves not rhythmic patterns themselves but the way in which they are executed, in particular rock and roll's generally more strictly adhered-to meter. While this is an essential component of rock and roll, its roots do not as clearly lie in the R&B tradition, which, as in blues and black gospel at the time, relies on the deliberate avoidance of an overtly strict, regular beat (Savage 1989, 72). Instead, these genres emphasized the "push-pull" of the beat rather than a metronome-like execution (Titon 2009). This creates a metric "swing" fundamental to the rhythmic enjoyment derived from the music. Rather than implied and manipulated, however, rock and roll's approach to "time" was (and continues to be) to attack it directly. Thus, E. Ward describes Sleepy John Estes's 1930s "Expressman Blues" as "eerily prophetic of rock and roll" primarily because of its "crisp 4/4 time," which places the tune "way outside" the blues mainstream of the times (1986, 29).

Writers who have observed this difference in the "swing" and "rock" styles typically characterize the latter as negative. Titon argues that when the triplet rhythm of slow blues is "accented monotonously, as in many rock 'n' roll songs from the 1950's, it becomes a cliche" (2009, 25). Likewise, Birchall sees the rhythm and blues of early rock transformed into "rhythm **without** blues—a drearily insistent and repetitive beat with no authentic feeling in it" (1969, 99, emphasis in original).

Chuck Berry's successful hybrid stylings are an excellent early example of the difference between the two approaches. Christgau (1992) notes that Berry was criticized for the repetitiveness of his style, the "orgasmic monotony" (Meltzer 1970, 78) of which Berry himself once said: "Really all I want to do is like **chop chop chop**" (Salvo 1989, 227, emphasis in original). But as Christgau adds,

"Repetition without tedium is the backbone of rock and roll" (1992, 62), and Campbell considers Berry the "architect" of rock and roll in large part due to his having developed its beat, one "completely purged of any swing influence" (2008, 112). On the other hand, the early Rolling Stones—who, although often called the best rock and roll band in the world, started out to be "simply a good R&B band" (Mick Jagger, in Smith and Fink 1988, 207)—are one of the rarer examples of the continued use of the more fluid R&B approach in rock and roll (although even in their case, the style is "simplified" [Beckett and Merton 1969, 109]).

Other Roots of the Rock and Roll Beat

The influence of pop music on what becomes rock and roll is typically viewed as that of "cleaning up" R&B on several fronts. One is structure, as pop and country have a more systematized verse-chorus relationship that Palmer (1992) discusses in terms of British folk music's song stanzas and the narrative ballad. Others are R&B's sexually overt lyrics, loose and rather rough ("spontaneous") lead and harmony vocals, and the beat, thought to be too rough and powerful to be palatable to the new teenage rock and roll audiences without dilution.

Analyses of "covers" of the R&B songs by white artists that were so important to the emergence of rock and roll into national prominence illustrate the point (Belz 1972; Shaw 1974; Stuessy and Lipscomb 2009). These recordings separated the various components, subordinated instrumentation to vocals, and in general diluted R&B's "total rhythm." Belz therefore argues that the early covers, in using this pop approach, provided a bridge to rock and roll for audiences with pop sensibilities (1972; also Shaw 1974, 126).

Typically, then, either R&B rhythm is perceived as making the jump directly to rock and roll, or rock and roll cover versions are perceived as R&B rhythms tempered, if not weakened, for white teenage consumption (although, see Campbell [2008] for a more nuanced view). But pop, country, and their European American antecedents are also strongly rhythmic, and it can be argued that it is exactly their approach to rhythm that gives rock and roll its almost mechanical, inexorably steady pulse, what Belz (1972, vii) calls "the most persistent feature of rock." Thus, while it is true that many rhythmic patterns in rock come from R&B roots, it might be the way they are "straightened out" in rock and roll that makes the latter so musically effective. From this perspective, the direct British influence on rock and roll in later years only accentuates a process begun with the genre's inception.

A closer examination of early rock and roll hits supports this view. While some covers were attempts to exactly mimic the R&B originals, others were (perhaps inadvertently) transformed. A good example may be heard in two versions of "Shake, Rattle and Roll," as performed by Big Joe Turner (R&B) and Bill Haley and the Comets (rock and roll). The Haley version replaces Turner's slower original, which featured a "persistent, heavy afterbeat," with an "up-tempo, four-to-the-bar" approach, and turns "Turner's earthy R&B version into exuberant, teen-age R 'n' R" (Shaw 1974, 137).

"Queen of the Hop," performed by Bobby Darin, although not a cover, is another good illustration. Its simple, inflexible, almost monotonous drumming is very different from the "looser," more syncopated and flexible R&B drumming of the same period, and "drives" exactly for that reason, in what is now a commonplace rock and roll technique. The structured, almost mechanical, approach of the rest of the rhythm section in the song only reinforces this inflexibility and differs from the more unstructured overall sound in R&B. And the result is strikingly similar to much subsequent rock of any period, which derives its rhythmic power from the simple, inexorably steady and predictable pulse that links it to early rock and roll and separates it quite distinctly from R&B. Meltzer has called this an "invincible relentlessness," and attributes it to mechanical repetition not only in rhythm, but in lyric, style and thus overall concept as well (1970, 118).

In fact, this "straightening out" of the beat can be argued to occur in other American hybrid styles. Western swing, for example, while strongly influenced by jazz and blues rhythms (Wilgus 1970), preserves a country approach to the execution of these styles, to the point that its "swing" is not like swing in jazz at all: syncopation is reduced, and a more regular, staccato emphasis of the 1 and 3 beats replaces the 2 and 4 upbeat emphasis of jazz. In addition, as in the case of Bob Wills and His Texas Playboys, the preeminent Western swing exponent, the drum kit, is reduced almost entirely to a closed hi-hat, snare, and bass drum, reinforcing rigidity in the sense that fewer percussive options are available (Boyd 2001).

Another example is the transformation of American (particularly Chicagoan) 1940s and 1950s electric blues by rock-era British blues musicians. The relatively fluid treatment of chord structure, instrumentation, vocal phrasing, and lyrics that characterizes the blues of Muddy Waters and Howlin' Wolf, for example, is replaced in British blues by a more organized, formal, repetitive strategy in everything but the ubiquitous guitar solos. More importantly in this context, the rhythmic figures in British-style blues, although fundamentally identical to those utilized in pre-rock American blues, are simplified, "regularized," and stripped of the relaxed, breathing character of the originals. The swing is replaced, as in rock and roll, with a "drive" created by the certainty of the tempo, the figure, and fills. A good example is "Further on up the Road" as performed by Eric Clapton, when compared to the same song in the 1957 version by Bobby Blue Bland or to most other versions of the classic Texas shuffle.

As in rock and roll, this transformation in other genres can be viewed as simply a different technique for expressing power and excitement rather than, as some would argue, the result of unsophisticated or racially decontextualized musicianship (Baraka 1999; Rudinow 1994). The delightful tension felt as a cause of rhythmic flexibility is replaced by the equally delightful satisfaction of rhythmic inexorability. Thus, it's not that rock and rollers don't swing because they can't, as some have argued; it's that they're not trying to. The point is to "rock." Or, as Willis argues, rock and roll succeeds because it "subverts the bar form, and actually replaces it with a continuous pulse or basic primitive, standardized rhythm. This regular beat . . . is the basic organizing structure of the music" (1990, 53). While R&B obviously utilizes elements of this approach as well, the "drive" in rock and roll, arrived at by the rigidity and simplicity of rhythmic form and execution, takes it further. Listening to almost any up-tempo rock song from the 1950s to today confirms Willis's observation that rock and roll's drive often precludes even linear order and temporal structure: "Rock and roll music can be stopped or started at any time; it can be turned back or forward; it can be suspended here and carried on over there; it can be interrupted . . . one of the commonest end-piece forms is the fade, the diminution of a constant beat into nothing—an impossible concept for any previous musical form" (1990, 53).

It can be argued, then, that much of rock and roll's rhythmic approach in fact stems from attributes in both European American and earlier British traditions. This view is in marked contrast not only to conventional wisdom regarding R&B but to also wider scholarly views of the relationship of European and African influences in popular music. For example, Savage (1989) sees in popular music two "converging traditions: the European 'classical' practices from which we also draw much of our harmony, melody, and sense of form; and African folk idioms and ideas, which have brought to American music the vital elements of spontaneity and syncopated rhythmic freedom" (1989, 67). Nettl points out that the "rather regular alternation of stressed and unstressed syllables [in many Anglo-American ballads] produces a fairly regular metric structure in the music" (1976, 42). He also finds simple, regular rhythms, like 4/4 and 3/4, very common in British and German folk music. In contrast, African elements are more rhythmically subtle, flexible, and syncopated (Nettl 1976, 91-97). Titon (2009) compares "Amazing Grace" as sung in a black American church and at an Appalachian revival. In the former, the congregation follows the implied beat loosely, and the leader sings in such a way that the beat is difficult to count but easy to feel. In the latter, the leader signals the beat precisely, with hand gestures, and the congregation is strict in its interpretation of that time.

Inasmuch as European American musical influence can be identified and compared to African American influence, one can argue that there is a difference in the perception of rhythm, how it is to be interpreted and manipulated and to what effect. This in turn could be linked to differing cultural norms regarding the relationship between music and society more broadly, including worship, social control, and sexuality (e.g., B. Ward 1998). In American musical forms, a blend of these perceptions inevitably results. What we think of as a rock and roll rhythm is thereby as much "European" as it is "African," and the European component is a strength, and not a weakness, of the musical style.

Conclusion

There is, of course, no single rock and roll beat, whether the focus is on meter, tempo, accents, or overall approach. Nor are any of rock and roll's rhythmic features directly identifiable as contributions from any social or racial group. As with any other American popular music genre, rock and roll and its artists arose as a consequence of complex relations among many groups, a dynamic that is often ignored because it does not reflect larger social and racial constructs (Waterman 2000). The point of the above discussion is simply to show that as good a case can be made for rock and roll's beat being "white" as "black." But, if in fact the rock and roll beat is ultimately uncharacterizable in racial terms, why bother?

Just as genres are defined socially by means of presumed markers that involve racial and other social-group characterizations, so too are racial, ethnic, and other groups themselves socially defined by means of agreed-upon markers, of which music is an important category (e.g., Killick 2001; Manuel 1994; Trimillos 1989). And the relationship between music marked by race and race marked by music applies as much to popular music and race today as it did in the early 1950s. As Wicke (1990, 4) puts it, "The assumption of a completely separate development of Afro-American and European American music is . . . a racist argument that (still) legitimizes the established barriers between the races" (see also Tagg 1989).

Rock, country, contemporary R&B, hip-hop, jazz, and other current styles are still racially marked and as historically and musically inaccurate as ever. By the 1960s, rock and roll had become rock, and "white music" (although with its black rhythmic origins dutifully noted by scholars and critics), and so it remains. As a consequence, in the 1980s, it was a "breakthrough" for MTV to show videos by black artists (Rowland 1989). The hard rock band Living Colour had early troubles being signed by a record label because its members are black (Flanagan 1989). You can pick your examples of the social consequences of the marking of music by race, and they take many forms: Wynton Marsalis, in his early years as director of the Lincoln

Center Jazz Orchestra, famously presented a series of concerts featuring virtually no white performers or composers (Balliett 1991; L. B. Brown 2004). And although hip-hop has become a global music, the white rapper is still a problematic figure to many who view the genre as intrinsically black (Hess 2005).

Overly simplified views such as that of the relationship of race to rhythm in rock and roll are not harmless. Americans' perceptions of their musical genres are as racialized as their views of Americans themselves—and as unfounded. As Marvin Harris has put it, "All racial identity, scientifically speaking, is ambiguous. Wherever certainty is expressed on this subject, we can be confident that society has manufactured a social lie in order to help one of its segments take advantage of another" (1974, 56). In the case of rhythm and rock and roll, the social lie is subtly racist in both directions: it implies that blacks cannot compete with whites in the more "developed" areas of melody, harmony, and structure, while whites can only be imitators in the area of rhythmic sophistication.

Stuart Hall notes (in Jhally 1997) that we are "readers" of race, which requires "territories of cultural knowledge" obtained through conventional wisdom and popular culture but also supported by cultural institutions (such as the press and academia) that are presumed to be more legitimate. Perhaps noting the extent to which early rock and roll rhythm is a true and complex hybrid of American and antecedent traditions is not as unnecessary as it might at first glance appear.

Acknowledgments

I am grateful to Stephen E. Young and Bruce Tomaso for their comments and suggestions.

References

Altschuler, Glenn C. 2003. *All Shook Up: How Rock 'n' Roll Changed America*. New York: Oxford University Press.

Balliett, Whitney. 1991. "Jazz." *New Yorker*, October 14.

Baraka, Amiri [LeRoi Jones]. 1999. *Blues People: Negro Music in White America*. New York: Harper Perennial.

Beckett, Alan, and Richard Merton. 1969. "Stones/Comment." In *The Age of Rock: Sounds of the American Cultural Revolution*, edited by Jonathan Eisen, 109-17. New York: Vintage Books.

Belz, Carl. 1972. *The Story of Rock*. New York: Harper and Row.

Birchall, Ian. 1969. "The Decline and Fall of British Rhythm and Blues." In *The Age of Rock: Sounds of the American Cultural Revolution*, edited by Jonathan Eisen, 94-102. New York: Vintage Books.

Boyd, Jean A. 2001. *Oral Memoirs of Johnny Cuviello and Steve Hathaway*. Waco, TX: BaylorUniversity Institute for Oral History. Transcript, http://digitalcollections.baylor.edu/cdm/ref/collection/buioh/id/1228.

Brown, Charles T. 1983. *The Art of Rock and Roll*. Englewood Cliffs, NJ: Prentice-Hall.

Brown, Lee B. 2004. "Marsalis and Baraka: An Essay in Comparative Cultural Discourse." *Popular Music* 23(3): 241-55.

Campbell, Michael, with James Brody. 2008. *Rock and Roll: An Introduction*. 2nd ed. Boston: Schirmer.

Christgau, Robert. 1992. "Chuck Berry." In *The Rolling Stone Illustrated History of Rock and Roll*, edited by Anthony DeCurtis and James Henke, with Holly George Warren, 60-66. New York: Random House/Rolling Stone Press.

D'Anjou, Leo. 2003. "The Riddles of Rock and Roll." *Soundscapes: Journal on Media Culture*, April 6, http://www.icce.rug.nl/~soundscapes/VOLUME06/Riddles_rocknroll1.shtml.

DeCurtis, Anthony. 1996. "Is Rock 'n' Roll a White Man's Game?" *Time* 147(18): 78.

Evans, David. 1987. "Blues and Modern Sound: Past, Present, and Future." In *Rock Music in America*, edited by Janet Podell, 8-17. New York: H. W. Wilson.

Ewen, David. 1977. *All the Years of American Popular Music*. Englewood Cliffs, NJ: Prentice-Hall.

Flanagan, Bill. 1989. "When Hits Were Hip: Top 40 Experiences its Second Golden Age." *Musician*, November.

Friedlander, Paul, with Peter Miller. 2006. *Rock and Roll: A Social History*. 2nd ed. Boulder, CO: Westview.

George, Nelson. 1989. *The Death of Rhythm and Blues*. New York: E.P. Dutton.

Gillett, Charlie. 1996. *The Sound of the City: The Rise of Rock and Roll*. New York: Outerbridge & Dienstfrey.

Gracyck, Thodore. 1996. *Rhythm and Noise: An Aesthetics of Rock*. London: Tauris.

Hamilton, Michelle. 1999. "Review Article: The Lure of Black Style." *Journal of Contemporary History* 34(4): 641-51.

Harris, Marvin. 1974. *Patterns of Race in the Americas*. New York: W. W. Norton.

Hatch, David, and Stephen Millward. 1987. *From Blues to Rock: An Analytical History of Pop Music*. Manchester, UK: Manchester University Press.

Hess, Mickey. 2005. "Hip-Hop Realness and the White Performer." *Critical Studies in Media Communication* 22(5): 372-89.

Horowitz, Irving L. 2010. "Rock, Recordings and Rebellion." In *The Anti-American Generation*, edited by Edgar Z. Friedenberg, 137-60. New Brunswick, NJ: Transaction Books.

Jhally, Sut. 1997. *Race, the Floating Signifier, Featuring Stuart Hall*. Northampton, MA: Media Education Foundation. Transcript, http://www.mediaed.org/assets/products/407/transcript_407.pdf.

Kamin, Jonathan. 1975. "Parallels in the Social Reactions to Jazz and Rock." *Black Perspective in Music* 3(3): 278-98.

Killick, Andrew P. 2001. "Music as Ethnic Marker in Film: The 'Jewish' Case." In *Essays on Film and Popular Music*, edited by Pamela R. Wojcik and Arthur Knight, 185-201. Durham, NC: Duke University Press.

Manuel, Peter. 1994. "Puerto Rican Music and Cultural Identity: Creative Appropriation of Cuban Sources from Danza to Salsa." *Ethnomusicology* 38(2): 249-80.

Marcus, Greil. 1997. *Mystery Train: Images of America in Rock 'n' Roll Music*. 4th rev. ed. New York: Plume.

Martin, Linda, and Kerry Segrave. 1993. *Anti-Rock: The Opposition to Rock 'n' Roll*. Cambridge, MA: Da Capo.

Meltzer, Richard. 1970. *The Aesthetics of Rock*. New York: Something Else Press.

Moore, Allan. 2002. "Authenticity as Authentication." *Popular Music* 21(2): 209-23.

Morrison, Craig. 1996. *Go Cat Go! Rockabilly Music and its Makers*. Urbana, IL: University of Illinois Press.

Nettl, Bruno. 1976. *Folk Music in the United States*. Detroit: Wayne State University Press.

Palmer, Robert. 1992. "Rock Begins." In *The Rolling Stone Illustrated History of Rock and Roll*, edited by Anthony DeCurtis and

James Henke, with Holly George Warren, 3-16. New York: Random House/Rolling Stone Press.

———. 1995. *Rock & Roll: An Unruly History*. New York: Harmony.

Peterson, Richard A. 1997. *Creating Country Music: Fabricating Authenticity*. Chicago: University of Chicago Press.

Plasketes, George. 1989. "Great Balls of Fire!" *Popular Music and Society* 13(3): 75-80.

Redd, Lawrence N. 1985. "Rock! It's Still Rhythm and Blues." *Black Perspective in Music* 13(1): 31-47.

Rowland, M. 1989. "Ebony Meets Ivory: Crossover and MTV Remake the Rules of the Game." *Musician*, November.

Rudinow, Joel. 1994. "Race, Ethnicity, Expressive Authenticity: Can White People Sing the Blues?" *Journal of Aesthetics and Art Criticism* 52(1): 127-37.

Salvo, Patrick William. 1989. "Chuck Berry, 1972." In *The Rolling Stone Interviews*, edited by Peter Herbst, 224-35. New York: St. Martin's Griffin.

Savage, Steve. 1989. *The Billboard Book of Rhythm*. New York: Watson-Guptill.

Shaw, Arnold. 1974. *The Rockin' 50s: The Decade that Transformed the Pop Music Scene*. New York: Hawthorn.

Smith, Joe, and Mitchell Fink. 1988. *Off the Record: An Oral History of Popular Music*. New York: Warner.

Stuessy, Joe, and Scott Lipscomb. 2009. *Rock and Roll: Its History and Stylistic Development*. 6th ed. Englewood Cliffs, NJ: Prentice-Hall.

Szatmary, David P. 2000. *Rockin' in Time: a Social History of Rock and Roll*. 4th ed. Englewood Cliffs, NJ: Prentice-Hall.

Tagg, Philip. 1989. "Open Letter: 'Black Music', 'Afro-American Music' and 'European Music'." *Popular Music* 8(3): 285-98.

Titon, Jeff Todd. 2009. "North America/Black America." In *Worlds of Music*, edited by Jeff T. Titon, 107-42. New York: Schirmer Books.

Tosches, Nick. 1999. *Unsung Heroes of Rock and Roll: The Birth of Rock in The Wild Years Before Elvis*. New York: Da Capo.

Trimillos, Ricardo. 1989. "Music and Ethnic Identity: Strategies among Overseas Filipino Youth." *Yearbook for Traditional Music* 21:9-21.

Ward, Brian. 1998. *Just My Soul Responding: Rhythm and Blues, Black Consciousness, and Race Relations*. Berkeley: University of California Press.

Ward, Ed. 1986. "The Fifties and Before." In *Rock of Ages: The History of Rock and Roll*, edited by Ed Ward, Geoffrey Stokes, and Ken Tucker, 17-246. New York: Rolling Stone Press/Summit Books.

Waterman, Christopher A. 2000. "Race Music: Bo Chatmon, 'Corinne Corinna,' and the Excluded Middle." In *Music and the Racial Imagination*, edited by Ronald Radano and Philip V. Bohlman, 167-205. Chicago: University of Chicago Press.

Wicke, Peter. 1990. *Rock Music: Culture, Aesthetics and Sociology*. New York: Cambridge University Press.

Wilgus, D. K. 1970. "Country-Western Music and the Urban Hillbilly." *Journal of American Folklore* 83(328): 157-79.

Willis, Paul. 1990. "The Golden Age." In *On Record: Rock, Pop, and the Written Word*, edited by Simon Frith and Andrew Goodwin, 35-45. New York: Pantheon Books.

Does Our Being There Change What We Come to Study?

Lindsey King

Abstract

While documenting an ex-voto tradition in a small Roman Catholic shrine town in Northeast Brazil where pilgrims craft mimetic offerings in payment for a spiritual healing, I began to see subtle changes in the manufacture of and interest shown in these offerings. Was this just a coincidence or did my traveling from the United States with expensive cameras and recording equipment spark this change? In this discussion, I examine the "art" of anthropology, delving into the question of how our gaze may be changing the material traditions that we travel to study and what linking changes this may bring to that culture.

As cultural anthropologists, we go to live with folks who do not know us and depend on their good grace to allow us to work with them, live with them, write about them, and hopefully turn our experiences into something that garners us employment. In the best of cases, we build lasting relationships and have a project that will sustain us at least until we get tenure, if not throughout our entire career. As is the case with most of us, my life has been profoundly changed by my experiences in the field. That fieldwork changes us is nothing new. The documentation that we undertake doesn't stop with our target population. It also forces us to spend a whole bunch of time with ourselves, giving us a particular insight that many people don't have the opportunity to gain.

The fact that culture is not static is also nothing new. It is one of the first aspects of culture that anthropologists learn. It must change in order to stay viable. With this in mind, we realize that even as we are studying a culture it is changing. There are many reasons for culture change to occur: diffusion, innovation, politics, economics, even the physical environment. These changes are often predictable and recognizable when we revisit our field sites. However, are there other changes that we did not predict; and to what extent are we, the researchers, responsible for some aspect of these changes? What I wonder—and have wondered since my first field experience—is how did my being there affect not only people I came to love but also the very traditions that I came to document? Did my being there effect a change in more than with a few people? Did my documenting a religious folk tradition in a small Roman Catholic shrine town in northern Brazil actually change the tradition itself?

My fieldwork in Brazil focuses on a material tradition found in what has been called folk Catholicism and is centered on the offering of mimetic art that represents a social or physical "dis-ease." These offerings, called *milagres* (*milagros* in Spanish and *tamata* in Greek) fall under the broader umbrella of offerings called *ex-votos* (meaning "from a vow" in Latin). This tradition was found in pre-Christian Greek and Roman societies and traveled through Europe with the Roman Empire. Examples of this tradition can still be found in parts of Europe, throughout Latin America, and in cities in North America with substantial Hispanic, Portuguese, or Greek populations.[1]

These offerings are usually small base metal representations of parts of the human body, animals, cars, houses, and other objects of modern life and are given to a patron saint in payment for intercession in the healing of a problem. A spiritual contract is made between an individual and a saint called a *promessa* (Portuguese and Spanish), which translates in English as to "promise." In this spiritual contract, the individual vows to repay the saint for his assistance. The contract can be fulfilled by making a pilgrimage, by tithing, by slaughtering an animal, or in any other way that is "agreed" upon by the supplicant and the saint. In Brazil, the contract is most often repaid by the making and offering of a *milagre*. This word means "miracle" (*milagro* in Spanish), and this word choice reflects the strong belief system held by the practitioners of the saint's efficacy in the making of miracles.

Dr. Adalberto Barreto, a native of Brazil and professor at Universidade Federal do Ceará in Fortaleza has been a pioneer in researching this tradition for many years. A few non-Brazilian researchers have also visited my field site for short periods of time. However, I am the first non-Brazilian anthropologist to spend several field seasons there. Could I, a North American who spent every day for months at a time talking with pilgrims and taking pictures of their offerings, influence the local population to regard the tradition differently? Can our being there change what we come to study? The Hawthorne Effect, which roughly states that people's behavior will change when they are aware that they are being studied, suggests this outcome to be highly likely (Roethlisberger and Dickson 1939). Using my own research as a case study, I will discuss this idea in this chapter.

Canindé, my field site, is a small Roman Catholic town in northeast Brazil in the state of Ceará. It is located about one hundred kilometers inland from the coastal capital of Fortaleza. Situated in the inhospitable backlands of the *sertão*, small farmers in this region have been plagued by shortages of water. Past cycles of drought have resulted in malnutrition and related diseases, and over half of the instances of infant mortality in Brazil occur in this northeast region (Nations and Rebhun 1988). In fact, northeast Brazil has been compared to the Australian Outback because of its extreme environment, and it encompasses what was once labeled the largest area of poverty in South America (Pang 1989). It is to this dry barren region that I first came to study the tradition of milagres. My introduction to this tradition was in a Medical Anthropology course. My professor had spent a day at the shrine in Canindé while visiting a Brazilian colleague in Fortaleza. He brought some wooden objects to class that had been given to him by the Franciscan *freis* (brothers) at the shrine. As a class project, we were given the task of trying to identify the problems depicted by the objects. For example, one of the figures was covered in red spots of paint, depicting a tropical rash. Another figure was a piece of wood that had been carved into a rough heart shape with the photograph of a young boy glued onto it. We decided this meant the young boy had been born with a cardiovascular problem. These potent objects captivated me on the spot, and I am still captivated by them all these many years later.

My first field season and the eventual subject of my dissertation and later research combined my past knowledge of art with my anthropological interest in social justice. Because institutional medical care was not then widely available in this region of Brazil, I wanted to research the vitality of this votive tradition and see if the making of a promessa as a healing strategy was still viable. As it turns out, it certainly was then and continues to be today.

For the most part, I spent my days in Canindé sitting and waiting, something that I never imagined anthropological fieldwork would be like while growing up reading issues of *National Geographic*. My primary concern has been documenting the art of the milagres that is produced by individuals who come to the shrine to fulfill their part of the promessa with the shrine's patron, St. Francis. Westerners know this saint as St. Francis of Assisi, but locally, he is called São Francisco do Canindé (St. Francis of Canindé) or São Francisco das Chagas (St. Francis of Wounds). Reportedly, having been the first person to receive the ritual wounds of Jesus Christ, St. Francis is often depicted with stigmata. From these images, he received this vernacular name. St. Francis is also associated with thaumaturgy, the practice of miracles. As previously mentioned, milagres are often small objects made of metal that replicate social or physical problems. Wax molds are also used in many parts of the world to make these offerings. However, one of the most fascinating aspects of this tradition found in northeast Brazil is that the milagres are most often made by or for each individual and artistically depict their special physical or social problem through the manipulation of materials such as clay, wood, cloth and even recycled objects (photograph 11.1). Many milagres graphically depict a medical problem by showing a gaping wound or a misshapen limb. With other milagres the problem may be harder to discern, and talking with the pilgrim is the only way to understand what is being described. A great portion of my time in Canindé found me in the Casa dos Milagres (House of Miracles) where pilgrims come to deposit their milagres. This is a small building adjacent to the Basílica de São Francisco (Basilica of St. Francis). Since this ex-voto tradition is considered by the clergy to be outside the dogma of the Catholic Church, offerings are not left in "sacred" spaces such as the Basilica. At other Roman Catholic shrines throughout the world, similar offerings are remanded to a separate building or a minor chapel.

During my first field season, even though not in a "sacred" setting, I was hesitant to talk with pilgrims when they offered their milagres, not wanting to encroach upon what I assumed was a private moment. Soon it became clear to me that the quiet, meditative behavior that I expected to accompany the deposition of an ex-voto did not necessarily happen and that people enjoyed my approaching them and asking them about their milagres and the stories behind the creation of them. Pilgrims told me that they considered milagres *arte popular* and that what they considered examples of sacred art

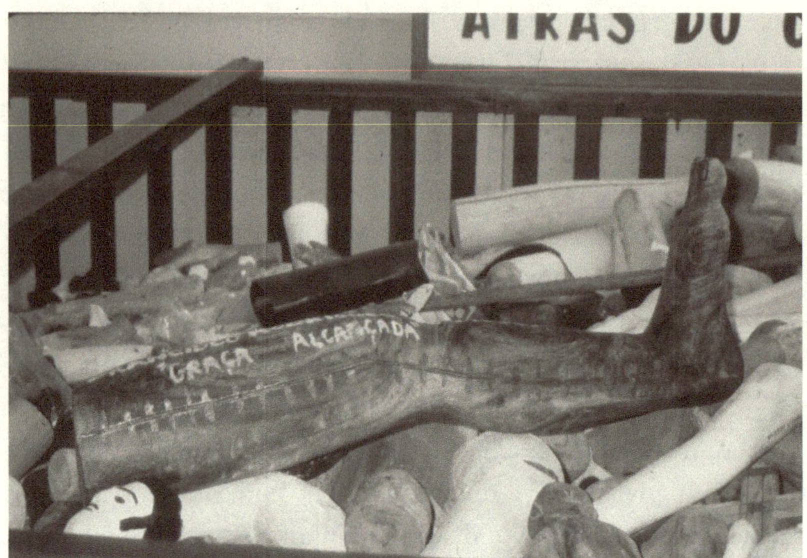

Photograph 11.1. Many milagres graphically depict a medical problem by showing a gaping wound or a misshapen limb. (Photograph by author)

were the plaster religious statues that could be purchased at all the souvenir shops that surround the Basilica. Interestingly, whenever people purchased these statues, they brought them to a priest to be blessed, which does not happen in the offering of a milagre. From this, I have come to believe that it is the priest's blessing that "activates" the sacredness of the statues, while it is the promessa, the vow, that is sacred in the votive tradition and not the milagre itself.

The behavior of the pilgrims around the milagres varies. Some people get down on their knees and pray when they make their offering; some people cry. Other people run in and literally throw their ex-votos in the bin, the receptacle for the offerings, and leave. In most cases, behavior does not seem to visually change during the act of deposition. Many times the individuals may have a friend take a photograph of themselves in the act of leaving their offering. Usually the individuals will place their ex-voto in the bin and stand there looking at other offerings. Sometimes they will pick up other milagres and discuss among themselves the purpose of the object—what it is supposed to depict.

The variation of the objects themselves is endless. For someone interested in folk art and especially in how people might envision and craft an image of their "dis -ease," being in the Casa dos Milagres is like a new exhibit and psychological study every day. An ongoing problem for me, however, is how to define the aesthetics of a genre that has no distinctive aesthetic criteria. An individual, who in most cases, has little familiarity with art other than religious statuary and images crafts each object. When I first began traveling to Canindé, the milagres were not made with the idea of being critiqued and put on display. In most cases, the "life" of an ex-voto was a brief one. At the end of each pilgrimage season, the milagres were destroyed by being burned. The reason for their destruction, I was told by one of the Franciscans, was the sheer mass of offerings deposited each year. A few were saved, selected in most cases for their technical merit, in other words, the innate ability of the person who made it to craft an object that was pleasing and meaningful (in the traditional aesthetic of Western art). In most cases, these milagres were of wood and were more polished and finely finished. These select few were added to the small collection in the local museum run by the Church, and even fewer were added to the collections of museums and individuals around the world.

When I have asked pilgrims about the destruction of their offerings, they usually reply that they are not disturbed by it. Most people respond that the ex-votos are forgotten once they are deposited. From these responses, it would appear that the milagres are created purely to fulfill the contract made between St. Francis and the individual and, as such, can be viewed as a type of spiritual currency used to pay off a divine debt. Further discussion with the pilgrims revealed that while aesthetics may influence the object's creation, it is not the foremost criterion. According to what I have been told, a successful image is one that can be recognized as representative of the problem, regardless of the artist's technique. While it is true that some people examine the milagres deposited in the bin and judge them to be *bem* (good) or *feo* (ugly), this evaluation usually refers to an arbitrary value or taste rather than to artistic ability. The pilgrims deem some of the milagres that I think are wonderful "unsuccessful." Because I have had training in art and because I have been influenced by other aesthetics, I see certain aspects in some milagres reminiscent of African masks or Southern "Outsider" artists and think they are wonderful. Yet, when I ask pilgrims in the shrine about these particular pieces, the objects are often not praised because the pilgrims say the angles are not human-like or that the face looks distorted. I often struggle with the idea of how I, as an outsider in the culture, in the faith, and in the ex-voto tradition, can work with these objects without looking at them with Western value judgment. Can I see them in the same light as insiders, or does the bias of a Western-trained art historian/folklorist/cultural anthropologist come to the field with me? In the years I have been studying these offerings, I have grown and developed a new lens from which to view these objects, a view which as we know only comes through seasons of experience. It is called "field sight." Through this lens, we as seasoned anthropologists endeavor to obtain the emic viewpoint of what we study. But even so, is it ever truly their viewpoint?

When I first went to Canindé in the summer of 1994, the Casa dos Milagres had a single large room where pilgrims came to fulfill their promessas (photograph 11.2). A large bin, into which a variety of ex-votos could be placed, filled most of one side of the room. These ex-votos ranged from the mimetic milagres to crutches, eyeglasses, candles, prosthetic limbs, leg braces, discarded leg or arm casts, x-rays,

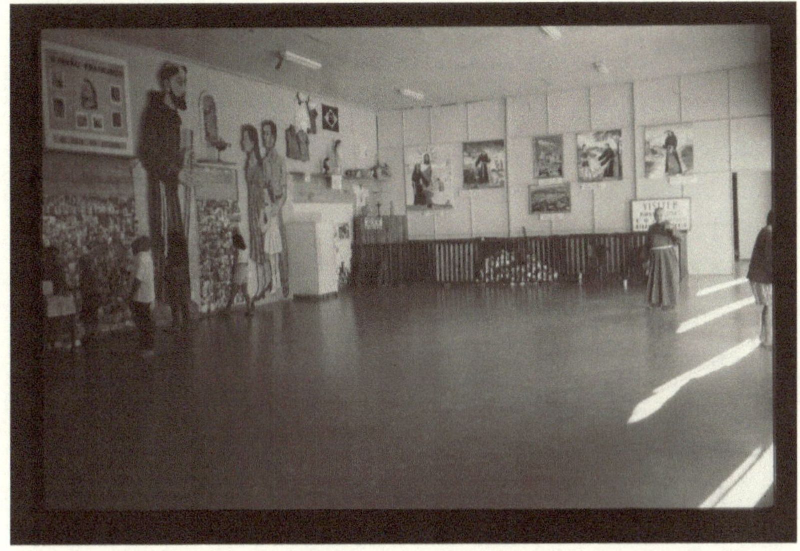

Photograph 11.2. The Casa dos Milagres had a single large room where pilgrims came to fulfill their promessas. A large bin, into which a variety of ex-votos could be placed, filled most of one side of the room. (Photograph by author)

containers of exuvial matter, bottles of *cachaca*, broken religious statuary, and many other items. Periodically, when the bins were filled to overflowing, they were emptied and their contents taken to an enclosed property owned by the monastery to await burning. Women who had pledged to cut their hair or their children's hair had a special bin just for their shorn locks. When the bin filled with swatches of different people's hair, the Franciscans emptied it and sold the hair to wig makers. The *batinas*, the traditional brown costume worn by pilgrims coming to Canindé that mimic those worn by Franciscan freis, were placed in another bin, washed, and then redistributed throughout the parish. On the walls of the Casa dos Milagres were random snapshots brought to the shrine by pilgrims.

Photographs are often brought by pilgrims to "reinforce" their promessa. Pilgrims who are paying a promessa in proxy for another person who, for whatever reason, could not make the trip themselves also often bring photographs to the shrine. Some shots depict injury, while others depict new cars, farm animals, deceased in coffins, soccer teams, soldiers, or newborns. These photos were placed on the walls in a haphazard fashion. Day in and day out, I would sit in a chair alongside the bin with Maria and D'Assis (two individuals who worked as docents in the Casa dos Milagres) and talk with pilgrims. We were instructed by the freis to remove crutches and eyeglasses that were offered by pilgrims to give to people in the parish who could use them.

Canindé is a small town, and it quickly became common local knowledge who I was, why I was in Canindé, and what I was interested in. Maria and D'Assis would make sure that each pilgrim talked with me, and if for some reason I wasn't there, they would be sure to show me all the new milagres that were deposited in my absence. Since I would sometimes take different genres of milagres out of the bin and photograph them, often just to relieve boredom during a slow day, both the locals and the pilgrims gradually seemed to show more interest in the objects themselves. I noticed that locals and pilgrims would often watch as I selected milagres to photograph and many times would suggest additional milagres for me to shoot. Also, it became more frequent that while I interviewed pilgrims, other pilgrims or workers in the Casa dos Milagres would stand close by to hear and comment on their stories. Another very interesting phenomenon occurred toward the end of my field season in 1996. Since Canindé is a pilgrimage destination, most of my research population is comprised of transient pilgrims staying in Canindé for only a few days. However, a handful of locals are known to carve milagres for other people. One day while looking at the milagres, I noticed that one particular carver had begun signing her carvings just like an artist signs a piece of art. As far as I know, this was previously unknown, at least at this particular shrine. Why did this carver begin to sign her carvings? Did my attention to this art form influence this act? Did she want people to recognize and appreciate her carving? Also toward the end of my 1996 field season, one of the Franciscans asked me to be on the lookout for any "good" milagres to pull from the bin to be added to the collection at their small museum. This museum had been created in 1969, and very few milagres had been added since then. I was thrilled at the time to have this "curatorial" assignment, but in retrospect, I am a bit uncomfortable with my being asked to do this rather than Maria or D'Assis. Why was it decided to add to the collection then, after almost thirty years, and why was I asked rather than someone who was a practitioner of the ritual? I chose milagres that I found to be very expressive, but are they really the same ones that a practitioner would have saved from the fire?

I returned to Canindé during the summer of 2011, fifteen years after my last visit, and I knew there would be changes to the town and probably the shrine. When I was previously in Brazil in 1996, the economy was in a very fragile state. The *real*, the currency of Brazil, was so unstable that from one day to the next its local buying power was subject to change. Now Brazil's economy is stable and quite strong. Evidence for this can be seen in many ways, especially in Canindé. The sleepy little town with one policeman in 1996 now has several jeeps full of policemen dressed in flak jackets and carrying semiautomatic weapons. Also, all of the residents who work for the parish now wear uniforms of brown shirts embroidered with the logo of the Basilica and denim jeans instead of their own clothes. Further evidence of prosperity and change includes several local businesses offering Internet access, and happily, my room at the monastery now had air conditioning rather than an oscillating fan. However, the most striking change was in the Casa dos Milagres. I am sure that my jaw dropped when I first walked in. Along the wall where I used to sit by the big bin of ex-votos is now a shiny glass and metal gift shop selling religious statuary, rosaries, religious literature, and jewelry (photograph 11.3). The bin for depositing milagres has been moved to a center wall and is the first thing one sees when entering. The original rear wall of the room has been taken down, and a second room devoted to the milagres now exists. Hanging on this wall are now hundreds of examples of offerings (photograph 11.4.)

There are clear display cases of wedding dresses, sports uniforms, and military uniforms. There are shelves of handmade houses and trucks and beneath them milagres that are too large to hang or shelve. The bins for offerings of hair and for the batinas still exist. However, now there is a cubicle where one can change out of the batina in private, rather than just disrobing in the middle of the room as was done previously. On at least two walls are photographs, but rather than being haphazardly arranged, they are now organized and grouped into genres. One can find groupings of pets, mastectomies, babies, and sports teams, all in different sections rather than intermixed as before.

Another change has to do with one of the vernacular religious icons. When I first came to Canindé people would come up and ask me where the *meninha* was. Meninha means "little girl." For a while, I was confused that so many little girls were lost and why people would think I would know where they could be. I was then told about the Meninha dos Amazonas, a doll that was kept in the museum, which had become an important icon to the followers of St. Francis. A family had reportedly brought the doll to the shrine many years ago in thanks to St. Francis for finding their little girl who had wandered into the jungle as they were clearing their land. The story, which is considered part of the informal liturgy of the followers, tells of the child being lost for several days, and then after a promessa was

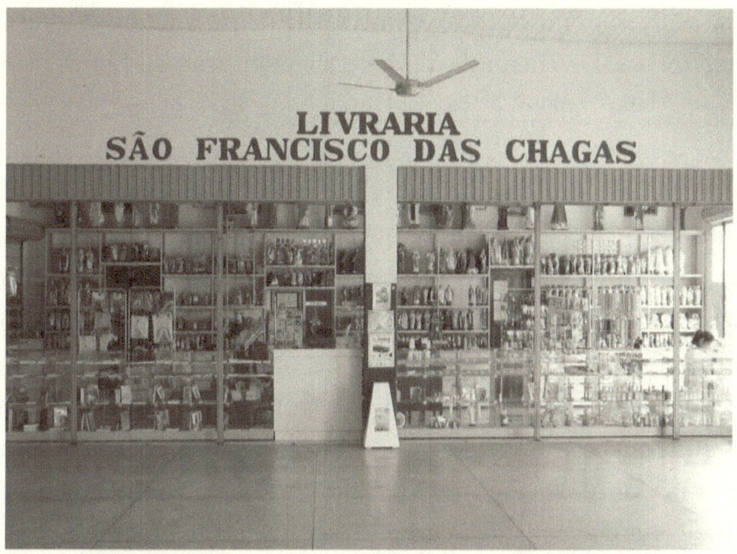

Photograph 11.3. Along the wall where I used to sit by the big bin of ex-votos is now a shiny glass and metal gift shop selling religious statuary, rosaries, religious literature, and jewelry. (Photograph by author)

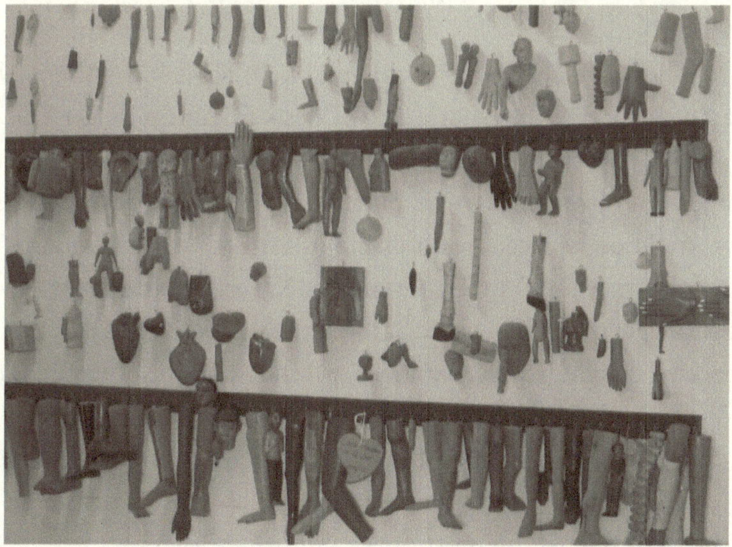

Photograph 11.4. The original rear wall of the room has been taken down, and a second room devoted to the milagres now exists. Hanging on this wall are now hundreds of examples of offerings. (Photograph by author)

made with Saõ Francisco, she soon walked into her family's yard no worse for wear. When asked where she had been and how she had survived, she replied, "This old man took care of me." When her family came to Canindé to repay St. Francis, reportedly upon entering the basilica and seeing the ceiling mural of St. Francis, the child exclaimed, "That is the old man who took care of me." This story is now very famous, and all pilgrims pay a visit to see the Meninha when coming to Canindé. The original Meninha, or at least the one that had been in the museum for the past forty years or so, was a rather dusty plastic commercial doll from the 1950s or 1960s, so I was quite surprised when I saw the current version of the Meninha. She is no longer in the museum and has her own designated area in the Casa dos Milagres complete with a plaque telling her story. However, the dusty plastic doll of the previous years has been cleaned and is dressed totally differently. I did not even recognize her and when I questioned the change, I was simply told that this version was "prettier."

Needless to say, all these changes were a bit more than I had imagined. I knew that Maria and D'Assis might no longer work at the shrine (Maria is retired, and D'Assis has become a Franciscan brother who lives in another part of Brazil), but I never dreamed they would be replaced by an official information kiosk manned by an employee of the church in uniform. Nevertheless, I knew several of the people who still worked at the shrine, and when asked, they all expressed delight with the modern gift shop and the other changes.

When I left Canindé in 1996, there had been a bit of a rift within the brotherhood as to the future of the shrine. Some of the members wanted things to stay as they were and to protect the shrine for the poor who make up most of the pilgrims. Others wanted to join with some local businessmen to promote the shrine as an international religious tourism destination. During the years, the leading proponent for the poor was transferred and sadly has passed away. The monastery has had an infusion of new brothers since my last trip, and they are working diligently toward increasing the profile of the shrine and drawing international visitors. Mass is now broadcast throughout Brazil via television, and there is a Franciscan who works full time to create liaisons with local and national governments to aid in the promotion of the shrine. The modernization of the Casa dos Milagres is part and parcel of this desire.

The Catholic Church is very enthusiastic about increasing the profile of Canindé as a world pilgrimage site. However, Canindé is a small town, and there is no infrastructure for tourists. Pilgrims who do come to Canindé are usually Brazilians from lower economic brackets and are comfortable hanging a hammock in the campground owned by the monastery. Because I do not relish living in the campground for long periods of time, I have had the pleasure of living at the monastery with the freis during my field seasons. As a tall North American woman, I initially stood out as a stranger, and even though I did not know everyone in town, everyone knew me and knew I was there to study the "art" of the ephemeral milagre tradition. With the current change of hanging the milagres on the wall in the Casa dos Milagres instead of burning them at the end of the pilgrimage season, the milagres are no longer ephemeral works. They are now placed on the wall to be admired and judged by others.

It is not my intention to say that my trips to research the milagres definitively led to these changes. In fact, they may have had nothing to do with them. As we know, change is inevitable. However, I wonder if we as cultural documenters realize that we may be instigators of change. Would the milagres in Canindé still be burned at the end of the pilgrimage season if I had not come to study them? Is the fact that I was viewed photographing them every day the reason they aren't destroyed and are now put on the wall for display? Are other milagre makers signing their work? More importantly, have these outward changes eroded or changed the spiritual tradition itself? Does this permanent "exhibition" change the process of creation of milagres in any way? Has this changed the "currency" of this tradition? Do different aesthetics enter into the worthiness of the offering now, and if so, did my aesthetic decisions have any bearing on this? These are the questions that I will probably never know the answers to, but they are questions that I will take to the field with me with each new field season and that will impact each new field project. I will always wonder, did my being there change what I came to study?

Note

1. Please see the work of the following: Barreto personal papers (n.d.); Bercht (1989); Cardoso (1983); Cassar (1964); Cátedra (1988); Davidson (1998); della Cava (1970); Deyts (1988); Dörner (1962); Dubisch (1995); Egan (1991); Finucane (1977); Forman (1975); Frota (1989); Garbini (1966); Greenfield (2001); Greenfield and Cavalcante (2005); Gross (1971); Hansen (1968); Jackson (1988); King (2005); Lanciani (1967); Marinatos and Hirmer (1960); Medeiros (1987); Meirelles (1968); Merrifield (1987); Mota (1968); Nolan (1991); Nolan and Nolan (1989); Oettinger (1990, 1992, 1997); Oktavec (1995); Pina-Cabral (1986); Radford (1949); Romano (1965); Rouse (1902); Saia (1944); Sanchis (1983); Scott (2010); Slater (1986, 1990); Toor (1947); Turner and Turner (1978); Wilson (1983).

References

Barreto, Adalberto. n.d. "Ex-votos: Os Milagres dos Santos." Unpublished manuscript. Universidade Federal do Ceará, Fortaleza.

Bercht, Fatima. 1989. *Miracles: Votive Offerings in Northeastern Brazil.* New York: Americas Society. Exhibition catalog.

Cardoso, Carlos Lopes. 1983. "Ex-voto, uma expressao ambigua." In *Primeira Exposicao Nacional de Paineis Votivos do Rio, do Mare do Alem-Mar.* Lisbon: Museu de Marinha.

Cassar, Paul. 1964. "Medical Votive Offerings in the Maltese Islands." *Journal of the Royal Anthropological Institute of Great Britain and Ireland* 94(1, 2): 23-29.

Cátedra, María. 1988. *This World, Other Worlds.* Translated by William A. Christian Jr. Chicago: University of Chicago Press.

Davidson, Hilda E. 1998. *Roles of the Northern Goddess.* London: Routledge.

della Cava, Ralph. 1970. *Miracle at Joaseiro.* New York: Columbia University Press.

Deyts, Simone. 1988. "Ex-voto de Guerison en Gaule." *Historie et Archologie* 23:82-87.

Dörner, Gerd. 1962. *Folk Art of Mexico.* New York: A. S. Barnes.

Dubisch, Jill. 1995. *In a Different Place: Pilgrimage, Gender, and Politics at a Greek Island Shrine.* Princeton: Princeton University Press.

Egan, Martha. 1991. *Milagros: Votive Offerings from the Americas.* Santa Fe: Museum of New Mexico Press.

Finucane, Ronald C. 1977. *Miracles and Pilgrims: Popular Beliefs in Medieval England.* Lanham, MD: Rowman & Littlefield.

Forman, Shepard. 1975. *The Brazilian Peasantry.* New York: Columbia University Press.

Frota, Lelia Coelho. 1989. *The Ex-Voto of Northeastern Brazil: Its Antecedents and Contemporary Expression*. New York: Americas Society. Exhibition catalog.

Garbini, Giovanni. 1966. *The Ancient World*. New York: McGraw-Hill.

Greenfield, Sidney M. 2001. "Population Growth, Industrialization and the Proliferation of Syncretized Religions in Brazil." In *Reinventing Religions: Syncretism and Transformation in Africa and the Americas*, edited by Sidney Greenfield and André Droogers, 55-70. Lanham, MD: Rowman & Littlefield.

Greenfield, Sidney, and Antonio Mourão Cavalcante. 2005. "Pilgrimage Healing in Northeast Brazil." In *Pilgrimage and Healing*, edited by Jill Dubisch and Michael Winkleman, 3-24. Tucson: University of Arizona Press.

Gross, Daniel R. 1971. "Ritual and Conformity: A Religious Pilgrimage to Northeastern Brazil." *Ethnology* 10(2): 129-48.

Hansen, H. J. 1968. *European Folk Art in Europe and the Americas*. Translated by Mary Whittall. London: Thames and Hudson.

Jackson, Ralph. 1988. *Doctors and Diseases in the Roman Empire*. Norman: University of Oklahoma Press.

King, C. Lindsey. 2005. "Pilgrimage, Promises, and Ex-Votos." In *Pilgrimage and Healing*, edited by Jill Dubisch and Michael Winkleman, 49-68. Tucson: University of Arizona Press.

Lanciani, Rodolfo. 1967. *Pagan and Christian Rome*. Boston: Houghton, Mifflin.

Marinatos, Spyridon, and Max Hirmer. 1960. *Crete and Mycenae*. New York: Harry N. Abrams.

Medeiros, Aderson. 1987. "Ex-voto e Romaria." In *Brasil: Arte Popular Hoje*, edited by L. Frota. Editoração-Publicações E Comunicação Ltda.

Meirelles, Cecília. 1968. *As Artes Plásticas no Brasil: Artes Populares.* Rio de Janeiro: Edições de Ouro.

Merrifield, Ralph. 1987. *The Archaeology of Ritual and Magic.* New York: New Amsterdam Books.

Mota, Mauro. 1968. *Votos Ex-Votos: Aspectos da Vida Social do Nordeste.* Recife: Universidade Federal de Pernambuco.

Nations, Marilyn K., and L. A. Rebhun. 1988. "Angels with Wet Wings Won't Fly: Maternal Sentiment in Brazil and the Image of Neglect." *Culture, Medicine and Psychiatry* 12:141-200.

Nolan, Mary Lee. 1991. "The European Roots of Latin American Pilgrimage." In *Pilgrimage in Latin America*, edited by N. Ross Crumrine and Alan Morinis, 19-49. New York: Greenwood Press.

Nolan, Mary Lee, and Sidney Nolan. 1989. *Christian Pilgrimage in Modern Western Europe.* Chapel Hill: University of North Carolina Press.

Oettinger, Marion Jr. 1990. Folk Treasures of Mexico: The Nelson A. Rockefeller Collection. New York: Harry N. Abrams.

———. 1992. *The Folk Art of Latin America: Visiones Del Pueblo.* New York: Dutton Studio Books.

———. 1997. *Folk Art of Spain and the Americas: El Alma del Pueblo, San Antonio Museum of Art.* New York: Abbeville Press.

Oktavec, Eileen. 1995. *Answered Prayers: Miracles and Milagros Along the Border.* Tucson: University of Arizona Press.

Pang, Eul-Soo. 1989. "Agrarian Change in the Northeast." In *Modern Brazil: Elites and Masses in Historical Perspective*, edited by Michael L. Conniff and Frank. D. McCann, 123-39. Lincoln: University of Nebraska Press.

Pina-Cabral, João de. 1986. *Sons of Adam, Daughters of Eve: The Peasant Worldview of the Alto Minho*. Oxford: Clarendon Press.

Radford, U. M. 1949. "The Wax Images Found in Exeter Cathedral." *Antiquaries Journal* 29:164-69.

Roethlisberger, F. J., and William J. Dickson. 1939. *Management and the Worker: An Account of a Research Program Conducted by the Western Electric Company, Hawthorne Works, Chicago*. Cambridge, MA: Harvard University Press.

Romano, Octavio Ignacio. 1965. "Charismatic Medicine, Folk-Healing, and Folk Sainthood." *American Anthropologist* 67(2): 1151-73.

Rouse, W. H. D. 1902. *Greek Votive Offerings: An Essay in the History of Greek Religion*. Cambridge: Cambridge University Press.

Saia, Luiz. 1944. *Escultura Popular Brasileira*. Sao Paulo: Edicoes Graveta.

Sanchis, Pierre. 1983. "The Portuguese Romarias." In *Saints and Their Cults: Studies in Religious Sociology, Folklore and History*, edited by Stephen Wilson, 261-90. Cambridge: Cambridge University Press.

Scott, Robert A. 2010. *Miracle Cures: Saints, Pilgrimage, and the Healing Power of Belief*. Berkeley: University of California Press.

Slater, Candace. 1986. *Trail of Miracles: Stories from a Pilgrimage in Northeast Brazil*. Berkeley: University of California Press.

———. 1990. "Miracle Stories and Milagres in Northeast Brazil." *Journal of Latin American Lore* 16(1): 109-27.

Toor, Frances. 1947. *A Treasury of Mexican Folkways*. New York: Crown.

Turner, Victor, and Edith L. B. Turner. 1978. *Image and Pilgrimage in Christian Culture*. New York: Columbia University Press.

Wilson, Stephen. 1983a. "Cults of Saints in the Churches of Central Paris." In *Saints and Their Cults: Studies in Religious Sociology, Folklore, and History*, edited by Stephen Wilson, 233-60. Cambridge: Cambridge University Press.

———. 1983b. Introduction to *Saints and Their Cults: Studies in Religious Sociology, Folklore, and History*, edited by Stephen Wilson, 1-54. Cambridge: Cambridge University Press.

PART IV
Art and Anthropology in Our Classrooms and Colleges

Arts Integration as Critical Pedagogy

Elizabeth A. Sheehan

Abstract

This chapter discusses arts integration in K-12 education as a form of critical pedagogy, a way to create a "curriculum within the curriculum" that meets the demands of standardized testing while encouraging students to make meaningful connections to the material they are taught. Arts integration allows teachers to use a wide range of art forms to teach core subjects, including those emphasized by statewide standardized tests. Focusing on an arts integration project for fourth graders at a Title I elementary school in Richmond, Virginia, the chapter describes how the study of African American history in the former capital of the Confederacy was positioned within the required yearlong Virginia History curriculum. Through field trips and with the guidance of their teachers, an architectural historian, a photographer, and a poet, the children created their personal responses to the story of black Richmond and explored their own and their families' relationship to this story.

"How did they get the jail underground?" This was the question a fourth grader at a Richmond, Virginia, elementary school asked an architectural historian who had just presented a slide show of significant sites in the city's history, including the notorious Lumpkin's Slave Jail. The question was excellent in a straightforward way. How *did* Lumpkin's Slave Jail, a place where thousands of people were once penned before being sold on the auction block, end up buried so far beneath today's streets? But the question was also a metaphor for how often history, especially history that is uncomfortable to think about, is obscured below the surface of official records, textbooks, and public memory.

The historian was one of a team of visiting artists and specialists who worked with two classes of fourth graders and their teachers in the 2010-2011 school year on a project called "Studying the Past to Embrace the Future." The project was funded by Partners in the Arts (PIA), a program of the University of Richmond's School of Professional & Continuing Studies that since 1994 has provided teacher training in arts integration as well as grants to support arts integration initiatives in regional schools. The Kennedy Center's *ArtsEdge* program defines arts integration as "an approach to teaching in which students construct and demonstrate understanding through an art form" (Kennedy Center ArtsEdge 2013). PIA's definition is broader and more ambitious, seeing arts integration as a cross-curricular, project-based pedagogy that may use several art forms to teach thematically linked content across two or more subjects. These definitions do not reveal the pedagogy's deeper purpose, however. PIA's goal is to help Pre-K-12 educators infuse the curricula with meaningful creative activities that spark students' interest, draw on students' diverse learning styles, and demonstrate the power of collaborative intellectual work. The benefits of arts integration are not confined to students. A study of PIA's impact on several schools in the Richmond area carried out in 2005-2006 showed that training in arts integration renewed teachers' interest in their work, making them more open to new teaching approaches, and helped non-art teachers gain confidence in using the arts to teach their subjects, whether those be math, science, or social studies (Horowitz 2007).

Each summer, PIA offers a course at the University of Richmond's Joan Oates Institute, which provides Pre-K-12 teachers with intensive, hands-on training in arts integration theory and practice. Over a thousand teachers in the greater Richmond area have attended the institute. They and other teachers are encouraged to apply for PIA grants that allow them to implement arts integration projects in their schools. These projects support required course content but also connect two or more subjects that otherwise would be taught in isolation from each other and almost certainly from art classes. "Studying the Past to Embrace the Future" was a project that brought together reading and creative writing, social studies, architectural history, and photography to give African American fourth graders the opportunity not only to create art related to black history in Richmond but also to enter into and engage with this history, from slavery to the civil rights era.

While it is commonplace to speak of the arts as enriching every child's life, PIA's mission goes beyond that. The program seeks to create sustainable change in Pre-K-12 education at a time when standardized curricula and testing have drastically altered the culture of the classroom and forced teachers to comply with policies that discourage inquiry and innovation in an effort to meet standardized criteria. Arts integration is process-oriented rather than product-oriented, relieving teachers and students of the need to create a finished product, to cross another goal line. It is more important that students share a learning journey with their teachers and the visiting artists who work with them.

Here I suggest that arts integration can be a form of critical pedagogy, an approach that education theorist Henry Giroux describes as seeking to "help students develop consciousness of freedom, recognize authoritarian tendencies, and connect knowledge to power and the ability to take constructive action" (2010, 1). In addition to providing an on- (and beneath-) the-ground examination of an important part of Richmond's history, "Studying the Past to Embrace the Future" invited the fourth graders to understand their relationship to this history, start to think about why things are the way they are today and, perhaps, about how they might be changed.

Policy and Practice

While efforts to standardize curricula and testing in US public education began in the mid-1960s, it has greatly accelerated as a result of the No Child Left Behind Act (NCLB) of 2001 (US Department of Education 2004), signed by President George W. Bush. The stated purpose of NCLB is to give all students equal opportunity to receive a quality education, a goal no one would question. Quality will be achieved by increasing accountability for students' performance and introducing standardized assessment practices in all states by 2014. Under NCLB, teachers "must use evidence-based practices, not unproven teaching methods that waste time and resources and do not work" (Chapman 2005, 6). But as Mulcahy and Irwin have pointed out, "Federal education policy is virtually closed to scholarly debate. Policy authors rarely submit their findings and scholarship to peer-reviewed journals" (2008, 202). The main architect of NCLB, former Secretary of Education Margaret Spellings, a Bush appointee, "has no formal training in education and has never worked as a classroom teacher" (Mulcahy and Irwin 2008, 202).

NCLB's focus is on meeting standards for reading and math, which are also priorities at the state level, whether the state is using its own standards to reach NCLB goals or has adopted the Common Core State Standards, an effort to create national assessment standards that correspond to NCLB but emphasize students' abilities to understand content in depth and in context rather than simply memorize facts (Common Core State Standards Initiative 2012). In 2011, the

Department of Education began to allow states to apply for a waiver that extends the deadline for meeting NCLB national benchmarks from 2014 to 2017 (US Department of Education 2013). The waiver also takes into account the greater challenge students from poorer families may have in meeting these benchmarks. Virginia received the waiver in 2012, relieving some of the time pressure of NCLB, but federal funding of public schools remains linked to the results of state-level standardized testing, a strong incentive for schools to adopt standardization in all subjects to meet national mandates and train students, and teachers, in this prevailing approach to pedagogy.

Public school teachers across the country almost literally race through the school year trying to cover detailed lists of facts and skills upon which student competency is evaluated. Indeed, the prefabricated lessons and unit plans make up what are called "pacing charts." These charts are intended to help teachers stay on track but also discourage taking advantage of opportunities for useful reflection and deeper understanding. Teachers must teach to the test. In Virginia, these examinations cover the state's Standards of Learning (SOLs). As with NCLB, the SOLs are meant to ensure a consistent curricula and basis for assessment. Teachers in most public schools have little time to introduce alternative teaching methods, although many try. One regional high school teacher sums up the challenges: "Teachers are too busy to collaborate, parents are too critical to become creative, and there simply are no funds to step outside the small structured world of our curriculum—which is intensely and unforgivingly assessed, with the students losing if we don't do a good job" (Bingham 2012, 2).

Education theorist Ken Robinson has written, "Creativity depends on interactions between feeling and thinking, and across different disciplinary boundaries and fields of ideas" (2001, 200). This is hardly a revolutionary observation; all of us know the truth of it based on our own experience. However, Robinson's statement seems antithetical to the nationally established and enforced policies of public education in the country today. To add to the stress, severe budget cuts in the past few years have resulted in teacher layoffs and increased class size. In this setting, art classes are marginalized, despite NCLB having designated art as a core subject. Especially in struggling schools, art may be viewed as an extra, an expensive add-on to the "real" curriculum. Some full-time art teachers are forced to work in more than one school while part-time art teachers, who may lack certification but often provide the only courses in string instruments or dance, are laid off altogether.

The increased segregation of subjects and erosion of art instruction have led to what has been called a "creativity crisis." The crisis has implications beyond limiting student opportunities for personal expression. An analysis of national scores on the Torrance Tests of Creative Thinking carried out by Kyung-Hee Kim of William & Mary College shows that while IQ scores continue to rise, creativity has steadily decreased in Americans of all ages since 1990 (2011). Kim's research suggests that students who score lower on standardized tests actually may be more creative than those who scored high. "If we neglect creativity in school because of the structure and testing movement," says Kim, "creative students cannot breathe, they are suffocated in school—then they become underachievers" (quoted in Zagursky 2011). Ongoing research by Luke Rinne and colleagues at Johns Hopkins University demonstrates that integrating art activities into learning improves students' long-term retention of content, evident on test scores (Rinne et al. 2011). However, the creativity crisis is also a crisis of low expectations for socioeconomically disadvantaged children and a serious deterrent to their developing skills seen as necessary to compete in the twenty-first century labor market. These skills include critical thinking, communication, collaboration, and creativity.

In his classic 1977 book *Learning to Labor: How Working Class Kids Get Working Class Jobs*, Paul Willis described the social reproduction, generation after generation, of male high school students who rejected school and its useless knowledge, who believed they were permanently disenfranchised from middle-class society, and who could envision no other career prospect than the manual labor their fathers and grandfathers had engaged in. In the United States today, of course, most high school graduates would be lucky to get any kind of job at all. Willis's research fits within a wider stream in critical education theory that since the 1970s has addressed the hidden curriculum, the body of knowledge and rules about social identity and behavior, that is transmitted along with formal course content. As elsewhere, the hidden curriculum in American education helps shape young people's sense of their place in the world as they internalize the message that they are powerless or, less often noted, preordained to exert power over others. To help achieve this end, the hidden curriculum may devalue the history and culture of the most disadvantaged students or else depict these as subordinate to the mainstream narrative of American identity and experience. Giroux writes that a critical pedagogy must provide students "with the skills they will need to locate themselves in history, find their own voices, and provide the convictions and compassion necessary for exercising civic courage" (quoted in Scott 2008, 103). But, learning time and again that their cultural references have no bearing on what counts as knowledge, young people also may learn that there is no alternative to the circumstances of their lives and that they cannot challenge what seems to be fixed and inevitable. Rigid and culturally narrow curricula also undermine teachers' hard-won expertise and make irrelevant the insight they have gained into their students' lives. The teacher's experience and knowledge become part of the problem that standardization must overcome.

These grim circumstances have inspired some educators to call for a complete rejection of the current system, scrapping the curriculum. For most public school teachers, however, even covert discussion among peers about what is wrong with public education can be risky. Observed deviation from required content and approved methods of instruction may lead to formal reprimands and write-ups by school administrators. Consequently, teachers may opt for what seem like SAT-prep strategies for gaming the system, techniques for just passing the damn exam. "Model how to answer constructed response items"; for example, make sure students can tell you, "What are three reasons that. . ." (Tankersley 2011). This technique is certainly effective, for preparing to compete on *Jeopardy* as well, but dispiriting for both teachers and students who must approach education this way, every day, for years on end.

This is not a situation that can be resolved Hollywood movie-style by a brave teacher and his students standing up to the authorities. I recently heard a charismatic art educator, quite Hollywood-style himself, speak to a group of art education students who attended a public university. The guest speaker talked about how he would decide on occasion to take his young students out on informal field trips so they could interact with the community and understand art-making as a collective, reciprocal process. His comments were in response to a question about how public school art teachers could break away from the strictures of standardization, but they were almost useless. All I could think of was liability (Did families know that their students were wandering the streets with this man? Had the school approved these random excursions?) and the frustration such unplanned group absences would have caused other teachers waiting in the building for their next class to show up. As it turned out, the guest speaker had never taught in a public school.

"Points of resistance and alternative approaches to public schooling are difficult to unearth," Mulcahy and Irwin write (2008, 206). This is "a testament to the effectiveness of the control mechanisms in place. Where they do exist, they often cannot announce their presence" (Mulcahy and Irwin 2008, 206). Arts integration, however, is not a subversion of what exists. It is more like a curriculum within the curriculum, a transparent demonstration of how Pre-K-12 education can be better, even in the age of standardized teaching and testing. Below, I provide examples of how an arts integration curriculum was structured and carried out in "Studying the Past to Embrace the Future." The project did not have to be disguised within the fourth grade curriculum, which in this state includes Virginia Studies. It allowed teachers and students to trace a rich historical seam embedded in and therefore compatible with the existing curriculum, as long as the "overlying" content was also taught. Arts integration is a method, not a particular body of knowledge, and as such can be used in almost any Pre-K-12 setting where teachers and students are given the time and support to implement these projects.

The Project

The Richmond Public Schools instructional specialist who conceived "Studying the Past to Embrace the Future" had long been interested in how Richmond's past is represented and misrepresented in statues, monuments, and architecture. At first, she thought the project would be best suited to middle school students, but an elementary school principal convinced her that it would be perfect for her school's fourth graders, especially given the enthusiasm of that grade's teachers. Why not insert this project into the state-mandated Virginia Studies curriculum and in doing so give students a deeper, more contextualized, and more interactive learning experience? Entirely by coincidence, the project was carried out during the same year that Richmond was beginning its commemoration of the Civil War Sesquicentennial, lasting from 2011-2015. The commemoration has particular resonance for Richmond, the former capital of the Confederacy. The events scheduled for the first year included community-based discussions of race that were inclusive and questioning, meant to open up sensitive issues rather than assume that they had been resolved and could be incorporated into a good-to-think-with narrative.

Although a much different place now than it was in 1961, when segregation was in full force, Richmond's Jim Crow discrimination has been replaced by the discrimination of enduring poverty among many of the city's black residents, who in 2011 made up slightly more than half of the population. Poverty has increased in the past thirty years; at present, about 22 percent of the city's residents live below the poverty level, but another 44 percent try to survive just above it. More than 32 percent of school-age children live in poverty (Moeser n.d.). Richmond has the densest concentration of public housing projects south of Washington, DC, most of them clustered in one neighborhood that is only a ten- or fifteen-minute walk from the city center. However, a local highway "wraps around the entire area, successfully positioned as a moat, or wall, which isolates the concentrated urban poverty from the resources of greater Richmond" (Sarvay 2011). Inadequate public transportation makes it difficult for residents to apply for jobs in the shopping centers and chain restaurants west of the city. The city center itself is a dead zone once its workers, many of them civil servants and social service agency employees, go home in the early evening. The liveliest place in the neighborhood after dark may be the emergency room of the nearby public hospital.

The students at the south Richmond public school where "Studying the Past" was implemented are luckier than most children who live in the projects on the north side of the James River. Their neighborhood has historical continuity and a distinct identity. Many students live in single-family homes, low bungalows with small backyards. The commercial streets are lined with shops; even so, there is no supermarket for miles. The school is a century old and is a landmark in the community, rising graciously above the surrounding houses. Yet its students are far from privileged in socioeconomic terms. More than 47 percent of local households have incomes of less than $25,000 (DataShare Metro Richmond 2010). At the time that the PIA project was carried out, all of the school's students were eligible for free or reduced-fee lunches. As in other poor neighborhoods, the students' addresses and caretakers may change a few times throughout their years in elementary school. It can be difficult for the school to keep track of who is enrolled, where they live, and what adult is responsible for them. Many of the fourth graders who participated in the PIA project probably had never been to downtown Richmond, where the most important sites associated with the city's black history are located. In living apart from the more depressed sections of Richmond, the children lacked even passing familiarity with these sites and the stories they told.

These were the circumstances—not the culture—of the fourth graders who participated in "Studying the Past to Embrace the Future." The PIA grant was modest, less than $7,000, with funds used mainly to pay the visiting artists. The grant also covered the small cost of journals for each child and basic art supplies. Richmond Public Schools contributed ten digital cameras for the students to share as they recorded images of the sites they visited. The project had an exceptionally dedicated group of people collaborating to bring the project to life. First were the two fourth grade teachers, who knew their students well and were willing to do the extra work required to make this a truly meaningful experience. The architectural historian, a man who had spent years protecting buildings and sites associated with Richmond's black history, was enthusiastic about sharing his knowledge with these children. He did not need an audience of scholars and city planners to feel he was making a difference. The creative writer on the project had been a social worker in Richmond schools, experience that added another dimension to her interactions with students. The other visiting artist was a young photographer. He understood that his role was to provide basic instruction and some onsite guidance but otherwise to encourage the students to explore what was possible with the digital cameras.

Close planning for the project began in the summer of 2010, with everyone involved at the table: the teachers, the visiting artists, the instructional specialist, and, on one occasion, me as well. I offered advice when asked but did not take the lead in any way. As with any collaborative effort, an arts integration project cannot be successful without shared understanding, goals, and commitment among those actually carrying out the project. The group created a schedule for the coming school year: what field trips would take place and when, which lessons or unit plans the visiting artists would be involved in, and what kinds of assignments would allow students to demonstrate the facts they had learned as well as their interpretation of these facts. While following one line of Richmond's history, albeit a line relevant to all of US history, the teachers also had to meet the content goals of the Virginia Studies curriculum, which included the state's role in the American Revolution, the Civil War, Reconstruction, and twentieth- and twenty-first-century Virginia. Where relevant, connections between Virginia Studies and "Studying the Past" would be made, entailing additional work for the teachers, but this addition led to the development of the students' critical thinking skills and ability to make connections across what seemed like separate lessons and topics.

A week after his presentation at the school where he was asked how the slave jail had ended up underground, the historian led the students and their teachers on a walking tour of sites in Shockoe Bottom. They had already seen images of most of these places in the slideshow. Shockoe Bottom is lowland along the north side of the James River that was the city's first commercial area and the center of one of the largest slave trading enterprises in the United States, second only to New Orleans. Enslaved Africans were brought in ships up the James to a landing and then forced to walk to the slave markets in the Bottom. After the importation of slaves was banned in 1807, Richmond's trade was based largely on the resale of slaves to plantations in the Deep South; these people were literally "sent down the river." The historian led the children into a passageway that opened into a lot where slave jails and auction houses once stood. "You are walking in the footsteps of the men, women, and children who were sold as slaves," he said. "The same sky that is over you was over them." As I stood among the students, I had the impression that they were really feeling what it would have been like to be a slave, on that very spot, with no possible escape from the passageway. They touched the crumbling brick wall of a nineteenth-century building next to them and tried to look through its small, filthy windows. Perhaps they were thinking that slaves could be someone their age, not just grown-ups. The lesson, in part, was about the reality and power of slavery in Richmond. But it was also about empathy, the capacity to understand someone else's experience, to enter into that experience and consider its possible connection to yours.

The historian led the children further on to the site of Lumpkin's Slave Jail. Archaeologists have been gradually excavating the jail since 2008, when the building's foundation was uncovered, but a large sign in front of the site has a drawing of what the building originally looked like. Using a shallow plastic bin filled with sand and some Lego blocks, the historian demonstrated how the small hill behind the jail had been re-graded several times, with the dug-up earth thrown down the slope and covering the base of the building. Erosion had done its work as well, and as the building deteriorated, its fallen pieces had been covered by dirt. Finally, tons of land had been thrown down the hill in the 1950s to create the Richmond-Petersburg Turnpike, which later became part of Interstate 95. Nothing of the jail and its foundation could be seen at this point. The fourth graders gathered around the historian, fascinated as he demonstrated, with a few simple and inexpensive props, how "they"—generations of urban developers—had gotten the jail underground. At the same time, the students were standing in front of its foundation and could see how it was being uncovered and forced back into public consciousness.

Architectural history gave the students a sense of what had been created in the past, but photography gave them the chance to create something themselves. The professional photographer who worked with the students combined the discipline of learning how to use a camera with the freedom to move beyond technical skills. One might expect that at their age and with only simple instruction most of the fourth graders would shoot blurry, incorrectly lit and poorly framed images, but this was not the case. Many of the photos were stunning in their sophistication and technical quality. Some were of symbolic images, such as sections of a mural at the African Burial Ground depicting rows of people in coffins. Some focused on the architectural details of the Hippodrome, Richmond's historic black theater. Photos of the recently unveiled civil rights memorial near the state capital were shot at angles that added drama to the tableau of eighteen black Virginians who had fought for equal rights. The most compelling photographs, for me, were interior scenes of the

Maggie Walker House, where the first American woman of any race to found a bank had lived and died. Some of these photos conveyed an eerie sense that Maggie Walker had just left the room, that the rocker in the foreground had just stopped rocking. In other photos, the sun filtered through curtains and cast a haze across photos and mementos on the wall, an effect that professional photographers would be happy to achieve. Of course, there also were many photos of the kids just clowning around, cramming into group shots.

In addition to photography, creative writing offered a way for students to respond to the project's lessons, building their language arts skills as they wrote poems, biographical essays, and short stories. There was no "What are three reasons that. . . " in these assignments. At the end of the school year, the visiting writer collected the pieces and put them into a stapled booklet for each child to own. Among the most moving was an essay called "You Can Leave but I'm a-Staying," an imagined account of why a young girl had decided not to join other slaves in running away. The girl would miss her family; she might be caught, and the consequences would be terrible. For now she would stay. The student's essay showed a nuanced understanding of how some enslaved black people, including children, had weighed the pros and cons of escaping. This is an understanding that even now many adults might not consider when thinking about slavery. The creative writer, with her background in social work, also observed or felt something that might have been overlooked in another kind of classroom, where teachers are rushed to get through the day's lessons. She thought that some of the children had become sad as they began to understand the enormity and cruelty of slavery. She advised the teachers to emphasize even more the accomplishments of black Richmonders such as Maggie Walker and the people depicted in the civil rights memorial, some of whom had been high school students, six or seven years older than the fourth graders, who had fought for integrated schools in the 1950s.

It is difficult to measure the academic impact of the students' participation in "Studying the Past to Embrace the Future." For good reason, school systems do not release test scores for individual classes but, instead, cumulative scores for elementary, middle, and high schools. The lead teacher's assessment of the project was realistic but positive. In her report, she noted the great deal of extra work involved in carrying it out, despite the support she and the other fourth-grade teacher had received from the principal. This problem will remain as long as teachers are forced to follow their pacing charts no matter what other opportunities for reflective learning arise in the school day. But the teacher had been pleased to see that the visiting artists were also teachers, that they were at ease interacting with the students, and that they shared responsibility for the success of the project. She also observed that the students made meaningful connections between what they learned from the formal Virginia Studies curriculum and what they learned from the project's parallel curriculum. One example of this was their recognition of the difference between the slave burial ground at Thomas Jefferson's Monticello and the burial ground in Richmond, near Lumpkin's Jail. Jefferson had provided stone markers for the dead; in Richmond, the burial ground is unmarked and anonymous. In fact, at the time that the students visited it, much of the burial ground was covered by a parking lot—yet another example of how history that is uncomfortable to think about is obscured and in this case literally paved over.

Conclusion

Arts integration is not the answer to the problem of excessive faith in and enforcement of Pre-K-12 education's "drill and kill" methods. But I believe that, even in small ways for now, it can be transformational in any school where teachers are willing to work together and are given time to plan and execute a project. This pedagogy is most needed in public schools that are financially challenged and often located in underserved neighborhoods, where students are less likely to have consistent opportunities to create art. In these schools, art integration projects can give students and teachers the opportunity to collaborate in the acquisition and interpretation of knowledge. In particular, projects that explore history and culture can empower students to claim the authority to interpret their own lives. To quote Giroux once more, "Critical pedagogy is about offering a way of thinking beyond the seemingly natural or inevitable state of things, about challenging 'common sense.' It is a mode of intervention" (2010). This is intervention on behalf of students but also intervention that students can bring to the world around them.

On one of their field trips, the fourth graders visited the Reconciliation Statue in Shockoe Bottom. The statue is one of three identical memorials to those who suffered under slavery, in Richmond, in Liverpool, and in Benin, three points of the triangle trade. The historian pointed out to the students the words at the base of the statue: "Acknowledge and forgive the past, embrace the present, shape a future of reconciliation and justice." "Shaping the future," he said, "that's your job."

Acknowledgments

I would like to thank everyone who helped implement "Studying the Past to Embrace the Future" and made it so meaningful: the fourth grade students, their two teachers, the project's visiting artists and specialists, and the school principal. Given Richmond Public Schools' sensitivity about individual school achievement, I have not used any of the participants' names. I also want to thank my colleague Robert S. McAdams for his many contributions to the development of Partners in the Arts in recent years and Dean Patricia Joy Johnson Brown of the University of Richmond School of Professional

& Continuing Studies for her thoughtful oversight and heartfelt support of the program.

References

Bingham, Barbara L. 2012. "Current Struggles with Cross-Curricular Instruction: Arts Integration and Lowered Expectations." Unpublished manuscript.

Chapman, Laura H. 2005. "No Child Left behind in Art?" *Art Education* 58(1): 6-16.

Common Core State Standards Initiative. 2012. "Implementing the Common Core State Standards," http://www.corestandards.org/.

DataShare Metro Richmond. 2010. http://www.datashare.vcu.edu/DataReport.aspx?Type=Income_And_Poverty&Geo=Swansboro-Belt%20Center&tract=&blk_grp=&NavType=RichmondCityNeighbor&Format=.

Giroux, Henry. 2010. "Lessons from Paulo Freire." *Chronicle of Higher Education*, http://chronicle.com/article/Lessons-From-Paulo-Freire/124910/.

Horowitz, Rob. 2007. "Partners in the Arts Teacher Training and Assessment Program (TTAP)." *Evaluation Final Report.*

Kennedy Center ArtsEdge. 2013. "What is Arts Integration?," http://artsedge.kennedy-center.org/educators/how-to/arts-integration-beta/what-is-arts-integration-beta.aspx.

Kim, K. H. 2011. "The Creativity Crisis: The Decrease in Creative Thinking Scores on the Torrance Tests of Creative Thinking." *Creativity Research Journal* 23:285-95.

Moeser, John V. n.d. "An Overview of Poverty, Race and Jurisdiction in Metropolitan Richmond," http://www.connectrichmond.org/portals/1/UpdatedMoeser.pdf.

Mulcahy, D. E., and J. Irwin. 2008. "The Standardized Curriculum and Delocalization: Obstacles to Critical Pedagogy." *Radical History Review* 102:201-13.

Rinne, L., E. Gregory, J. Yarmolinskaya, and M. Hardiman. 2011. "Why Arts Integration Improves Long-Term Retention of Content." *Mind, Brain, and Education* 5(2): 89-96.

Robinson, Ken. 2001. *Out of Our Minds: Learning to Be Creative.* Chichester, England: Capstone Publishing Limited.

Sarvay, John. 2011. "Windshield Tour Drives Home the Problems of a Community," http://www.floricane.com/pergula/post/windshield_tour_drives_home_the_problems_of_a_community.

Scott, David. 2008. "Henry Giroux and Critical Pedagogy." In *Critical Essays on Major Curriculum Theorists*, 103-14. New York: Routledge.

Tankersley, Karen. 2011. "But They Knew That! How to Help Your Students Show What They Know on State Assessments." *Virginia Journal of Education*, http://www.veanea.org/home/967.htm#toc.

US Department of Education. 2004. "No Child Left Behind Act Executive Summary," http://www2.ed.gov/nclb/overview/intro/execsumm.html.

———. 2013. "ESEA Flexibility," http://www2.ed.gov/policy/elsec/guid/esea-flexibility/index.html.

Virginia Department of Education. 2012. "NCLB Waiver Approved by US Department of Education," http://www.doe.virginia.gov/news/news_releases/2012/jun29.shtml.

Willis, Paul. 1977. *Learning to Labor: How Working Class Kids Get Working Class Jobs*. New York: Columbia University Press.

Zagursky, Erin. 2011. "Smart? Yes. Creative? Not so Much," http://www.wm.edu/research/ideation/professions/smart-yes.-creative-not-so-much.5890.php.

The Art of Teaching Anthropology: Examples from Biological Anthropology

Susan Kirkpatrick Smith, Laura D. Lund, and Marilyn R. London

Abstract

Teaching in a college or university setting has many challenges, including often-inadequate preparation in graduate school and the requirement to develop new courses, often in a short period of time. Anthropology faculty are at a particular disadvantage because anthropology lacks any discipline-specific journals for the publication of articles on the scholarship of teaching and learning. Many anthropology faculty desire to have more resources available for course and assignment development. In this chapter, we present several examples of course syllabi, class activities, and a sample student paper that faculty can use as they develop or revise anthropology courses.

Teaching is an art that should be nurtured and allowed time to grow and mature. The reality of teaching in American colleges and universities today, however, does not usually allow for this slow, careful development of teaching expertise. Graduate teaching experiences vary widely, ranging from the lucky students being given purposeful pedagogical training to others being thrown into a classroom and given no guidance at all. Many new faculty members are hired to teach three or four new courses, or more, in one semester, while juggling their other new responsibilities in service and research. New faculty may have access to sample syllabi, or even to general classroom management techniques through university-sponsored workshops, but the "how to" of structuring a class that meets required learning outcomes, providing for the development of critical thinking skills, promoting writing across the curriculum, and creating a class that students want to take is often missing. Here is where young faculty, or indeed experienced faculty, who are developing new courses or wanting to improve their pedagogy need to learn from others in their own discipline. And it is here that anthropology faculty are at a disadvantage.

Many journals exist that are devoted to discipline-specific teaching. Many liberal arts disciplines, such as English, Geography, Biology, Foreign Languages, Chemistry, and Psychology, have such journals. (Pusateri 2013). Anthropology is in the unenviable position of having no outlet for discipline-specific Scholarship on Teaching and Learning (SoTL), and more important, no source for faculty looking for specific ways to improve their own teaching. This does a disservice to our profession, our students, and our faculty, who are forced to reinvent the wheel when faced with new course development.

I must point out that the Royal Anthropological Institute (RAI) of the United Kingdom began publishing an open-access, peer-reviewed journal entitled *Teaching Anthropology* in 2011. This journal, which has published four issues as of 2013, "promotes dialogue and reflection about anthropological pedagogies in schools, colleges and universities. . . . We also aim to stimulate scholarly discussions about the relationship between pedagogy and its social, institutional and political contexts."[1] The focus of many of the initial articles is on teaching in the British tutorial setting, which is quite different from the most common American lecture-based classes. Anthropology in the United Kingdom means social anthropology, or cultural anthropology as it is more commonly known in the United States. Therefore, this journal will not be a resource for US professors teaching in a four-field anthropology department or teaching biological anthropology, linguistic anthropology, or archaeology.

Some additional resources are available for teaching anthropology at the college level. The American Anthropological Association (AAA) has a site to which faculty members can upload examples of their teaching resources.[2] As of 2013, of the 125 submissions, only 8 were student assignments or activities. The remaining examples were syllabi. These resources are a good start, but they do not provide the level of detail and discussion found in SoTL journal articles. Rice, McCurdy, and Lukas (2011) have published *Strategies in Teaching Anthropology*, which covers all four subfields of anthropology and provides examples of class activities and assignments for encouraging students to engage with anthropological content. The book is now in its sixth edition, so presumably it has done well. But the publisher, Pearson, does not prominently promote it at professional conferences; nor have publisher representatives made it a priority to discuss it when making office visits.

On the other hand, publishers are quite good at promoting their own packages of web-based lesson content. Pearson has MyAnthroLab; Cengage has CourseMate. Other packages can be accessed, sometimes with a separate fee, by students to supplement their course texts. However, the activities on these websites are usually more geared toward knowledge and comprehension rather than higher-order learning, such as analysis and synthesis. What faculty need are examples of exercises that promote these higher levels of interaction within the field of anthropology.

New Approaches for Sharing Teaching Strategies

Workshops on teaching biological anthropology have been offered at the past two meetings of the American Association of Physical Anthropologists (AAPA) (London, Smith, and Madden 2012, 2013). These workshops were developed to address the needs discussed above for more exchange of teaching ideas and concepts among faculty members. At the AAPA meeting in 2013, thirty-five people attended and twenty-eight completed post-workshop evaluations. Of the respondents, twenty-one out of twenty-eight rated the workshop as very useful or useful, (answering "1" or "2" on a 5-point scale) while all twenty-eight responded that they would attend another teaching workshop at future AAPA meetings (Smith n.d.). These data suggest that faculty, from full professors to graduate student teaching assistants, are eager for anthropology teaching resources. The topic of the 2012 workshop was on course development in multiple settings (for example, online, classes for majors, general education). The workshop leaders presented detailed syllabi and course resources for innovative class topics or structures, then had workshop participants develop their own courses and share them with the rest of the participants. In the 2013 workshop, the focus was on in-class activities. Again, the workshop leaders presented examples of tested activities and then had the participants generate their own. Appendix 1 has examples of exercises from both the workshop leaders and participants.

An Extended Example: Lab in Forensic Anthropology

Given the problems discussed above and the lack of resources, we have included with this chapter an example of a detailed class assignment, including a sample student paper (appendix 2). What follows is a discussion of teaching activities developed for a senior-level lab in a forensic anthropology class for anthropology majors. These activities have been refined over several years of teaching the course, and they are based on formal and informal feedback from students.

Forensic anthropology courses have become a staple in many anthropology programs and are often seen as a way to attract students to the discipline of anthropology in general. A sampling of anthropology programs in the 2011 issue of the AAA's *AnthroGuide* shows that 20 percent of departments with an anthropology major have a course, faculty member, and/or concentration in forensic anthropology. Forensic anthropology classes are also found in community colleges (Mott Community College 2013), as are certificate programs in Forensic Anthropology (University of Hawai'i, West O'ahu 2012). Students are drawn to the field of forensic anthropology due to the popularity of television shows such as *Bones* and versions of the *CSI* franchise. While the large number of television shows with a forensic focus has glamorized the field of forensic anthropology and has drawn students to this field, there is almost no work in forensic anthropology that is available to students with only a bachelor's degree (American Board of Forensic Anthropology 2008). Even though forensic anthropology courses can be a boon for departments needing to boost their numbers, having the resources available for teaching the course can be difficult in these times of budget cuts. The research project discussed below fosters the development of scientific writing, critical thinking, and public speaking. Anthropology programs can capitalize on public enthusiasm for courses related to forensic sciences and use this excitement as a springboard for teaching critical thinking and writing. The learning objectives that are addressed with this research project include the following:

At the end of the assignment, students will demonstrate the ability to:

1. Create a testable hypothesis or research question related to forensic anthropology
2. Conduct original research in order to test their hypothesis
3. Write an original research paper using appropriate disciplinary conventions
4. Present their research in a professional manner, either as a poster or as an oral presentation

The Assignment

Students in the Lab in Forensic Anthropology are required to conduct original research based on a testable hypothesis or research question developed by the student in consultation with the professor. Examples from previous projects include: Is it possible to differentiate between sharp-force traumas to bone after cremation? How does soil pH affect decomposition? How does ammunition size affect bone traumas? What are the patterns of blunt-force traumas on a dog that has been killed by a car (appendix 2)?

The Process and Outcomes

1. Students submit a hypothesis or research question they wish to investigate. They discuss this with the professor and refine it until it is an acceptable topic.
2. Students submit a research plan, including methodology, materials, and timeline.
3. Students submit a bibliography of sources for the literature review of the research paper.
4. Students submit a rough draft of the complete research paper.

5. Students submit a final draft of the research paper.

6. Students present the paper in a conference-style paper or poster.

The majority of students have conducted their research projects using pork products purchased at a grocery store or butcher shop, because of the anatomical and size similarity between adult humans and pigs (Swindle and Smith 1998). However, other students have conducted their research on pets they have buried in their yard and that have sufficiently decayed. Either of these sources provides students with an inexpensive source of bone on which to cause trauma, burn, or decompose, and it has the added benefit of providing our lab with a teaching collection for future classes. It is difficult to purchase any human skeletal material for teaching collections and virtually impossible to acquire any with examples of specific trauma or postmortem damage. While casts of these types of cases do exist (France Casting 2013), seeing a gunshot on bone is not the same as seeing it on a cast. The best case is when labs can have casts of human bone, with the animal bone from the research projects to supplement the collection. After assigning this research project only five times, with a class size ranging between ten to twenty students, the teaching collection now includes excellent examples of blunt force trauma, sharp force trauma, gunshot wounds from different weapons, and vehicular trauma, as well as examples of postmortem damage to bone resulting from dismemberment or cremation.

Conclusion

Anthropology needs to join the ranks of other social sciences and establish an easily accessible forum for sharing teaching strategies, innovative assignments, and examples of best practices. This is particularly important as the classroom is changing because of technology. Conference presentations, such as the AAPA workshops discussed above (London, Smith, and Madden 2012, 2013) and an invited session at the AAA in 2012 on distance education (Dixon and Gonlin 2012; Aguilar 2012; Hunt 2012; Smith 2012; Tessandori and Dixon 2012), are beneficial for starting conversations about teaching but do not provide the handy references needed by faculty who are developing new courses or bringing new life to tired assignments. We can get some suggestions from teaching texts devoted to innovative assessment techniques (Angelo and Cross 1993) or from guides to incorporating more writing in the classroom (Bean 2001), but discipline-specific resources are even more needed.

Appendix I: Sample Syllabi and Class Exercises

I. Plagues, Pathogens, and Public Policy: The Anthropological Perspective

Marilyn R. London

Course Description

The impact of diseases on populations from prehistoric times through the present will be examined, along with public perceptions of disease, scientific breakthroughs on treatment and prevention, and the ways that politics and public health policies can enhance or impede the advancement of disease treatment. The natural history of disease, population structure, and immunity will be discussed. The class will address emerging and reemerging diseases and the ways that first responders, researchers, and policy makers may affect the outcome of an outbreak.

Each student is required to write a short paper (5 to 10 pages) on a disease discussed in class or another disease approved by the instructor and to give a 5-minute class presentation on the disease. To write the paper, students are required to read at least one book about the disease or at least two scientific papers and answer a series of questions about the disease. These questions are: Identify the symptoms, pathogen, transmission pathway, susceptible populations, historic and current prevention measures, historic and current treatments, and the natural conditions that encourage or discourage the spread of the disease. How has public policy affected the spread or containment of the disease? How has the disease modified the course of history (including medical history)? What conditions could make this disease a current problem or threat? Identify the cultural aspects of the disease transmission and/or treatment. For the final exam, community roles will be assigned at midsemester, and each student is required to write a disaster plan for his or her community organization or agency. These plans will be presented at a "Town Meeting" the week before the final. The final is a "mass disaster" that includes an epidemiological component, and the students are required to follow their disaster plans (until they do not work anymore) to respond to the disaster and a series of reports and "phone calls" (I use 3 X 5 cards) about incidents related to the disaster. The written part of the exam is an "After Action Report," a commonly used government form that asks for a summary of the situation, explanation of actions taken, and evaluation of what worked, what did not work, what will be done differently in the next event, etc.

Text

Sherman, Irwin W. 2007. *Twelve Diseases that Changed our World.* Washington, DC: ASM Press.

I'm also considering adding the following text:

Krasner, Robert I. 2010. *The Microbial Challenge: Science, Disease, and Public Health.* 2nd ed. Boston: Jones and Bartlett Publishers.

Course Schedule

Week 1: Basics of disease and epidemiology: terminology, pathogens, scope of course

Week 2: Influenza

Film: *American Experience: Influenza 1918*

Film: *Influenza: Aiming at a Moving Target* (from the European Scientific Working Group on Influenza, which also has other resources at http://www.eswi.org/)

Reading: Sherman, Chapter 10

Week 3: Hemophilia, Porphyria, and other genetic diseases

Film: *Bad Blood: A Cautionary Tale* (http://badblooddocumentary.com/)

Reading: Sherman, Chapter 1

Week 4: Cholera

Reading: Sherman, Chapter 3

Week 5: Smallpox

Film: *History's Mysteries: Smallpox* (History Channel)

Reading: Sherman, Chapter 4

Week 6: Bubonic plague

Film: *The Black Death* (BBC Documentary) (http://www.youtube.com/watch?v=BsCkgX2epFw)

Reading: Sherman, Chapter 5

Week 7: Malaria

Film: *India's War against Malaria* (Createspace, 2007, 22 min.)

Reading: Sherman, Chapter 8

Week 8: Guest Speaker

Dengue Fever

Week 9: AIDS

Frontline: *The Age of AIDS* (http://www.pbs.org/wgbh/pages/frontline/aids/)

Reading: Sherman, Chapter 11

Week 10: Yellow fever; Potato blight

Film: *American Experience: The Great Fever* (http://www.pbs.org/wgbh/amex/fever/)

Reading: Sherman, Chapters 9, 2

Week 11: Diabetes and other chronic diseases

Week 12: Syphilis, Tuberculosis; Leprosy
Reading: Sherman, Chapters 6, 7

Week 13: Polio
Film: *American Experience: The Polio Crusade* (http://www.pbs.org/wgbh/americanexperience/films/polio/)

Week 14: Town Meeting: Planning for Disasters and Disease Outbreaks

Week 15: Final

Note on Videos

Many of the films are available online, or from PBS. I have even downloaded one from iTunes! There are also informational videos online such as http://www.youtube.com/watch?v=kVhtV6_Rdog&feature=related, which is a training film for nurses on how to care for polio patients who are being kept alive in an iron lung. Search for talks on the diseases on TED.com. The students seem to like the mix of lectures and audiovisual presentations.

Additional Readings

Fiction

Alvarez, Julia. 2007. *Saving the World.* Algonquin Books of Chapel Hill. (SMALLPOX)

Barrett, Andrea. 2008. *The Air We Breathe.* W. W. Norton. (TUBERCULOSIS)

Behrens, Peter. 2006. *The Law of Dreams.* Random House. (POTATO BLIGHT)

Faulks, Sebastian. 2005. *Human Traces.* Vintage Books. (MENTAL ILLNESS)

Lamb, Wally. 1999. *I Know this Much is True*. Harper Perrennial. (SCHIZOPHRENIA)

Lowenthal, Michael. 2007. *Charity Girl*. Mariner Books (Houghton Mifflin Company). (SYPHILIS)

Mullen, Thomas. 2006. *The Last Town on Earth*. Random House. (INFLUENZA)

O'Farrell, Maggie. 2006. *The Vanishing Act of Esme Lennox*. Harcourt. (MENTAL ILLNESS)

Roiphe, Anne. 2006. *An Imperfect Lens*. Shaye Areheart Books. (CHOLERA)

Willis, Connie. 1993. *Doomsday Book*. Spectra. (BUBONIC PLAGUE)

Nonfiction

Barry, John M. 2005. *The Great Influenza: The Story of the Deadliest Pandemic in History*. Penguin Books. (INFLUENZA)

Black, Kathryn. 1997. *In the Shadow of Polio: A Personal and Social History*. Da Capo Press. (POLIO)

Crosby, Molly Caldwell. 2006. *The American Plague: The Untold Story of Yellow Fever*. Berkley Books. (YELLOW FEVER)

Greenberg, Michael. 2008. *Hurry Down Sunshine: A Father's Story of Love and Madness*. Vintage Press. (MENTAL ILLNESS)

Johnson, Steven. 2007. *The Ghost Map: The Story of London's Most Terrifying Epidemic—and How It Changed Science, Cities, and the Modern World*. Riverhead Trade. (CHOLERA)

Mankell, Henning. 2004. *I Die, But the Memory Lives on . . . A Personal Reflection on AIDS*. Harvill. (HIV/AIDS)

Parascandola, John. 2008. *Sex, Sin, and Science: A History of Syphilis in America*. Praeger. (SYPHILIS)

Ramirez, Jose P. 2009. *Squint: My Journey with Leprosy*. University Press of Mississippi. (LEPROSY)

Rosen, William. 2007. *Justinian's Flea*. Penguin. (BUBONIC PLAGUE)

Rosenberg, Charles E. 1987. *The Cholera Years: The United States in 1832, 1849, and 1866*. University of Chicago Press. (CHOLERA)

Sacks, Oliver. 1990. *Awakenings*. Harper Perennial. (SLEEPING SICKNESS)

Shilts, Randy. 2007. *And the Band Played On: Politics, People, and the AIDS Epidemic*. 20th anniversary ed. St. Martin's Griffin. (HIV/AIDS)

Shreve, Susan Richards. 2008. *Warm Springs: Traces of a Childhood at FDR's Polio Haven*. Mariner Books. (POLIO)

Slater, Leo B. 2009. *War and Disease: Biomedical Research on Malaria in the Twentieth Century*. Rutgers University Press. (MALARIA)

Styron, William. 1992. *Darkness Visible: A Memoir of Madness*. Vintage. (DEPRESSION)

White, Neil. 2009. *In the Sanctuary of Outcasts: A Memoir*. William Morrow. (LEPROSY)

II. Anthropological Study of Mummies—ANT 380

Gwyn Madden

Course Description

This course will cover the history of mummy studies, environmental impact, and current research methodology. Natural and artificial mummies will be surveyed globally, including the potential cultural components involved. Ethical use of mummified remains and representation of mummies in the media, literature, and museum settings will complete the course.

Required Course Texts

Arriaza, B.T. 1995. *Beyond Death: The Chinchorro Mummies Of Ancient Chile.* Washington, DC: Smithsonian Institution Press.

Carter, H., and A.C. Mace. 1977. *The Discovery of the Tomb of Tutankhamen.* Mineola, NY: Dover Publications.

Glob, P.V. 2004. *The Bog People: Iron Age Man Preserved.* New York: New York Review Books Classics.

Journal articles; located on Blackboard (see list under "Readings" tab)

Grading

Syllabus quiz	1 x 25 points =	25 points
Discussion notes	20 x 10 points =	200 points
Topic paper	1 x 100 points =	100 points
Presentation	1 x 50 points =	50 points
Group assessment project/paper	1 x 100 points =	100 points
Midterm	1 x 100 points =	100 points
Final	1 x 100 points=	100 points
Total points		675 points

Grading Scale

90% = A

80% = B

70% = C

60% = D

Below 60% = F

Objectives

Student will be able to. . .

1. Discuss in depth the historic, religious, and cultural reasons that cultures choose to mummify

2. Identify the geographic locations in which mummies are found worldwide

3. Identify environments that improve preservation or enhance decomposition

4. Identify modern forms of technology appropriate for mummy studies

5. Discuss the issues associated with the ethical handling of human remains

6. Discuss accurately the historic discovery and treatment of mummified remains

Discussion Notes

Students are required to write discussion notes for each reading assigned. The notes are due in class on the same day the assigned reading is to be completed, as indicated in the course schedule (see Readings page on Blackboard). Discussion notes consist of four sections:

Books and Historic Readings

1. Respond to the reading: what initial thoughts or feelings did the reading provoke?

2. Summarize the main point(s) of the reading in two or three sentences.

3. Draw connections between the assigned reading and other readings, films, discussions, and lectures covered in class.

4. Pose two questions to generate classroom discussion about points the readings make.

Methodological Readings

1. Define the methodology used in the reading.

2. Identify the sample size and describe the sample population.

3. Discuss any problems you see in the methodology.

4. Pose two questions to generate classroom discussion about points the readings make.

Complete all four parts for each discussion note assignment. Use an outline format rather than paragraphs; fully formed thoughts and coherent writing are expected. The notes must be NO longer than one page; typed, double-spaced, 12-point font, with the name, date, and reading assignment title in the upper right corner. Each reading should have a separate discussion notes page turned in.

Discussion notes are designed to:

1. Prepare you to discuss the readings in class

2. Improve your critical reading skills and help you build your own interpretations of the course materials

3. Increase your control over your grade

Notes will be graded on a 10-point scale. To receive 10 points, the notes must be complete (i.e., include the four required components), and they must reflect time spent reading and thinking about the assignment. Partial credit will be given for notes failing to meet these requirements and for notes that are too general or vague. Emailed or late notes will be NOT accepted.

Exams

There will be a midterm and a final exam. The final will be comprehensive. You will be evaluated on your understanding of the lecture material, text readings, labs, and videos. The exams may consist of fill in the blank, true/false, listing, multiple choice, matching, and short answer.

Topic Papers

Each student will select a topic to research (methodological, historic, or cultural), write an 8-10 page paper on the topic, and present his or her findings to the class. An A paper will require no less than 10 primary sources, a B paper no less than 8, a C paper no less than 6, a D paper no less than 4; less than 4 sources will result in an F on the paper. NO Internet sources are allowed. You may not use Wikipedia, the dictionary, or encyclopedia as a primary source. The papers should be typed, double-spaced, and a 12-point font should be used. A title page should be used, including your name, the topic of the paper, the course information, and date the paper is due. Papers are due during class time on the due date; NO late papers or emailed papers will be accepted. Citations must follow the style guide on Blackboard under the "Course Documents" tab.

Topic Presentations

ALL presentations should be PowerPoint and must be emailed to the professor by 8 am the day the presentation is to be given. Citations should be used within the text of the presentation, and all photographs/images are required to be cited in the text. A reference page should be the final slide on the PowerPoint. The presentation should be 12-15 minutes long; shorter or longer papers will be docked points. You will be graded on clarity of the material presented, applicability of the images, grammar, organization of the material and slides, and depth of knowledge on the topic.

Course Schedule—Subject to Change

Dates

Week 1	Definition of mummy—natural vs. artificial processes Syllabus Quiz
Week 2-4	History of mummy studies
Week 5-7	Mummy studies today—methodology
Week 8	Midterm
Week 9-13	Mummies by culture
Week 14-15	Ethics in the study of human remains Representation of mummies in the media/literature/museum
Week 16	Final

References

Allison, M. J., and E. Gerszten. 1982. *Paleopathology in South American Mummies: Application of Modern Techniques.* Richmond: Virginia Commonwealth University.

Arriaza, B. T. 1995. *Beyond Death: The Chinchorro Mummies of Ancient Chile.* Washington, DC: Smithsonian Institution Press.

Aufderheide, A. C. 2003. *The Scientific Study of Mummies.* Cambridge: Cambridge University Press.

Barber, E. W. 1999. *The Mummies of Urumchi.* New York: WW Norton.

Cockburn, A., E. Cockburn, and T. A. Reyman, eds. 1998. *Mummies, Disease and Ancient Cultures.* 2nd ed. Cambridge: Cambridge University Press.

David, A. R., and R. Archbold. 2000. *Conversations with Mummies: New Light on the Lives of Ancient Egyptians.* New York: Madison Press.

Hart Hansen, J. P., and H. C. Gullov, eds. 1989. *The Mummies From Qilakitsoq: Eskimos in the 15th Century.* Man & Society 12. Copenhagen: Meddelelser Om Gronland.

Spindler K., H. Wilfing, E. Rastbichler-Zissernig, D. zur Nedden, and H. Nothdurfter, eds. 1996. *Human Mummies: A Global Survey of Their Status and the Techniques of Conservation.* New York: Springer Wien.

Turner, R. C., and R. G. Scaife, eds. 1995. *Bog Bodies: New Discoveries and New Perspectives.* London: British Museum Press.

III. "Introduction to Anthropology—Four Fields: Online Assignments"

Susan Kirkpatrick Smith

I have created an online introduction to anthropology that requires the students to conduct research in each of the four subfields of the discipline. Below are examples of the exercises I have created. While these were specifically created for an online class, they can be used in a regular course as well.

Cultural Anthropology—Introduction to Culture

- Watch one of the four movies listed below.

- Watch the movie as an observer of cultural practices, not just as a movie lover. Report on the cultures you observed as if you were an anthropologist engaged in participant-observation. Describe the non-American culture(s) to a reader who is unfamiliar with them.

- If you were going to do a longer-term study of one of the cultures presented in the text, what kind of questions would you like to answer about the culture?

- How do people from the different cultures in the movie react to each other? Are there examples of ethnocentrism? Are there examples of cultural relativism? Discuss these concepts in your paper, then address how they are or are not exemplified in the movie.

- You must make specific references to the appropriate chapters in your textbook in your essay. The point of this assignment is to show me how you are applying what you have learned in the course to your analysis of the movie.

Movie Options

1. *Bend it Like Beckham* (Gurinder Chadha, dir., 2002, Fox Searchlight)

2. *Fiddler on the Roof* (Norman Jewison, dir., 1971, United Artists)

3. *Mosquito Coast* (Peter Weir, dir., 1986, Warner Bros.)

4. *The Gods Must Be Crazy* (Jamie Uys, dir., 1980, 20th Century Fox)

Biological Anthropology—The Concept of Race

For this project, you will survey people's attitudes about race. I want you to ask 20 people the following questions and record their responses in a table.

- How many races are there?
- What are they?
- What is your race? (Do not give them choices to pick from.)
- What is your sex?
- What is your age?

After you have collected your data, analyze the results. Do you find that there are any cultural factors that influence people's attitudes about race? Do people of different age/sex/self-described race have different attitudes about race? Do the words people use fit any of the discussions from the text? Do any of your informants bring up any of the issues addressed in the textbook or in the other class readings? If so, what are they? If not, why do you think they do not? How could this research be used to discuss why race is not a valid biological concept?

Archaeology—Garbology

For this project, you will explore the relationship between people's behavior and the material remains they leave behind. Find a friend who is willing to let you look through his/her trash. Taking proper health precautions, record everything you find in the trash. Then try to make inferences about the behavior that resulted in the particular accumulation of garbage before you. For example, the presence of 78 beer cans might indicate a party.

Next, interview your friend about what actually went on in the house, apartment, or room during the period of garbage accumulation. Does the account of the garbage owners match with what the garbage indicated to you? Think about what you have read about archaeological research and address some of the issues involved when archaeologists attempt to infer behavior from material remains, especially from other cultures.

Requirements for the garbage selection process

• The garbage cannot be from your own home or a home where you spend most of your time.

• Tell your garbage donor that you need to have at least a full "kitchen" sized garbage can to work with.

• Do not ask how long the garbage has been accumulating.

• Do not ask any other questions about the garbage before you begin to analyze it.

Requirements for the paper

• Description of the "site." Where in the house was the garbage located? What kind of container was it in? How long did the garbage seem to have been accumulating? Any other important information about the situation of the garbage itself?

- Provide a *detailed* list of what you found in your excavation.
- Analyze the garbage.
    - Who do you think made the garbage? Can you tell any thing about the age and sex of the person who threw it away?
    - What does the garbage tell you about the behavior of the person who threw it away?
    - What can you infer about the events that occurred during the period of garbage accumulation at this location?
    - Base this discussion strictly on what you have found, not on what you know about the owners of the garbage. This should be written before talking with the garbage owner(s).
- Present your analysis to the garbage owner(s) and ask them to confirm or refute your findings.
- Report on your conversation with the garbage owner(s). How well did your interpretations match up with their reporting of what happened during the time period that the garbage accumulated?
    - What happened that you were able to document from the garbage?
    - What happened during the time of the garbage deposition that did not leave any evidence in the garbage?
    - What kinds of misinterpretations did you make?
- How does this experience relate to what research archaeologists do? What kind of mistaken assumptions did you make that you think an archaeologist might make?

Linguistic Anthropology—Gender and Conversation

You will be observing a conversation between a female and male for this assignment to see whether they use different communication styles. Before you begin the assignment, you will need to read the class readings on linguistic anthropology from the textbook and the article by Deborah Tannen.

- Observe a conversation between a male and a female. You must be an observer and not a participant in the research.

Requirements for the Paper

- Describe who the participants of the conversation were. Give the age of each person, location of the conversation, relationship of participants to each other, etc. If you do not know the participants, then make your best guess about the characteristics of the conversation participants.
- Describe what the conversation was about and give specific details about how the conversation relates to the text and article readings. These details may either support or disagree with the discussion of language differences between males and females you read about for linguistic anthropology.
- Does your research agree with the concepts presented by Tannen? Be specific.
- Next, discuss the kinesic, phonological, grammatical, lexical—or other—language differences you see between males and females (see textbook).

Reading

Tannen, Deborah. 2001. "The Power of Talk: Who Gets Heard and Why." In *Anthropology: Contemporary Perspectives*, 8th ed., edited by Phillip Whitten, 169-77. Needham Heights, MA: Allyn & Bacon.

IV. Modern Human Variation

Course organization created by *Teaching Biological Anthropology in the 21st Century Workshop Participants*, 2012

The course will be divided into three main sections:

1. Climatological Adaptations
    a. Skin color and race
        i. Explore this important topic by comparing multiple phenotypic traits in the class.
        ii. Have the class get in groups based on these traits:
            1. Skin color
            2. Hair color
            3. Blood type
            4. Ability to curl tongue
        iii. As the groups change members, use this as a way to discuss concordant and disconcordant trait characteristics.
    b. Body proportions
        i. Have students research how athletes for certain sports exhibit certain body proportions and what the trends are for world-class athletes from certain countries.
        ii. In class, discuss variation in body proportion related to Bergman's and Allen's Rules, as well as how cultural factors, such as training for a particular sport, affect body build.
2. Nutritional Adaptations
    a. Evaluation of fad diets
        i. What do you eat on each fad diet?
        ii. Does that meet the nutritional requirements discussed in class?

b. Food-Stamp challenge

i. Send students to grocery store with the amount of money from food stamps.

ii. What could you buy?

iii. Address the balance between meeting caloric versus nutritional needs.

iv. Discuss the biocultural causes of obesity in the United States.

3. Pathological/Biological Adaptations

a. Infectious disease

i. Activity: Choose random biological and cultural traits in your class and then "kill" people because of them. Examples:

1. If you are over 6 feet tall, you die.

2. If you have long hair, you die.

3. If you are wearing a red shirt, you do not die.

ii. Then see who survives and determine the difference between cultural and biological factors that affect survival.

iii. How might biological and cultural factors change due to this disease?

V. Stone Tool Making and Tool Use

Marilyn London

Courses: Introduction to Biological Anthropology, Human Origins

At the end of the assignment, the student will demonstrate the ability to:

1. Use flint-knapping techniques to manufacture a stone tool
2. Identify the best use of the tool
3. Demonstrate the use of the tool to other students
4. Describe the manufacture and use of the tool in a short essay

Making tools from raw materials can provide the student a better understanding of how to choose resources (the type of stone chosen), the difficulty of manufacturing a usable tool from raw materials, and how to manufacture tools that will meet the needs of the situation. You (the teacher) may have a selection of rocks and minerals available to you, and you may have some skills in flint knapping; if this is the case, you are in the minority. You can use heavy glass as a substitute for obsidian. You can obtain videos on flint knapping, even online (these vary in length and quality), or you can find a local flintknapper to help you. Many local archaeology clubs have a toolmaker who is willing to come and demonstrate to your class. *The Oxford Companion to Archaeology* (Silberman 2012) and other publications have detailed descriptions of the basic methods used. Or you can borrow stone tools for use in your class. Be sure that anyone who is handling the raw materials or making the tools has protection (leather gloves, goggles).

Students are given several raw foods to prepare. Working together as a class, they assess the tools available and choose the best tools for the tasks. The object is to cut the food into small enough pieces that it can be eaten (or cooked quickly). Provide cutting boards or a protected surface for the students to use. The foods should include tomatoes, onions, garlic bulbs, jalapeño peppers, limes, cumin seeds, and cilantro. If all goes well, the results of the activity can be mixed together to make salsa. Provide corn chips so that the students can sample their creation.

Questions to ask the students

1. What kinds of tools were used for the food preparation (scrapers, awls, blades, etc.)? How well did the tools work?

2. Which foods were easiest to prepare? Which were hardest?

3. Does this exercise change your perception of early hominid tool use? Why or why not?

4. Do you think chimpanzees or other great apes might be capable of creating stone tools like you made? Why or why not?

Reference

Silberman, Neil Asher, ed. 2012. *The Oxford Companion to Archaeology*. 2nd ed. New York: Oxford University Press.

VI. What Does It Mean To Be Human?

Susan Kirkpatrick Smith

Course: Human Origins

1. Have students write four times during the semester what they think it means to be human. I ask students to write a half page in class. Following each writing assignment, we discuss their comments. These discussions can take place in small groups or as a large-group discussion. I take up their writing and give them a participation grade. I do not grade the content.

   a. Day 1:

      i. I do not provide the students with guidance other than to write what they think it means to be human and to take a half page to provide their answer.

      ii. I ask the students to share some of their answers and I put them on the board. We then talk about which of these traits of humanness would leave evidence in the archaeological record.

      iii. We then discuss which type of anthropologist studies each of these types of data and what the data then suggest about when the students believe that "humans" first appear in the archaeological record.

         1. Note: Because many students enroll after the first day of class, I ask all late enrollees to participate in an online discussion of the topic. They must write the same original posting and then discuss their postings online with others who enrolled late.

b. After modern primates:

i. For this discussion, I ask the students to make sure that they refer to information they have learned in class about primates.

ii. We have small-group discussions (3-5 students per group) about how the students' views of what it means to be human have changed since the beginning of the semester.

iii. The small groups share what they discussed, and we talk about why studying nonhuman primates is important in a human origins class.

c. After early hominins (usually after we discuss *H. habilis* or *H. erectus*):

i. Again, students are asked to talk about what it means to be human, and they are asked to refer to material they have learned about early hominins.

ii. Large- or small-group discussions focusing on what features of humans they are seeing so far follow.

d. After arrival of anatomically modern humans:

i. Final in-class discussion of what it means to be human.

ii. I ask the students to center their discussion on the various archaic forms (Neanderthals, *H. heidelbergensis*, etc.) and whether they believe that they are "human."

2. Essay on final exam: "How have your views of what it means to be human changed over the course of the semester? What have you learned in the class that caused you to change your views? If you have not changed your views, what have you learned in the class that has reinforced your views? Make sure you have specific references to course material in your answer."

a. I hand back their original writings before the final exam so that they can refer to them while studying.

b. I let them know that this question will be on the exam.

3. What does this address?

   a. Writing Across the Curriculum initiatives:

      i. Students "write to learn" rather than write to show what they have learned.

      ii. Students are graded on participation (which often includes discussion of what they have written afterward) but not on content.

      iii. The final exam essay is where they are graded on this concept.

   b. "Enduring Questions" initiatives:

      i. Helps with "why do we need to know this" types of questions.

      ii. Moves beyond memorizing taxa.

4. Learning objectives:

   a. Student will develop and articulate a statement on "what it means to be human" supported by concepts learned in class.

   b. Student will demonstrate how disparate areas of physical anthropology contribute to the field of human origins.

VII. Play the Feud

Contributed by *Teaching Biological Anthropology in the 21st Century Workshop Participants*, 2013

Courses: Introduction to Anthropology, Introduction to Biological Anthropology, Human Origins

This assignment is a good way to review material that is new and often confusing to students. Start by explaining the rules of *Family Feud*. If you or the students are not familiar with this popular TV show, you can find the rules online.

Create several different polls.

1. 100 female Neanderthals were asked: "What do you find attractive about male Neanderthal faces?

    a. Possible answers:

        i. Occipital buns

        ii. Wide noses

        iii. Large supraorbital tori

2. 100 *Homo erectus* were asked: "What is your greatest cultural achievement?"

    a. Possible answers:

        i. Fire

        ii. The Acheulean hand ax

        iii. Being able to survive outside of Africa

3. 100 New World Monkeys were asked: "What is your favorite food?"

   a. Possible answers:

      i. Fruit

      ii. Insects

      iii. Leaves

This exercise is a good way to review factual material in a fun environment.

APPENDIX 2: Sample Student Paper for Forensic Anthropology

"That Poor Dog": Vehicular Trauma Analysis of a Dog by Applying Forensic Anthropology

Laura D. Lund

Abstract

This research is a case study analyzing trauma, sex, age at death, and time since death, of a domestic dog (*Canis familiaris*) suspected of being hit by a vehicle. A man who gave it a proper burial in his parents' backyard found the deceased dog on the side of the road. I excavated the burial using archaeological field techniques and recovered most of the skeletal remains, lots of hair, some skin, and six claw sheaths. Severe blunt force trauma consistent with vehicular trauma was documented. The damage was primarily isolated to the skull and the right side of the dog's hind limbs. I used the same trauma methods Forensic Anthropologists use with human victims when determining individual identification and details surrounding a victim's death. These analyses are crucial in the investigation of the death of human victims, and this research was done to apply these methods to the death of a domestic dog. Forensic anthropology students are unable to use human remains in this type of study. As a student, I must turn to nonhuman subjects when studying forensic methodology. Analyzing the remains of this domestic dog that died in a manner consistent with vehicular trauma provided such an opportunity as a useful substitution for human remains.

Introduction

About 5,000 pedestrians are killed every year in the United States. According to the Georgia Highway Safety Statistics Information (GHSSI), approximately 150 pedestrians are killed each year in Georgia within the last 20 years. The physical evidence is crucial when it involves hit-and-run cases (Beddoe 1958).

The National Highway Transportation Safety Administration reported on the statistics of child pedestrian fatalities between 1992-2001 and found that 6,679 pedestrian fatalities were between the ages of 0-15, which is 12.6 percent of all pedestrian fatalities. Adult pedestrian fatalities represented a much larger number.[3] A study in Oxford, Britain, reported on pedestrian vehicular trauma from different road accidents. There were 27 pedestrian fatalities out of 500 victims involved in some form of vehicular trauma. Only four of those victims were under the age of 20 (Atkins et al. 1988). A population level Rhode Island study of vehicular trauma was done assessing age patterns (Rockett et al. 1990). Between 1984 and 1985, 5,769 vehicular trauma cases were detailed and categorized by road-use type. The highest percentage was motor vehicle occupant and the lowest percentage was pedestrians and pedal cyclists. Among the pedestrians and pedal cyclists, the highest number of fatalities was between the ages of 5-14 (Rockett et al. 1990).

The Not-in Traffic Surveillance System (NiTS) has collected fatality information from traffic accidents since 1975 in the Fatality Analysis Reporting System (FARS). However, hit-and-run accident information is not collected. Therefore, I am unable to report population-level information on total number of vehicular homicide victims or age patterns involving hit-and-run accidents in the United States or Georgia. I have attained, however, two court cases involving hit-and-run situations that occurred in Georgia. In both cases, the physical evidence was heavily utilized and resulted in convictions for both cases. The first case, Klaub versus The State of Georgia, occurred in 2002. Klaub had taken his wife's car late one night and returned to tell his wife that he had hit a dog. The next morning Joeann Edwards Swift was found dead. The physical evidence was analyzed and ultimately was responsible for the conviction of two counts of vehicular homicide, hit and run, and driving with a suspended license. They were able to compare the automobile pieces and paint chips in the victim's clothing to the 1986 Mercury Topaz belonging to Klaub's wife (Klaub vs. The State of GA, 564 SE2d 471 [2002]).

The second case was Henry versus The State of Georgia. This case occurred in 2007, in which Henry was convicted of vehicular homicide for hitting two fourteen-year-old boys. He had a passenger with him after leaving a bar. The passenger pleaded for the driver to return to the scene when Henry hit the two boys, and he refused. One boy was killed on impact and the other was found hours later with severe injuries resulting in several surgeries. Henry was convicted with felony hit and run, a lesser charge than vehicular homicide, based on the lack of presentation of the physical evidence (Henry vs. The State of GA, 645 SE2d 32 [2007]). This is an example of the importance of retrieving the physical evidence completely and accurately to help ensure enough information is present to seek justice for these victims. Forensic anthropologists, medical examiners, and crime scene investigators have a responsibility to collect detailed information regarding cases of vehicular accidents, especially those of vehicular homicide. In these cases, the physical evidence is vital in the progression of identifying the victim and narrowing a possible driver. This paper discusses the forensic methodology used for human victims of pedestrian, and hit-and-run accidents.

As a forensic anthropology student, I am unable to use human remains in this type of study. I must turn to nonhuman subjects to apply forensic methodology. I was able to locate and analyze the remains of a domestic dog (*Canis familiaris*) that died in a manner consistent with vehicular trauma, which provided a similar substitution for human remains, especially those of children because of size and height.

I was able to do a full excavation of a domestic dog that had been buried after being found on the side of an urban road (photograph 13.1). My purpose for excavating the dog was to forensically assess the trauma it had sustained and analyze the skeleton for other factors such as age at death, time since death, and sex. The analysis of the skeletal remains of victims that have sustained vehicular trauma is methodical and time consuming. A useful report of a hit-and-run case was written to detail the analysis of the remains of a vehicular trauma victim to examine the body and other physical evidence (Beddoe 1958).

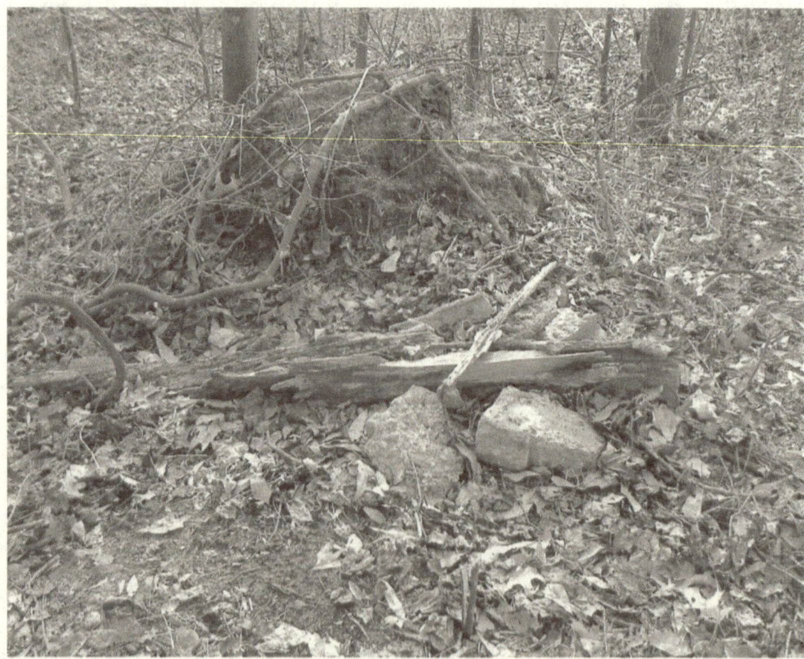

Photograph 13.1. Dog buried under the concrete slabs. (Photograph by Laura Lund)

Excavation

A full excavation of the domestic dog burial was completed using standard archaeological techniques in March 2010. During the excavation process, there were two important details to consider for the analytical portion of this research. Shortly after digging, the feature of the burial was exposed (photograph 13.2). The soil was inconsistent with the rest of the Unit. When pressure was applied, the root clusters and soil would give with a spongy feeling. As the hole was opened to the size of a cantaloupe, there were visible clumps of hair. The soil was blackened from the decomposition of soft tissue. The remains of the dog, labeled TPD-2, were retrieved carefully and methodically. Unfortunately, because of the tremendous thickness of the roots, the full skeleton could not be exposed without disarticulating it as it was uncovered. I had to photograph and extract the remains as they were uncovered. The bioturbation from the roots had disturbed the skeleton from the original placement at the time of the burial. However, the skeleton remained articulated for the most part even with the presence of bioturbation.

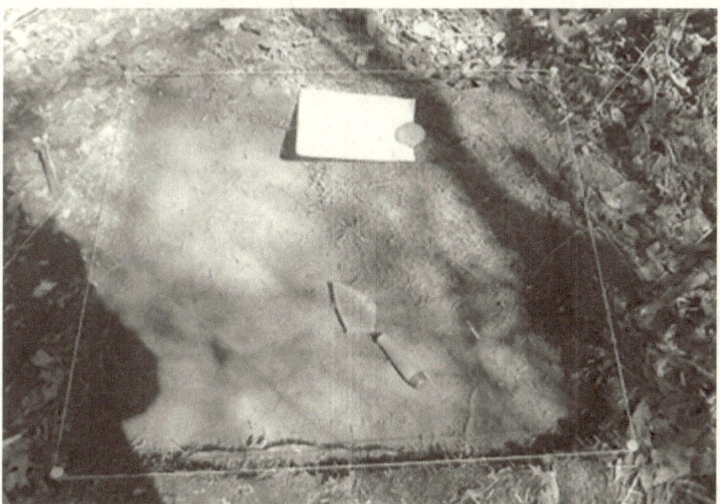

Photograph 13.2. Excavation Unit 1 - Feature 1. (Photograph by Laura Lund)

Methodology

After all the remains of the dog were uncovered, through both excavation and screening, they were cleaned with Oxy Clean and warm water. They were not soaked in the water-Oxy Clean mixture, but were dipped in the mixture and gently scrubbed with a toothbrush. The postcranial remains were then rearticulated in order to assess the skeleton for sex, age at death, time since death, and trauma. The skull was so fractured that articulation proved to be more difficult than the postcranial skeleton. I used a line drawing of a coyote skull to shade in the fragments of the skull that had been recovered (figure 13.1).

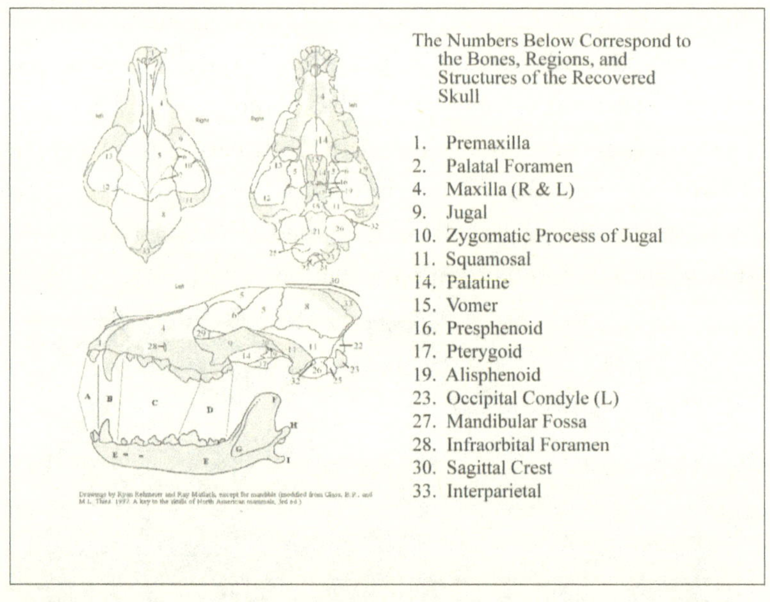

Figure 13.1 Line drawing of skull fragments. (Permission by Diane Warren)

Results of Skeletal Analysis

The dog's skeleton was intact, except for the skull (photograph 13.3), and there were no signs of scavenging. I was able to conclusively determine the dog's sex as a male by the presence of the *os penis* (penile bone) that was recovered. The age at death was determined from the epiphyseal growth plates of the iliac crest. Neither epiphyseal growth plate was fused completely, but there were signs of partial fusion. This indicated that the dog was approximately 6 months to 2 years old. The time since death was determined by the seven stages of preservation characteristics (table 13.1).

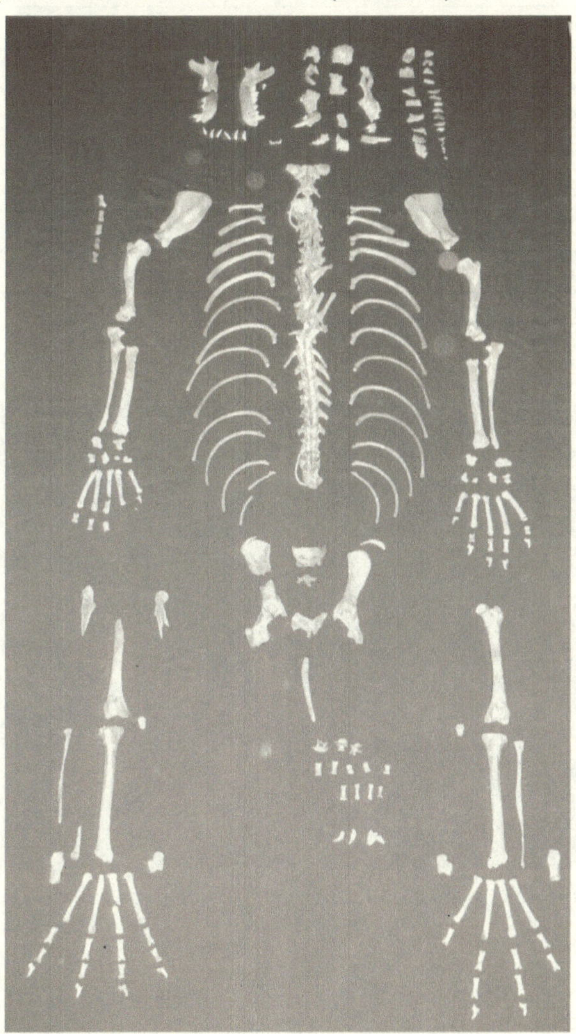

Photograph 13.3. Skeleton of TPD—2. (Photograph by Laura Lund)

Table 13.1 - State of Preservation Characteristics of Skelton TPD-2		
	Contemporary	Non-Contemporary
Color	Light	Dark-X
Texture	Smooth - X	Grainy
Hydration	Wet & Greasy - X	Dry
Weight	Heavy - X	Light
Condition	Whole - X	Fragmented
Fragility	Tough - X	Fragile
Soft Tissue	Present - X	Absent

Table 13.1. State of Preservation Characteristics.

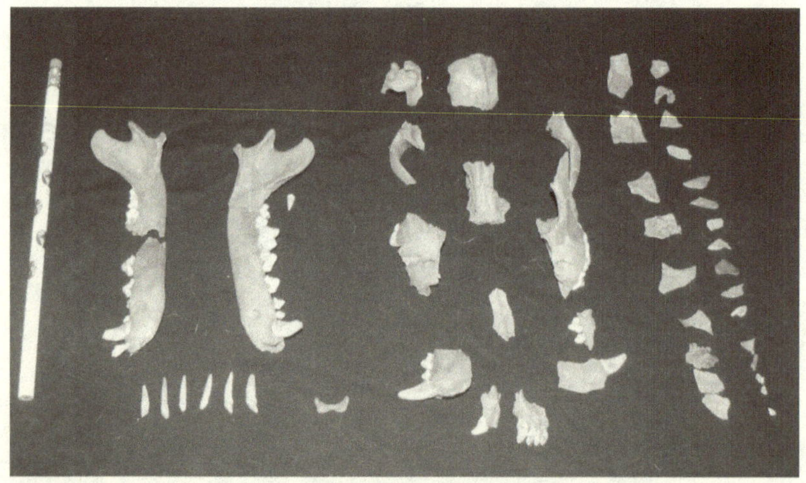

Photograph 13.4. Recovered skull fragments. (Photograph by Laura Lund)

Trauma

The cranium was very fragmented. There are 23 unidentified possible skull fragments that were recovered. However, there are a few skull fragments that I was able to identify (figure 13.1 and photograph 13.4). A fragment of the sagittal crest and the interparietal were recovered with fragments of the right and left parietal bones. The left maxilla, jugal, and squamosal bones were recovered. The left jugal bone has a comminuted compression fracture at the suture, and the left squamosal bone also has a comminuted compression fracture. The right squamosal bone has a fracture.

There was extensive blunt force trauma to the mandible and maxilla of the dog. The right mandible has a perimortem compression fracture anterior to the ramus and posterior to the alveolar process at M3 (M – molar). The right I3 (I – incisor), I2, and I1 were also not recovered. The left mandible also had a perimortem compression fracture at M1, in which the tooth had also fractured off. P2 (P – premolar) was also broken, but appears to be antemortem. There is a dark cusp and a white cusp that is still present. The left I3 was still present, but I2 and I1 were not. The maxilla had more signs of trauma on both sides. I2 was found as a loose tooth. There were four separate comminuted compression fractures on the left side of the maxilla. The right side had three separate comminuted compression fractures, and all teeth were in the maxilla except P3, P4, and M2, which were not recovered (figure 13.2).

The right *os coxae* (hipbones) has a perimortem comminuted compression fracture of the shaft of the ilium, and there is also a caudal acetabulur fracture. The left *os coxae* has a comminuted compression fracture at the ischium and an epiphyseal fracture of the iliac crest. The sacrum's coccyx has a comminuted fracture and

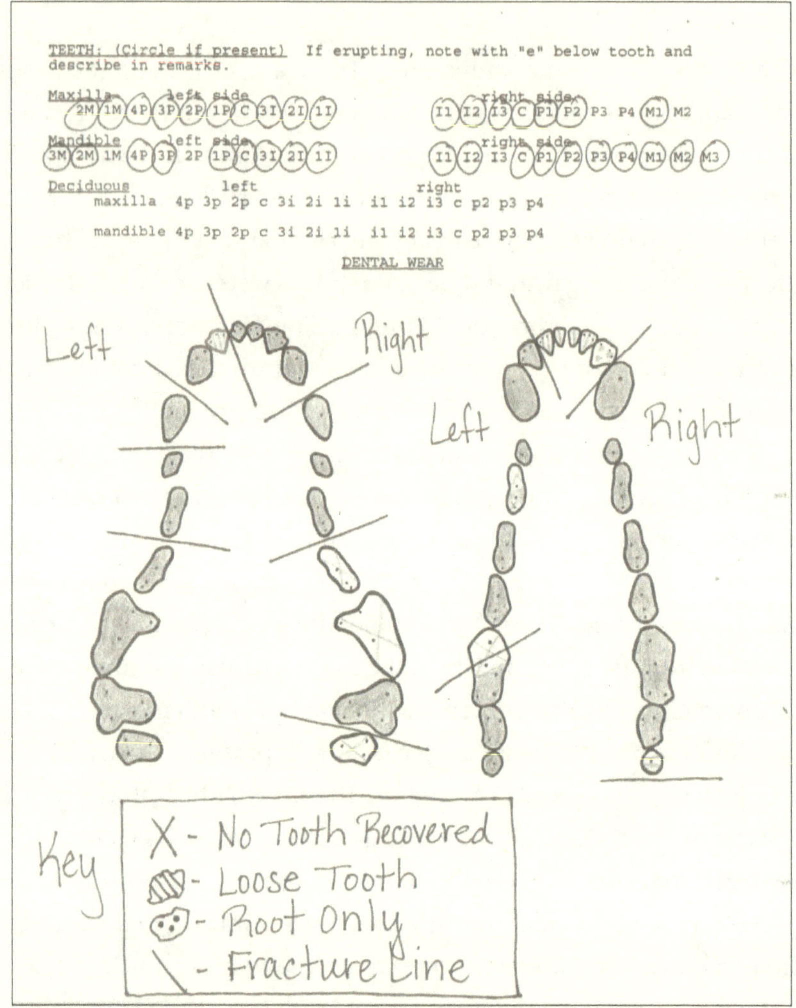

Figure 13.2. Line drawing of teeth recovered. (Data sheet created by and used with the permission by Diane Warren)

the pubic symphysis has fractured away from both the left and right *os coxa* (photograph 13.5). Consistent with the fracture to the right acetabulum, the right femur is in three pieces. The trauma is present with two proximal comminuted fractures that split both the femoral head and greater trochanter apart from the shaft. The right fibula has a distal fracture approximately 2 centimeters proximal to the lateral malleolus. The medial malleolus of the tibia is also fractured. The left femur, tibia, and fibula had no signs of fractures (photograph 13.6).

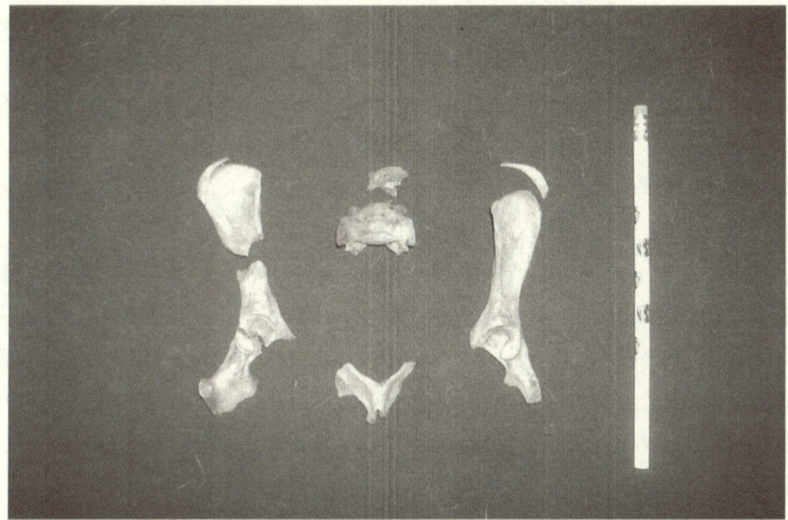

Photograph 13.5. Pelvic trauma. (Photograph by Laura Lund)

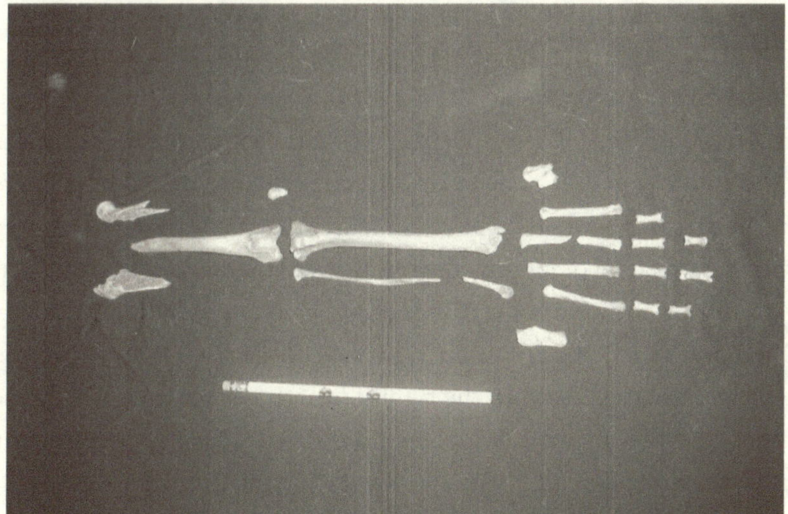

Photograph 13.6. Right hand limb trauma. (Photograph by Laura Lund)

Secondary trauma was also observed on the postcranial skeleton. The right floating rib has one perimortem comminuted compression fracture and a possible antemortem shearing fracture posterior to the tubercle on the same rib. T1 (T – thoracic vertebrae), T2, T9, and T10 all had perimortem comminuted compression fractures at the spinous processes. The right transverse processes of the thoracic vertebrae numbers T10 and T12 were fractured as well. More transverse processes were fractured on the left side of the thoracic vertebrae; numbers, T10, T12, and T13. The transverse processes of the lumbar vertebrae (L) were also fractured on L1 and L2.

There is no trauma evident to the long bones of the forelimbs; however, both the right and left spines of the scapulae are fractured. The left scapula has more trauma than the right. The spine was almost comminuted, only attached at the superior end of the spine. There are two radiating fractures from the spine to the infraspinous fossa, another to the supraspinous fossa and finally another to the subscapular fossa.

Discussion

Based on the skeletal analysis of TPD-2, it is consistent with vehicular trauma. The majority of primary trauma was to the skull and most likely would have been the direct cause of death. It appears to be the primary area of the blunt force trauma and would have caused severe damage to the brain. The fractures to the right *os coxa* and the right side of the long bones also indicate primary blunt force trauma. There was more damage to the right side of the skull than to the left, which is also the case with the right side of the long bones of the hind limbs and the *os coxae*, which can aid in concluding the direction of force. It appears that the dog was facing slightly laterally on the right side with the force of the vehicle to the dog's head. All of the dorsal fractures to the vertebrae and scapulae appear to be secondary fractures from the dog flipping over on its back repeatedly from the initial force of the vehicle's first blow to the head and right side of the body.

Using a nonhuman subject was beneficial for practicing forensic methodology. Animals, particularly dogs, are good substitutions for humans because both humans and dogs are regularly affected by blunt force vehicular trauma (Simpson et al. 2009). However, there is not a National Trauma Data Bank for dogs in veterinary medicine like there is for humans. A study evaluating 239 dogs sustaining vehicular trauma in 2001 was done in an attempt to answer age pattern questions and severity of trauma and outcome (Streeter et al. 2009). This was the first study to analyze the associations with survival from dogs suffering vehicular trauma. The majority of the 239 dogs sustaining vehicular trauma were young (n=149), and 33 dogs died as a result of their injuries, but there was no significant difference between the nonsurvivors and the three age groups (Streeter et al. 2009). A similar study was done using 235 dogs arriving at a vet hospital in California between 1997-2003 with varying types of blunt force trauma, including vehicular trauma. They were assessed to determine what caused the trauma in the animals. Ninety-one percent of the dogs that came into the hospital sustained blunt force trauma from motor vehicle accidents. The average age was two and a half years old, and out of the 235 who entered the hospital with blunt force trauma, only 29 died, while 14 of the 29 suffered severe head trauma (Simpson et al. 2009). These studies reflected the nonsurvivor characteristics of similar vehicular trauma that TPD-2 had sustained and represented the largest age group in both studies that were nonsurvivors. This indicates that younger dogs are more likely to stray into the streets and therefore more likely to be exposed to vehicular accidents.

Using the same trauma assessment used in human hit-and-run cases (Beddoe 1958), I was able to answer questions regarding age at death, time since death, and the physical evidence of a hit-and-run case. In the case of TPD-2, the only physical evidence left is the skeletal remains. If this were a human hit-and-run case, it would be difficult to create a case based on the remaining physical evidence. However, establishing the age at death, between 6 months and 2 years old, the time since death, approximately, 2-3 years, the sex as male, and the physical evidence of vehicular trauma, I could narrow the missing persons down to a smaller data set. This would be imperative to identifying a possible victim and possible driver.

Acknowledgments

Thank you to Hope Morris for her assistance in researching forensic anthropology programs and courses in American colleges and universities. Thank you also to the participants in the AAPA workshops on *Teaching Biological Anthropology in the 21st Century* for providing exciting new course and assignment ideas. We would also like to acknowledge the Hoover Family for providing permission to excavate the dog in their yard. Also, thank you to Dr. Diane Warren from the University of Oklahoma for granting permission to use her line drawing of the teeth.

Notes

1. RAI's *Teaching Anthropology* (http://www.teachinganthropology.org/)

2. AAA's "Teaching Materials Exchange" (http://www.aaanet.org/customcf/syllabi/search_form.cfm)

3. See www.nhtsa.dot.gov, accessed April 17, 2010.

References

Aguilar, Madeline. 2012. "Crossing Borders: Teaching American Students from Abroad—Using Blogging as a Teaching Tool while Traveling and Teaching Online." Paper presented at the annual meeting for the *American Anthropological Association*, San Francisco, CA, November 13-18.

American Board of Forensic Anthropology. 2008. "What is Forensic Anthropology?" http://www.theabfa.org/forstudents.html.

Angelo, Thomas A., and K. Patricia Cross. 1993. *Classroom Assessment Techniques: A Handbook for College Teachers.* San Francisco: Jossey-Bass.

Atkins, R. M., W. H. Turner, R. B. Duthie, and B. R. Wilde. 1988. "Injuries to Pedestrians in Road Traffic Accidents." *British Medical Journal* 297(3): 1431-34.

Bean, John C. 2001. *Engaging Ideas: The Professor's Guide to Integrating Writing, Critical Thinking, and Active Learning in the Classroom.* San Francisco: Jossey-Bass.

Beddoe, H. L. 1958. "Hit-Run Murders: Examination of the Body." *Journal of Criminal Law, Criminology, and Police Science* 49(3): 280-84.

Chase, K., D. R. Carrier, F. R. Adler, T. Jarvik, E. A. Ostrander, T. D. Lorentzen, and K. Lark. 2002. "Genetic Basis for Systems of Skeletal Quantitative Traits: Principal Component Analysis of the Canid Skeleton." *Proceedings of the National Academy of Sciences of the United States of America* 99(15): 9930-35.

Dixon, Christine C., and Nancy Gonlin. 2012. "Bringing the Past into the Classrooms of the Present: Crossing the Borders from the Society of American Archaeology to the American Anthropological Association." Paper presented at the Annual Meeting for the *American Anthropological Association*, San Francisco, CA, November 13-18.

France Casting. 2013. Pathology and Anomaly Casts, http://www.francecasts.com/casts/humans/pathology_and_anomolies/.

Hunt, Katharine D. 2012. “Crossing Barriers: Teaching Linguistics Online.” Paper presented at the Annual Meeting for the *American Anthropological Association*, San Francisco, CA, November 13-18.

London, Marilyn R., Susan Kirkpatrick Smith, and Gwyn Madden. 2012. “Teaching Biological Anthropology in the 21st Century.” Workshop presented at the Annual Meeting for the *American Association of Physical Anthropologists*, Portland, OR, April 11-14.

———. 2013. “Teaching Biological Anthropology in the 21st Century.” Workshop presented at the Annual Meeting for the *American Association of Physical Anthropologists*, Knoxville, TN, April 10-13.

Mott Community College. 2013. “Course Descriptions,” http://www.mcc.edu/programs_courses/course_desc.php?coursecode=ANTH-210.

Pusateri, Tom. 2013. Teaching Journals Directory, http://cetl.kennesaw.edu/teaching-journals-directory.

Rice, Patricia C., David W. McCurdy, and Scott Lukas. 2011. *Strategies in Teaching Anthropology*. 6th ed. Upper Saddle River, NJ: Pearson.

Rockett, I. R. H., E. S. Lieberman, W. H. Hollinshead, S. L. Putnam, and H. C. Thode. 1990. “Age, Sex, and Road-Use Patterns of Motor Vehicular Trauma in Rhode Island: A Population-Based Hospital Emergency Department of Study.” *American Journal of Public Health* 80(12): 1516-18.

Simpson, S. A., R. Syring, and C. M. Otto. 2009. “Severe Blunt Trauma in Dogs: 235 Cases (1997-2003).” *Journal of Veterinary Emergency and Critical Care* 19(6): 588-602.

Smith, Susan Kirkpatrick. 2012. "Student Research in an Online Learning Environment: Some Suggestions for Introduction to Anthropology." Paper presented at the Annual Meeting for the *American Anthropological Association*, San Francisco, CA, November 13-18.

Streeter, E. M., E. A. Rozanski, A. de Laforcade-Buress, L. M. Freeman, and J. E. Rush. 2009. "Evaluation of Vehicular Trauma in Dogs: 239 Cases." *Journal of the American Veterinary Medical Association* 235(4): 405-8.

Swindle, M. Michael, and A. C. Smith. 1998. "Comparative Anatomy and Physiology of the Pig." *Scandinavian Journal of Laboratory Animal Science* 25(1): 1-10.

Tessandori, Anthony S., and Christine C. Dixon. 2012. "Crossing the Border From the Lab to the On-Line Classroom: A Successful Pedagogical Story of Adapting a Biological Anthropology Lab Course to a Virtual Classroom Environment." Paper presented at the Annual Meeting for the *American Anthropological Association*, San Francisco, CA, November 13-18.

University of Hawai'I, West O'ahu. 2012. "Applied Forensic Anthropology Program Information," http://westoahu.hawaii.edu/forensic.

The Art of Anthropology at a College in Crisis: Exploring Some Effects of Neoliberalism on Higher Education

Vincent H. Melomo

Abstract

This chapter addresses the increasing pervasiveness of neoliberal ideologies in our culture and focuses on the implications of these ideologies for the future of anthropology in higher education. More specifically, the chapter considers how these ideologies pose a particular challenge to anthropology's more humanistic dimensions, which include both the art of anthropology and an anthropology of art. Throughout the chapter, the author tells the story of how reductions were made recently to the anthropology program at his institution in response to converging economic crises. He analyzes the context of these changes and the process by which they were made in order to raise questions about the broader implications of neoliberalism for the discipline of anthropology. The chapter closes by suggesting measures anthropologists could take to resist and survive the threats brought by an increasingly neoliberal higher education environment.

Introduction: Anthropology, Art, and the Humanities, Under Attack

Anthropologists generally agree that one of the most distinctive traits and unique strengths of our discipline is its integrative and in-between relationship to the sciences and the humanities (Feinberg 2009). While the broad field of anthropology has most consistently been positioned as a science, many cultural anthropologists in particular have considered their practice as closer to the humanities and as more of an art. Although this perspective has roots in the work of Boas and his students from early in the twentieth century, it has become much more prevalent since the Geertzian (1973) interpretive and then postmodern turn in anthropology toward the end of the twentieth century. These later theoretical shifts first encouraged anthropologists to look at cultures as texts and then encouraged us to look more critically at the texts that we produce and at ourselves as producers of those texts (Clifford and Marcus 1986). As a result, many cultural anthropologists have come to see ethnography as a socially and politically situated form of expression. Even more relevant to the focus of this volume, the ways ethnographers express their knowledge have become more experimental and artistic (Marcus and Fischer 1986), and artistic expressions themselves have become more accepted objects of ethnographic inquiry (Morphy and Perkins 2006).

This relationship between anthropology and the arts and humanities, an important one worth preserving, ties the issues raised in the rest of this chapter to the other chapters in this volume. This chapter draws from the specific example of the anthropology program at my university to explore what might happen to anthropology broadly and to the art of anthropology and an anthropology of art more specifically as the existence of the liberal arts and the humanities are increasingly called into question. It is not hyperbole to say that the liberal arts, humanities, and more specifically anthropology, have been under attack in recent years. The discipline of anthropology has recently made headlines in a way that it rarely does, but for the most unfortunate of reasons. The most visible of these attacks have come from several governors of large states who questioned the logic of supporting specific programs in the liberal arts, including anthropology, in their public universities (Z. Anderson 2011; Stancill and Frank 2013) and from a leading business magazine that announced anthropology as number one in its list of "The 10 Worst College Majors" (Goudreau 2012). This chapter argues that these attacks on the liberal arts, the humanities, and on anthropology nationally are linked to the specific example of changes made to the anthropology program at my university by a neoliberal logic increasingly prevalent in higher education and in our society more broadly.

Tying in with the volume's focus on the art of anthropology, this chapter is intended to be a kind of storytelling. Like most anthropological storytelling, I try to ground the story in context and theory and thus try to give the story a purpose (Clifford 1986, 98). The story is in the end intended to be a cautionary tale, representing a kind of reflexive public anthropology that encourages us to consider more critically our place as anthropologists and agents in an American society and culture. The focus of the story is the anthropology program at William Peace University (formerly Peace College), where I teach, and the trials and tribulations we encountered in the 2010-2011 academic year.[1]

In sum, in early January 2011, the college's administration decided that a relatively new and promising anthropology major would be reduced to a minor with the loss of 25 percent of the full-time faculty, or one half of two full-time positions.[2] The news was devastating to the anthropology faculty and students and a surprise to many in the college. In this chapter, I discuss my experience and understanding of the process by which this happened. I try to tie this story into other issues in higher education and in our culture at large. In the closing, I reflect and ask the reader to reflect with me, on the possible implications of this story to the discipline, perspective, and body of knowledge that we love.

Neoliberalism, Higher Education and the Economic Crisis of 2008

The news of the decision to reduce the program forced me to face the difficult problem of how to explain why this had happened. I needed to be able to provide an answer for my own understanding but also to respond to the various others both inside and outside of academe who would inevitably ask. The possible reasons for the reduction of the program are various. Perhaps the most obvious explanation could be that we did not have a successful program by many measures or that we failed to represent the major and discipline effectively to the administration. While this is of course possible, as I explain further below, I believe strongly that this is not the case, and colleagues inside and outside of our discipline and our institution thought our program and the program review documentation that we produced was very good. Another possible reason for the reduction of the program is that we were subjected to an arbitrary decision made by an imperious administration blindly cutting expenses in many areas. This is an explanation popular with some at our university, but I do not think it is a sufficient one. As cultural anthropologists know, even seemingly arbitrary decisions by those in power typically reflect unspoken cultural values and perspectives not unique to those exercising their power. As Ortner (2006, 130) states, social actors, even those in relative positions of power, "are always involved in, and can never act outside of, the mulitiplicity of social relations in which they are enmeshed." The third possible explanation for the cuts, the one that I seek to explore further in this chapter, is that the decisions made about the anthropology program at Peace were to a significant degree the result of the cultural logic of neoliberalism.

As discussed by Richland (2009, 170), cultural anthropologists studying a wide variety of topics have in recent years increasingly brought attention to "what they see as the creeping expansion of neoliberal logics." Scholars in other disciplines have also written much in the past decade about neoliberalism as an ideology that has shaped higher education in particular in significant and dramatic ways (Archer 2008; Davies and Petersen 2005; Olssen and Peters 2005).[3] This chapter is yet another then echoing this concern, but it is different by offering a firsthand reflection on how this reality may be shaping our own discipline of anthropology and, at least in some institutions, even threatening its existence. In this chapter, I explore how neoliberalism was a key force in shaping the context and events of our story and consider how neoliberalism provides an explanation that has implications for anthropology and the art of anthropology beyond William Peace University.

Neoliberalism is a concept that has been defined with varying degrees of specificity. The concept is most closely associated with economic globalization and particularly with the imposition of free market policies on "developing" nations. Neoliberalism emphasizes a laissez-faire role for governments with regard to regulating markets but at the same time requires of governments an active role in encouraging business and market concerns. The term is also sometimes used more generally, as I intend to use it here, as a kind of shorthand for a way of thinking about the place of economic and business concerns in a society. In my broad use of the term, I am thinking of neoliberalism as the ideology and rhetoric justifying the increasing primacy of market concerns in all areas of life—from governments to health care to education. Neoliberalism, at an extreme perhaps, is the idea that the economic sphere should not be constrained to serve social needs but that argues that all other areas of society and culture should be brought in line with economic concerns and that the market and the rationalities of business best govern institutions of all kinds. As Olssen and Peters (2005) discuss, neoliberalism has significantly affected higher education in numerous ways, in terms of educational purpose, organizational structures, social relations, and professional identities. They write, "The ascendancy of neoliberalism . . . has produced a fundamental shift in the way universities and other institutions of higher education have defined and justified their institutional existence. The traditional professional culture of open intellectual enquiry and debate has been replaced with an institutional stress on *performativity*, as evidenced by the emergence of an emphasis on measured outputs: on strategic planning, performance indicators, quality assurance measures and academic audits" (Olssen and Peters 2005, 313, emphasis mine). *Performance* as defined by neoliberalism, thus bears little resemblance to the creative, aesthetic, and affective dimensions of performance as the term is used in an artistic context but has more to do with the "performance" of a financial investment, or a machine. Neoliberalism as a dominant cultural logic thus shapes the higher educational environment in a variety of ways, and as I discuss further, it also shapes the specific processes and decisions that reduced the anthropology program at Peace.

Before outlining the specific institutional factors that shaped the reductions at Peace, it is important to first address the broader cultural and political context in which these reductions occurred. To do so, it is necessary to address the role of neoliberalism in the immediate economic crisis and the responses to it. The economic crisis of 2008, now several years old, was undoubtedly the product of numerous and diverse factors. However, at least when it began, there was a clear consensus that it was to a significant degree because of the failure of governmental regulatory oversight in the financial industry (Bardhan 2012; Milanovic 2012). This failure of regulatory mechanisms can be generally attributed to the dominance of neoliberal policies in the United States, endorsed by both Republican and Democratic administrations over the past several decades. These policies privileged the financial markets, their freedoms and flexibility, and achieved this through a deemphasis on regulation and enforcement. This privileging of the financial sector, as time has shown, was arguably done at the expense of other areas of society.

Years after the downturn occurred, the news was still filled with stories of the effects of and responses to the economic turmoil that followed. These responses most typically emphasized cutting budgets and cutting services to virtually all institutions that serve the public in some fashion, both public and private—cuts to workforces, cuts to pensions, cuts to health care services, cuts to athletic programs, and most relevant to this volume, cuts to the arts and cuts to education. As we all have learned, even chancellors and presidents of higher educational institutions have responded by cutting their budgets and services out of claims of necessity. To use the dominant locational metaphors of the discourse about the economic crisis, the uncontrolled fiscal policies of "Wall Street," a product of neoliberalism, have trickled down in dubious ways to affect "Main Streets" across America. What seems the most strange and sad paradox of our current context is that it often seems that the loudest political voice and the conventional wisdom that has emerged from this crisis brought on by neoliberalism is a call for more neoliberalism. As seen throughout the 2012 election cycle and as outlined in their party platforms on their respective websites, the Republican Party and the emergent Tea Party in particular have exploited the unhappiness and insecurity created by this crisis to paradoxically continue to argue for less government regulation and more support of "free markets." However, in addition to these specific groups engaging in such policy rhetoric, many public leaders and administrators of all political stripes have, by proclaimed necessity, embraced a politics of austerity that has in effect furthered neoliberal perspectives and policies.

What is most relevant to the story of anthropology at Peace is how these calls for a more business- and market-based approach have shaped so many of our institutions, not just those areas more conventionally thought of as "businesses." To put it perhaps too simplistically, but to the point, the response to the problem of our society's having given too much privilege to market ideas and business concerns has been to try to *further* enforce market ideas and a business mentality on *even more* areas of society and culture, particularly in education. How this is relevant to a story about anthropology at William Peace University and to the volume's focus on art and anthropology is what I hope to clarify. While a much more expanded discussion of the broader political and policy landscape and the rhetoric, values, and money that shape it is warranted, I will now return to the story of the college in crisis and address the more immediate role that neoliberal ideas played in shaping our anthropology program.

A College's Response to Converging Crises

William Peace University is a private, coeducational university located in the heart of Raleigh, the capital city of North Carolina. Although the university has traditionally and still does emphasize the liberal arts, it has in recent years placed increasing emphasis on developing its professional programs, and the liberal arts have been in decline. William Peace University, like many institutions in higher education, has been in a crisis mode for several years. This crisis very significantly results from the economic downturn that began in 2008 and the pressures that it has put on institutions, governments, endowments, families, and students across the country. However, in addition to the challenges posed by the economic downturn, Peace's crisis has also resulted from struggles with enrollment. Until the summer of 2011, William Peace University was a women's college, Peace College. The college was very small, with a full-time enrollment of around seven hundred students in 2011. Like many women's colleges over the past several decades, the university struggled to grow its enrollment. While Peace transitioned from a two-year to a four-year college in the late nineties and grew its number of majors from six to seventeen, the college was not able to consistently meet its enrollment goals. Though Peace's endowment was healthy, as a small, tuition-driven college, it was particularly vulnerable to changing market conditions in higher education. Low enrollments meant high stress, and when the economic collapse of 2008 hit, a difficult situation was made much worse.

The crisis reached a head in the second half of 2010 under the direction of a new college president. In the summer of 2010, a new president was hired with an apparent mandate to "right size" the college and make it more "responsive" and "flexible," to use the all-too-familiar neoliberal euphemisms. When we returned to campus in the fall of 2010, we were met with significant staff layoffs, a gloomy state-of-the-college address, and a call for *all* academic programs in the college to undergo an internal review. Essentially, every program (and by extension, the few faculty within them) was asked to argue for its own existence. The already scheduled rotation of academic program audits was disregarded, signaling the dramatic changes to come. For this program review process, each program coordinator was asked to produce a document providing basic data about such things as class enrollments, numbers of students majoring and minoring, and program cost, and to respond to a number of questions addressing the strengths and significance of the programs for the present and future. In line with neoliberal concerns, the specificity of the data requested and the questions posed provided little room for the artful construction of a persuasive narrative. As I will discuss further, the art of anthropology simply seemed to be irrelevant to the process.

While the call for the program review was most unwelcome, I was reasonably optimistic that our program would survive. It was just in 2006 that Anthropology at Peace had gone from a concentration in the liberal studies major to a stand-alone major. The program was still one of the newest majors on campus, and although it had grown slowly at first, it had grown steadily in the prior two years (from eight to sixteen students majoring in 2009-2010, to approximately twenty-five students majoring in the 2010-2011 academic year). These numbers, while unimpressive for a larger school, made us the seventh-largest major on campus, out of seventeen. Our courses were generally well enrolled, satisfied many of the college's liberal education requirements, and were listed as electives in several of the other college's majors. We were also one of the most visible majors on campus because of the activity of our faculty and students, and particularly because of the success of our engaged learning opportunities. Specifically, one faculty member led a long-running and very popular summer program in Mexico and another ran a well-publicized and self-funded archaeological field school at a historic site in North Carolina. These summer programs were regularly used in promotional materials, and the anthropology faculty were even often asked to represent the college to outside groups. We were also an especially efficient major, offering four concentrations with only two full-time faculty and a few adjuncts. We did this by having a two-year rotation for many upper-level courses, by counting courses from other disciplines toward our concentrations, and through our summer programs. To use the rhetoric of neoliberalism, we tried to be as "flexible" and "responsive" as possible in order to help recruit and retain students; one of our concentrations—forensics—was specifically created to increase our marketability to today's students. Unlike some majors, we even brought in extra moneys to the college, particularly by drawing students from other colleges and universities to enroll in our summer programs. After outlining all of this in our program review document, I thought we were safe.

However, just before the start of the spring 2011 semester, we were notified of the outcome of the review process in individual meetings with the provost and president. I was initially most relieved to learn that I still had a job and that I would remain employed as a full-time faculty member in anthropology. However, I was then very surprised to learn that my senior colleague was asked to continue as a half-time faculty member, and I was even more disheartened, and increasingly so with time, to learn that starting in the fall of 2011, an anthropology major would no longer be offered for incoming students at Peace. In sum, we had been reduced to where we had been five years earlier. An anthropology major that we had worked on for years to birth and help grow would again only be a minor and concentration within a liberal studies major. We were confident that even in this incarnation, we could and would still serve our students well, but the turn of events made us disheartened for ourselves, for our students, for the college, and for the discipline.

Critical Reflections on Neoliberalism and Anthropology

So, how does this story of anthropology at William Peace University relate to neoliberalism, and what does this have to do with anthropology and art? In the program review document that was submitted to the administration, I discussed anthropology in ways that would be familiar to any dedicated student and practitioner of anthropology.

I argued that anthropology offers a unique understanding of human biological and cultural diversity and offers an important historical, contextual, and holistic perspective on the human experience. These are some of the most basic, noble, and humanistic tenets of the discipline. However, when reviewing the document and reflecting on the process for this volume, it became sadly clear to me how both the process itself and the arguments that I offered in response were shaped by neoliberal concerns. In the end, throughout most of the program review document, I found that I was justifying the discipline less in terms of any intrinsic philosophical or humanistic value, less for its value in helping to promote a more civil society or global understanding, and even less for its value in promoting a deep awareness of self and other. While these concerns were not entirely absent, the document seemed to all come back to a kind of "dollars and cents." How much did our major cost, and how many students/customers did it serve? How would our major contribute to recruiting and retaining students who could pay for college? How could our discipline help students get jobs? How efficient were we?

I came to understand that the program review process was based on the neoliberal perspective that the college is a business, the business has a market, and since the college is doing poorly as a business, it needs to reshape its product to best capitalize on its share of the market. The key academic piece relevant to gaining market share is to have majors that draw students/consumers and to have majors that parents/consumers know will lead to a job so that they can economically rationalize their investment. Recognizing the need to appeal to the neoliberal logic governing this process, I argued that anthropology can indeed do such things as attract students and help students get jobs and do these tasks pretty well. I consulted the Bureau of Labor Statistics website on projected job growth for anthropologists; I drew from the career materials on the American Anthropological

Association's website; and I heralded the ways in which our major could help anthropology students get most any kind of job and how any student in most any job would benefit from having had at least some anthropology. I offered specific examples from the few majors we had already graduated—students working in education and government and in graduate school, and I offered specific examples of students we had successfully recruited and retained. I even cited Harvard business review articles that argued for training more anthropologists (Anderson 2009; Davenport 2007; Radjou 2009).

Again, what I felt I was asked to do and what I was sincerely trying to do with my program review was to *sell* the discipline and to sell ourselves through our work within it. I felt compelled to market anthropology to our administration, to turn it into an attractive product they should want to buy, to make it seem like a good investment with strong returns. I was positioning students and parents as the consumers, the college as the business, and our program as the vehicle that would bring them together. I was doing neoliberalism, and I thought I was doing it well.

However, I am writing this chapter because I want to highlight that although my serving this neoliberal logic was obviously necessary, in the end it is also by some measure problematic that I did so. Even more importantly, I want to bring attention to the fact that it did not work anyway. Why precisely this was the case I cannot know, as the operations of those in relative positions of power are typically kept secret from those who are subject to such power. As Cohen (1974, 110) asserts, "The more privileged a group is in society, the more secretive and mystifying it tends to be about its organization and strategies." However, based on the general direction of the university and the decisions made, it seems that in the end, numbers beyond our immediate control may have sealed our fate. The simple most important fact that likely shaped our viability as a major at our college is that very few high school students know enough about anthropology to choose it as a major that they would seek out in applying to colleges. Because our major was not one of those that are highly ranked by high school students in such surveys, from our administration's perspective, our major could not effectively recruit new student-consumers to boost enrollment, despite some of the recent success we had had at doing so. And also importantly, because a degree in anthropology does not explicitly and necessarily translate into a career in the areas of greatest projected job growth, the parent-consumers of potential students would not likely seek out anthropology for their children. And finally, our chief administrator was likely not sufficiently aware of and invested in the value of the discipline of anthropology herself for it to matter. In the end, my interpretation of our story is that the survival of anthropology at Peace was not just a matter of how well anthropology fit into the neoliberal logic of the institution but of how well others perceived the discipline of anthropology to satisfy the neoliberal logic of our society and culture.

Of course, it was not just anthropology that was affected by these changes at our college, and anthropology in fact was affected much less than some other disciplines. Perhaps predictably, the humanities suffered most, with reductions in history, music, art, and Spanish. Relevant to this volume's theme, the major in art, which had already been paired with the more marketable "graphic design," was phased out. Another significant response to these pressures was the revision of the existing liberal education curriculum. What emerged was a curriculum that was intended to place greater emphasis on marketable skills rather than areas of disciplinary knowledge. Most significantly, mirroring the neoliberal emphasis on constructing social agents primarily as consumers, the new liberal education curriculum clearly emphasizes that students are consumers of higher education almost exclusively to gain access to professional opportunities. In the revised curriculum, students are required to take four years of preprofessional classes, with limited explicit emphasis on making them more globally conscious or more critically self-aware human beings.

What follows from these market-driven, neoliberal shifts, is that there is less opportunity for institutions of higher education, and for those who teach in them, to be independent agents shaping society and culture. Such institutions and the people within them will to a significant degree be and teach what "the market demands." The potential role that anthropology in particular can have in transforming people, society, and culture is lessened if anthropology is done only in service to the economy or, taken to the extreme, if anthropology does not exist in such institutions at all.

Throughout the crisis of the fall semester, while I was struggling with how to explain and defend the discipline to the college administration, coincidentally, another episode occurred in anthropology's perpetual struggle to define itself. The age-old question of whether anthropology is or should be considered more of a science or art was revisited again in response to the revision of the American Anthropological Association's (AAA) long-range plan. The discussion was overblown in the press, and the AAA in the end disavowed neither science nor art, and as it always does, instead embraced both.[4] However, the issue made me think further about my own characterization of anthropology in relation to this volume's theme and made me consider further how the discipline represents itself and is understood by a broader public.

In looking back at the final program review document I produced, I realized that I did not give much consideration to the art of anthropology. While I definitely do conceptualize the broad discipline of anthropology as a practice of both art and science, and I have a general interest in and respect for the anthropology of art, this was not easily apparent in my writing. I placed a clear emphasis on the more "scientific" aspects of the discipline, and I emphasized specific skills and perspectives in the discipline that can be construed as having a particular use value for those interested in business (e.g., having a global perspective and the combination of quantitative and qualitative skills). The necessity of arguing for the value of anthropology according to a neoliberal logic seemed to leave less room for the aesthetic, the interpretive, and the creative. If my task was to sell anthropology, in retrospect it seems I thought I would do that best primarily by highlighting its affiliation with the more scientific approaches to understanding humans and by highlighting its more practical and utilitarian dimensions.

Though this topic needs much further consideration, what I am suggesting is that neoliberal pressures, while challenging to anthropology generally, may have harsher implications for the art of anthropology (and even an anthropology of art). As it is the humanities that most consistently suffer under the logic of neoliberalism, it is the more humanistic side of anthropology that is perhaps likely to suffer as well. As a field that is most simply defined as the study of humans, an anthropology without a humanistic emphasis is very hard to imagine. It has been clear to anthropologists for decades now that a "practical" anthropology, best seen in its applied forms, is necessary and should be promoted. However, a less "practical" anthropology, one that sees value in continuing to tell stories of the variety of human expression and experience, and in continuing to seek to address the eternal question of what it is to be human, is no less needed. As this chapter has intended to convey, it is most unfortunately getting easier though to imagine a society that does not see the value of encouraging a humanistic anthropological perspective in its higher educational institutions.

Concluding Thoughts on Resisting and Surviving

In concluding this chapter, I want to prompt discussion of two important questions that were raised for me through this process and to offer some ideas about how to respond to our current situation. The first question is the one more relevant to this volume's theme, and that is, What is the place of an art of anthropology in a higher education environment shaped by neoliberalism? And, the second question, which was more of the chapter's focus is, What is the place of anthropology in higher education and in our society in this same environment? In answering these questions, we are forced to consider how we will define our discipline and to define ourselves in the future—engaging in an ongoing social construction of valuation.

My own reflection on these recent events at my institution and on their implications for anthropology generally has led me to offer three broad suggestions for how we anthropologists might direct our energies going forward.

The first suggestion is that as a discipline, and as individual professionals, we perhaps need to respond better to the demands of neoliberalism and find better ways to publicize and market ourselves. While we are all quite cognizant of what anthropology is, what anthropologists do, and the relevance of the discipline, we need to do a better job of educating others about us—from schoolchildren to parents, politicians to college presidents. More than a decade after his call for a more public anthropology, Borofsky may find even more reason to "cry" today about the place of the discipline in the public sphere (2000; see also Vine 2011). Anthropologists need to embrace the spirit of Borofsky's public anthropology and take it further by positioning ourselves and thus the discipline to have a larger role in shaping popular discourse and public policy. In doing this, anthropology would become more visible and better regarded by the larger population that is increasingly instrumental in shaping our survival. Anthropologists should seek to have roles that are more active on school boards, in the media, in politics, and in leadership positions in our own institutions and across society. Unless more people see anthropologists, hear from anthropologists, and read about the work of anthropologists, we will always be engaged in the Sisyphean task of declaring our own relevance.[5]

The second suggestion, which speaks to a related issue that I did not discuss further, is that in response to the neoliberal pressures of assessment and accountability, we need to collectively better define what are the goals of our teaching (and research), what learning outcomes we expect, and perhaps necessarily, how these goals and outcomes serve economic or practical concerns. How do we better define and measure how such things as awareness, understanding, and sensitivity are increased through courses in anthropology? If we are to respond to the pressures of neoliberalism, these goals and outcomes need to be expressed in ways that are clear and accessible, and most importantly in the language of assessment, they need to be "measurable."

My third suggestion for responding to our current context is that we need to sharpen our critical tools and rhetorical weapons and wage war. We need to offer a clear, strong, rational, and passionate voice critiquing the rhetoric and logic of neoliberalism and how it is shaping our society, culture, and our selves. This third response is related to the first in that we need to do a good job of making this argument not just among fellow anthropologists and academics, but we also need to be speaking from positions of authority and leadership so that we can call upon a broad audience to listen. We should strive to do what anthropologists perhaps do best, and that is to remind people that there are other ways of thinking and being and that they are sometimes better.

Whether the reader is persuaded to consider choosing at least one of the above, or what I think is my course of action, all of the above, it has recently become more clear to me at least that we have to do some things differently if we are going to thrive or even survive in the current environment. In a humanistic spirit, we should recognize our kinship with others in our contemporary world who are also struggling to maintain their agency. As Ortner (2006, 147) describes, we must do this "by resisting domination in a range of ways, but also by trying to sustain . . . a certain kind of cultural (or for that matter, personal) authenticity 'on the margins of power.'" The unfortunate alternative is to continue to become academics who are "divided, disillusioned and distressed individuals whose ability to carry out the work they 'love' is constrained and subverted by the infiltration of neoliberalism" (Archer [2008, 268], drawing on Davies and Petersen [2005]).

Notes

1. Since the writing of the first draft of this paper for the Southern Anthropological Society meetings of 2011, "Peace College" became "William Peace University." The name change occurred in the summer of 2011, as part of larger changes to the college, the most significant of which was the transition from being a college for women to being coeducational.

2. The reductions to the anthropology program at William Peace University were not unique, though I was not aware of what was happening at other institutions while initially working on this project in March 2011. I later learned that during the same period discussed in this chapter, the anthropology program at Howard University was threatened with reductions that had much more significant implications for our society as a whole, given the historical significance and ongoing important work of their department (Bugarin et al. 2010).

3. For a thorough discussion of the political philosophy and economic theory that has shaped the role of neoliberalism in higher education, see Olssen and Peters (2005). For a discussion of how neoliberalism in higher education is affecting the identities and subjectivities of academics, see Archer (2008).

4. See the American Anthropological Association's (AAA) website for the "Long Range Plan" (http://www.aaanet.org/about/Governance/Long_range_plan.cfm, accessed June 26, 2013); and, see the "Correspondence" section of the February 2011 *Anthropology News* (52[2]: 3-4) for letters protesting the perceived changes and for the AAA's official response. This response is also available on the AAA website at http://www.aaanet.org/issues/press/AAA-Responds-to-Public-Controversy-Over-Science-in-Anthropology.cfm, accessed June 26, 2013.

5. The response by anthropologists to the Governor of Florida's attack on anthropology (Z. Anderson 2011) offers a very positive example in this direction. The prompt response by the AAA leadership (Dominguez and Davis 2011) to challenge his statement is exactly what was needed, but his comment should provoke a broader, more organized, and sustained effort. Along these lines, Charlotte Noble and the students at the University of South Florida responded to Governor Scott by creating a wonderful online resource that highlights the variety of important research projects they are conducting in his state (http://prezi.com/vmvomt3sj3fd/this-is-anthropology/, accessed June 26, 2013). Writing for the *Huffington Post*, Paul Stoller (2011) and Rachel Newcomb (2011) also quickly took issue with Governor Scott, with Stoller discussing the politics surrounding a liberal arts education today and Newcomb arguing that anthropology does have great economic value, as is recognized by China and India. Finally, the new AAA President Leith Mullings (2012) offered

an overview of some of the important ways anthropologists have responded to Governor Scott's statement and also noted that anthropologists have provided unique critical analyses of the economic crisis.

References

Anderson, Ken. 2009. "Ethnographic Research: A Key to Strategy." *Harvard Business Review*, March, http://hbr.org/2009/03/ethnographic-research-a-key-to-strategy/ar/1.

Anderson, Zac. 2011. "Rick Scott Wants to Shift University Funding Away from Some Degrees." *Herald Tribune*, October 10, http://politics.heraldtribune.com/2011/10/10/rick-scott-wants-to-shift-university-funding-away-from-some-majors/.

Archer, Louise. 2008. "The New Neoliberal Subjects? Young/er Academics' Constructions of Professional Identity." *Journal of Education Policy* 23(3): 265-85.

Bardhan, Ashok. 2012. "The Twin Excesses—Financialization and Globalization—Caused the Crash." In *The Globalization Reader*, 4th ed., edited by Frank J. Lechner and John Boli, 203-5. Hoboken: Wiley-Blackwell.

Borofsky, Rob. 2000. "To Laugh or Cry." *Anthropology News* 41(2): 9-10.

Bugarin, Floridez T., Eleanor King, Mark Mack, and Arvilla Payne-Jackson. 2010. "An Impending Death for Anthropology at Howard University." *Anthropology News* 51(8): 28.

Clifford, James. 1986. "On Ethnographic Allegory." In *Writing Culture: The Poetics and Politics of Ethnography*, edited by James Clifford and George E. Marcus, 98-121. Berkeley: University of California Press.

Clifford, James, and George E. Marcus. 1986. *Writing Culture: The Poetics and Politics of Ethnography*. Berkeley: University of California Press.

Cohen, Abner. 1974. *Two Dimensional Man, An Essay on the Anthropology of Power and Symbolism in Complex Society*. Berkeley: University of California Press.

Davenport, Tom. 2007. "The Rise of Corporate Anthropology." *Harvard Business Review*, November 28, http://blogs.hbr.org/davenport/2007/11/the_rise_of_corporate_anthropo.html.

Davies, B., and E. B. Petersen. 2005. "Neoliberal Discourse in the Academy: The Forestalling of (Collective) Resistance." *Learning and Teaching in the Social Sciences* 2(2): 77-98.

Dominguez, Virginia R., and William E. Davis III. 2011. "Letter to Governor Rick Scott," http://www.aaanet.org/issues/policy-advocacy/upload/letter-to-gov-scott.pdf.

Feinberg, Richard, 2009. "Bridging Science and Humanism." *Anthropology News* 50(9): 4-8.

Geertz, Clifford. 1973. *The Interpretation of Cultures*. New York: Basic Books.

Goudreau, Jenna. 2012, "The 10 Worst College Majors." *Forbes*. October 11, http://www.forbes.com/sites/jennagoudreau/2012/10/11/the-10-worst-college-majors/.

Marcus, George E., and Michael H. J. Fischer. 1986. *Anthropology as Cultural Critique*. Chicago: University of Chicago Press.

Milanovic, Branko. 2012. "Grounded, Income Inequality and Speculative Investment Led to the Financial Meltdown." In *The Globalization Reader*, 4th ed., edited by Frank J. Lechner and John Boli, 200-202. Hoboken: Wiley-Blackwell.

Morphy, Howard, and Morgan Perkins. 2006. "The Anthropology of Art: A Reflection on Its History and Contemporary

Practice." In *The Anthropology of Art, A Reader*, edited by Howard Morphy and Morgan Perkins, 1-32. Malden, MA: Blackwell Publishing.

Mullings, Leith P. 2012. "Anthropology Matters." *Anthropology News* 53(1): 13.

Newcomb, Rachel. 2011. "To Governor Rick Scott: What Anthropologists Can Do for Florida." *Huffington Post*, posted October 13, http://www.huffingtonpost.com/rachel-newcomb/to-governor-rick-scott-wh_b_1008964.html.

Olssen, Mark, and Michael A. Peters. 2005. "Neoliberalism, Higher Education and the Knowledge Economy: From the Free Market to Knowledge Capitalism." *Journal of Education Policy* 20(3): 313-45.

Ortner, Sherry. 2006. *Anthropology and Social Theory: Culture Power and the Acting Subject*. Durham: Duke University Press.

Radjou, Navi. 2009. "R&D 2.0: Fewer Engineers, More Anthropologists." *Harvard Business Review*, June 10, http://blogs.hbr.org/radjou/2009/06/rd-20-fewer-engineers-more-ant.html.

Richland, Justin B. 2009. "On Neoliberalism and Other Social Diseases: The 2008 Sociocultural Anthropology Year in Review." *American Anthropologist* 111(2): 170-76.

Stancill, Jane, and John Frank. 2013. "NC Governor Wants to Tie University Support to Jobs, Not Liberal Arts." *Charlotte Observer*, January 29, http://www.charlotteobserver.com/2013/01/29/3821498/mccrorys-call-to-revamp-higher.html.

Stoller, Paul. 2011. "The Limited Good of Rick Scott's Anthropology." *Huffington Post*, posted October 17, http://www.huffingtonpost.com/paul-stoller/the-limited-good-of-rick-_b_1012356.html?ref=email_share.

Vine, David. 2011. "'Public Anthropology' in Its Second Decade: Robert Borofsky's Center for a Public Anthropology." *American Anthropologist* 113(2): 336-40.

About the Contributors

SUSAN FALLS has a PhD from CUNY-Graduate Center and teaches anthropology at the Savannah College of Art and Design. Her work focuses on the intersection of material culture, semiotics, and political economy, especially as it relates to art and design. She is particularly interested in exploring alternative visual technologies and practices for ethnographic research and presentation.

MARGARET WILLIAMSON HUBER, Distinguished Professor Emerita at the University of Mary Washington in Fredericksburg, Virginia, has a DPhil from the University of Oxford. Her publications include studies of the Kwoma of the Sepik River in Papua New Guinea; of the Powhatan Indians of Virginia; and of popular culture, most recently "Analogical Classification in the Wizarding World" in *Semiotics* (2011).

DANIEL W. INGERSOLL JR. is Professor of Anthropology, Emeritus, St. Mary's College of Maryland. He earned a BA in anthropology from Harvard College and a PhD in anthropology from Harvard University. His interests include American culture, experimental archaeology, and material culture analysis. He served as the past Secretary-Treasurer (1997-2000) and President-Elect and President (2003 and 2004) of the Southern Anthropological Society. He has also served as the SAS Webmaster (2000-2006) and is the current SAS Archivist with Carrie B. Douglas.

Kathleen Butler Ingersoll is the Principal at ReAdapt, LLC. She earned her BA from St. Mary's College of Maryland, her MA in anthropology from College of William and Mary and her PhD from the University of York, UK. Her research interests include environmental archaeology, gardens and food production, and historic preservation. Her Southern Anthropological Society service includes the Mooney Prize Committee and the Student Paper Prize Committee. Her most recent SAS meeting paper (2013) was coauthored with Daniel W. Ingersoll, titled "Healing a Culture's Reputation: Challenging the Cultural Labeling and Libeling of the Rapanui."

Lindsey King is an Assistant Professor of Anthropology at East Tennessee State University. Her specialties include religious material culture and its use in healing strategies, Native American studies, and visual anthropology. Her most recent research interest is in the traditional art of dowsing and its function in contemporary society.

Vernon James Knight Jr. is Professor of Anthropology and Curator of Southeastern Archaeology at the University of Alabama. He is an archaeologist, having published on fieldwork and museum studies in the eastern United States and the Caribbean. His research interests include prehistoric social archaeology and the archaeology of early European-Indian contact. Recent books include *The Search for Mabila* (editor, 2009, University of Alabama Press), *Mound Excavations at Moundville: Architecture, Elites, and Social Order* (2010, University of Alabama Press), and *Iconographic Method in New World Prehistory* (2013, Cambridge University Press).

Marilyn R. London earned her MA in Biological Anthropology at the University of New Mexico after receiving her BA in Anthropology from George Washington University. She has worked as a human skeletal analyst for medical examiners in New Mexico, Iowa, and Rhode Island, and for the Repatriation Office at the Smithsonian. She is a Lecturer in the Department of Anthropology at the University of Maryland and team-teaches a course at George Washington University annually with David R. Hunt. Ms. London is a Fellow of the American Academy of Forensic Sciences, a Fellow and Past President of the Washington, DC Academy of Sciences, and a member of the American Association of Physical Anthropologists. In 1998, she coedited the book *Anthropology Explored* with Ruth Osterweis Selig; in 2004 the Smithsonian Press released a revised and expanded edition of the book (with additional editor P. Ann Kaupp).

LAURA D. LUND is a Graduate Research Assistant at Georgia State University working toward her Biological Anthropology Master's degree. She received two BS degrees in Psychology and Anthropology from Kennesaw State University. Her thesis is focused on the estimation of body size and weight of the earliest hominid, *Sahelanthropus tchadensis*, by using the correlation of molar size and body size as compared to humans, extant apes, and australopiths. She has presented at the Georgia Academy of Science and two posters at the 15th and 16th Annual Symposium of Student Scholars and Undergraduate Research Reception at Kennesaw State University.

BRANDON D. LUNDY is the Interim Associate Director of the PhD Program in International Conflict Management and Assistant Professor of Anthropology at Kennesaw State University, Georgia. He received his PhDs from the State University of New York at Buffalo and the Université des Sciences et Technologies de Lille, France. He is a specialist in ethnography, cultural anthropology, Portuguese-speaking West Africa (Cape Verde and Guinea-Bissau), and the Atlantic World. His current research interests include the impact of globalization on livelihood strategies, food systems, and cultural identity in Guinea-Bissau. Dr. Lundy recently coedited *Teaching Africa: A Guide to the 21st-Century Classroom* (IUP, 2013) with Dr. Solomon Negash. He has published in *Ethnopolitics* (2012), *Culture, Agriculture, Food and Environment* (CAFÉ) (2012), *Migration Letters* (2011), and the *Anthropology News* (2010).

Vincent H. Melomo is Associate Professor of Anthropology at William Peace University in Raleigh, North Carolina. He researches and teaches in both sociocultural anthropology and archaeology. His research has primarily been on the children of immigrants from India and their struggles to carve out unique identities and cultural forms in an American context. However, he also conducts research in historical archaeology in the southern United States, on the colonial period and the Civil War. His work in these very different areas is married by an overarching interest in the global interactions that have created the ethnic and cultural diversity of the United States in the present and past.

Robert C. Philen is Associate Professor of Anthropology at the University of West Florida. He is also literary executor for his late partner, the prolific poet and essayist Reginald Shepherd. One of Philen's key areas of scholarly and creative interest is the intersection of art, ideas, culture, and individual agency, with this interest no doubt shaped in part by his interactions with Shepherd, as well as with his current partner, painter Carlos Goebels.

Hector Qirko is an Assistant Professor of Anthropology in the Department of Sociology and Anthropology at the College of Charleston.

ELIZABETH A. SHEEHAN is director of Partners in the Arts, a program of the School of Professional & Continuing Studies at the University of Richmond. Her research interests include the role of artists and intellectuals in social change and the culture of academic institutions. She received her PhD in cultural anthropology from the City University of New York Graduate School and University Center.

SUSAN KIRKPATRICK SMITH is an Associate Professor of Anthropology and Chair of the Department of Geography and Anthropology at Kennesaw State University. She received her MA and PhD in Anthropology from Indiana University. She conducts research on human skeletal remains from archaeological contexts in Greece. She has also presented at multiple conferences on anthropology pedagogy in online and in-class settings.

JESSICA STEPHENSON is Assistant Professor of Art History in the School of Art and Design, Kennesaw State University, where she teaches courses on non-Western art. Before joining Kennesaw State University, Dr. Stephenson served as the Curator of African Art at the Michael C. Carlos Museum at Emory University. Her research foci are the emergence of novel art forms in contexts of social rupture and change and histories of museum collecting and display of southern African art.

RACHEL SYKA holds a bachelor's degree in anthropology from the University of Virginia. Her research interests encompass the connection between materiality, heritage movements, and current efforts toward environmental and cultural sustainability. She plans to continue to pursue anthropology, whether in the form of a higher degree within the field or amongst the peoples and places that enliven the discipline itself.

JENNIFER VOGT is a recent PhD graduate of the anthropology program at Vanderbilt University. At Vanderbilt, Vogt's research primarily focused on how local actors build and negotiate relationships in the evolving context of state projects among potters in Quinua, a rural village in the southern Andes of Peru. Her research has investigated how local artisans accommodate, adapt, and divert state-supported projects, which encourage small-scale capitalist enterprises alongside traditional technologies and cultural identities for national competitiveness in global markets. Vogt's research interests include cultural economics, business and entrepreneurship, community development, rural livelihood strategies and diversification, and local and collective experiences of current economic policies. She currently holds a mentor position in the College of Arts and Sciences Pre-major Academic Advising Resource Center at Vanderbilt University.

Index

A

D

E

G

H

I

M

N

T

X

Y

Z

www.ingramcontent.com/pod-product-compliance
Lightning Source LLC
LaVergne TN
LVHW050917080826
845145LV00001B/112

* 9 7 8 0 9 8 4 6 4 4 5 6 8 *